THE CIVILIZATION OF THE AMERICAN INDIAN SERIES

EMPIRE
OF THE INCA

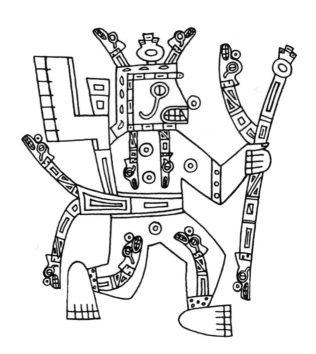

EMPIRE
OF THE INCA

BURR CARTWRIGHT BRUNDAGE

With a Foreword by Arnold J. Toynbee

UNIVERSITY OF OKLAHOMA PRESS

Norman

BY BURR CARTWRIGHT BRUNDAGE

Juniper Palace (New York, 1951; Petersburg, Fla., 1976)
Empire of the Inca (Norman, 1963)
Lords of Cuzco (Norman, 1967)
A Rain of Darts: The Mexica Aztecs (Austin, Texas, 1972)
Gian Carlo (Petersburg, Fla., 1975)
Two Earths, Two Heavens: An Essay Contrasting the Aztecs and the Incas
    (Albuquerque, N.Mex., 1975)
The Fifth Sun: Aztec Gods, Aztec World (Austin, Texas, 1979)
The Phoenix of the Western World: Quetzalcoatl and the Sky Religion (Nor-
    man, 1981)

International Standard Book Number: 0-8061-1924-1

Library of Congress Cataloging in Publication Data

Brundage, Burr Cartwright, 1912–
    Empire of the Inca. With a foreword by Arnold J. Toynbee.
[1st ed.] Norman, University of Oklahoma Press [1963]
    396 p. illus. 24 cm. (The Civilization of the American Indian series)
    Includes bibliography.
    1. Incas. 2. Peru—History—To 1548. I. Title.
F3429.B84   985.01   63–18070
ISBN: 0-8061-1924-1   MARC
Library of Congress   [r72]rev   Lim

Empire of the Inca is Volume 69 in The Civilization of the
American Indian Series.

7   8   9   10   11   12   13   14   15

To My Beloved Wife

FOREWORD

PROFESSOR BRUNDAGE'S HISTORY of the rise and fall of the Inca Empire is based on a thorough study and mastery of the sources of information. He has seen with his own eyes the Peruvian landscape which was the theater of this historical tragedy; he has visited the principal surviving monuments of the Pre-Columbian civilization of the Andean world; and he has made a critical analysis of the only written sources for Andean history that there have ever been, namely the Spanish conquerors' obituary notices of the empire and the culture that they themselves had destroyed. The Inca regime must have accumulated vast archives, not of written documents but of *quipus* (a mnemonic device that served the same purpose as medieval Western tallies); but these have mostly perished, and the key to the interpretation of the surviving specimens has been lost.

All military and political power is intrinsically transitory; and the history of its temporary acquisition is therefore always ironic. The history of the Inca power brings out the inherent irony of imperialism sensationally, since the Inca Empire's time-span was unusually brief. Its second founding, after the Incas' desperate conflict with the Chancas, was taken in hand less than a hundred years before the rapidly built but, to all appearances, solid structure was suddenly destroyed. Some synchronisms are dramatic. During the thirty years before the Incas and the Spaniards actually crossed each other's paths, they were rushing to collide with each other, without yet being aware of each other's existence. Topa Inca, the second of the two Inca arch-conquerors, died in 1493, one year after Columbus had made his first landfall in the Antilles; Topa Inca's successor Huayna Capac started to extend Inca rule from Peru into what is now Ecuador in 1511, two years before Balboa discovered the Pacific. Huayna Capac died in 1526, which was the year of Pizarro's second voyage of exploration along the Pacific Coast of South America. Pizarro's third voyage, which ended in the Spanish conquest of the Andean world, was launched in 1531, when the war between Huayna Capac's rival heirs, Huascar and Atahualpa, was in full swing (an extraordinary stroke of luck for the Spanish adventurer, whose ridiculously tiny force might have been overwhelmed by the sheer weight of a united and unexhausted Inca Empire's man power, notwithstanding the immense disparity in the potency of Spanish and Andean weapons). By 1533, all was over.

The story is not only a fascinating one in virtue of its dramatic quality; it is also illuminating for the comparative study of would-be world empires. This is one of the most fruitful approaches to a general study of human history; and it is also an approach that is particularly significant for the present generation of mankind. In the Atomic Age the permanent political unification of mankind on a literally world-wide scale is evidently the only alternative that we have to the infliction on ourselves of a catastrophe of unprecedented and immeasurable dimensions. All past attempts at establishing world peace are therefore of topical interest for us today.

The Inca attempt is also specially instructive for an inquirer who is studying the would-be world empires by the comparative method. This is an attempt that was made quite independently of the classical attempts in the Old World, e.g., the Persian, Chinese, and Roman empires. The likenesses and differences in experience and in structure between these experiments and the Inca experiment throw light on the nature of this kind of polity. Professor Brundage is well qualified for taking a synoptic view of the Inca Empire and its Old World counterparts, since he was a student of the early empires of the Old World before entering on his present work.

One of the keys to an understanding of empire-building is the role played in it by innovations in the field of religion. This aspect of the creation of the Inca Empire has been treated by Professor Brundage systematically, and this is one of the most valuable features of his book.

In retrospect the Inca Empire may look not only orderly but humane by comparison with its Aztec parallel and its Spanish sequel. Against either of those two dark foils, perhaps any empire might acquire a specious sheen. Professor Brundage's narrative brings out the grim truth that the Inca Empire, too, was built up by brutal methods and was almost always a house divided against itself. This seems to be the nemesis of any attempt to unite the world by force.

ARNOLD TOYNBEE

Grinnell, Iowa

PREFACE

"Ñaupa pacha," so the Inca tellers of tales began their public recitals: "Once upon a time . . . ."

This book tells the story of a people who, hatched in a small pocket of the Peruvian sierra, rose in the end to become the architects and chief beneficiaries of an empire they called Tahuantinsuyo, the Four Quarters. Tahuantinsuyo was a peculiarly sacred empire; its territorial aggrandizement was simply a function of its religious mission while, reciprocally, its thirst for power dictated what were to be the lineaments of its most holy beliefs. No carping distinction was made between the two concepts. When the sense of divine election began to fail, the empire incontinently collapsed—a fall more sudden and resounding than that of savage Assyria.

It has been my hope to avoid two particular pitfalls in the reconstruction of this piece of man's history: one, the error of reading Tahuantinsuyo as a mere prelude to the Spanish conquest; the other, the error of seeing in the Incas precursors or practitioners of the polities of today. Theirs was an antique empire owing inspiration to previous Andean models. It was merely the most successful of the competing and expansive states of its day, and because it was the only one to absorb them all, it was unique and *sui generis*.

Because no system of writing supported this formidable state, he who would reconstruct it must go to the published Spanish material, much of it crude and partial. All of this has been combed through and as complete a picture as possible of the political history and its supernatural sanctions is hereupon presented. The Incas produced something that is worthy of being considered, in all of its *longueurs*, by every educated person. No thumbnail sketch can do justice to Tahuantinsuyo and none is intended.

I wish to acknowledge a deep debt of gratitude to Captain and Mrs. George Casanova, whose hospitality opened for me the gates of Peru. My thanks are also due to my own institution, Florida Presbyterian College, for the aid it provided in the preparation of the manuscript.

BURR CARTWRIGHT BRUNDAGE

St. Petersburg, Florida

CONTENTS

———————

ILLUSTRATIONS

between pages 174–75

Macchu Picchu / Tambo Machay / Inca Doorway
A *Huaca* / Ruins of Viracocha Inca's Villa at Pisac
Temple Entrance at Vilcashuaman
Terracing over the Urubamba / Gate at Sacsahuaman
Kenko / Ruins of Topa's Palace at Chincheros
A Corner of Coricancha / Cuzco Today

MAPS

EMPIRE
OF THE INCA

Because the Romans and the Greeks were exceedingly wise as well as enterprising, one does not marvel that they did things worthy of commendation and great praise. Nevertheless I believe the Incas should be no less praised for the mighty things they performed, while having none of the knowledge possessed by Greek and Roman. In truth if the Incas had had chroniclers who remembered and wrote down the deeds of their captains and doughty soldiers, all this would be known to us.

—Gutiérrez de Santa Clara, III, 62

To attempt to deal with the origin and early years of Peru and the first kings of the land, is indeed a hard and demanding task. Inasmuch as neither histories nor other memorials have survived of it, so much the greater is one's inclination to disbelieve whatever we may write. Few are those who can testify to the truth.

—Román y Zamora, II, 11

IN THE BEGINNING . . .

———————

IN THE DAYS of their unchallenged grandeur, the imperial Incas gave out that, before their ancestors had appeared on the scene, before—that is—their immense cultural mission was made evident to the world, all had been confusion and misery in the sierra. Tribal skirmishes decimated the populations; cannibalism, incest, and devil-worship kept them in deep ignorance. No longer safe in the valleys, the people perched up in their fortress-towns on the flanks of high mountains fearfully eyeing bands of warriors scouting the tilth beneath them.

This is very neat, partially true, and of course made the subsequent *Pax Incaica* stand forth vividly and advantageously by comparison. Huaman Poma (Hawk Lion), descendant of a long and venerable line of non-Inca chieftains, gives us however a broader and perhaps more just view.

The mists of pre-Inca history, we are informed, veil from our eyes four successive epochs. The people of the first age were the *Pacarimoc runa* (Beginning People). Simple wandering agriculturists of white skin, they inhabited caves and lived at peace with each other and with the beasts of the field. Though primitive they were blessed in their religion, for they worshipped Viracocha, the Creator, as the one and only god. In short, this was the age of innocence. The later division of mankind into ruling aristocratic groups and commoners is attributable to them, for the descendants of their older and legitimate sons became the former, while the commoners of the Indian world were the offspring of their bastards.

The age which succeeded was one of these latter commoners, called the *Huari runa* (Origin People). They emerged from their caves and took up a more toilsome life, organizing in the process terrace and irrigation agriculture. They learned to erect beehive huts and began to wear skins. They were still peaceful and had begun to elaborate ideas concerning the trinitarian aspect of the Divine.

The third age saw the appearance of the *Purun runa* (Wilderness People), commoners also. Thatched stone huts appeared and the weaving of garments began—there was now evolved in fact the full paraphernalia of civilization: law, land divisions, herding, metallurgy, massive engineering projects, marriage, kingship, and the rich ceremonialism of war. Populations rapidly increased, and the masses spawning in the sierras poured down into the lowland valleys, carrying their culture and their quarrels with them. A great diversity of languages and customs was the result of these migrations.

The fourth age was the logical outcome of this, but was no longer one of commoners. The increasing incidence of war placed a premium on the ruthless, the strong, and the cunning. This was the age of the *Aucapacha runa* (Wartime People), heroic and distinguished captains who everywhere began to claim emoluments and dignities. Many of the tribes of the sierra moved reluctantly up onto the barren heights, leaving the valleys to become arenas in which these gladiators might exercise their violent arts. Culture, nevertheless, progressed and learned men called *amauta* (clever, sage) appeared to inculcate the arts. The high world of the Andean sierra was divided into roughly four realms which (according to our informant) corresponded exactly with the later four quarters of the Inca Empire. It was only after this fourth or Heroic Age that the Incas came upon the stage of history.

If we now scan Huaman Poma's scheme of pre-Inca time carefully, we find that the essentials in it are as follows:

(1) The primacy of civilization in the highlands, and the derivative nature of the coastal cultures.

(2) The antiquity of a deeply felt caste system among the Peruvians.

(3) An agreement with the often repeated official Inca line that, just preceding their rise to power, the highlands were prey to unregulated wars. Huaman Poma specified that these were carried on by competing war-chiefs, *sinchis* (strongmen) as they were called.

(4) Absence of any mention of Cuzco.

The value of Huaman Poma's outline is that it presents to us a theory of sierra prehistory not wholly discolored by the pervasive tinting of the Inca apologists. As such it may therefore broaden our understanding of that past. Though naïve, it is a comprehensive and indeed a daring view of history and is worthy of our consideration. Furthermore, it is about all we have.

Therefore if we interpret it in our own terms, we should say that the Incas appeared in an already very old highland world in which for centuries a yawning social chasm had existed between the lordly class and their subjects, and which additionally had memories of the former imposition of techniques (and perhaps of rule) upon the valleys of the coast; that in this world the Incas were lifted out of obscurity by certain *sinchis* who, because they were not strong enough to seize an older imperial state, perforce had to create one, which they called Cuzco.

PART ONE
FONS ET ORIGO

ONE.
THE SETTLEMENT OF CUZCO
IN LEGEND AND FACT

In the basement of their history the Incas had placed a keystone of heroic size upon which the whole structure was made to rest. The removal of this one stone would have allowed the imperial edifice to collapse into rubble. This was the official tale of their origins in Pacaritambo (Origin Lodge): it was their Exodus in that it related to their going forth in obedience to divine oracles and their *Aeneid* in presenting the foundation of their capital, Cuzco, as the mythical culmination of their wanderings. The singular place of this tale in justifying the legitimacy of the Inca imperium is attested by the efforts made by later Spanish officialdom to discredit it.

Pacaritambo was a site some eighteen miles southeast of Cuzco and in Father Cobo's day could still present archaeological evidence of the attention lavished upon it by the last Inca emperors. Here in a hill was the Inca *pacarina*, the "place of appearing," three caves named respectively Tambotoco, Marastoco, and Sutictoco, where *toco* means "hole."

Out of this sacred mountain following the flood there had emerged crawling into the light eight gorgeously bedizened and heroic beings. Theirs was a singular destiny for Inti, the sun-god, who was their father, had commissioned them to establish dominion over the world, to conquer, to despoil, and to administer in his name. These beings were conceived as propagators of his truth, militant soldiers of a new and exclusive gospel.

There were four brothers, Ayar Cachi, Ayar Ucho, Ayar Auca, and Manco Capac, each in the company of a sister-wife, Mama Cora, Mama Rahua, Mama Huaco, and Mama Ocllo. The names of these ancestral eight contain, for the brothers, the word *ayar* (the wild grain *quinoa*) and for the sisters *mama* (Lady); *cachi* is salt, *ucho* is chili pepper, *auca* is warrior, *capac* is chief, *cora* is weed, and *ocllo* is pure. Manco, Huaco, and Rahua have no certain meanings in Quechua.

The deeds of these precursors were to be full of hidden meanings as they moved ambivalently between heaven and earth, between the serenity of the divine command which was sending them forth and the coming exigencies of Inca history. In their possession was a golden staff whose peculiar property it would be to inform them when their mission was at an end by remaining fixed in the soil of that as yet unknown but promised land toward which they were journeying.

En route difficulties developed with the oldest and most troublesome of the brothers. Ayar Cachi was cast in a Homeric mold. He carried a golden sling by means of which in fits of demonic ferocity he would re-create earth-forms by hurling great rocks about him, gouging ravines out of the mountain sides and tumbling high peaks down. His other name was Huanacauri (Rainbow). To frustrate the evident danger from this member of the band, the other brothers prevailed upon him to return to the place of origin at Pacaritambo in order to retrieve some of the golden vessels they had failed to bring with them. Deluded by this trick he re-entered the cave, whereupon the brothers walled him in with great slabs of rock. In spite of his plutonic writhings and attempts to break loose, this was the end of his earthly existence.

Yet he was to reappear miraculously to the group at the site which thenceforth took his name, the ridge of Huanacauri on the south side of the Huatanay (Halter) Valley. This was the Mount Pisgah of Inca history from which Cuzco, the Promised Land, was first glimpsed below. Hovering above the ridge on splendid and iridescent wings, Ayar Cachi appeared to them with the injunction that they should descend into the valley and there found Cuzco as the seat of a mighty empire. He added that, henceforth resident on this mountain as a *huaca* (idol), he would be known to them as Huanacauri and that they were to offer sacrifices to him as their tutelary genius, bringing their young men to him for the rites of tribal initiation. After this momentous oracle, from which all Inca history was to flow, Ayar Cachi was transformed into a rude stone, perhaps the most holy single object in Inca ritual. Ayar Ucho, the second brother, was also metamorphosed into a magnificent winged being. Reciting the previous omen from the deep spaces of heaven, he was correspondingly changed into a sacred stone at near-by Matahua.

Matahua was a meadow on the slopes of Huanacauri, about six miles from Cuzco, and was the one site where the Incas on their trek resided an appreciable time. Here they scratched their meager potato patches out of the thin soil and from here they descended to continue their ineluctable destiny.

In those days the upper Huatanay Valley—present-day Cuzco—was already dotted with the farmsteads of resident groups. One of these pueblos belonged to the Hualla Indians. Mama Huaco set the pace in the penetration of their cultivated lands, leading the way in a berserker attack that nothing could resist. She is reputed to have killed a lone Indian, torn out his lungs, inflated them, and with the horrid object ballooning from her mouth to have rushed in upon the tiny Hualla hamlet. The terrified Huallas fled far away into the snowy Andes—to the valley of Pisac and beyond. Triumphantly following Manco Capac and their blood-stained Hippolyta, the remaining members of the band took possession of the abandoned settlement called Huaynapata (Youth Terrace), for here in the waving grass of the narrow ridge between the Huatanay and the Tullumayo (River of Bones) the golden bar had sunk into the earth telling them that this was Cuzco. Their next move was against the Alcaviza (Black and White) Indians whose settlement lay beside the Huatanay crossing. They were subdued according to the legend by the mere proclamation of the holy Inca mission.

One step further was to be taken in order to complete the seizure of all the land between the streams. Accompanied by Ayar Auca and the sisters, Manco Capac removed to a spot magnanimously granted him by the Alcaviza chieftain. Here on the spur of land formed by the confluence of the two streams was to arise Manco Capac's residence. Here also this first Inca chieftain and his heroic kinfolk sowed the maize they had brought from Pacaritambo. On this spot was one day to be situated Coricancha (Gold Enclosure), a home for the gods and the holiest edifice in Tahuantinsuyo.

Upon the demise of the last of his brothers two years later Manco Capac inherited all the sisters. When his son Sinchi Roca was come to manhood Manco, dying, designated him as his heir and successor.

《 2 》

IN ITS BROAD OUTLINES the above represents the official version of the Sacred Legend. For the Incas it did three things. It stated to the world their right to be in Cuzco. It offered them a simplified yet comprehensive history and geography to contemplate. Finally it established incontrovertible proof that the powers of heaven were of a different order than generally conceived to be—the heavens were made new as was to be the earth.

Not all of this can be considered historically accurate as it stands, and it therefore calls for interpretation. To discover a probable account one must turn to competing, nonofficial, euhemeristic, or even hostile versions of these same events. Luckily for us the Spaniards were interested in preserving these, solely because they served the purpose of undermining the legitimacy of Inca rule and thereby lending a seeming correctness to the Catholic kings' own unprovoked attack upon that regime. Because the long rancors felt by the earlier inhabitants of the valley of Cuzco against the men of Manco never wholly vanished, these fragments of their memories give us a more consistent, possible, and less idealized picture of the actual events.

Our sources tell us that before the appearance of the men of Manco there were several meager communities living in the upper Huatanay Valley sharing the not overly rich meadows. Among these were first the Huallas, who, as their personal names show, spoke a non-Quechua language. They were the only Indians we know to have considered themselves indigenous to the valley, for their own special cave of origination was located here. They tended to cluster on the higher ground at the base of the interfluvial triangle and the steep meadows just back of present-day San Blas. Inca memory was to refer to the pre-Inca sierra population as just such timorous groupings dwelling above the flatlands but ready at an instant to scatter up onto the defensible heights above them. These Huallas were by all accounts considered unwarlike. They were never to form any official part of the later Inca nation, but it is likely that "Cuzco" was their name for the land.

This was the period of ethnic upheaval in the Peruvian world, a period when it was customary for tribes threatening or threatened by their neighbors to choose war-leaders to act for the duration of the danger. This leader was the *sinchi* and he could even be invited in from an alien group if his reputation was impressive enough. If he achieved true eminence, he was given the honorific title *capac* (splendid, rich) which was tantamount to chieftain. These captains were not *condottieri* for their services were not hired. With that exception, however, and in a more barbarous context, they resembled those lethal and calculating captains of the Italian Renaissance. When the need had passed they were supposed to relinquish their leadership yet some seem to have set up tyrannies. Manco is to appear cast as such a leader. It is said that while he had been elected to a leading position, it was his later great successes which earned him the coveted title of *capac*. We have little doubt that this early custom of electing war leaders explains the curious feature in Inca royal history which we will study later: each ruler had his own lineage of descent or *panaca* which excluded that of his royal successor—for in the beginning the successor of a *sinchi* was often unrelated to him.

Into this little world of the Huallas at an unstated time in the past invading bands began to burst, either in successive waves or occasionally allied in weak confederations. To unravel this complicated ethnic situation is a formidable task, and the picture we present is not the only possible one. Inca orthodoxy admitted with reluctance at least four groups who contributed their blood to the formation of the Inca people.

The Sauasiray (Needle Peak?) people appear to have been the first to irrupt into the interfluvial triangle, where they took up their residence along the ridge on that piece of ground later to become famous as the site of Coricancha, dominating the confluence of the two rivers. Here on the site of this original and diminutive Cuzco they built Quinticancha (Hummingbird Enclosure), and three other building complexes. They appear to have been a fairly numerous people, and in the troubled days to come were led by a redoubtable *sinchi* called Copali Mayta. Their particular *huaca* may have been Ayar Cachi. Their cave of origination in the Sacred Legend is said to have been Sutictoco; the name Sutic (Name) is that of a mountain of Paruro, next to Pacaritambo, and we may thus surmise that the Sauasirays had close connections with Contisuyo; they were probably of complex origins.

Coincident with this invasion, or very shortly thereafter, there entered the Antasaya (Copper Region) folk who probably came from the near-by Anta Basin and may thus have been the people of Maras who formed a significant part of the early Cuzqueños—Maras the pueblo is near the Plain of Anta. Because the apex of the interfluvial triangle was held by the Sauasirays they took for themselves the Hualla lands at the base, called Huaynapata, along with the flat terrace of Collcampata (Granary Terrace) just above. This certainly means that they possessed also the steep heights above as a place of refuge. Their *sinchi* was named Quisco, and they seem to have had amicable relationships with their neighbors below them. Ayar Auca may have been their *huaca*.

The two robust peoples were not long to possess the ridge without a contest, however. The ancient track in from the northwest, the famed Chinchaysuyo (Lynx Quarter) road, in dropping down the steep face of Carmenca met the track in from the southwest, the Contisuyo road, at the Huatanay crossing. This junction produced a natural market place where goods from the four regions of the sierra world around were traded, later to be known as Cusipata (Joy Square). Here at the crossing the Huatanay was shallow enough to have formed a small marsh along the northern bank. When later filled in during the days of empire-building, this riparian flat became the memorable Haucaypata (Leisure Square) facing the market area just across the stream. Today it is the Plaza de Armas. Having crossed at this point the road led down the sloping ridge, passing the site of the Sauasiray hamlet on the right to turn down to the passage

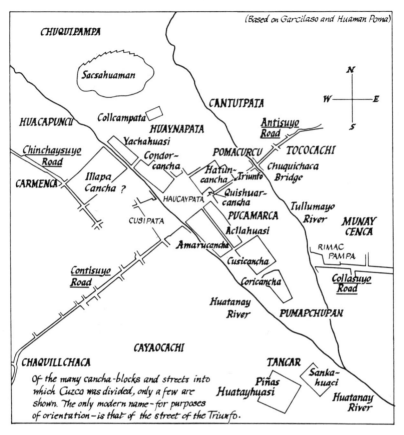

(Based on Garcilaso and Huaman Poma)

CHUQUIPAMPA

Sacsahuaman

CANTUTPATA

N
W —— E
S

HUACAPUNCU

Collcampata
HUAYNAPATA
Yachahuasi
Condor-
cancha

Antisuyo
Road

POMACURCU   TOCOCACHI

Chinchaysuyo
Road

Chuquichaca
Bridge

Hatun-
cancha   Triunfo

CARMENCA

Illapa
Cancha ?

HAUCAYPATA

Quishuar-
cancha

Tullumayo
River

MUNAY
CENCA

CUSIPATA

PUCAMARCA
Acllahuasi

Amarucancha

RIMAC
PAMPA

Cusicancha

Contisuyo
Road

Coricancha

Collasuyo
Road

Huatanay
River

PUMAPCHUPAN

CAYAOCACHI

CHAQUILLCHACA

TANCAR
Sanka-
huaci

Piñas
Huatayhuasi

Huatanay
River

Of the many cancha-blocks and streets into
which Cuzco was divided, only a few are
shown. The only modern name – for purposes
of orientation – is that of the street of the Triunfo.

Plan of Modern Cuzco with Some Inca Sites Identified

over the Tullumayo. Here at this second ford was an open field which
would become for the Incas the square of Intipampa (Field of the
Sun), today Limac Pampa a short block northeast of Santo Domingo.
Once across the stream the road became the main artery of com-
munication down the valley and indeed to the far lands to the south,
the Collasuyo road so named.

The importance of these two crossings is thus evident. The Sauasirays controlled that one over the Tullumayo while a new people, the
Alcavizas, who had crossed into the triangle and settled a compact
pueblo of some thirty thatched huts beside the marsh, held the passage over the Huatanay. They called their hamlet Pucamarca (Red
Town), and we can guess that the indistinguishable shards and cold

ashes of these people lie today under the church of La Compañia sited on the great square. The Alcavizas were hardy and able to hold their own in this chaotic little world of change. They may have been originally from Contisuyo, the vast broken area south of Cuzco within which was located Pacaritambo. Ayar Ucho of the Sacred Legend was their national *huaca*.

Some kind of an equilibrium was established among these three pueblos, undoubtedly a loose confederation of sorts. With the entrance of the war band led by Manco, everything was to change. Like a fine pinch of some catalyst dropped into a brew, the presence of the men of Manco was to throw this remote valley into a turmoil that lasted until a vast empire arose to claim for itself the immobility of perfection. It was indeed a historic entry, though made by only a handful of men. The year is unknown, as is the occasion, but it needs no great imagination to behold their dark faces and the bared, sinewy arms, the loaded slings and the war maces ready, as in their hunger these dispossessed of the earth first gazed into the hollow where the hamlets of Cuzco slept, while behind them stood their unkempt women, uncomprehending and enduring, the mothers of one of the great nations in history. Who were these folk, and who was their leader?

The clearest indication of Manco's affiliation comes from the following statements in our sources: that the Sun created the Tambo (Lodge) Indians; that Manco was himself a Tambo Indian; that his father was Apu Tambo (Tambo Captain); and finally that he appeared from the cave of origination called Tambotoco (Hole of the Tambos). The Sacred Legend places this cave in Pacaritambo, but Pacaritambo was both a mythical concept designed to impose a unity of provenience upon the diverse peoples making up the Incas, and a strictly geographical location. We know that the earlier home of the Tambos was over the watershed to the north in the Urubamba Valley. This being the case, they entered Cuzco via the Anta Basin, probably adding some more folk from Maras to their migration, for the second of the three caves of Pacaritambo was Marastoco. The Tambos are said to have consisted of about sixty families.

The first group they met were the Antasayas at the base of the triangle. Manco seems to have coexisted with them, perhaps for a number of years, before pushing farther into the triangle. In the process he acquired the field of Collcampata from them, giving rise to the persistent Inca tradition that the golden bar of settlement was first tested here. Later he and his folk moved some hundreds of yards further down the slope of the ridge to Huaynapata, from which they dispossessed the Antasayas, whether by war or prearrangement we cannot tell. A detail of the Sacred Legend says that when Manco was at Huaynapata, he ordered the third of the brothers Ayar Auca, the ancestral *huaca* of the Antasayas, to fly ahead of him to Cuzco where, upon alighting, he became the community stone called Cuzco Huanca (Field Guardian of Cuzco). The Tambos had thus pressed the Antasayas out of the base of the triangle and into the center. Priority for the Antasayas in the seizure of the land at the apex is attested by the statement that Ayar Auca lived on the site of Cuzco proper two years before he died, leaving the four sisters and the rule to Manco, while another source identifies the first "Inca" to conquer Cuzco as Cuzco Huanca, who died however before he could acquire enough power to become king. These movements imply the subjection of the Sauasirays and a subsequent *modus vivendi* which allowed the three peoples to exploit the area together. This explains why there were three caves of origination subsumed under the myth of Pacaritambo: from the leading cave, the Capactoco or Tambotoco, came the Tambos; from the Marastoco came the Antasayas; and from the Sutictoco came the Sauasirays. The Sauasiray *sinchi* Copali Mayta escaped into the Andes, perhaps with some of his people, uttering as he left these valedictorian words: "Whenever you gaze upon those masses of snow, you may well declaim that the fugitive Copali Mayta is there."

Because of their original possession of the area both the Antasayas and the Sauasairys were to be known as Cuzcos. Their primacy, with the Tambos who followed, is attested in the specific and official statement from the palmy days of the empire to come that Inti the Sun was the father of "Tambos and Cuzcos."

But the hamlet of Pucamarca was still held by the Alcavizas, the fourth element, who seem to have been strong enough to refuse to combine with that league of three which now formed under a leader called Sinchi Roca, Manco having died.

With the celebrated Ayar Ucho, their communal *huaca*, as their rallying point, the Alcavizas withstood the pressures of the coalition under the rule of Sinchi Roca and of his successor, probably a Cuzco Indian. Only when the fourth "Inca" war leader appeared to head the coalition were its harassments of the Alcavizas finally successful. Those Alcavizas who submitted, their dwellings, and their lands were then incorporated into the union as the fourth and last of the basic ethnic elements of the new little state. This is why, though there are only three caves of origination in the Sacred Legend, there are four ancestral brothers: Ayar Ucho the Alcaviza, Ayar Auca the Antasaya, Ayar Cachi the Sauasiray, and Manco Capac the Tambo. And because of the long-lasting dualism between the three allies on the one hand and the Alcavizas on the other, we have the two urban modes in Cuzco, each controlling a river crossing on the same great road, Haucaypata and Intipampa.

But there cannot be the slightest doubt that the Alcavizas and the *ayllus* (lineages) later formed from them represented to both the preimperial union and the later imperial royal line a major threat, for when Pachacuti, the second founder of the empire, was remaking the entire social fabric of Cuzco he banished the descendants of the Alcavizas to a suburban area—and this in spite of the fact that they had become organized as the Ayar Ucho *ayllu* which by legendary sanction thus could claim Incahood almost to the same degree as the Tambos and Cuzcos. These Alcavizas possessed and continued to cherish a separate history of their own which retailed the deeds of their many great *sinchis*, describing how they had heroically retained their freedom—which meant control of the crossroads—down to the time of the fourth Inca ruler, when the trickery and deceit of the men of Manco finally overcame them. However the facts may have been, the animosity of the Alcavizas for the later legitimate line of emperors was deep and abiding, remaining vocal for at least forty years following the Spanish conquest.

« 3 »

THE READER IS FAMILIAR ENOUGH with the foundation legends of Rome to realize that until quite late in its history there was no such thing as a "Roman." At a swampy river crossing on the Tiber's bank Latins, Sabines, Etruscans, Aeneadic pirates from Lavinium, and uncounted other groups settled, conquered, struggled, lost or won out in a long and serpentine historic process, lending each their ancestral tales and heroic wonders to the manufacture of a single and deceptively combined legend of the origin of a great and holy city. This is no less true of the Inca origins. As far as we can identify the four brothers from Pacaritambo, they thus represented not only different ethnic groups but different periods of entry and of dominance. And in fact it is certain that more than four peoples were involved. Out of it all however was finally to emerge a city which disposed of a new form of political power, empire, and this imposed integrity was to necessitate a single myth. Though the elements of that myth had once been the disparate property of the diverse groups, the needs of the new state were to fuse them finally into one orthodox and official account; disparity could not be admitted, and so the "Incas" appeared just as if there had never been a time when they had not existed as one people. Nevertheless it is clear that the men of Manco had the lion's share in the stitching together of the myth.

The Pacaritambo itinerary is of interest, insofar as it is possible to salvage it, though its historical value is highly debatable. If the Tambos really came from the Urubamba Valley, then the journey from Pacaritambo belongs to another of the four groups, and the most likely candidates are the Sauasirays, who seem to have originated in Contisuyo, the correct general area.

After leaving Pacaritambo, the "Incas," so goes the Sacred Legend, had settled a small place en route which they called Tamboquiru (Tambo Teeth); here Mama Ocllo bore to Manco Capac the son Sinchi Roca whom we have already noted as the second ruler in the Inca king list. Most noticeable in the itinerary are the long stopovers to establish temporary habitations, a typical aimless, marginal-subsistence way of life for a neighborhood group too weak to build up a prosperous field-system of its own or to acquire rights near established communities in good land. The consequences for these uprooted folk were that they were squeezed up onto the barren heights to become desultory llama-herders, potato-growers, and sullen witnesses of the greener life lived in the river bottoms below.

Traditionally their whole trek, though only a short distance, took them at least eight and possibly more than twenty years to complete.

The settlement of Matahua was apparently decisive. Here the warlike orientation of these footloose people was first evidenced; from here they appear to have become adept at raiding the valley below, sometimes in conjunction with other groups. The unrelenting harshness of the cold highlands was increasingly stamped into the pattern of their *mores*, while the smallness of their group no doubt taught them to substitute for the weight and prestige of numbers the simplicity of policy and unquestioned obedience to a capable war leader. The residence in Matahua was of sufficient duration for tradition to make it the locale of their first tribal festivals (later to become great state ceremonials), especially the *huarachicoy* (breechcloth ceremony), the rite by which the Inca youth became a man and a member of the society.

When it came time for them to change raiding into something resembling conquest, they wisely mated policy with war. Sinchi Roca had taken as wife Mama Coca, daughter of Sutic Huaman (Name Hawk) of Sañu, a valley pueblo.

This union brought them the positive benefits of an alliance, and when finally the group moved in on Cuzco the people of Sañu accompanied them in their ranks to take up homesteads near by. The Sañu element in early Inca history is important: it is probably that element which brought the "Sutic" tradition into the Sauasiray complex. If so, Sinchi Roca will have been not a Tambo but a Sauasiray chieftain.

The pueblo of Sañu is to be identified with the present San Sebastián, three miles out of Cuzco. It is noteworthy that Huanacauri, the sacred mountain upon which the wandering Incas had just settled, was a *huaca* of the Sañu people before it ever became a part of the Inca orbit. The cause for Inca appropriation of that site and of its sacred lore can perhaps be seen in the fact that they could not erase from their tales the confusion of *two* Huanacauris, Ayar Cachi and Ayar Ucho—two stone *huacas* both claiming the same ancestral properties and protective qualities, though the former was undoubtedly the original Sañu *huaca* identified with the mountain. In this area there were economically important salt pans, and San Sebastián today lies on the confluence of the Huatanay and the Cachimayo (Salt River)—which may or may not have indirect reference to the presence of Ayar Cachi in the myth. The road down from Matahua debouched into the Huatanay Valley opposite the site, which was thus a command point against those wishing egress from the mountain. In the official itinerary we are finally told that, besides settling at Matahua on the slopes of Huanacauri, the ancestral eight also settled in the valley at its foot in a pueblo called Quirimanta (Made of Wounds), probably across the river from Sañu. From here, through Sañu, they entered Cuzco.

« 4 »

THE RELIGIOUS ELEMENT in the foundation legends is inextricably woven into these far-off events. We must believe that when the various groups left each their own *pacarina*, they took with them the usual meager complement of cults, of which the most pervasive, though not the most dynamic, was that of the Earth Mother. In the official legend this divine power hides under the name Mama Huaco, or epithetically under the name Mama Ocllo; both are mentioned as consorts of Manco. Mama Huaco is generally credited in the tales with being the giver of victory; she is the one who brought the mission to an end by sinking the enchanted wand deep into the earth, her own element. She it was who inspired her shamanistic priestess to read oracles from inflated lungs and to incite the warriors to their sanguinary tasks, much like an Old Testament Deborah. Her role however has been muted by the later reconstruction of the Inca myth along the lines of an exclusive sun worship.

Her overriding importance in the period of the foundations becomes evident when we inquire closely into her functions. Her true name was simply Mama (The Mother), which has been the name of the Magna Mater in every land under the sun and in every age down to our own. One of our sources explicitly equates Mama Huaco with the sierra goddess Pachamama (Earth Mother) when it states that she was the mother, not the sister, of Manco Capac. She was uncreated; she lived in the cave of Tambotoco and was a famous witch and shape-shifter. Spirits attended her; she cast enchantments; she was a powerful oracle for she conversed familiarly with the things of the earth, trees, rocks, and lakes; in fact it was she who created all the *huacas* in the world. She was connected with serpents, being herself of the race of *amaru* (serpent, dragon). She bore the child Manco to an *amaru*-demon and then entrusted him to a mysterious and vivid bird of the montaña who nurtured him for two years within the cave. Mama Huaco mated not only with her son Manco but promiscuously with any man she desired. She was far more powerful than Manco, her son and consort; she was very beautiful and beloved by all, especially by the poor of Cuzco.

Accordingly when we note from another source that the name of Manco's mother was Pachamama Achic (Earth-Mother Witch) the identification becomes complete. Mama Huaco was then the Earth Goddess, changeless, eerie, and especially manifest in her female practitioner, the sorceress. But the Incas did not own her exclusively for she was the common possession of all sierra Indians. Even the later all-consuming effulgence of Inti could not veil her forms. It is true that she was demoted in the Sacred Legend to become the sister instead of the mother of Manco and was cast in the role of a lusty Amazon instead of that of a pristine deity, but her hold upon the folk, the "poor," was never loosened for they continued to live and die in her bosom.

Manco Capac is said to have turned both the captured Huallas and their lands over to Mama Huaco. This is merely another way of saying that her cult, enriched by the forced labor of the conquered, was established on those *chacras* (tilled fields) which had formerly belonged to them and which lay under the heights at the head of the valley. It is perhaps of some interest that the only church at present in this part of Cuzco belongs to St. Anne who, in Catholic hagiology, is the most venerable of the great female saints. Do we perhaps have in the rotten adobes of this sleazy edifice today the shrine of the Earth Mother's successor? Santa Anna is a very old parish in Cuzco.

The Inca origination tale specifically glorifies the sun-god Inti. It is his divinity which floods the recital in the light of transcendence. The question which intrigues us here is whether it was a fully developed cult of the sun which the Tambos or Cuzcos brought in with them. And did they really claim to be his sons from the beginning?

We know that Manco brought with him the sun-falcon, a fetish carried about in a primitive wicker reliquary which gave to its possessor the power of rule—the implication being that this puny *huaca* was all that Manco possessed of a personal cult at the time. The amazing use to which it was later to be put, its expansion into a militant imperial church is a tribute to the religious daring of these people. The growth of this Inti cult, glacial at first, must have begun as soon as the occupation of the site of Coricancha, for the tradition of Inca hostility to the local *huacas* around them is persistent and reflects the constant posture of defense which the invaders adopted one against the other in the interfluvial triangle. The Inti cult must have been deeply implicated in that posture.

In ruffling these faded and almost illegible pages of Inca history we are reading a remote lesson whose runic obscurities provide few certainties for him who reads. Our excuse for trying is that wherever the spirit of man has flickered into light, it merits recollection. The earliest pinpricks these particular people made upon the Andean palimpsest have been badly smudged by time, but what there is to read is here recorded.

TWO.
THE FIRST SEVEN RULERS

«   I   »

WHILE AN INFANT INCA STATE was being thus painfully nurtured on
the site of Cuzco at the northwestern end of the Huatanay Valley,
the remainder of the valley was occupied by equally active communities. Sañu we have mentioned as being in league with one or
more of the invaders of Cuzco. Beyond Sañu were many pueblos,
mainly of Ayamarca (Mummy Town) affiliation, ranging in size
from twenty-five to one hundred households. How cohesive those
Ayamarca groups were we do not know, but they were able to contest power with the sixth Inca ruler on more than equal terms, under
a *sinchi* who made an indelible impression on early Inca history, the
formidable Tocay Capac (Complete Chief).

One of the most important of the valley states not included in the
Ayamarca confederation was Muina, some twelve miles distant from
Cuzco and situated strategically close to the opposite end of the
valley. Further along, still on the trunk road south but outside the
Huatanay Valley proper, was Huaro, a place of some power. It was
six miles beyond Muina.

As the traveler today leaves the Lucre Basin, which rounds off this
end of the long valley, to continue on the road south to Bolivia, he
moves up over a low saddle of hills, a route older than the Incas who

24

utilized it. At this spot and fully as strategically located as Cuzco—
though holding the eastern instead of the western gateway to the
valley—is the site today of the wide ruins of Pikillacta (Flea Town—
a modern name), an archaeological site hot and uncommunicative in
the midday sun and most lonesome in the chilling rains. From its
pirca walls one's glance sweeps effortlessly down the treeless slopes
to Lake Lucre. All around the hills are stepped with ancient terraces.

From the evidence of its ruined stones Pikillacta was constructed
just previous to the Inca conquest, and there is indeed every evidence
that it was a major hub of military and cultural influences radiating
outward. Before Cuzco was formed, it played the role of a Cuzco
at the opposite end of the valley. Though nothing in the scanty
records prompts us to believe that it was still flourishing at the dawn
of Inca history, its mantle must have fallen to some one of the adjacent communities, perhaps to Huaro, perhaps to Muina. With its
peculiar doorless houses, its extensive ceremonial areas, the exactitude
of its ground plan, Pikillacta hints at significant events preceding the
rise of Inca power without in any sense satisfying us with the certainty
of knowledge. We do not even know the true name of this vast and
silent city.

A short way beyond the ruins, in a constricted section of the road,
the Incas were later to construct a toll house and check point, today
called Rumi Collca (Stone Bin). When the traveler has passed
through this to the south he has left the Inca heartland as it was in
the palmy days.

<< 2 >>

WE ARE AT A POINT where we must consider the word "Inca" and
its meaning, for upon this some of our historical interpretation must
depend. Sarmiento says the word "Inca" is Quechua and means
"Lord." Huaman Poma says it means "Conqueror." Ramós Gavilán,
without translating it directly, says the term was used as a title like
that of pharaoh or sultan, but he adds that Manco Capac himself invented the word, implying thereby that he knew of no specific meaning for it. Zárate says that the rulers bore the name"Inca" in the same
fashion that the Roman emperors bore the title "August." Matienzo

says that it means "King" or "Great Lord." Gutiérrez de Santa Clara
has it "Caesarians." Fernandez gives it to us as "something like
Lord" and Oviedo, "Emperor, Monarch or King of Many Realms."
The Chumbivilca Indians interpreted it as "Lord" or "Eminence."

From the above it would seem reasonable to suspect that the word
"Inca" was an honorific term which has no remembered etymology;
it was therefore not necessarily a Quechua word. If we assume this,
then the historic Incas must have borrowed or stolen an honorific
title already in use in a previous period. Huaman Poma flatly states
that this was so, and it would seem to be further attested by the fact
that of the first seven historic "Inca" rulers in Cuzco, one alone bore
the title "Inca." Not until the reign of Inca Roca is the name seemingly a permanent appanage in the family. But if "Inca" were a title
from a previous level of history, it must have been reserved for a
very high status indeed, for it was not ordinarily borne by a Peruvian
sinchi until the groups in Cuzco seized upon it. Whatever then may
have been the original meaning of the word "Inca," we are aware
that it was a title coveted by and finally acquired by those groups,
Tambos, Cuzcos, Sañus, Mascas, etc., who were involved in the
process of building up a viable state in the Huatanay Valley.

Driven by the double logic of consolidation and expansion, this
state began its growth as a loosely federated cluster of hamlets and
canchas, and soon was organized sufficiently to turn its combined
and hostile gaze against the more powerful pueblos farther down the
valley—in which process, and after much time had elapsed, the
Cuzco magnates received or took the fortunate designation of "Inca."
Upon such groups in the environs who may have previously used the
title and whom the people of Cuzco came finally to conquer, they
rebestowed the title either as an act of policy or military necessity—
or else withdrew it as a punitive action. This appears to have been
the origin of the class of Hahua Inca (Outer Inca) or "Incas by
adoption," as we call them.

As far therefore as we can see, through the artificialities of the
Sacred Legend and the details of the later royal genealogies, the
"ancestral eight" and their early successors were not considered Incas
while they were initially building up the Inca state. The designation
"Inca"—like the word "Roman" in somewhat similar circumstances

—was to mean finally, an inhabitant by right of the holy city of Cuzco.

In spite of the fact that Inca rule was built up on the office of *sinchi*, the principle of which was elective, the fiction was later created and maintained that from the days of Manco Capac to the close of empire, primogeniture—or at least the hereditary principle—was the sole rule of succession in the royal line. The presence of competing groups in the formation of the small state, with all the tumults, pressures, and duplications implied, would seem to preclude such a settled method of succession in the beginning, and we can be sure that the early Inca rulers included in the official list were not all Tambos, though such is the dynastic illusion which the list would foist on us. Sarmiento indeed shows us an early but self-conscious constitution in Cuzco which was remarkably military. Election seems not to have been fully given up until after the great schism in the latter years of the reign of the eighth ruler, Viracocha Inca, when a cabal of captains used it for the last time in setting up as his successor a prince of their own choosing.

Because of this and because of the fact that Viracocha Inca was the first ruler to envisage the possibility of empire based on occupation and tribute, we split the royal line at this point. In this chapter we are considering only those Inca chieftains who preceded him. Within this early group there appears to the historian a further division; from Manco Capac through Mayta Capac, the fourth ruler, we have the period of entry into the interfluvial triangle accompanied by confederation and skirmishing and ending in the unification of Cuzco and its road crossings; from Capac Yupanqui to Yahuar Huacac, the seventh ruler, the new state of Cuzco begins to impinge upon the world around it, expanding the area of its war-arm as well as the reach of its alliances, a modest new wealth making this possible. Following this, and beginning with Viracocha Inca, as mentioned above, empire is adumbrated, then formed, to last intact until the disastrous civil commotions between Huascar and Atahualpa.

« 3 »

THE ANNALS OF THE FIRST SEVEN RULERS, though brief and uncertain, present some points of broad interest. Manco Capac we have already discussed. We must leave him in a kind of limbo, for the indications are that, though he led the Tambos into the valley, he himself did not lead the other groups as *sinchi* in their combined efforts. The historicity of this man is not as important however as his place in the Inca legend. He was the Aeneas who personified the piety of the race as well as the divinely inspired Numa who poured over them the sweet vials of his wisdom.

Sinchi Roca is more palpable, and we tentatively assign him to the Sauasiray group. Born during the historic trek, he improbably is said to have assumed the leadership at the age of fifteen. While holding his people together at Matahua, he succeeded in breaking open the lock of the valley below him by that crucial marriage with Mama Coca of Sañu. By her, the legend says, he had a son in Matahua who was called Manco Sapaca but who did not become his successor. This has the appearance of a contest for the *sinchi*-ship in which the Tambo candidate (for Manco was a Tambo name) lost out to a more acceptable Sauasiray contender. It is interesting that our sources consistently classify Sinchi Roca as unwarlike—an undesirable characteristic in this little world of fierce ambitions.

Sarmiento is aware of a hitch in the succession at this point for he mentions the nonaccession of Manco Sapaca with some curiosity. Whether Lloque Yupanqui, the next ruler, was a younger brother, as stated, can perhaps be brought into question though there is no proof that he was not. The name Lloque means "Left-handed." In official Inca historiography he is classed as both a do-nothing and a coward, which enables us to make a guess that the so-called negotiations he entered into with neighboring pueblos down the valley are euphemisms for his inability to make headway against them. Sañu, the pueblo of his mother, is mentioned in this regard, showing that it was confederate with Cuzco—certainly not subject. Beyond Sañu was Huaro, powerful in those days, and when we hear that two of its *curacas* (headmen) had occasion to come to Cuzco, our own feeling is that this was no friendly embassy but a hostile onslaught on the puny Inca state.

What Cuzco looked like at this time is a matter of pure speculation. One imagines it as a series of adobe *canchas* and field systems scattered loosely about the headwaters of the Tullumayo, the Huatanay, and the Chunchulmayo. The ineradicable xenophobia of each of these pueblos would have made the aspiring presidency of Tambos and Cuzcos a most decisive factor, reflected in the aloofness of each community cluster. Real cohesion must have been the product of external circumstances, such as attack from without, rather than the results of an enlightened policy, and therefore was surely rare and intermittent.

Perched on the very lip of the bowl of Cuzco, high above the straggling group of hamlets, was the Inca *pucara* (hilltop fortress) or place of refuge, Sacsahuaman. No doubt in those days it was merely a roughly walled enclosure—later it would become the most formidable piece of military engineering in the Western Hemisphere.

The market place at the Huatanay crossing probably did more to advance a sense of singleness in the hamlets than any other cause. Here were exchanged the *quinoa* from the rich Plain of Anta above and behind Cuzco, the gaudy feathers of the Amazonian parrot, and the luxuries of the Yucay Valley neighboring on the north, with the salt, pottery, and staples of the Huatanay. This part of the life of Cuzco would go on whatever the political progress in the area.

Lloque Yupanqui is said to have remained childless until well advanced in years, at which time, in response to the solemn tones of an oracle, his people placed him, like the venerable David, in the embrace of his new young *coya*, or queen, Mama Cahua (Prudent Lady) who awakened his vigor and bore him a son, Mayta Capac. But his senility finally made it necessary for the magnates to appoint two of his brothers as regents to act for him. He died about the time when the drive to unify all the pueblos of Cuzco under one leader was becoming an imperative, for the vigilance of the microscopic state had been dangerously relaxed in the days of his dotage, thus allowing the stubborn Alcavizas to become a major threat.

《 4 》

MAYTA CAPAC was a three months' child and born, adds the gargantuan tale, with all his teeth. At the age of one he was already close to his adolescence, and at the age of two he was engaging in brutal physical encounters with the other young braves of Cuzco. All sources mention his extraordinary and somber aggressiveness.

29

It is evident that Mayta Capac stood for something different in the official historiography than did his predecessors. He was the first to express fully the arrogant pride of the Inca, and it was he who put a terminus to the inchoate and fumbling beginnings of the Inca state. After him Cuzco was a name of decided local importance. He is the first of the heroic Incas.

The events which introduced the rule of Mayta Capac recall to us, though in the tiniest of miniatures, the widespread and bloody revolt of the confederate Latins against the suzerainty of the Roman *civitas*. It appears that the simmering pot of race in Cuzco boiled suddenly over, presenting these incipient Incas with the alternatives of bringing to ripeness a policy of local coercion and subjugation, or of drifting aimlessly about in the small ethnic eddies of the valley like the rest of the clans in the sierra. Lloque Yupanqui was content to espouse the latter course. The young Mayta Capac forced the adoption of the former.

The situation came to a head when the Alcavizas, who controlled the crossing of the Huatanay and were still partially outside the federation, organized other dissident Cuzco groups in a common front against those Incas strung out along the interfluvial ridge above them. The site of Coricancha was the earliest center of the federation's power in the triangle, and here was resident the *fainéant* and lingering Lloque Yupanqui, blocking all efforts to prepare the defenses of his home. What happened then has all the appearances of a revolt led by the virile young Mayta Capac and the group of champing braves who supported him, for they accosted the old man with insulting demands that he resign his position as *sinchi* forthwith. Lloque Yupanqui submitted and Mayta now set about preparing his feeble hamlet for the ordeal ahead. We do not know whether Mayta Capac was a Tambo or a Cuzco Indian—his name brings him into close connection with the Sauasiray *ayllu*, for many of this lineage were to bear it in the years to come.

Mayta attacked the Alcavizas down by the Huatanay ford and thereby provoked a nearly successful retaliation. It was no easy struggle and continued over an appreciable period of time. Nevertheless the numbers involved were absurdly small and enable us to see that, after all, it was only a minor skirmish on the sierra and unworthy of reporting were it not pregnant with future meaning. The abortive Alcaviza raid on Coricancha was delivered by ten warriors; Mayta's victory was achieved with something over fifty. So impressive was this deliverance of the Inca pueblo from peril that the spot where Mayta made his decision to fight was sacred thereafter in the eyes of the Incas, a *huaca* of peculiar sancity commemorating their first victory of note. Slowly the Incas were acquiring a history.

A policy of studied terror is attributed to this triumphant Inca *sinchi*. He is reputed to have prepared an infamous torture chamber known as Sancahuasi and to have cast the defeated Alcaviza leader into it, with the gruesome result that he was never heard from again. The concentration of Alcavizas in the interfluvial triangle was at last broken up, their influence was severely reduced, and their best lands were taken. It is Mayta Capac, furthermore, who is credited with the introduction of the spy-in-residence technique of control, called the *"mitmac* system" that was to prove so useful to the future empire. By means of this constant Inca surveillance inserted into their councils and communities the Alcavizas—and no doubt whatever allies had risen in revolt with them—were shorn of much of their capacity for conspiracy. The Incas had thus created almost unconsciously a new system of power in Cuzco, which no longer depended only on federation and mutual toleration but to some extent also on force of arms and oppression. The *mitmac* system, though surely only in the germ, announced the change.

A corollary of this change in policy is the well-attested memory of Mayta Capac's hostility to the *huacas*, by which is meant those sacred sites, cult objects, and powers belonging to the recalcitrant pueblos of Cuzco and environs. To police the sullen thoughts of the conquered was not enough. Inca logic seems to have demanded equally the subjugation or at least derangement of the deeper sources of their cohesion and power, namely, their immemorial religious sanctions. It may be that we have here the germ of that amazing insistence upon a systematication of the divine which became a reflection in heaven of the domination of the Inca caste on earth.

Sarmiento retails a story which shows Mayta Capac initiating a new chapter in the cultic life of the Incas, for he says that the sacred fetish, the Inti-bird, brought into the valley by Manco Capac but never revered till now, was activated as a family oracle by Mayta Capac. Thus was stressed Mayta's charismatic inspiration in contrast to the lack of it in his predecessors. The same thing is negatively stated when we hear that the prestige of the local shamans (non-Inca) had been at a high point before him, and that, because of his suspicion of the *huacas* of these medicine men, Mayta Capac made a practice of consistently mocking them. To reorient these subjugated cults under the presidency of the necessarily higher Inti religion, he created the office of high priest and assigned it to his oldest son. We may be sure that this is the fountainhead of that astounding cere-monial development which will henceforth accompany the rising fortunes of Tahuantinsuyo.

Mayta Capac still ruled only a small area in and immediately around Cuzco. After crushing the Alcaviza threat there was no further need for warlike adventures, and Cuzco became an active sierra emporium with a modest increase in wealth that allowed Mayta Capac to rule on a more expansive scale than had formerly been the case. He continued however to live within the mud-walled enclosures of Inticancha (Enclosure of the Sun), the original name for Coricancha. He is the first Inca ruler whose personality, fiery and dour alternately, was impressive enough to be remembered. From Mayta Capac on we can correctly speak of an Inca nation.

« 5 »

THE FIFTH INCA RULER, Capac Yupanqui (Honored Chief) was installed in preference to an older brother whose physically repulsive appearance denied him the right to rule. We are led to believe that among the other sons of Mayta Capac also there was dissatisfaction with the succession, for Capac Yupanqui felt prompted to extract from them an oath in which they recognized him alone as the *capac*, the ruler. His power was soon secure, however, and the incident serves merely to explicate the growing self-consciousness of a ruling group. One brother, Tarco Huaman, became in his own right a famous captain without ever, to our knowledge, challenging the authority of his less gifted brother; again—revelatory of a new caste solidarity—when Capac Yupanqui left Cuzco on a military venture outside the valley, he was able to leave a brother as his lieutenant in Cuzco.

The rule of Capac Yupanqui holds an interest because of this campaign which he led in person. It is the first armed foray outside the valley of Cuzco mentioned in the records of the Incas, and shows that remarkable and arrogant people beginning to flex their thews. Most probably it was a raid into the Yucay Valley.

Earlier Inca rulers had dwelt in Inticancha. Capac Yupanqui was the first to leave the ancestral hearth and move into a new residence. We can guess where it was. His father had seized the holdings of the Alcavizas which ranked equally in stategic importance with the site of Inticancha. Cobo tells us that up to his time all Inca rulers had belonged to Hurin Cuzco (Lower Cuzco), which was the area around Inticancha; after him they resided in Hanan Cuzco (Upper Cuzco), around and above the Huatanay ford. It is not difficult to gather therefore that this first Inca "palace" was in Pucamarca, the site of some of the great *canchas* of the rulers of the empire. Inticancha, though we are not expressly so informed, was no doubt given over in charge of his brother the high priest—which move would have incidentally left Inti, the *huaca* of the royal house, as sole resident and possessor of Inticancha. The subsequent enrichment and development of the Inti cult can be partially traced to the freedom it thus acquired by the removal of the royal residence. A family naos now, Inticancha could in time become a state shrine and finally an imperial pantheon. From this time on it was the custom for each ruler on his accession to build and inhabit his own regal *cancha*. This new procedure is inevitably bound up with the creation of the royal *panaca*—mentioned from the following reign—the cultus of the ruler institutionalized as a household to carry on after his death.

《 6 》

CAPAC YUPANQUI left the usual number of sons, of whom the *Incap Sapay Churin* (Only Child of the Inca) or legitimate heir was Inca Roca. It is noteworthy that the title "Inca" is here once and for all adopted by these rulers. The pride of the sinewy little state had been aroused.

The events of Inca Roca's reign all revolve about his marriage with Mama Micay (Lady Round-Face), the lovely daughter of Sumac Inca (Handsome Inca), *sinchi* of Huayllacan, a pueblo in the Yucay Valley. A persistent story ran that it was she who was somehow responsible for the bringing of new irrigation channels down into Cuzco, thereby producing an immediate increment of agricultural wealth for the state. The explanation must be that the people of Huayllacan controlled certain headwater areas on the north side of Cuzco which could be tapped only if amicable relations existed between the two neighbors. The water is identified in the chronicles as the Spring of Tocori on Mount Chaca (Bridge). Various and colorful indeed are the miraculous stories related to the gushing forth of this source. When the Spaniards entered the area they found the *panaca* of Mama Micay and Inca Roca still in possession of full rights to the dispersal and control of this water.

This alliance with a foreign pueblo which could look down both into the Yucay Valley on the north and the Huatanay on the south was to become the center of a tangled web of intertribal complications. For the first time we can see Cuzco involved in relationships with neighboring pueblos. Our vision reveals—even though darkly—not a lack of militancy on the part of the small state but rather a lack of any directed policy of expansion. Inca Roca himself seems to have remained in Cuzco surrounded by evidences of the new wealth and immersed in the luxuries of a harem larger than that of any of his predecessors, while a warlike group of sons and brothers, exulting in their new nationality, moved fiercely about the country, developing their techniques of warfare and spreading broadcast the first careless handfuls of those seeds whose full harvest was to be—to all the people of Peru who were later forced to gather in its bitter sheaves—terror, tribute, and majesty.

Most notable of all these ferocious sons was the eminent and energetic captain, Vicaquirau, the very *summa* of the heroic and patriotic ideals which were at the foundation of the Inca state. While still young this Fabian seems to have been provided with his own Buccellarian band, a coterie of devoted warriors with whose help Muina, the key to the opposite end of the valley, was successfully raided. Similar in renown and family pride was Apu Mayta, the captain who attacked the Mascas and brought home their chieftain as a prize to Cuzco, the first Inca triumph of which we are informed. Raiding parties, dispatched out beyond Muina down the Collasuyo road, perhaps as far as Quiquijana, made tentative contact with the Canas and Canchas. These military adventures were not necessarily forerunners of empire, but they were at least hard-hitting forays, possibly in alliance with other strong pueblos.

The following interesting situation arose. The *coya*, who had brought as her dowry peace with the pueblo of Huayllacan, had originally been promised to the famous Tocay Capac, *sinchi* of the Ayamarcas. This leader had considered the change in arrangements as a breach of faith and had begun a period of intermittent hostilities with Huayllacan. It followed that relations were also strained with Cuzco. A three-way embroglio developed which was not settled until a peace was arranged between Cuzco and the Ayamarcas, by terms of which a daughter of Tocay Capac was married to the Inca heir apparent and Tocay himself was given an Inca princess or *ñusta*, to wife. From the above we can see that the Ayamarca people were too formidable in those early years to be met head on by the Inca state.

Much that is unclear about this passage in Inca history would be revealed to us if we knew the exact location of the Ayamarca communities and their central pueblo Ahuayrocancha. One has the impression that the key to their power lay somewhere in the Anta Basin and that they could thus extend their influence into either of the two fruitful valleys flanking it.

To get to the Plain of Anta you take the old Chinchaysuyo road leading northwest out of Cuzco. There lie the marshes and flatlands of Anta (Copper) partially closed in by hills and rolling downs. This pampa, a rich area then and heavily populated, is a high basin draining northward into the Vilcamayo, also called the Urubamba (Worm Plain). Bound about on three horizons the Andes slumber; reedy ponds and a bleak expanse meet the traveler's eye today, while the old imperial terraces of the Incas rim the land in amphitheatrical serenity. In early days it was all greener. The peoples here were to contribute their blood to the formation of the Inca state.

The relations between Cuzco and this productive basin must always have been close, but it is not until the reign of Inca Roca that we become aware of the extent, for it is that ruler who granted to the pueblo of Anta the coveted privilege of bearing the name "Inca" and of displaying their new caste by the use of the heroic earplugs. They are the first Incas-by-adoption of whom we hear. The granting of this honor implies that they were coequal confederates and not subjects newly conquered. Perhaps, in view of the feature that Inca Roca is the first Cuzco ruler expressly to be named an "Inca," there is even room for the conjecture that it was the people of Anta who granted to their Cuzco allies the privilege of wearing the title of "Inca" at this juncture and not the reverse, as later Inca historiography insisted. This we will never know.

Certain it is that from now on particularly favored pueblos which fell in line with the plans of Cuzco were rewarded with the boon of citizenship in the new caste system, a procedure in some ways comparable to the jealously guarded extension of the franchise by the growing *civitas* of Rome.

One other achievement, the meaning of which may be indissolubly linked with this portentous assumption of Incahood, is credited to Inca Roca. This is the creation of that unique institution, the royal *panaca*, a ceremonial and a cult coterie centered about the ruler and designed ultimately to serve him in death; it is often referred to also as the royal *ayllu*. Inasmuch as it is to be described later, it will be sufficient to note here that Inca Roca appointed a son to maintain his mummy, his rites, his palace, his continuing wealth, his table service and entertainment after death, and the continuity of his blood.

Inca Roca left a number of children. His chief pride and fame rested on the exploits of his energetic sons. His palace was probably near or on the great square, though it need not have been a particularly pretentious group of *pirca* and adobe buildings. Our only description of him is none too reliable and depicts him as a large and corpulent man with a voice like thunder, much addicted to gambling. On his death—of which we know nothing except that a single source says that it was "hastened by his sons"—many of his women performed the suttee by allowing themselves to be garroted with their own braids; their honorable positions as royal consorts by this act were confirmed.

« 7 »

THE SUCCEEDING AND SEVENTH RULER was named either Titu Cusi Hualpa (Liberal Joyous Cock) or Mayta Yupanqui but was more generally referred to by his astounding and colorful soubriquet, Yahuar Huacac (Blood-Weeper). There is indeed something peculiar about him: with a single exception, noted below, not one event is reported by the chroniclers from his reign, though we know that Inca rule in his day extended to the Urubamba Valley. Both our reliable and our more fanciful sources depict him as a ruler more or less sans history and let it go at that. The confusion in regard to his original name and the grotesquerie of his nickname may conceal a dynastic disturbance. At any rate the popular imagination busied itself with weaving amazing tales on the basis of his name, though it may mean nothing more than "Bloodshot."

It is Sarmiento who has preserved for us certain semi-miraculous, semi-historical material, which is worthy of being set forth here and contrasted with what the same source offers as the purely historical annals of his rule.

It will be recalled that the marriage of Mama Micay to Inca Roca had estranged the Ayamarcas from Huayllacan (undoubtedly Huayllapampa, Meadow Valley, which today is sited on the south side of the Urubamba across from Yucay). Having territory with a common border the two peoples found it all too simple to carry on hostilities against each other, in the course of which a curious intrigue was conceived. Mama Micay in the meanwhile having given birth to the prince Tito Cusi Hualpa, her former Ayamarca suitor Tocay Capac agreed to an advantageous peace with Huayllacan, providing they would abduct the Inca heir and deliver him over. Being the weaker of the two, the pueblo of Huayllacan felt compelled to agree to this arrangement. Needless to say this decision represented a dangerous treason on their part, as by marriage they had acquired an almost kinship status with Cuzco, being now avuncular relatives of the Inca house.

But like many poisons this treason spread until it had tainted the Inca magnates themselves. The town of Paullo, belonging to the Huayllacas, lies to the north of Cuzco on the steep southern declivities of the Urubamba Valley. Here lived a brother of the Inca ruler named Inca Paucar (Gaudy Inca) who was acting as the *sinchi* of that community. Either he or, unbeknownst to him, his sons, agreed to act as agents in the plot. Inca Roca was accordingly informed that the people of Huayllacan wished to strengthen their blood ties with Cuzco by commending their lands and goods to the young prince, who was accordingly invited to a series of kinship festivities to seal this resolution. Not suspecting treachery from his *coya*'s pueblo, and confident of his strong position in the Urubamba Valley, Inca Roca sent the young prince and heir, now about eight years old, under a suitably impressive guard of picked Inca warriors, to his mother's people.

The first version of the tale fully implicates Inca Paucar and the people of Huayllacan in a subterfuge in which a pretense of slackness was put on during which the Ayamarcas, lurking near by, swooped down, seized the prince, and carried him off. The other version is less damaging to the reputation of the Inca house, inasmuch as it specifies that the only guilty ones were certain sons of Inca Paucar who had become jealous of their royal cousin and who themselves directly treated with Tocay Capac and delivered the boy up to him.

The now fully armed Huayllacas of Paullo, led by Inca Paucar, caught up with Tocay's party in Ayamarca territory, and a feigned attack was delivered. Inca Paucar is supposed to have seen to it that victory lay with the Ayamarcas, who were thus enabled to escape with their prize. All the warriors in the Inca prince's bodyguard perished in this affair.

In a version in which Tocay Capac was not himself the leader of the raid, the kidnapped prince was brought before him in his residence in Huayrocancha. Here occurred the miraculous event which so impressed itself upon later Inca history, for the child, informed by the cruel Tocay that he was to be destroyed, began suddenly to weep tears of blood; this so appalled his captors that they dispatched the prodigy to the obscurity of hard service on their llama ranches rather than take the obviously dangerous step of killing him out of hand.

Yahuar Huacac lived a year among the Ayamarca shepherds, badly treated and in close custody. But opportunely one of the women of

Tocay Capac took pity on the young captive and sent word of the site of his detention to her father, the *sinchi* of Anta. The Anta braves, answering the appeal of their kinswoman, covertly gathered at the designated spot on a prearranged day, outwitted the vigilance of the Ayamarca guards, and carried the boy off. A savage encounter occurred at Lake Huaypu when the pursuit caught up with the Anta warriors fleeing southward; the Ayamarcas were defeated.

Yahuar Huacac was royally feted in Anta, but his escape from Tocay Capac was not made known to the Incas for another year. When Inca Roca was finally informed of the whereabouts of his heir, he sent a spy disguised as a beggar to ascertain if indeed it was true. When the happy discovery was reported back, Inca Roca dispatched an important embassy with costly presents to Anta petitioning the return of his son. In a spirit of neighborliness the Antas returned the gifts; they sent word that their only desires were to serve Cuzco, but that the return of the royal heir was nevertheless contingent upon their being granted the full aristocratic status of Incas of the blood. In gratitude Inca Roca went in person to Anta and greeted the people as his Inca kinsmen.

Back in Cuzco, Yahuar Huacac was given as a bride Mama Chiclla (Selected Lady), a daughter of the great Tocay Capac himself, thus healing the breach that had brought tragedy to so many pueblos. Tocay Capac in reciprocity married an Inca princess. An alliance of great importance to Inca expansion had thus been cemented. Two years after his return to Cuzco, Yahuar Huacac assumed the coronal fringe, his father having died. At the time he was nineteen years of age.

Picturesquely blending elements of diplomatic and military history with miracle and romance, this tale has a value in providing an oblique view of the actual situation towards the close of the reign of Inca Roca.

The situation as presented is complex. Inca military power was able at this point to control some of the pueblos in the close vicinity of the Huatanay Valley and had reached north along the Antisuyo road as far as the Urubamba River—as such it had challenged the Ayamarca power in the Anta Basin. However, when the royal heir was abducted by a coalition between Ayamarca and those pueblos subject to the Incas in the Urubamba Valley, Cuzco could only sit supinely by. The stalemate was broken when Anta, Huayllacan, and the Ayamarca falling out sent their warriors into the field against each other. Marriage, confederacy, and watchful waiting were perforce adopted by the small Inca state in preference to a full commitment on the field of battle.

Beside the picture of a subject community revolting, we find treachery among the Inca magnates themselves. The appearance of the cousins of the heir-apparent among the conspirators would point to a struggle over the Inca succession as at least one of the moving factors in the incident which forced Inca power back from the Urubamba. Ayamarcas inflicted a complete initial disaster on Inca arms with ease, and even in the end the Incas had to come to an arrangement through exchanged marriages with the formidable Tocay Capac. Diplomacy and arrangement were still the superior Inca weapons, though certainly not their only ones.

They had been forced to bow to the desires of the strong pueblo of Anta, and in a move that was to initiate a remarkable Inca policy and one of the intimate secrets of their power, they thus first extended their caste and prerogatives to a favored group by adoption or co-optation. The Antas became the first Incas by adoption. They were able to extort this desirable concession because of their position as potential members of the anti-Inca coalition that threatened to ring Cuzco in from west, north, and east. The significant point to be made is that, with insufficient military might, the Inca state was able to dissolve this hostile alliance and avert the impending avalanche. The above are permissable speculations which we can derive from the famous tale.

By his Ayamarca *coya* Yahuar Huacac had either two or three legitimate sons. After what may have been acute succession difficulties, the youngest son inherited.

The name of this prince, who thus became the eighth Inca ruler, was Hatun Topa Inca (High Royal Inca). He is better known to history, however, as Viracocha Inca. Inasmuch as there begins at this point a complete reorientation in Inca policy, we shall leave him for later consideration.

WE MUST CLOSE with a word on the absolute chronology of this early period. The official historians of Tahuantinsuyo had no interest in the mere addition of years, and their heirs, the Spanish chroniclers, were accordingly left to their own far-reaching fantasies on the subject. Briefly there is no exact knowledge at all, and each historian must guess where he is in these uncharted seas by whatever method of dead reckoning he prefers. Rowe has opted for 1200 A.D. as a rough date for the founding of Cuzco.

On the basis of a reconstruction of early Inca history, which essentially omits Manco Capac in the story of the actual founding, we have seven rulers to account for down to Pachacuti's accession date, which may be accepted, on Cabello Valboa's evidence, as 1438. Our own preference, based on the concept of four generations to a century and working back on this estimate from Pachacuti, gives a date for the first Inca entry into Cuzco, as recorded in the Sacred Legend, closer to 1250 A.D., but the difference is slight indeed. Interestingly enough for those who enjoy contemplating the coincidental, this is also the date given for the descent of those invading Nahuatl peoples who called themselves the Aztecs into the lake basin of Mexico which was to become their home.

THREE.
BASIC FORMS
OF PERUVIAN RELIGION

IT IS SCARCELY POSSIBLE at this distance to make a general assessment of Peruvian religion; considering the plethora of languages spoken there before the coming of the Spaniard, as well as the fact that there is not one but three Perus—coast, sierra, and montaña—we would be wise no doubt to stress the variety in religious formulations to be found therein. The exuberant grotesquerie of Mochica religion, as we apprehend it from their ceramic art, is certainly in no sense comparable with the order and dignity of the developed Inca cult. Statements like this are perhaps as far as we can go in the matter of noting differences in religious attitudes.

Father Cobo, who was closer to the sources than we and who is eminently worthy of respect, states that the Indians of Peru evinced a peculiar and most compelling impulsion towards the divine and a special curiosity about it, with the result that most of what they did, made, and—from vegetables to progeny—nurtured, was done and raised to offer to the gods. Intensity of religious feeling was therefore everywhere the norm.

Common patterns do appear in Peruvian myth and cult. Wherever we look in pre-Spanish Peru we find the importance of oracles, the popularity of pilgrimages, the prevalence of the *pacarina* cult, the

Flood story, and a tendency to accept the idea of a sovereign creator. The Incas naturally partook of this basic Peruvian religiosity, but as they moved up into the rarified levels of empire, they were to re-define radically and indeed to reconstruct it in its various elements. We may thus properly speak of imperial Inca religion as distinct from this more general type.

《 2 》

COBO GIVES US FURTHER TO UNDERSTAND that the two principal deities worshipped by the Peruvian Indians were the Sun and the Earth. The sun, *qua* sun, was not the most universally acknowl-edged god either on the coast or in the sierra before the Incas brought him into prominence, which leaves alone to Pachamama, Earth Mother, that high distinction. Nevertheless we have to state, in a seeming anomaly, that she figures hardly at all in the Inca imperial pantheon, that she never made "officialdom" as it were—in exactly the same fashion as we find the old Aegean Earth Mother Demeter having no real seat on Olympus. Plastic representations of her, spe-cifically identified as such, in museums are unknown to me, and only one is clearly mentioned in the works of the chroniclers. Nor could she claim any shrine in Peru comparable in wealth with those of the Inca Coricancha or the coastal Pachacamac (Earth-Maker).

I can see only one explanation which can unite Cobo's assertion of her primacy and the indecisive quality of our evidence, and this is that she represents a level of religious understanding so basic, so inchoate, so pervasive, so vast, so venerable, so protean, that the specialized cults of the Creator, the Sun, and the Thunder—more friendly to priestly manipulation and enrichment—offered her no stimulation and no reason to change. Pachamama never altered either her broad and bountiful, or her cruel and flinty, lineaments. She stayed down among the lowly potato-growing folk while daring leaders were creating imaginative political and theological formula-tions far above their heads. These leaders of course had no intention of denying her. To put it simply, it was because they so thoroughly accepted her as an all-in-all that she was not bent to specific priestly purposes.

43

As to how she was depicted in the minds of the Peruvian Indians, we may say that palpably she was the earth itself, and characteristically she was that mysterious sheaf of powers residing in the substance of the earth. By some she was worshipped as an open, tilled field, a *chacra*. By others she was seen as the soaring ranges of the Andes—whom therefore they called *Coya*, Queen—and in her precious essences she could be distilled out in the pure metals, gold and silver, to which metals in nugget form they reverently blew kisses, calling them "Mother." The mountains were thought of as her plenteous breasts, the milk of her waters flowing ceaselessly out of them to nourish her children, and for obvious reasons therefore the confluence of two streams always formed a superior *huaca*. Her most famous oracle stood where the Mama and the Chacalla joined (today the Rimac and the Santa Eulalia rivers behind Lima). Mother, mountain, and water were here one.

We have stated that no undeniable sculptured representations of Pachamama have come to our notice, yet there are figurines of nude "womanliness" which, like the Roman concept of Juno or the Syrian Astarte figurines, express the force that was particularly hers to dispense. Women naturally found her worship congenial to them. Though she bore and nurtured all humans, male as well as female, still to the latter she had given that special secret that was part of herself, the power to bear and rear.

From Huarochiri in the sierra comes a myth which reflects her cult practices. A certain god, Pariacaca (Sparrow Rock), succeeded in bringing water to the drought-stricken *chacra* of a woman named Chuqui Suso; in payment he demanded her favors and together they ascended his sacred mountain, there to unite in a deep embrace. That this is a decayed version of the rites of the down-pouring storm-god who awakens the earth below him to fertility is evident. Ritual mating on high places of the earth intended to mime, restate, applaud, and encourage the divine activities of Mother Earth are numerous in primitive cults.

We know more of Pachamama as she was conceived among the Incas than elsewhere in Peru. This is the deity whom in a previous chapter we identified with the Mama Huaco of the Sacred Legend. To the humble and composite folk of Cuzco she was a veritable

Witch of Atlas, a Morgan le Fey, a Circe, dangerous, enchanting, desired, but still recognizably the Earth Mother; this to be seen in her intimate connections with serpents, Mithraic cave-birth, rocks, and the unrivaled mystery of herself—for she was without a begetter. In the Cuzco cult she was the holy *chacra* first mentioned in the Sacred Legend. Here in her avatar as Mama Sara (Corn Mother) she appeared to the folk in the festival of the Aymoray, a harvest-home and one of the four central ceremonies of the imperial Inca state.

Throughout Peru another deity, Mamacocha, Mother Sea, appears to have been simply a special epiphany of the Earth Mother—as she was also in Syrian mythology. On the coast the Earth Mother was named Vis, while the Sea was Ni. The latter divinity fed the people of the valleys there with the same luxuriant hand as did Pachamama, but from the teeming shoals of the Pacific instead of the terraces of men. Around Lake Titicaca the Collas venerated that body of water as their mother, and their ancient claim was that they had sprung from her body. Everywhere in Peru springs were thought to be Naiads, "Daughters of the Sea," and after the sowing of the crops offerings of conch shells—pleasing and sympathetic objects—were made to them. Thus ran a Peruvian husbandman's prayer to one of these "Daughters of the Sea":

> O fountain of water, you who have watered my land so many years and thus bounteously have allowed me to gather in my sustenance, do the same this year also, and even more copiously for a harvest greater yet.

We are fortunate in possessing a myth which pertains to that aspect of Mamacocha worshipped in the coastal valley of Lurín at the shrine of Pachacamac. This is the myth of Coniraya and is treated more fully in the following chapter. Here it suffices to say that we learn of a great goddess called Urxayhuachac inhabiting the deeps of the Pacific who, like the foam-born Aphrodite, was called "Mother of Doves," and who possessed her own shrine in the temple complex of Pachacamac where was a tank containing a sacred fish, totemic of the edible fishes in the sea, and no doubt also an avatar of herself. The tale about her has a scarcely veiled reference to human beings

45

sacrificed in her cult by being hurled down from the headlands. Thus, like a true Aphrodite, she is reputed to have lured and charmed certain unfortunates to their deaths with caresses and loving words.

In her various forms the Earth Mother is to be found in the basement of all Peruvian religion. She was the Holy Mother (Mama Ocllo) and is at times indistinguishable from Moon Lady (Mama Quilla). Not only was she a deity, or rather a series of deities, and therefore capable of being mythologically and humanly understood; she was also a prodigious religious abstraction. She was "the experience" of the Peruvian Indian as he moved wonderingly, humbly, delightedly, and fearfully from the cradle to the grave. It is to be noted that, consequent upon the discovery of empire as a mode of organization by the Inca state, with its nice political demands, she seemed to sink deeper into the folk consciousness; serenely as always, because sure of her power, she could allow the architecture of a state pantheon to arise in noble and masculine proportions over the preserve of Nature, whose mistress she yet remained.

<< 3 >>

ONLY ONE OF OUR SPANISH SOURCES deigns to give us an account of the meaning of *huaca*, a concept basic to any understanding of Peruvian religion, so whatever we say about it is bound to be in some degree suppositious. We are aided analogically however by recalling from the broad pages of history and anthropology that almost every people has believed in "Power," an impersonal quality clotted in various centers in the real and the supramundane worlds, available to both gods and men in varying proportions, but peculiarly dangerous to the latter. Loosely this is the *kuranita* of the Australian Arunta, the Polynesian *mana*, the Vedic *brahman*, the Roman *numen*, the Christian *holiness*, the modern gambler's *luck*, though needless to say there are multifold differences in the special aspects and applications of all these. It would seem that the Peruvian *huaca* belonged to this rich, varied, and imposing family of concepts. Gómara explicitly states that the word refers to the wailing (*huaccay*) that was characteristic of all Peruvian worship, but it equally well can be connected with the Quechua *huac* ("apart") and *huaccay* ("to keep, to guard"), the stress being on otherness, inaccessability, the feeling of distance.

A *huaca* was both a localization of power and the power itself resident in an object, a mountain, a grave, an ancestral mummy, a ceremonial city, a shrine, a sacred tree, cave, spring, or lake of origination, a river or standing stone, the statue of a deity, a revered square or a bit of ground where festivals were held or where a great man had lived. The power which enabled skilled artisans to produce curious pieces of goldwork or fine tapestry or rich dyes or the like was also *huaca*.

Coca, the narcotic leaf from the montaña, was *huaca*. Mama Coca, so ran the saying, was once a lovely woman who had to be killed because of her sexual excesses. Her destroyers cut her up in bits, whereupon there sprang up the coca tree bearing for mankind its rapturous leaves. Coca is carried about in a woven bag but one cannot open the bag to chew the coca until after one has copulated with (i.e., opened) a woman in memory of the deity. Many Quechua girls were accordingly endowed with the name Coca as a thing of power. In this naïve bit of punning folklore from old Peru the tale of the personality known as Mama Coca shifts in rainbow fashion to become equally a statement of the *huaca* of coca. At this low level of Peruvian thinking about the supernatural we find them seeing power and personality simultaneously as two aspects of reality.

« 4 »

THERE WAS ONE CATEGORY of objects in which the quality of being *huaca* was particularly discrete, namely stellar and atmospheric configurations. These were the stars, the storm, the moon, the sun, and the rainbow.

There is much evidence that even before Inca arms forced the worship of their sun-god Inti upon the conquered provinces, there existed local sun cults in Peru. Nevertheless they seem not to have been of paramount prominence except in the far north. The reason for this was that the sun itself was often subsumed under a more generalized god of the sky and the storm.

Mountains in particular, the home and the buttress of the storm, were *huaca*. One etiological tale will illustrate this. The people of the Rimac area worshipped a certain *huaca* on the margin of a glacial lake near the heights of Pariacaca, the vast mountain shield behind them. Because they sacrificed women and children to this *huaca* who was called Huallallo, Pariacaca manifested himself to them and commanded that if they would transfer their adoration to him instead they need immolate only llamas in sacrifice. But the people were too frightened of their own *huaca*'s vengeance to initiate the act themselves. So Pariacaca, armed with thunder and great floods of hail and water, initiated a cosmic three-day battle against the adversary. From the waters unleashed in this conflict was created the present lake Pariacaca. As for Huallallo, he was flung out of the range and over into the opposing Andes just beyond Jauja, where as an isolated volcano he still continues to exist.

Such mountains were scarcely distinguishable from the storms they bred. Of all the male *huacas* in the sierra the "storm" or the "rain" was the most pervasive and dynamic. He was envisaged as a heroic figure in the heavens armed with supernal weapons. In his hand he held the rain, the hail, and the thunder, and the crack of his golden sling was the lightning bolt. To him were dedicated as future shamans all male children born in the open fields on a day of thunder —they were thought indeed to be his sons. Among the Incas he was Illapa (The Flashing One); in the province of Huamachuco (Exotic Bonnet) he was the famous and dreaded Catiquilla worshipped on a sacred peak. Functionally he differs in no important respect from the well-known Near Eastern Baals, givers of rain and wielders of the flood, with the exception that the extant fragments of his mythology never specify him in the role of the dying or disappearing god. After the Spanish conquest the Indian devotees of the storm-god refused to give him up, transmuting him instead into St. James; the drumming of the hoofs of his horse across the pavements of heaven easily explained the sound of the storm. The mounted Santiago today at any important Corpus Christi celebration is, after the Virgin, the most obvious saint in the processions, and he still brandishes aloft his lightning transmuted into a glittering Spanish sword.

There is much reason to suspect that an early form of this Peruvian sky-god was the great cat or jaguar, whose barbaric and highly stylized figure is in art generally portrayed side-on but with head turned to menace the beholder. In those versions where his figure is erect and semihumanized, he has a serpentine mane and grasps serpents, generally two-headed, in both hands (or claws). We have no difficulty equating these serpents of his with the lightnings carried by gods of thunder. The tusked god of Chavín and the erect god from Tiahuanaco are almost certainly prototypes of such later Peruvian thunder-gods as Illapa, at least in their atmospheric role. This would give him among Peruvian male deities perhaps the most venerable place of them all. Beside him the specific Inca sun-god would have been an upstart.

Today the Quechua-speaking Indian in southern Peru believes fervently and graphically in Ccoa, a vicious catlike figure resident among the peaks who commands the rain and all the horrors of the storm; his cruelty is well-known, and the hail bursts from his eyes and ears to spread havoc indiscriminately on the planted fields below and to bring hunger and misery. He is interchangeable in function with Santiago the Thunderer. In northern Ecuador, land of volcanoes, the modern Indian knows this thunder-cat as a fiery mountain demon who commits sodomy with women, strangles them, and then disappears in a rush of wind.

Stars possessed the powerful *huaca* of serving as the ideal simulacra of all species of birds and animals on earth, sustaining them and giving them the vigor to multiply. The Southern Cross, or Lyra, was thought to be a parti-colored llama from whom emanated all individuals of the tribes of llamas. One star presided over the mottled anacondas of the trans-Andean slopes, while another was the stellar progenitor of all bears and jaguars. The Pleiades present a more generalized application of this. Called Collca (Granary) in Quechua, they were held to be the foremost *huaca* in the night skies, creating and penetrating with their fertilizing powers all living beings, including the families of mankind, and providing their sustenance, whence they were worshipped with impressive sacrifices and referred to also as "Mother." In villages near Cuzco today observations are taken of their degree of brightness to determine the time of planting.

The true power of this constellation which possessed the secret of plenty can be seen from the fact that in certain valleys of the coast the year depended on its annual rising.

The fiesta of the Pleiades was called the Oncoy Mita (Disease Time) and was celebrated by many of the Peruvian tribes with confession and purification. It opened the calendrical year for these groups in June. In colonial days the rites of the Oncoy Mita were occasionally added to the end of Corpus Christi, the Indians even going to the extent of secreting the appropriate *huacas* under the voluminous skirts of the Virgin as she was carried along in procession.

The morning star, Chasca (The Dishevelled One), dispensed stores of freshness and loveliness upon flowers, princesses, and virgins below. She was the deity of the rosy cloud rack of morning, and when she shook out her long hair she scattered the dew upon the earth.

On the coast the moon was generally considered to be a *huaca* superior to the sun, ruling even such elements as the thunder, the sea, and the whirlwind. Her ardent patronage of women was well known; she was the divinity of queens, princesses, and of all women in childbirth.

《 5 》

IT IS SIGNIFICANT that the Peruvian Indians saw the heavens in the same terms as the earth, radiating holy influences. Stars and stones differed not at all in the intensity of their respective powers. One real difference, however, can be perceived on closer inspection btween the stellar and the chthonic, namely that the stellar *huacas* served more as repositories for the basic ideas and categories in creation, as blueprints and sources of all forms and shapes, whereas stone and earth possessed in a higher degree the vital element that infused these forms. No stone *huaca* for instance was thought to be the progenitor of all mankind; it was rather the ancestor of a particular tribe, more specific and less ideal. No star, on the contrary, is known as the ancestor of any specific tribe of men. The above generalization is useful up to a point, for *huaca* is always power, whether heavenly or mundane, but it does not explain the overriding position of the storm-god, whose uniqueness lay in the close dependence of Pacha-mama upon his benevolent rains.

The *huaca* in the earth, in stone, had a special meaning, of course, for it was the flesh of the Mother. The cult of stones is perhaps not older in the Peruvian religion than that of the heavenly bodies, but it seems to have been more pertinacious of its original forms. The solemn and noble concept of a supreme creator-god is a stellar con-cept; no mountain or rock was ever raised by the Peruvian priesthood to that eminence. The gray and lonesome *puna*, the gorges, moun-tains, and boulders meant something different. Some instances of these cults of stone will serve to make this clear.

At the lowest level were the *conopas*, generally quartz stones or unusual pebbles handed down in the family from father to son. They were the *lares* and *penates* of the Cuzco Indians and were also known as *huasicamayocs* (householders). In them resided the spirit of the family ancestors, each having its own name. The care and worship of these *huacas*, being purely private family cults, are therefore to be carefully distinguished from the public worship of the tribal an-cestor. Some families, no doubt the particularly notable ones, pos-sessed as many as four of these *conopas*.

On a broader level of social federation comes the standing stone *huaca*, placed as a rule in the center of the pueblo and acknowledged to be the mentor of the community. It was known as *huanca* (field guardian). In the sierra province of Huamachuco we are told that no pueblo was without its community *huaca* of stone.

An unusual *huaca* was that emerald "big as a goose egg" adored by the natives of Manta, which because of its uniqueness was called "the orphan" by the Spaniards. Though put to cruel tortures the Ecuadoran Indians never revealed its whereabouts, convinced that if they did the whole earth would sink and crumble and all men would die. In this stone there resided the *huaca* of the cosmic.

Sometimes these tribal *huacas* were on near-by sacred peaks, them-selves possessing a similar *huaca*. Such was the Inca Huanacauri already referred to. This crude stone was carried about by the Inca army in all its foreign conquests and returned to the site after the achievement of victory. The Inca state—as a special vehicle for the Inca caste—survived in war only because of the special *huaca* of martial vigor and prowess dispensed by this talismanic ancestor.

The tribal *huacas* were often grouped in divine families or local pantheons, which is to say that the male ancestral stone was given a consort and sons. An erect stone, some fifteen feet high, on a mountain near Hilavi was divided into a male and female portion, both back to back and entwined with serpents. This recalls the curious site of Kenko (Place of Winding Passages) on the height above Cuzco, a standing stone backed up against a great rock which has galleries cut through it and serpentine channels running down the sides (thought to be for offerings of *chicha* to the Earth Mother). A well-known *huaca* in Huamachuco had grouped about it ten others reputed to be its sons, as well as a female stone with her parts exposed—this latter being its wife, a *huaca* of multiplication for all the people around. When the Augustinian monks broke the redoubtable stone of Catiquilla into rubble and dispersed it, the "power" still resided in the bits, for one small pebble, on being interrogated later by an Indian wizard, replied, "I am Tantaguayanai (Ragged Swallow), son of Catiquilla." From Catiquilla's graveled remains in the days of the Spaniards some three hundred sons were eventually to be spawned.

The ancestral *huaca* with his procreative power, however, did not always need a consort hewn by frosts and sun out of the crags like himself. He sometimes demanded a human bride. There is information on record of a lovely fourteen-year-old virgin, married in a three-day fiesta held on an icy peak, to the stone *huaca* who watched over the prosperity of the folk.

Chimborazo, the snow-covered volcano in Ecuador, was the *pacarina* or place of origin of the Puruha Indians. To it they sacrificed their high-born virgins and finest llamas of the sacred herds. Chimborazo, a great male, was wedded to Mount Tungurahua, a female, on the opposite side of the valley; their visits to each other and their gigantic matings were a matter of record. Perhaps the most startling example of this familial arrangement of the stone *huacas*—though laid on an imperial scale and supporting the Incas' sun theology— was the marriage arranged by the tenth Inca ruler, Topa Inca, between the island of Titicaca, seen as male, and the near-by island Coati, female.

BECAUSE OF THEIR INTERTRIBAL PRESTIGE the most venerable oracles could be appealed to by the distant chieftains, by the rulers of civilized states, or by the commoner folk. These oracles were scattered the length of Peru, sometimes in vast artificial shrines like that of Pachacamac in the Lurín Valley south of Lima, sometimes in the most awesome natural surroundings as that of Apurimac. Their responses usually were available at certain stated times only, no doubt co-ordinated with seasonal festivities. They were generally consulted at night and under the most grisly and sibylline conditions; when their answer came, it came as a shriek or hiss out of the unlit chamber and was interpreted to the petitioner by the chief officiant at the shrine.

In the old and established valleys of the coast, such as Pacasmayo and Rímac (Lima), there were famous oracles, but none matched Pachacamac in venerability, influence, or wealth. This famous oracle, the nucleus of a population of twenty thousand souls, attracted vast numbers of pilgrims who came under a pan-Peruvian safe-conduct from as far as one thousand miles away. In the adobe-lined streets of this city by the sea mingled Indians of many nations, the poor carrying their pathetic offerings side by side with arrogant ambassadors from great rulers who arrived with sumpter trains of carriers laden with the stuffs of their provinces. The temple was built on an eminence overlooking the Pacific, but it was further artificially stepped up to a great height in a complex series of brilliantly painted adobe terraces and setbacks, a shrine so holy that protracted fasting alone could move the suppliant up from one level to another, twenty days being required to enter the enclosure and a whole year to gain the top. Only one gateway gave access to this startling edifice, at the summit of which was the naos of Pachacamac, an unwindowed, bloodstained, and fetid den. The oracular god inside was a *huaca* of origination, a wooden post or tree trunk known to have created the people of the area. His priesthood, arranged hierarchically under a high priest, had over the years developed his mythology to portray him as something more than a local ancestor; he controlled all beings, sustenance, and functions and possessed the power to destroy his creation by flood if and when he desired.

So impressive a male god, resident on his gray cliffs over the rolling waters of the Pacific, necessarily had to be brought into connection with Mamacocha, the Sea, and so the myth ran that they were wedded. Her name was Urxayhuachac, as we have already seen, and she may have had the form of a sea serpent.

In its intertribal aspects the cult of Pachacamac was typically oracular. *Curacas* and rulers sent their requests concerning threatened crops, diseases, and floods and offered the god gifts in return. The high priest who received their emissaries customarily sat in a morose silence with covered head. Animal sacrifices were offered over the north and south sides of the temple complex. In more difficult and onerous cases, human beings were destroyed as offerings on the precipitous side facing the sea. Priests charged with the question on the request of the pilgrim advanced into the naos in symbolic attitudes of servility with their backs to the idol. The blood of the sacrifice was then smeared over the crude features of the wood stock, in this way satisfying the deity's immortal hunger.

This cult may indeed stand as representative of much Peruvian custom, a *huaca* of local origination, which had the idea of creation implicit in it, alongside some form of the majestic Mother who out of her plenty feeds all humans. It differed from the typical only in being the most famous of them all as a pilgrimage center and the one most feared by the suspicious Incas.

Up on the sierra the three *huacas* specifically ancestral to the Incas were the temple of Coricancha, Huanacauri, and the Pacaritambo cave of origination. All three sites contained the petrified bodies of the male progenitors of the Inca line. The city of Cajamarca (Canyon City) possessed a famous *huaca*, as did Huamachuco in the thunder-oracle Catiquilla. South of Cuzco the supreme oracle was Coropuno, situated on a mountain eternally covered with ice and snow. Below Cuzco some sixty miles down the Royal Road towards Collasuyo was the wealthy shrine of Vilcañota, a supremely holy oracle lying under the mountain mass or "knot" of Ausangate, visible from the center of Cuzco and one of the best-known landmarks in this somber and theatrical land. Farther on lay the great lake of the Collas, itself a goddess, with several sacred islands studding its surface, Titicaca being paramount among them. Titicaca was a well-known *huaca* before the coming of the Incas, but inasmuch as it was they who organized its splendor and spread its fame to the confines of their world, we shall leave consideration of it until later.

Contrasting with the coastal Pachacamac was the sierra oracle of Apurimac on the Royal Road northwest of Cuzco. The Apurimac (Great Speaker) was the river separating the Quechua-speaking Indians from the Chancas and Vilcas to the west. On the rim of this great gorge stood a *temenos*. A sacred enclosure had been erected within which was a life-sized wooden post driven into the ground. This rudely fashioned idol, referred to as the Apu (Great One), was female, for it had breasts of gold, the fine garments of a woman, and a precious girdle. Grouped around stood a multitude of other sacred poles, all female, and all daubed with dried blood as was the Apu. Like the Peloponnesian Artemis, this sanguinary Peruvian goddess reveled among her attendant nymphs and in surroundings even more uncouth and savage. Conforming to the total femaleness of this divine family was her priesthood, for instead of being served by a high priest as was Pachacamac or the Inca sun-god, the goddess had a sybil called *sarpay* who interpreted her voice. The relationship of the female *huaca* to the great rumbling river spirit below is unclear —they may have been one and the same.

On their march of conquest west and north the Incas were to seize this famous site and to integrate it into their policy by installing one of the Inca ruler's sisters as the *sarpay*. This seems to have been the situation until the entry of the Spaniards, on whose approach the sybil, responding to the tragedy of the occasion, covered her face and, invoking the name of the Apurimac, threw herself from the lip of the gorge into the deity's vertiginous embrace below.

« 7 »

A DETAILED DISCUSSION of the many varieties of priests and sorcerers would be out of place here, but a general statement on the subject should be made because of its bearing on Inca cult and history.

A fundamental shamanism lies behind all sacred offices in ancient

Peru. Presumably there was some kind of an evolutionary line leading from the minor shaman of the community who invoked and
questioned his own *huaca* (a pebble, a spring, a tree), up through
the established office of the diviner for the important provincial
huaca, and finally to such institutionalized cadres as the priesthood
of Pachacamac or Inti. Perhaps to some such rough line of development corresponds that statement of Arriaga, wherein he shows the
three ways by which in Peru a person became a sorcerer or priest:
by self-election, by heredity, or by the suffrage of other priests.

Shamanism in ancient Peru, as among Siberian, Eskimo, and
American Indian tribes in general, was a calling as well as a skill.
A person who had become suddenly deranged or hysterical could
be thought proper for training in the abstruse art of sorcery. A person
who had narrowly escaped drowning had the *huaca* of the appropriate
water-spirit and could be trained up in that deity's oracular service.
A person who had been struck by lightning or one whose mother
had given birth in the open during a storm had been thereby claimed
to his service by Illapa, the thunder-god. In the southern Andes
today, so slow has been the decay of time that sorcerers, curers, and
thieves all are thought to have a special intimacy with Ccoa the
thunder-cat, who takes as his thanes those whom he has killed with
his lightnings.

According to most of our accounts the lower orders of the popular
shamans formed a wretched, greedy, and afflicted class, feared by
their own people while scorned and suspected by that Inca state
which held them in much the same odor as the medieval Christian
church held witches and other purveyors of the devil. They seem
not to have assumed their shamanistic functions until fairly old.
Cobo mentions the numbers of these shamans and practicing wizards
as being impressively large in every community—though we suspect
that an increase occurred after 1532, as a result of the removal of the
stern hand of the Inca.

The areas of specialization open to the shaman were many. There
were herbalists, generally women, whose knowledge of the local
flora was both curative and deadly, depending on the immediate case
before them. There were witches who divined in frenzies brought on
by heavy potions of *chicha* infused with *vilca*, a purgative herb;

others who discovered mysterious things by second sight, by shape-shifting, by aerial flights, or by incubation. Some divined the cause of disease, the whereabouts of a stolen article, or the adultery of a wife through the movements of spiders kept in jars; others did it by kernels of maize or by a voice from the flames. Others were illicit-love brokers or professional abortionists. To these ventriloquial wizards the local folk resorted on every occasion, public and private, for they alone had the ear of those powers feared by the people.

One group of these diviners must be singled out for special emphasis. This was the class of sorcerers, male and female, from Collao called the *ichuri* (Grass Men), who heard confessions of sin, imposed penances, and finally purified. It is highly probable that the confessional was indigenous in much of Peru, but finding it most prominently featured in Collao following their conquest of that province, the Incas may have deliberately exported that version of it for police purposes into their growing empire.

Among the Peruvians sin had a community connotation—affecting family, tribe, or state—wherefore a sin unconfessed by an individual could exert a blighting influence upon the larger group of which he was but a part. In its most extreme effects it could even cause the illness of his *curaca* or ruler or bring about his death. Any calamity to the pueblo or state if not immediately repaired might therefore entail a rigorous search for the secret sinner and his forced subjection to the confessional. Needless to say, the worst sin of all was falsely confessing. When the Inca ruler fell ill, he would sometimes order each province in the empire to confess en masse.

The confessional was supposedly secret, but one may be permitted strong doubts on this subject, for if the confessor had reason to believe that something was withheld or untruthful in a certain person's confession, he consulted his *huaca* for a verdict—then if need be the person was punished by the community. After a full confession a penance corresponding to the gravity of the infraction was imposed: exile for a stated period up in the passes, to live like an animal on grasses and roots, whipping, stoning, and of course *in extremis* death.

The usual procedures of penance and purification took place at recognized lavatories on riverbanks. Here the confessor could be found squatting, doubtless a ragged and unwelcome sight to all. Those who came to him confessed into a bunch of *ichu* grass. This he held in one hand while he savagely belabored them over the back with a sharp stone, the usual penance to be endured. But if the sin were egregious, the sinner could be sentenced to whipping by deformed and dwarfed Indians assembled on the riverside to perform that sorry duty. After this the sin was transferred into the handful of grass by spitting in it. Or, if the person confessing had brought instead red, white, and green powders for the sorcerer to arrange in checkers on a flat stone, they could then be puffed away into the air as placatory offerings to the gods. "Hear me, mountain peaks about, and plains, condors which soar, and owls, for I wish to confess my sins."

If the *ichu* rite had been used, then the contaminated grass was thrown into the water to be carried far beyond the reach of men, where its power could no longer be felt. A ceremonial baptism or bathing in the river followed.

The confessional, because of its analogy with the similar institution in the Roman Catholic Church, is on the surface one of the most curious aspects of ancient Peruvian religion. The amazing potential in the hands of this group of shamans charged by custom with confessing as a purificatory rite can well be imagined. That the Inca rulers were uneasily aware of this is evident.

FOUR.
PERUVIAN MYTHS
OF CREATION

《 I 》

A PEOPLE MUST ALWAYS REMAIN UNDISCOVERED by the historian until there is in his possession some knowledge of the ideas they held in regard to the source of being, and of the terms in which they described their own appearance upon the face of the earth. The mythology of creation is just this corpus of human speculation out of the past. Nor should the variety, the crudeness, and the concreteness of some of its pages blind us to its fundamental gravity. Our present-day sophistication has separated the idea of human history from the concept of creation which—thus removed into a kind of intellectual limbo—tends therefore to shrivel away. Other ages however have reversed the emphasis, viewing history as an adjunct of creation, a late face of it as it were.

We are fortunate in possessing some creation myths from Peru, which, taken all together, represent a geographical spread down the Andes from Ecuador to Bolivia. From Quito comes the story of the flood-serpent, and from around Cuenca the story of the Cañar Indian brothers and the two beautiful female macaws. From Huamachuco we have the tales of Ataguju the creator-god and Catiquilla, the *huaca* of the stormy peaks of the Cordillera Blanca. Farther south in the sierra we have the contrasting tales of the creator-god Coniraya on the one hand and of the storm-god Pariacaca and his son Huathiacuri on the other. In the valleys of the central coast, particularly Végueta and Huacho, there were told involuted legends of the creation of the world by the Sun, and a subsequent fashioning of mankind by one of his blood. From the area close to Cuzco comes the legend of the querulous llama and the Flood. The important myth of the creation of the world by Viracocha is Inca but looks to the Puno and the upper Vilcañota Valley. This is the sum total of Peruvian creation myths extant.

The simplest of these tales, not concerned strictly with creation but with survival after the Flood, relates that anciently a llama-herder's beasts ceased grazing and began to complain piteously while gazing insistently into the night sky. They finally revealed to their master that they read in the stars the signs of a great deluge close at hand. With this forewarning the shepherd and his children were enabled to escape up a sacred mountain which increased its height as the waters of the flood rose. From these fortunate few, the Cuyos were descended. This tale comes from an area close to Pacaritambo, the early home of the Incas.

The Quito myth concerns the three sons of a divine first being, Pacha. These three made war on a great serpent. Wounded with their many arrows, the serpent vomited up the waters which rose and flooded the world. The three sons of Pacha and their wives ascended Mount Pichincha to escape the deluge. They took with them many stores and many kinds of animals and preserved them up there in a house of canes.

The Cañar myth likewise begins *in media res* with a flood and a selective survival. Two brothers fled up a mountain which, as in the tale above, could adjust its height to the engulfing waters. After the subsidence they descended to scrape out a miserable existence on roots and herbs. One day they found, on returning to their hut, that deliciously prepared food and *chicha* had been mysteriously left for them. After a number of repetitions of this they finally hid in the hut to discover the cause of the bounty, and saw two lovely macaws fly in. The birds then changed into young Cañar women and set about preparing the day's food. When first surprised they flew away as parrots, screaming, but the younger brother finally succeeded in raping the younger sister, having by her children who became the ancestors of all the Cañar Indians. He married her and the other he made his concubine upon the death of his brother. The Cañars are thus explicitly said to be descended from parrots.

These origination myths stress the animal world, and one of them indeed may be interpreted totemistically. They share the concept of the flood at the beginning of things and the derivation of a particular tribe out of that catastrophe. In them the holy mountain, the tribal *huaca*, is connected with this origination.

《 2 》

THE AREA BETWEEN QUITO AND CUZCO has left us two major families of creation myths: the Catiquilla and Pariacaca stories from the sierra and the sun-god stories from the coast. Both sets differ markedly.

The most curious of these, because of its mixture of native creation elements and hostility to the Spaniards, is perhaps the tale connected with Catiquilla, the *huaca* of Huamachuco, the zone where the mighty peak of Huascarán, highest of the mountains of Peru, rears up above the quiet valley world of the Callejón de Huaylas. Hereabouts in antiquity the Indians adored Ataguju, who from his seat in the sky governed all things. This omnipotent god possessed no consort but ruled in consonance with two emanations of himself, servants and helpers, whom he had created *ex nihilo*, themselves without wives. In the tales about him we can discern both Inca and Spanish influences.

Ataguju sent down upon earth a certain personage to reside among a group of Christians, who in their hostility first enslaved and then destroyed him, but not before he had seduced one of their women. This woman bore two eggs from his embrace before she died, one of them to become the redoubtable *huaca* Catiquilla. Catiquilla dutifully recovered his mother's corpse and revived it, whereupon she gave him a sling which had belonged to his father and with which he now proceeded to kill the hated Christians. With the land freed of this pollution he then appealed to Ataguju to aid him in repopulating the land with Indians. In answer the Creator sent him to the sacred mountain, where with his golden digging stick he unearthed those first Indians from which all tribes were later to claim descent. The Huamachucos and Conchucos of this area thus look to Catiquilla, a thunder- and rain-god aloft on his snowy peak, as the source of their being. At the foot of the holy mountain there was a large religious community which worshipped him in company with his brother and his consort. It was this famous oracle which neither Atahualpa nor the Spaniards after him were wholly able to silence.

A somewhat similar and almost as notable god of the sierra high places was Pariacaca, whose eyrie was on the sacred crags of Condorcoto (Condor Mound) beneath which straggled the perilous and awesome road connecting Jauja with the coast. There are two versions of his myth. The most straightforward one relates that five eggs appeared on the summit of Condorcoto, out of which hatched Pariacaca and his brothers. Pariacaca's first act was to call down ruinous floods which carried away in a great wave of destruction a certain arrogant rich man who had set himself up as a god. Following this, Pariacaca had occasion to stop at a fiesta being celebrated in a pueblo near Huarochiri. Because clad in the habiliments of a beggar at the time he was neglected by all the merrymakers—with the exception of one compassionate girl who regaled him with *chicha* and other comforts. In gratitude he imparted to her the secret that five days thence he was going to destroy them all by a great flood, but that she and her children (no doubt by him, though this is not stated) and immediate family would be permitted to escape to higher ground and safety, if she would not divulge the secret. Having then ascended a great mountain above Huarochiri, Pariacaca sent down in wrath his consuming waters which destroyed all but those forewarned.

The expanded version is more folkloristic. Here Pariacaca is presented as the father of a personage disguised in the rags of an outcast and called Huathiacuri. In this version the rich man had fallen ill because his wife had unknowingly and inadvertently committed adultery. Huathiacuri cured the rich man and was rewarded with the younger of his two daughters. He used to make a daily ascent of Mount Condorcoto, where the five divine eggs were preserved, and there dally in love with this young bride. But an inimical brother-in-

law challenged him to a contest of cleverness, and his father Pariacaca, as one of the five mystic eggs on the heights, advised him in an
oracle to accept. The challenges in this contest, all of which Huathiacuri won, though not directly related to our subject, are of interest
as revealing how a basic myth can be patched and embroidered and
finally made into a vehicle for speculation and entertainment. The
first chore was to trick a fox and vixen out of their magical drum and
chicha jar, this taking place at a fiesta. At the celebration Huathiacuri's wife beat the drum in a manner superior to her rival (her
wicked sister?), making the earth shake under the dancers, while
Huathiacuri himself outdrank all his enemies, remaining sober as
they, when they tried to drain the magic goblet, failed and fell down
in drunkenness. The next contest was to see who could wear the most
splendid finery. Huathiacuri won by donning a dress of snow.
Another was a race to see who could first erect a suitable house.
Though the rich brother-in-law had many helpers, a host of small
birds and animals finished Huathiacuri's house first. Revenge was
finally exacted when Huathiacuri challenged his opponent to a special and difficult dance, but the brother fled from the test to become
the stag on the hills which is today hunted by man. As for the wicked
sister, Huathiacuri turned her into a stone shamefully displaying her
private parts to the world.

In both the Catiquilla and the Pariacaca myths, we have the common pattern of a storm-god, either born from or resident in a holy
egg on the sacred peak. Associated with him are brothers, helpers or
avatars of himself. This storm-god destroys an evil race with his
floods and then brings into being the present peoples of the earth.
These are then not strictly creation stories but re-creation myths referring to a postdiluvial survival. And both storm-gods are ambiguously joined to a creator-god (see below).

<< 3 >>

THE MYTH OF CONIRAYA must now be examined. The setting is
exactly the same as that for the Pariacaca stories, namely in the great
mountain chain between Jauja and Pachacamac, and we must therefore accept the fact of their close association, the main geographical

difference between the two myths being that the Coniraya tale oscillates between the highland zone and the religious site of Pachacamac on the Pacific. That the priesthood of Pachacamac had a control over the making of the myth we cannot doubt.

We are told at the beginning that Coniraya was in reality Viracocha the Inca Creator. He first appeared among men disguised in the filthy rags of a beggar, ordering for them the elements in their culture, their control of irrigation systems, the practice of agriculture in terraces, etc. He had one trait of particular interest: he was profoundly hostile to the local *huacas* worshipped by the people, maltreating and mocking them.

In those days there was a beautiful but disdainful virgin named Cauillaca, much sought after by the local *huacas*. Changing himself into a bird, one day Coniraya inserted his semen into a fruit which the girl ate. Thus she became pregnant without knowledge of her violator's identity. To discover this, when her child could crawl, Cauillaca summoned all the *huacas* to a meeting. Elegantly attired they appeared before her, with the exception of Coniraya, who was clad still in his tatters. The mother put her young son down in the silent circle on the assumption that he at least would know his paternity. When the child embraced the knees of the unprepossessing stranger, in utter horror at the indignity, the mother seized the child and fled down from the Cordillera into the sea off Pachacamac, where the two were metamorphosed into great rocks off the coast. Coniraya's pursuit of her—he was now resplendantly clad as a king and blazing in glory—was fruitless. As he followed her down from the mountains he blessed or cursed certain animals according as they prophesied his success or failure in the chase; thus condors, hawks, and lions are fortunate creatures whereas skunks, foxes, and parrots are undesirable.

Realizing at last that the mother and child were beyond his reach, he entered the famous shrine of Pachacamac on the coast. Within this sanctuary the two daughters of Pachacamac were guarded by a serpent. This monster Coniraya easily subdued, after which he proceeded to rape the first daughter; the second girl escaped his attentions by flying away in the form of a dove. The mother of the young women and the consort of Pachacamac, referred to as the Mother of

Doves, had gone down into the sea to visit Cauillaca. In those days the sea contained no fishes. In the mother's absence from the sacred site, Coniraya, still overwrought, produced out of the solitary fish kept by the goddess in the temple tank all the tribes of fishes that today fill the sea, an act of benefit for mankind. In wrath at Coniraya's presumption and criminality, the great goddess pursued him down the coast. On a particularly high headland she attempted to lure him with loving enticements and words to his death below, but on a pretext of relieving himself he escaped back into the highlands around Huarochiri.

Gutiérrez picked up a version of this myth where Cons the Creator is credited with the original creation of earth, the heavenly bodies, man, and all animals *ex nihilo*. This god passed through the lands ordering all things until he came to the sea where, by the power of his "Word," he created fish life. Then he returned to his place in the sky. He was followed by the more powerful god Pachacamac, who destroyed this creation in fire and flood, and transformed men into monkeys. After this Pachacamac remade the creation.

The full story of this secondary creation by the god Pachacamac is found in another myth, widely believed by the Indians of the central coast. In this tale the original creator is the sun, while the heroic coastal god involved in the process of re-creation is at one time Pachacamac and at another time his half-brother, a god formerly worshipped in the valley of Végueta whose name is given as Vichama. Because it is built on the traditions, possibly hostile, of two coastal valleys at some distance from each other, the myth presents a confused and poorly jointed appearance, with the same act sometimes appearing more than once in only slightly variant form. Its ritualistic features are of interest.

The Sun created the world and then, in the valley of Végueta, by his rays impregnated the exposed body of a woman. She bore a divine child. Pachacamac, the Sun's first-born, jealous of his father's intimacy with the woman, took her child and cut him into pieces. These pieces he sowed in the ground. From the teeth came corn, from the bones all edible roots, and from the flesh cucumbers, fruits, and trees. Thus Pachacamac brought food into the world so the woman would not starve. Yet perforce she had to nourish herself on the body of her child. From the preserved placenta of the child the Sun, to placate her, produced another child who took the name Vichama. When Vichama had attained a splendid manhood he left Végueta on a far journey; it was during this absence when Pachacamac completed his revenge upon his father the Sun by destroying the mother. He similarly cut her up and from the pieces now created men and women. On his return the dutiful son Vichama first reassembled her scattered remains and resuscitated her, and then in transports of wrath pursued his half-brother and his mother's murderer, Pachacamac, to his temple by the sea where he has since remained. Vichama appealed to his father the Sun to turn all the evil people of Végueta who had conspired with Pachacamac into inanimate stones. They are now either the stone *huacas* revered in the valley, or the rocks, headlands, and islands along the coast similarly worshipped. Then at Vichama's request the Sun sent down three eggs, one gold, one silver, one copper. From the first were reproduced *curacas* and nobles, from the second the womenfolk of the powerful, and from the third all plebians. The world after its ordeal had now been repeopled.

This is a myth which implies the periodic rite of the dismemberment of a child and the use of its flesh for the promotion of fertility. The woman, who is unnamed, will be, if not the Earth Mother herself, an avatar for her, for from her body alone springs humankind. Life is produced when the Sun warms her and stimulates fertility. Here the sun as a male force of procreation takes the place of a rain-god in the act of divine copulation. There are hints in the myth however that Vichama can be ambiguously viewed as a storm-god, for when enraged he bellows and emits flashes, while his ministrations (i.e., the bringing of water to the soil?) are needed to revive his fallow mother, the Earth.

One of the persistent patterns in all of the myths mentioned above is the destruction of an evil or contentious race of men by a flood. When specified this flood is sent by the lord of storms himself. The inhabitants of many Peruvian provinces could point to their mountain *pacarina*, out of which they had emerged as sole survivors from a divine flood. In Quechua this event was termed *uno pachacuti* (The Flood which engulfed the World). Nor were the Incas exempt from this pervasive tradition, for their Sacred Legend told that they had emerged from the cave of Pacaritambo following a flood.

Under this welter of myth we can descry a basic Peruvian story: creation, followed by the creator's destruction of mankind in a flood, and then their recreation or survival brought about by a bodily (and sometimes beggarly) son of the creator. The superficial resemblance to the Judaeo-Christian story is evident, and indeed one of the mysteries of the colonial period in Peru is why the friars did not make more of this.

《 4 》

THERE REMAINS TO CONSIDER that creation myth which the Incas appropriated and modified for their imperial uses. They referred to the creator as Ticci Viracocha (Foundation Lord or, perhaps better, Lord of Beginnings). No mother had brought him forth, and the two sons or emanations of himself who were to aid him in the great processes he now planned were created by him *ex nihilo*. He was invisible and had his seat in the sky. At a time when the earth was wrapped in impenetrable darkness, he descended to Tiahuanaco, from which sacred site he brought forth by his Word alone the luminaries of the sky. Daylight he created and mankind, animals, and maize.

As with the two different versions of the creation in our own book of Genesis, this refined and priestly concept is coupled with one more concrete, variegated, and folkloristic. This catchall version told how Viracocha, capping his gigantic task in Tiahuanaco of ordering the hosts of heaven, sent the sun to make his first appearance out of the rocky island of Titicaca to cancel forever the chaos of darkness. After this he essayed mankind, creating the first race of humans of his own heroic stature. When they became rebellious and disobeyed him, their punishment was on an equally grand scale, for in Tiahuanaco and Pucara they were changed to stone, where as huge and lifeless travesties they stood for all later ages to see. But others say that retribution overcame this wicked race in the flood which the creator sent upon them.

67

This flood was one of the most awesome apparitions of the creator. In Tiahuanaco the creator had shaped the varied tribes of men as figurines in clay or stone and painted them in the colors, headgear, and garments which as nations they were ultimately to adopt. Then, in a great passage of power, he gave them life and a law to obey and live by and sent them down into the earth from which, after the subsidence of the flood, they emerged at the selected place of origination, each one a prototype of his nation in dress and speech. These sites became *huacas* of supreme sanctity to each nation of the Peruvian world.

But the path of the creator was not to be smooth. Beside the two Viracochas whom he had made to aid him in his work, there was a third son, an evil one called Tahuapaca. It was he who cast disorder, unreason, and enmity into all the beautiful works which issued from the divine hand; mountains properly established he melted into loathsome and pestilential valleys, cool springs he withered into barren flats, while into mankind he inserted the corruption of evil. Because of his rebellion the creator ordered him bound, put in a balsa, and set adrift on Lake Titicaca. Cursing and threatening he was thus wafted away but he did not meet death; he still endures, for he floated out the Desaguadero outlet at the bottom of the lake and disappeared into the earth.

With all the tribes of men in their places the creator began his ministry among them: conjuring them up out of the respective *pacarinas*; ordering their societies; assigning to them languages, dances, and pastures; giving them knowledge of the names and properties of places, herbs, and fruits. But especially he enjoined them to obey him and practice charity towards each other. He himself went north up the sierra highway, while sending his two helpers respectively along the montaña road and along the coast that they might duplicate his work. In these travels he is described as a gigantic man, bearded, venerable, and clad in a long white robe.

He taught and preached first to the people of Collao and then passed northward inveighing against the *huacas* until he came to Cacha, the seat of the Cana people. Here the hostile inhabitants tried to stone him, but he cast fear in them by calling heavenly fires down to blast and melt the mountains around. Not until the Canas repented did he stop the fiery ordeal. Urcos was his next destination and there he was well received, speaking to the people from the peak of a high hill, henceforth a most holy *huaca*. When he came to Cuzco he gave the site its name and installed Alcaviza as its first *curaca*.

Thus was his progress until he emerged upon the Ecuadoran seacoast. Joined at this remote northern spot by the other two Viracochas, he spread his mantle and "like foam" rushed out, borne magically across the waves. He never reappeared among men.

With certain variations, this represents the main outlines of the Viracocha myth. But a most important addendum or interpretation was tacked on by the imperial Incas. This addition was used to bridge the gap between the creation of *all* men by Viracocha and the Pacaritambo Sacred Legend which belonged solely to the Incas.

With the retreat of the flood the first land to emerge was the island of Titicaca, in a deep orifice of which the Sun had taken refuge. After his glorious rising here to give light to the world, he called before him the son of his body, Manco Capac, revealing himself as his father and promising him dominion over the entire world. Therefore, before sending him underground to reappear from the cave of Pacaritambo, he invested him with the regalia of an Inca emperor and charged him to spread his cult over the lands. Then he, the moon, and all the heavenly bodies ascended from Titicaca to assume their eternal stations in the skies.

《　5　》

ANY ANALYSIS OF THE VIRACOCHA MYTH begins quite naturally with the vexed and cloudy subject of the site of Tiahuanaco. Little can be said about these extensive ruins lying at thirteen thousand feet above sea level on the southern margin of Lake Titicaca. When the Incas appeared the site was already in ruins. Almost certainly it had been before them a ceremonial and pilgrimage center rather than a true urban focus. It need not therefore itself have been the capital of an empire, but one tends to assume empire or something very like it to account for the labor and organization necessary to erect its structures. The Pacasa Indians in whose territory it was located had no memory of the original builders; they referred to it as Taypicala, meaning in Aymará "the central stone," and adored it as a *huaca*. The Collas at the north end of the lake stated that all the tribes of men after the flood had issued from Tiahuanaco's ruins.

It is easy to see that the towering monolithic statues among those early ruins could have given rise to the story of the creation by Viracocha of a race of giants subsequently petrified, his wrath being suggested by the neglect into which these remains had fallen. No doubt this attracted Viracocha's creation myth to the site in the first place. It is true that there are some superficial resemblances between Viracocha and the god depicted on the monolithic gateway there. Viracocha possessed an entourage of angelic warriors and helpers which could recall the forty-eight divine messengers depicted in the service of the Tiahuanaco god. Viracocha commanded fiery bolts down from the heavens, as we know from the Cacha story, while the Tiahuanaco deity is shown holding the double snakes which symbolize the lightnings. But these in themselves do not establish identity. Furthermore the benevolent and long-robed Viracocha, bearded and leaning on his staff, is a culture-god and the missionary of a new religion, a high priest in short, totally at variance with the blazing sun- and storm-god of Tiahuanaco. In his original nature—as he was worshipped at his aboriginal shrine in Urcos—Viracocha may have evinced the characteristics of a thunder-god wielding flood and thunderbolt, but that would have been long before he was taken over by the Incas. In brief we can find no real connection between him and the site of Tiahuanaco.

Nevertheless out of some such basic Peruvian *huaca* was formed finally the majestic Viracocha of imperial times. He was to become a god invisible, unproduced, needing no consorts—all of these non-popular concepts. He lived somewhere and anywhere in the sky, but he typically cared little for the tirades and specious tricks of an atmospheric or stellar god. His creation and destruction of the disobedient creatures whom he had called into being reveal him as a source of all order and, more vaguely, of morality. He created *ex nihilo* and by the incidence of his Word alone. He was completely sovereign, for he not only created all the other great *huacas*, assigning spheres to each, but he even evinced a pronounced hostility towards them. His sovereignty was neither local nor regional alone;

it was, at its highest, imperial. His full title was Illa Ticci Viracocha Pachayachachic (Resplendent One, the Foundation, the Lord, Instructor of the World).

Such an elaborate structure of priestly concepts rested on a basement of popular Peruvian myth and cult. Viracocha who created men from painted stone dolls is a barely disguised way of stating that men were evolved from the living rock, as the other myths inform us. The Flood tale permeated the mythic consciousness of Peru and consequently had to appear in the Viracocha story, no matter how awkward its appearance there. Viracocha's other selves or helpers reveal the primitive capacity of the Peruvian *huaca* for infinite self-multiplication, witness the spawning of the sons of Catiquilla mentioned previously. And Viracocha's rejection by the Colla merrymakers uses a motif we find also in the Pariacaca tales.

We have discovered enough perhaps to realize that there were at least two different levels in the Viracocha myth. The earliest is to be connected with the local atmospheric and mountain *huaca* of the Cana people, worshipped in Urcos, Cacha, and possibly in Pucara. This *huaca* was known to the inhabitants of Cuzco as early as the rule of the third Inca *sinchi*. The second level appeared after Viracocha Inca had attempted to make of this foreign god something of a suzerain over the other *huacas*, for by his time such a deity was becoming a necessity in the maintenance of the new conquests. Pachacuti was clearly to define this as full sovereignty, but the enriched myth would still remain impressively Peruvian at its core.

FIVE.
VIRACOCHA INCA
AND THE CHANCA WAR

((1))

THIS REIGN, so disturbing to the sierra of southern Peru and at the same time so revolutionary to the inner design of the small Inca state itself, has not yet claimed its proper share of Inca history. This is surely due to the stringent recodification of Inca annals in the succeeding reign which sought an indirect glory by blackening the past. The modern interpreter feels like a man admitted only to the threshold of a vast and darkened chamber. Standing there he may crane his neck about to identify, partly by their dim outlines and partly by their position in the room, the objects which furnish it. But to each of his identifications there will always attach a certain vagueness.

Cabello Valboa gives as the date of the deposition of Viracocha Inca the year 1438. It is certain that his reign had been fairly long, though whether he assumed the royal fringe as early as Cabello Valboa's 1386 is uncertain. Fifty-two years would be an extended reign in any period of history, and we would prefer the competing tradition of a thirty-six-year rule; nevertheless he is referred to as an aged man even before the Chanca war, so Cabello's date is not outside the realm of possibility.

Of the three legitimate sons of Yahuar Huacac, the prince Hatun

Topa Inca was the youngest and was therefore not the first one designated as the heir. He had been married to Runtu Caya (Pearly Dried-Oca) of Anta, the pueblo whose members had not long before been taken into the caste of Incas. His reign was enriched with the loot of his conquests, and in his own day, previous to the downgrading of his annals by his son and successor, he was widely famous. That he was industrious in the varied activities that go with rule is evident. Whether at the same time he was wise, learned, and amicable, as is stated, is not capable of proof, but the enduring success of his technique of conquest bespeaks abilities of a high order. For reasons which will appear, Inca imperial history has its true beginning with him.

Beside the ambition of this ruler, there were other reasons at that time impelling the state outward upon its new career. For one thing, the events of the preceding reign had sucked Cuzco deeply into the tumultuous affairs of her neighbors. The warlike posture which the Incas had then of necessity adopted ended by creating for them a cadre of active and cunning captains, veritable conquistadors. And finally, a broader basis of policy had been established when, to make their support permanent, the Incas had extended to deserving confederates the privilege of wearing the earplugs. From a small and despised pueblo the Incas had become a caste, flexible and powerful. Empire flows naturally out of such a potential.

Before he could move elsewhere, Viracocha Inca had first however to allay embers of unrest still burning in Cuzco. This he performed with studied cruelty and terror. This situation is consistent with Cieza's otherwise unsupported tale that the childless Yahuar Huacac, the preceding ruler, had been assassinated in the city as the result of a plot hatched in Contisuyo and that the city had been saved from sack and chaos only when the people in their straits elected Viracocha Inca to his place.

Having preserved, as he thought, the groundwork for a new military expansion, the new ruler began with an advance over the northern saddle into the Urubamba country. In personal command he first advanced upon the wealthy pueblo of Calca. Crossing the river here, he demanded their submission. The people of Calca, following the custom of the times, fled up to their *pucara* overlooking

73

their fields and accepted siege. The Incas stormed the fort and took it, a maneuver in which they were to become cruelly proficient with the expansion of their empire in the succeeding reigns.

So fierce had been the Inca assault, so thorough was the defeat of Calca, that Viracocha Inca could now impose upon the conquered a permanent tie with Cuzco. Heretofore, like the typical Peruvian *sinchi*, every Inca ruler had considered warfare as a sporadic series of raids and sacks. This had long been the common pattern in the sierra. Now however the Inca ruler was to burden himself with continuing administrative duties in regard to his conquests, each one to be firmly and permanently held and appropriately consolidated. He was, in short, already embarked upon a career of empire.

According to the arrangement Calca had to deliver to Cuzco an agreed tribute at stated times; she was to hold herself subject to an arbitrary *corvée* of labor, and she was to accept the presence and supervision of a resident commissioner or governor. In return Calca was to preserve her field system and be ruled by her native *curaca* under tribal custom. As a patent of his new imperial eminence Viracocha Inca was later to demand that a particular levy of men from Calca be employed in the construction of two palaces, one in Cuzco, and one, a pleasure resort, in a more distant setting.

In the same region he forced the surrender of another pueblo and sealed the understanding arrived at by endowing its *curaca* with the gift of an Inca girl. Under the impact of such successes other peoples in the valley came to offer their submission.

Arduous and bitter campaigning seems to have been the order of this new day. We next see the new conqueror farther to the south smashing the power of Muina, that ancient adversary which had formed a coalition with others to stem the Inca advance. This signal victory, by unblocking the eastern exit of the Huatanay, gave Cuzco uncontested dominion over her own valley.

((2))

WHILE VIRACOCHA INCA WAS ABSENT from Cuzco on these adventures, dissension in the city, which his police action at the beginning of the reign had not really extinguished, flared again into life. A

74

brother of the deceased Yahuar Huacac denied Viracocha Inca's right to the *mascapaycha*, the royal tassle, and along with a large number of partisans in Cuzco he rose in revolt. Inca Roca, a prince whom the ruler had placed in charge of the city, was murdered and a brief reign of terror ensued. Bathed in blood, the city now apparently split along the lines of the two moieties of which it was composed—which may or may not have reflected those serious cultic differences to be mentioned later. Innocently involved were those concubines whom Viracocha Inca had left behind in Cuzco, for they were brutally slaughtered by the insurgents in an attempt to extinguish the ruler's line. But when Viracocha Inca wheeled his forces around and in a swift column moved upon the capital, the revolt incontinently collapsed. The usurper and his entire household destroyed themselves, and their bodies received condign treatment, being thrown out for the creatures of carrion to gnaw and glut upon. A thorough purge cleaned out what remained of the usurper's partisans, and Cuzco settled down to an exhausted and trembling peace.

The steady growth in the external power of the state could not mask a profound internal weakness. The divisiveness of so many and such disparate tribal traditions in the city of Cuzco itself, the heart of the state, was constantly sharpened by the lack of a fully established principle of succession. Inca rule had emerged out of the elective and limited office of *sinchi*. No emperor could of course ultimately accept the principle of election, but as yet the imperial office was too raw to have provided its own proper substitute. This would be clarified to some extent in the following reign.

At some later time Inca war groups, well equipped and with a garrisoned Muina now behind them, pushed farther up the Vilcañota, overwhelming first the Cavinas, then the Canchas, and lastly the Canas. The latter were reduced without a fight after the Canchas had proved unable to halt the Inca juggernaut in a trial of arms. This important thrust carried the Inca Empire beyond the pueblo of Quiquijana and rested it now up against a dangerous frontier, that of the Collas who controlled the northern Puno.

While the Incas had now arrived at the edge of the great Peruvian intermontane basin in the center of which lay Lake Titicaca, they were not to secure a foothold in the area until well into the following reign. The situation in the Puno at the time of Viracocha Inca's advance was fluid and reflected that tendency found everywhere in the Peru of the day to carve large political structures out of the chaos of competing tribes and city states. The tough and sinewy state of Chucuito on the shores of the lake certainly had such pretensions. Here from his seat in the pueblo of the same name a Colla war lord had just battered the power of the Canas so roughly that, on the approach of the Inca armies from the opposite direction, the Canas had as we have seen surrendered to or at least made common cause with the men of Cuzco. The Cana surrender was no doubt a conditional one, and because of their exposed position now as a border march they appear to have received special treatment at the hands of the Inca. At any rate the previous victory of Chucuito over the Canas had endangered the security of that other powerful Colla state beside the lake, with its capital at Hatun-Colla, and had brought on hostilities between the two.

Cieza has it that the army of Viracocha Inca did advance into this den of lions but was hastily withdrawn. This was because, following a fierce and memorable battle between the two Colla armies, it was seen that Chucuito the victor now ruled with uncontested power throughout the basin. Cuzco and Chucuito, both so evenly matched in prestige, thereupon made a treaty of friendship. We are not convinced by Cieza's testimony concerning the presence of Inca armies in Collao during Viracocha Inca's reign, but the nonaggression treaty may be accepted as an event logically occasioned by the new common border established between the two states. The heavy campaigning in which both sides had so recently been engaged explains why a truce of this kind was acceptable.

<< 3 >>

BY THE END OF VIRACOCHA INCA'S ACTIVE MILITARY CAREER the infant empire of Tahuantinsuyo had been born and Cuzco had become the center of a turbulent and aggressive *politique*. It exercised dominion over the rich Plain of Anta, over a buffer area southwest of Cuzco, and it controlled the Urubamba from Calca to well beyond

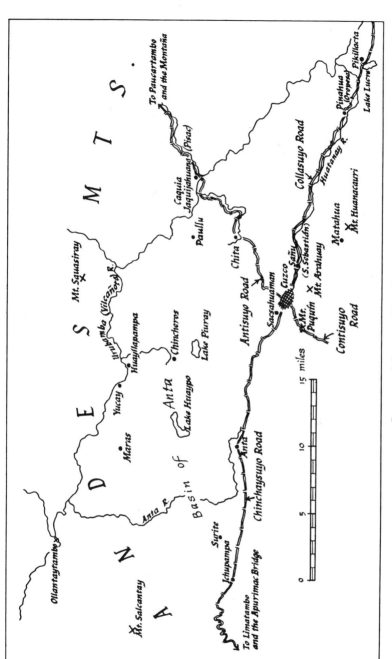

Cuzco and Surrounding Area

Quiquijana. But these buffer areas were not as steadfast as they looked. The entire western front was to bulge in and finally give way in the last days of the reign under the repeated blows of the equally aggressive Chancas, and in that crucible of war the Inca state was to be recast.

This first stage of Inca empire-building had been erected on the scaffold of a prince's ambition and carpentered in the fierce energies of trained captains. With this initial consolidation the need for new sanctions began to be apparent. The honorific titles of the *curacas* so far conquered—as well as of the Inca rulers themselves—had been usually *capac*, somewhat the equivalent of "duke." After the Cana surrender and thus at the culminating point of his imperial career, we find our prince taking the throne name by which he was thereafter known to history, Viracocha Inca. This must mean, on our previous showing, "The Lord Inca," and will therefore be roughly the equivalent of the Persian title King of Kings. Thus did this first Inca emperor announce his pre-eminence over all other subservient or competing Incas. Henceforth the title of Inca was permanently held in the royal line as the Sapa Inca (the Sole Inca).

But the full meaning behind this assumption of a ripe imperial titulary is more complex. To bring this out we must go back to the first meeting of the Inca armies and the Canas. Just beyond the village of Compapata, the scene of the defeat of the Canchas, was situated Cacha, a pueblo of the Canas. Here, long before the advent of the Incas, had existed the famous *huaca* of the god Ticci Viracocha, whose stone statue was to survive the depredations of the Spaniards long enough to be described by Cieza. The actions which the Inca ruler now took are of great interest in this connection for, upon receiving the Cana offer of surrender at the border, before anything else he first took possession of this god; in fact he passed several days in the temple before he was ready to meet the Cana *curacas* to formalize a treaty.

Reading between the lines, we can see that this was a period of temple incubation to seek the god's oracle in dreams. The story runs that on the morning when the ruler emerged he summoned his counselors and captains to hear the glorious news that the god Ticci

Viracocha Pachayachachic had appeared to him and that the whole imperial future of the Incas held up to his gaze had been certified to him and his descendants forever. Overcome by the portentous announcement, which naturally sanctioned and encouraged their careers of conquest, the magnates now hailed their leader as "Viracocha Inca," which name he immediately assumed formally. The rationale of empire was now evident—the god had foreordained it. In gratitude Viracocha Inca ordered the enlargement of the Cacha shrine in adobe brick, and the installation in it of a new and more splendid statue of the Delphic god.

The adoption of the name Viracocha Inca is thus susceptible of a dual interpretation, one stressing the overlordship of the Inca ruler and the other the imperial protection proffered by that special creator-god. It is our feeling that the latter emphasis is perhaps somewhat predominant.

When Viracocha Inca returned to Cuzco he brought with him more than an increase of prestige; he brought a problem. Who was now the paramount god of the Incas? Inti, the family fetish and identified with the Sun, was their father. From Manco Capac down, the line had subsisted because of his good will. There had never been any question of his ultimate sovereignty in the line. But was it not now equally evident that Viracocha had given them the empire? We may as well state here, at the risk of anticipating, that this momentous question was not to be solved until the following reign.

Our sources are chary of facts on this subject, and yet we perceive outlines of the cleft riven deeply through Inca society by the elevation of this new god. First it must be understood that the cult of Viracocha had not been unknown in Cuzco previous to this time, and Viracocha Inca may therefore have made his decision to aggrandize this god before he left on his upper Vilcañota campaign. In this case the attack on the Canas will have been a crusade directed to securing the holy places of the cult. This would explain the ruler's eagerness to enter so precipitously the divine presence, there to receive his imperial commission.

Also it is not improbable that the office of Villacoma (Advising Sorcerer) or high priest was introduced into Cuzco at this time, or at

least refashioned, to point up this religious reorientation. That the
state suffered upheavals in the process is a statement found in only one
source, which attributes the rebellions to the noble families who held
sacred offices. It is our reading of these faint signs that the newly
invigorated Viracocha cult was engaged in a series of moves, possibly repressive to the other city cults, and more certainly designed
to achieve for itself a controlling position. That this cult will then
have been an arm of Viracocha Inca's policy seems obvious when we
recall the hostility, in myth, of the Creator to all the local *huacas*.
The Inca emperor had announced himself as his earthly instrument.
Huaman Poma tells us in a fascinating passage that the ruler "ve-
hemently" worshipped Ticci Viracocha and that he was prevented
from the enormous act of burning all the other *huacas* only at the
coya's urgent intercession. She pointed out to him the certainty of his
deposition if he should carry out his mad intentions.

A curious and unplaced fragment of popular notions concerning
the reign points in the same direction. A two-year drought in the
land had persisted in spite of copious sacrifices. Viracocha Inca thereupon ordered all the *huacas* brought into the great square of Cuzco.
While the multitudes watched, he stepped in among the idols armed
with his golden mace. Three times he demanded that the powers tell
him why they persisted in allowing the people to perish. When they
maintained their obdurate silence, he proceeded to smash them into
bits. And at that moment a divine voice was heard from the heavens
announcing that if the folk would worship him as god, the famine
would be brought to an end. Humbly acquiescent, the people prepared an idol of this god—quite obviously Viracocha—whereupon
rain came and the drought ended.

It is easy enough to see a Viracocha faction crystallizing in this
reign, but much harder to identify the opposition. Logically it would
of course have included the *huacas* of the varied groups in the city
who were not of the *ayllu* of Viracocha Inca; it may have included the
huacas of confederate Incas outside the city proper. But where did
Inti stand?

Though Cobo says that Viracocha Inca ordered that the Creator
be preferred to Inti, the times were apparently not ripe for such a

clarification of the long-standing ferment. The cultic strife in part reflected the discontent of those pueblos both in and outside Cuzco who felt most cruelly the goads of the dour Incas. The empire was still too new to have its power and ruthlessness fully developed, and so the god who was its sanction was not everywhere accepted.

This mixture of fact and speculation takes on a consistency if one adds to it the pectin of the pre-Inca past. We have seen that an earlier period in Peru was known when all men believed in the god Viracocha. Archaeology points to a period preceding both the Incas and the period of local wars before them when both cult and conquest carried a special high god throughout southern and central Peru. This was the Tiahuanaco culture, and the ruins of Huari, near modern Ayacucho, are tentatively thought to be the stones of *its* Cuzco. The Huancas remembered that before the Incas came they had adored a creator of all things. The Rucanas near Andamarca related to the Spaniards facts concerning a pre-Inca people called Viracochas who came conquering among them, few in numbers but saintly. The Rucanas had been forced to build a great city for them and to help to bury them in their whitewashed tombs.

Here was a pre-Inca empire, centered in the highlands northwest of Cuzco and resting its pretensions on a great *huaca* of imperial stature. Supposing this to be true, we may then more easily understand why the newly honored god of Viracocha Inca was so violently opposed by a portion of the Incas in Cuzco. For the Inca ruler to have taken this foreign god—if indeed it was he—as his peculiar *huaca* and to have used him for imperial purposes was to announce that purely local Inca interests were henceforth to be secondary to the grandly expansive designs of the reigning house. Community was to be displaced by state, tribe by emperor, and the comfortable *chacras* of Cuzco by the windy wastes and tribulations of a widened world.

Such a theory may serve to define more closely the opposition. And that the fears of the opposition were justified will readily be seen in the sequel, for the historian can only believe that Tahuantinsuyo did consciously model herself in part on a blueprint from the past, open to her then and still readable, but lost to us today.

IT WAS AGAINST THIS BACKGROUND that a dangerous conspiracy within the royal family itself now developed. As might be expected, it concerned the succession. Viracocha Inca had produced a number of sons, of whom Inca Urcon (Llama Buck Inca) had already been fully designated as his father's choice. Another legitimate and younger son was Cusi (Joy, Good Luck) who had been given at the period of his tribal initiation the full name of Inca Yupanqui (Honored Inca). He had been born in Cusicancha, possibly a women's establishment, close to Coricancha, and thus was fully a Cuzqueño. These two princes were to be protagonists in a drama of lurid power.

The emperor had long since accomplished his most pressing campaigns to the south and east. He was now old and weary. For some years he had been building a royal retreat and fortress at Pisac in the Urubamba Valley high above the valley floor. Pisac had an outstanding strategic value as it stood midmost on the only road that led from Cuzco into the montaña of Paucartambo. This eagle's nest he called Caquia Jaquijahuana, rich, remote, and perfectly secure, a world of precipices and hanging footpaths unbelievable unless seen. It was towards these villas that he had turned his thoughts when he announced the co-optation of his son Inca Urcon as a second emperor. This son had been placed in charge of Cuzco during his father's involvement in the Vilcañota campaign, and was familiar with the rule.

Sarmiento says that in deciding upon this action Viracocha Inca was moved by his passion for the beautiful concubine, Cori Chulpa, who had borne him the prince Inca Urcon. This tale makes Urcon out an illegitimate claimant to the succession, and his selection by his doting father was therefore an insult to the legitimate *coya*.

Whatever the truth of this, the divisive effects of his coregency are abundantly evident. With the old emperor now in semiretirement and following his own formal investiture as an Inca ruler, Urcon began his summary and ill-starred rule, from which history has preserved for us little else than sneers and slanders. It was he nevertheless who seemingly first instituted the tradition of brother-

sister marriage to insure the purity of the royal line. This development—a phenomenon found in other royal lines in history— must
be interpreted, because of its chronology, as being connected with the
new ideas of empire.

Inca Urcon is reputed to have been indifferent to the affairs of state
and besotted in the seductions of harem and fiesta. When he finally
abandoned the thin air of Cuzco for more remote havens of refinement and lubricity, he left behind as his appointed governor his
brother the legitimate prince Inca Yupanqui—or as we shall henceforth call him in anticipation, Pachacuti (Earthquake). This appointment, along with the serious weakness now evident in the direction
of affairs, nourished the seeds of treachery, never slow in growing in
the soil of the Inca state.

Standing at restless attention, waiting as it were for the now slack
and indifferent state to employ again their lethal skills, was a close
group of hard-bitten Inca captains. They were all close kinsmen, and
it was they who had so brilliantly guided the armies which had up to
now carved out the beginnings of an empire. Expansion was in their
blood. Old war-dogs, their dissatisfaction with the current apathy
was understandable—and dangerous. Furthermore the Chanca peril
that was steadily maturing beyond the chasms of the Apurimac,
shortly to be mentioned, could no longer be blinked at, and their concern was heightened correspondingly.

Out of these resentments grew the ugly flower of conspiracy.
The prince Pachacuti had previously campaigned with distinction
under the tutelage of two of the most famous of these warriors,
Vicaquirao and Apu Mayta. Of these two champions, bringers of
splendid victories, it is said by Sarmiento, "They were the initiators
of that fearsome dominion which subsequently the Incas exercised."
All sources agree that they were the heart and soul of the generals'
cabal. At least three sons of Viracocha Inca were also included: Inca
Roca, oldest legitimate prince; Topa Huarochiri, earlier a war-leader
and later, by appointment, the high priest of the state cult; and a
certain Viracocha Inca Paucar (Lord Inca Flower). In all there are
variously said to have been seven to twenty Inca magnates involved,
not including those of the old emperor's concubines who had been

seduced in both their loyalty and their virtue by the fierce Apu Mayta.

Pachacuti was selected as the standard-bearer of the group, he being both popular with the generals and legitimate in his ancestry. The task of the plotters was made the easier by the absence of any constituted sovereign from the city, for both coemperors had departed, one to wear out a quiet old age, the other to solace the fires of lust. The ultimate objective of this group must have been at the very least the unseating of Inca Urcon, and possibly even the assassination of the old ruler. In all this Pachacuti stands shrouded in the obscurity of his intentions, and we can only believe that those who correctly assessed the prince as an apt pupil of expansion still had no sight of the lonelier and more appalling pinnacles of his spirit, shrouded as they were by the drifting cloud-racks of war and rebellion.

<< 5 >>

A CURIOUS HISTORICAL COINCIDENCE was looming over the state. While domestically the hearth was being piled high with combustibles, out beyond the hills a hurricane was preparing its blasts to scatter the ashes of that foyer to the four winds. The state had two enemies at once. This great wind was the Chanca power then rehearsing its forces for the cyclonic days just ahead.

The little knowledge we have of the Chancas shows them to have been a sierra people typical of their time and place. Their traditions, their arrogance, and their expansiveness were those of a nation in most respects like the Incas. They differed from them only in their lack of a charismatic leader and consequently of final success. Their *huaca* of origination was Choclococha (Fresh Corn Lake), a small body of water near the western border of the province of Vilcas, on the shores of which they performed their appropriate tribal rites, even as the Incas did at Pacaritambo and Huanacauri. Alternatively they were said to have been descended from a lion, as the Incas seem to have been descended from a serpent. Their legends told of a wandering and a final settlement up against the flank of the Quechua (Salubrious Land) nation, where their abounding vitality sent them skyrocketing into prominence. In a contest of arms with the Quechuas in the very early part of the fifteenth century they secured a memorable victory, and were thus enabled to push into the warmer valleys of Andahuaylas (Copper Meadows) and make it the center of their power, just as the Incas had seized the Huatanay.

Defeated in their homes and squeezed eastward, the Quechua tribes seem to have been welcomed as confederates by the Incas, who happened to speak the same tongue. Amity between the two nations was indeed imposed by stern necessity, for the Chancas were now close enough to the Apurimac crossings to directly menace Cuzco. Vaguely we can discern an ominous increase in this pressure from the west, and we must surmise that the border, just under the towering abutments of the Vilcabamba Andes, was the scene of alarms and bloody forays in the earlier part of the reign of Viracocha Inca, and that as it grew in savagery so it increased in tempo. Sooner or later the sons of the lion would face in ultimate battle the sons of the day-star.

In the light of this the historian can see a partial logic in Viracocha Inca's campaign to impose empire on Muina and the Vilcañota pueblos behind him. Thus was formed a wall of allies against which the Inca back would some day have to lean.

Sometime about the year 1438 the energetic rulers of the Chancas deployed the full strength of the nation against Cuzco. The *sinchis* who led the two moieties were Hastu Huaraca and Tomay Huaraca (Circling Sling); the names of their revered ancestral mummy which they brought with them into battle was Uscovilca (Sacred Cat).

It was an overwhelming display of power. Having effected the formidable crossing of the Apurimac, and with parties now fanning out widely to outflank and divert Cuzco on the north and south, the two experienced captains moved the main body directly against Cuzco. At the Pass of Vilcaconga (Sacred Neck) they paused to send a laconic demand to the Inca ruler demanding his submission.

The aged Viracocha Inca was at the time in a pleasure villa in the Plain of Anta directly in the path of the advancing horde. No longer was his grip on the helm as vigorous as formerly, and his only recourse was withdrawal. He and his son Urcon moved back upon the city of Cuzco but only for long enough to organize a massive retreat, a move which would never be forgotten in the annals of Inca infamy. Accompanied by some of the magnates and sections of the pueblos which made up imperial Cuzco, the coemperors fled up over the Antisuyo road to the sanctuary of Viracocha Inca's hilltop station in the Yucay Valley.

The crisis forced upon the members of the Pachacuti conspiracy the necessity of an immediate decision. If they also fled, they would be implicated in whatever fate had in store for the Urcon party. If, conformable to the official position of their candidate as the duly accredited governor of Cuzco, they openly announced their intention of remaining, they were throwing against very long odds indeed— they would have to take upon their shoulders the heavy burden of defending the state at a juncture when the two emperors had defected and morale in the city was partially shattered in consequence. Failure would spell either destruction by the Chancas or reprisals at the hands of the Urcon faction, who would be fully apprised of their plotting. But victory could bring in a double harvest; they would not only probably win the succession *de facto*, but they would throw open limitless vistas of empire to the north.

Behind the imposing figure of their prince and governor, they cast the die for the hardier course. Cuzco was to be defended. This large decision took the place of the conspiracy and in fact made it a dead letter. If events went well, the full extent of their disloyalty need never be known.

« 6 »

LATER INCA GENERATIONS were to remember this moment, for it was subsumed for them in the following tales.

One, the Exiled-Prince motif, related that the old emperor had banished the young prince Pachacuti, who had been arrogant and difficult, forever out of his sight. For three years the youth was condemned to the lonely life of a herder guarding the llamas of the Sun on the downs of Chita. While there one day, nodding in the shade of a great rock, he was accosted by a bearded man in a long robe, who announced himself as a god greater than the Sun. Prophetically he advised the prince of the Chanca danger gathering strength over the horizon, and he promised to the young herder full victory in that coming conflict. Disregarding the possible anger of his

86

father the king, the young man returned to the court to pass on the somber warning. Here the magnates sided with the brave and patriotic youth, but the rancorous old king thought him mad to enunciate such frightful predictions, sent him back into exile, and ordered that thenceforth his name should never be mentioned among the living.

This tale stresses the incapacity of the incumbent king, the patriotism and piety of Pachacuti, the split in the councils of state, and the justification of Pachacuti by sanction of the Creator himself. It refers by innuendo to the cultic controversy which divided the Incas and displays the rightness of the Viracocha cult as against the lesser one of Inti. The scene of the revelation is placed in Chita, between Cuzco and Pisac.

The Magic Mirror version of the story was also widely known. It relates how Pachacuti was on the road to his father's palace when his course was arrested at the spring called Susurpuquio. He saw a crystal mirror fall from the heavens into its waters, whereupon, gazing into the depths of the mirror, he saw a personage from whose head spread out a halo of three rays. Serpents twined about his shoulders, on his forehead was the royal fringe, and he wore huge earplugs. His cloak was the pelt of a lion with the paws crossed over his chest. This apparition announced to the frightened prince that he was the Sun and his father. Thereupon in the kaleidoscopic depths of the mirror he revealed to him all the provinces he was destined to conquer. He cautioned the prince to hold him in honor, and he promised him support in the defense of Cuzco against the Chancas. Thereafter wherever he went Pachacuti always carried with him this mirror in which all things near and distant were available to his gaze.

The Magic Mirror tale puts no particular stress on the obduracy and ineptness of Viracocha Inca. It refers to Inti, the fetish of the royal house, as the source of the divine aid, and it plainly identifies him as an Inca king. No particular hostility toward the Viracocha cult is evident.

These two tales enshrined and sanctified the new Inca *politique* which was to arise out of the ruins of the Chanca war; and they carried further that history of revelation in the annals of the Incas which had begun with Manco Capac.

So slender were the human resources left for the military defense of Cuzco that an attempt to secure additional help was the first order of business for Pachacuti. A request for aid was sent to the main body of Incas who had fallen back into the Vilcañota country, and this may have brought forth some small increment to the last-ditch group. Similarly the previously aligned peoples in the valleys round about were approached, among them the Canas and Canchas. Though technically confederated with the Incas in empire, at this stormy crossing for the Inca state, these had to be hired—not commanded— to come. What were the terms which these mercenaries had made for themselves is unknown but they probably involved greater privilege. They seem to have been detached from Viracocha Inca's service to help shore up the defense of Cuzco. Reinforcements from the peoples of Contisuyo—Quechuas, Aymaras, Cotapampas, and others —having so recently been struck by the advancing Chancas were especially counted on, and in this Pachacuti was not to be disappointed. In sum it was a motley defense; only superb leadership could have held it together.

The Chancas were now rapidly closing in on the city. They must have been somewhat surprised by the presence in Cuzco of a rump state while at the same time the formal Inca sovereignty had taken up a rearward position in the Yucay Valley. They of course treated with both powers in the usual pre-battle menaces and calls to surrender. The legitimate state replied evasively, but Pachacuti issued from his beleaguered Andean Troy a ringing negative and a challenge.

The nadir of his fortunes had now been reached. Legend later embroidered upon it with the moving and pathetic picture of a heavily burdened and disheartened prince on the dark eve of battle. He and his three immortal Horatians, each accompanied by a faithful and aristocratic squire, were all that was left of patriotism and virtue on this *Noche Triste* of the Incas. In the dead of darkness, it was said, Pachacuti sallied out, enjoining on his small band that they remain behind, for he went to seek apart and in dreams the comfort and assurances of his god Viracocha Pachayachachic. It was at that point that the famous revelation and prophecy were made to him. In the dawn he appeared to his followers with the glorious news of the certainty of triumph, while to their questions he answered only that certain beings would appear in time to succor them. It is of course not at all impossible that Pachacuti undertook converse with the god in the customary rite of incubation. He did succeed in inspiriting the defenders of Cuzco with hope of aid, unspecified whether divine or human.

The Chancas now moved out from their base at Ichupampa (Grass Valley), on the sierra road just west of the Plain of Anta, and arrived at the lip of the valley of the Huatanay. The Incas were aroused to the sudden danger by a vociferous alarm brought posthaste by a defector or a spy from the Chanca camp. On a spot named Quiachilli (Open Wound), lying up beyond the broad bosom of Carmenca, the Chancas halted to make their demonstration. This in part had its intended effects. The more timorous of the Cuzqueños, on beholding these first Chanca scouts looking down upon them from the pencil-sharp skyline, panicked and broke away up the mountainsides, where they were to remain throughout most of the battle, fascinated and fearful witnesses to the drama about to unfold.

The first violent skirmishes occurred when the Chanca vanguard with ear-splitting howls poured down against the several mud-walled villages that made up the city of Cuzco. As it turned out, they were unable to break in as far as the Huatanay crossing, possibly because of the ultimate menace of the early fortress of Sacsahuaman on their flank. The Incas who had already had their Paul Revere now produced their Molly Pitcher as well, for in the savage fighting that erupted in one of the barrios of the city, a certain Inca woman was seen valiantly defending her home in hand-to-hand encounters with the Chanca braves. The story is not improbable, for we know that Pachacuti, having taken the unorthodox decision to meet the enemy head-on rather than retiring with all his people to the fortress above the city, had indeed expected to fight at the very gates of the city; he had already mined the approaches to it with pits and barricades of sharpened chonta stakes.

The day's struggle was inconclusive. The night which ensued saw the Chancas still encamped up on Carmenca while the Incas fitfully slept on their arms in the villages below. The gloom of this night was not to be repeated until it was the turn of the Pizarros in 1536 to sleep in the burned-out embers of Cuzco, swords in hand and

horses saddled, with Inca warriors ululating on the heights around—
a full century later.

In these desperate straits Pachacuti's true mettle showed, for with
the coming of dawn his forces still stood ready and willing to continue the unequal combat. At some period indeed a strong ray shot
into the darkened valley as twenty or so small parties of warriors
mainly from Contisuyo filtered in from the south and east to swell
the defenses.

The Chancas decided to hurl their full fury down on Cuzco with
the dawn. But Pachacuti, clad in a lionskin and personally engaging
the enemy, had forestalled them and had led his forces heroically up
and over into the very teeth of the opposition. No quarter was asked
or given that day, and the slopes across which the Incas fought were
known from that time forward as Yahuar Pampa, the Field of
Blood. Around midday that indefinable umpire of battles, panic,
struck the Chanca forces with his eerie weapon and they broke and
fled. Though exhausted and badly mauled themselves, the Incas
pursued closely. In a bloody six-mile pursuit no prisoners were taken
but all overtaken were slain. Needless to say those Indians who had
been sitting on the fence now threw in their lot with the victors,
swelling their ranks. The Chancas fell back upon their camp at
Ichupampa.

The above is the traditional account of the salvation of Cuzco.
It is based upon broken bits of folk memory, on Spanish selection
and reinterpretation, on shifting and uncertain localizations, and on
miracle mixed with fact. An uncontaminated account such as would
satisfy today's military historian is obviously impossible. The general
course of the battle is clear nevertheless, and the fierce anxiety of the
encounter can be sensed by the historian from the wisps of facts that
seem still to hover like dust above the spot.

Pachacuti later insisted that the very stones on the field of this
battle had been metamorphosed into warriors invisible to all but
him. They sprang up at the command of the god who had promised
his aid, and in ghostly ranks they fought indomitably to bring
him his hard-won deliverance. They were the celebrated *pururauca*
of story, a word meaning in Quechua, "stones hurled from heights
upon the enemy." Another etiological account relates that in the

earlier stage of the battle things had gone badly for the forces of Pachacuti, penned up in their mud walls, because he had failed to equip himself with the *topayauri*, the golden scepter of rule. From the sky a voice came down warning him that he must carry it if he was to fulfill the conditions of his destiny. He returned to Coricancha and there ceremonially assumed that most important part of the Inca regalia. Meanwhile the high priest had lined up a file of great stones and accoutered them in helmets, shields, and battle clubs to simulate friendly warriors. Turning back from the melee to summon reinforcements, Pachacuti saw the figures from a distance, and believing them to be a contingent of his own troops, called out to them in a voice of great power. As one, they took life, arose, and strode forth, divine automatons whose inexorable regiments crushed all before them. Heaven had patently intervened to save the Inca state.

Cuzco had indeed been saved, but there still remained the final task of thrusting the Chancas back across the Apurimac, where they would no longer be an immediate threat. At Ichupampa they had reconsolidated their forces, calling in their flanking parties which had been sent out north and south of the city.

When Pachacuti was finally able to move against them (and it may well have been a matter of a year or more before the depleted state could organize an offensive), he did so equipped with the indefinable prestige of one of heaven's minions, for he had announced himself both as the son of the Sun and the recipient of Viracocha's protection. Still dangerous, the Chancas replied defiantly. Logic now had cast the Inca army in the role of the attacker, and for long the bitter scales of war hung evenly poised. When two of the Chanca chieftains were finally killed and their heads brandished aloft on the points of Inca javelins, the defenders broke. Resistance at the walls collapsed, and in the turbulent wake of retreat the valiant Chanca captain Hastu Huaraca alone was swept away to escape for more memorable deeds yet.

Ichupampa was a turning point in Andean history. By demoting the power of the Chancas, it insured that Cuzco would dominate at least the central sierra, and it taught the Peruvian world beyond this to shudder at the martial renown of the Incas. To the Incas themselves it was to reveal that the cultic strife which had been a source of weakness and bewilderment to them could be resolved. But they knew also that the security they enjoyed was due to the presence among them now of a new and a most awesome personality.

PART TWO
THE ROLE
OF CAESAR

SIX.
PACHACUTI
FATHER OF VICTORY

THE CHANCA VICTORY is presented to us in the sources as the most striking event in all Inca history—the year one, as it were. This is because we know Inca history only through Pachacuti's rewriting of it, and he would certainly have so described it in any case. Yet in a real sense it is true. Impressive as is the long reign of Viracocha Inca in quarrying, marking, and assembling the massive blocks of empire, he had not indeed convinced his world to raise them up, course upon course, until a wholly new edifice should appear. It was Pachacuti who did this; victory over the Chancas swept clear the stage and introduced the architect onto the scene, a fully matured man confident of his vast powers of design.

On the field of battle due vengeance was taken upon the captured Chanca magnates. They were mocked, insulted, tortured, and finally destroyed, while their skulls were prepared to provide drinking bowls for the victor, in which he would toast both his own success and his enemy's disgrace. The final humiliation to the corpses was to make them into *runatinyas* (man-drums). The skins were stripped off and stuffed with dried *ichu*-grass; flutes were tucked into their mouths; and their mummied hands, now empty of the scepters of rule, were so placed that, when pounded upon the distended drum-

95

heads of their bellies, they would hollowly sound forth the tattoo of their own ignominy. These gruesome trophies were housed in a building erected on the site and were later to be seen by the Spaniards.

The continued existence of an Inca state in the Yucay Valley posed an initial problem, for in that place resided the living and legitimate source of authority, the two defecting coemperors still with their retinue of Inca magnates. Pachacuti possessed Cuzco, overwhelming military strength, and the prestige of great success. All that he lacked was legitimacy. To gain this, Pachacuti had to dispose of Urcon and be accepted in his stead.

What emerges clearly from the records is that the hated Urcon, declared an outlaw by the Cuzco assembly of notables, was hunted down, defeated at the head of the remnants of his forces, and killed, probably in the Vilcañota country. His warriors were either dispersed or absorbed. It is probable that Pachacuti, in his incessant pursuit of authority, now married Urcon's wife and sister, the *coya*, who had had no children by him. An embassy was then dispatched to the aged father demanding that he pass on the *mascapaycha*, the royal headdress, to Pachacuti as the notables of the tribe had decreed. Having lost Urcon, his son and sole supporter, Viracocha Inca could only accede.

The doors of the old emperor's final abasement were flung open at Pachacuti's coronation festivities. Treated with the full reverance due to his exalted office, yet despised for his cowardice in deserting his city and mocked for his senile sorrow over the loss of his favorite son, the old man was perforce carried and bumped in his litter back over the hill road to Cuzco. He was an imperial prisoner, his use at the moment being to serve the interests of that new conqueror on the sierra scene who was at the same time his son.

As was to become customary in the royal line, the coronation of the Inca ruler was also a royal wedding. For ten days Pachacuti and his intended *coya* retired into complete seclusion, meanwhile rigorously fasting each in their separate establishments while the magnates and kinsmen purified themselves in similar ways.

This completed, the bride in sandals and headband of gold was ceremonially presented to Pachacuti, who formally accepted her as his *coya*, after which he presented her to the clans for their similar acceptance and as a prerequisite of her positon endowed her with the income of certain designated pueblos. He gave her ladies for her entourage, and the people at large offered her sumptuous gifts.

But the core of the ceremony was in this case the actual transmission of the sovereignty. Betanzos gives a curious but circumstantial account of this passage of power. At the proper moment the aged Viracocha Inca arose and before the awed multitude which was gathered in the sacred plaza announced his resignation of the royal fringe and then handed it over into the possession of his son. Having done so, he gave to him the throne name by which history was thenceforth to know him, Pachacuti.

Duly invested and with the supreme power at last firmly in his hands, the thunderbolts of Pachacuti's delayed vengeance were now hurled into the scene. He commanded a filthy pot such as was used only for ordure and other filth, to be brought, filled to the brim with *chicha*, and presented to the stunned old man. The terrible son, in the strained silence that succeeded, made clear that because his father had acted like a woman he had consigned him henceforth to drink from unclean vessels, and he ordered him to drain the revolting potion to the last drop.

Viracocha Inca, no longer great, no longer indeed fully an emperor, was deprived of his manhood by this shameful action. He did as commanded and then prostrated himself helplessly at his son's feet, begging what small mercies might come his way. From this point on in the three months of ceremonies, sacrifices, and feasting connected with the coronation, Pachacuti treated Viracocha Inca with condescension and a kindness perhaps more brutal than scorn. Everything the old father ventured to ask was granted, including, finally, his request to return to Caquia Jaquijahuana, his favorite villa and refuge.

A few years later, still attended by a devoted following, Viracocha Inca, founder of Tahuantinsuyo, died and was given an honorable place in the genealogy of rulers. In the years that followed his mummy, sumptuously accompanied, was often borne on an imperial litter over the bleak *puna* to enjoy the many fiestas of Cuzco, the city to which he had given life in his reign and the city he had abandoned in his fearful old age. This mummy was later to be hidden

97

along with others from the ruthless inquiries of the Spaniards. Gonzalo Pizarro found it and burned it, though the ashes were secretly salvaged and revered by the Indians of his lineage. Polo de Ondegardo later succeeded in locating these ashes and had them sent down to Lima, where, with other Inca royal mummies, they were interred in a courtyard of the Hospital of St. Andrew. No doubt they still rest today somewhere in this uncongenial lowland soil.

« 2 »

THE BOY CUSI, who had come to his princely manhood as Inca Yupanqui, now stood before the world as the emperor Pachacuti. The titles he took were Capac Inca (Chief Inca), Intip Churin (Son of the Sun), and Huachaycoyac (Lover of the Poor), and as such he was saluted on his exit from the great shrine by all the Inca nobles, *curacas* of neighboring tribes, and residents of the villages of Cuzco.

With unequaled energy the new emperor set to work to refashion the world he knew, moving ahead on three fronts simultaneously: imperial expansion, administrative integration, and ceremonial sanctification. Only the first concerns us in this chapter.

By this time the old war-dogs Vicaquirao and Apu Mayta, whose adherence had helped to raise Pachacuti to the throne, had dropped out of the picture, and he was to depend on the battle skills and loyalties particularly of two of his brothers, Inca Roca, a man feared above all for his toughness, and the brilliant Capac Yupanqui. These were the first of his great captains. The greatest of all was to be finally his younger son and successor Topa Inca, but this was still far in the future.

We must not suppose that the world fell into Pachacuti's lap immediately. Many of the groups around Cuzco had seized upon the Chanca invasion to defect from the authority of the Incas. Muina and Pinahua, the two most recalcitrant of such communities in the valley, had to be crushed—now for the last time. Ayamarca pueblos close by were struck with fearful power while even more savage treatment was reserved for the Cuyos and Cavinas, who had entered together upon a conspiracy to block Inca reconsolidation of the Vilcañota and upper Apurimac by destroying the new tyrant. The plot had been hatched in great secrecy. While being entertained during a heavy *chicha*-drinking by the Cuyo *sinchi*, Pachacuti was suddenly set upon. A servitor suborned for the purpose struck him heavily on the head, injuring him seriously, so much so that the deep scar from the encounter was later visible to the Spaniards on his mummy. The Inca captains, frightened and infuriated at sensing a magnificent future under their warlike leader so nearly extinguished, began such a campaign of killing and torture among the Cuyos and in the general area round about that, when their Hunnish ferocity finally subsided, the Cuyos as a people had ceased to exist and that whole part of Contisuyo lay in bloody and smoking ruin. The lesson of this reprisal was not lost on the world. If the sierra tribes had trembled after the Chanca defeat, now they existed, silent and submissive, in the very penumbra of terror.

Having recovered from the attack, Pachacuti turned his gaze to that part of the lower Vilcañota around Calca generally referred to as the Yucay country. To the Spaniards the area of the Yucay was considered "more beautiful than Aranjuez," and the early Christian householders of Cuzco were more than once in the succeeding centuries sorely tempted to remove lock, stock, and barrel to that neighboring valley; indeed they often sent their sons and daughters to be raised there. The traveler of today, descending into the warm trench of the valley with the austere chill of Cuzco still upon him, can only echo these eulogies from the past. The effect of the sharp teeth of the Andes rising almost vertically from the east side of the valley to over twenty thousand feet, with the lovely valley drinking in the spillings of their snows, is indeed unforgettable. Ruins of the Inca period dot the valley floor and the crags above. From Viracocha Inca to the end of the dynasty every Inca ruler fell in love with the Yucay; they walled the river side, stepped up rich and arable terraces, and constructed fortresses, temples, bridges, villas, and garrison points. And so isolated and timeless is the life of the poor here today that some of them are born, live, and die within the dark, andesite chambers and apartments built by Pachacuti and his successors, the only notable change being that they are roofed now with Spanish tile instead of Indian thatch.

Pachacuti launched his captains against Ollantaytambo, the strongest point here, a community which was to defeat even the determination of the Pizarros a century later. Though seriously wounded here, the famous Inca Roca led his *orejones* in a superb escalade which brought about the fall of the fortress city. It was razed to the ground as a chastisement, and only after some time did it rise again, this time as an Inca city consciously designed to play a leading role in the life of the new empire.

Ollantaytambo was one of the gateways to an amazing world—the montaña—for it commanded two of the three possible and arduous routes into the Vilcabamba (Sacred Valley) country. Here was the major source of those desultory consignments of gold dust and nuggets which occasionally made their way up into the near-by sierra. Stretching uncharted up and down the eastern face of the Andes, the montaña also provided the chromatic wealth of feathers from hummingbirds and macaws, jaguar skins, monkey hair, and—most valuable of all outside of its gold—the narcotic leaf of the coca bush, grown only in those humid and broken *quebradas*.

It was to organize this source of unequaled wealth, so that it might more consistently serve the needs of the great state he was contemplating, that Pachacuti had kicked open the door at Ollantaytambo. There was the additional reason of security, for the savage Campas of the upper jungles occasionally threatened those passes. But essentially it was the same hunger which led both Inca and Spaniard into this land. Pachacuti sought gold, for gold was divine, being thought of as the "teardrops of the Sun." An empire such as he envisaged must possess vast stores of it and the supply must be constant.

Accordingly the army moved up through the pass of Panticolla behind Ollantaytambo and down into the Lucumayo Valley paralleling the Vilcañota to the northeast. There was a well-recognized trail, but the difficulties of icy heights followed by steaming thickets were immense. But no contretemps of height or weather could halt the ardent Inca flood. Pachacuti was met at a place on the frontier called Cocospata by emissaries from Vitcos, the central pueblo of Vilcabamba. In accepting their offers of submission Pachacuti insisted that the gold-washings be greatly expanded. He sent out his own prospectors, organizers of gangs, and road surveyors to make certain of the same, and arranged the annual delivery of a stated quantity of both silver and gold. Leaving a governor in the new provincial capital of Vitcos and the beginnings of a building program, he then turned the head of his army about and returned the way he had come.

《 3 》

ALL OF THE CAMPAIGNS of Pachacuti were logically conceived. His scattered and intial activities in the greater Cuzco area, against Muina, the Cuyos, and others, had produced the reconstruction of that infant empire left to him by his father. Conquest of the Yucay country secured him a rich agricultural patrimony, while the montaña campaign laid the foundations for that largesse which alone can attract support to a barbaric state. The Vilcas campaigns, now to follow, represented the sheer hard work connected with a final settlement of the Chanca question and the first testing of Inca power in an area in which, up to that time, it had been wholly foreign. It must be remembered that, though Pachacuti had previously defeated the Chancas in his own territory, he had not been able to follow up with a thrust into theirs. But he had already made certain policy moves designed to prepare the ground for an attack in that direction, notably by granting to Quechua and Cotapampa magnates the Inca prerogative of wearing the earplugs. This was in recompense for the aid which these buffer peoples had extended during the Chanca danger. He wanted a solid ground of loyalty behind him.

It will be remembered that one of the Chanca *sinchis*, Hastu Huaraca, had made a daring escape from the disaster of Ichupampa and had fled back to his people. He had succeeded to an extent in reinspiriting them. Pachacuti was thus moving against an old and most formidable enemy. Leaving one of his brothers as regent in Cuzco, Pachacuti led out a sizeable force of allies, both subjects and Inca *orejones*. That it was the first massive uncoiling of the Inca state taking possession of those territories promised to it by the gods and not a simple raid could be seen from the fact that the *coya* and the harem traveled with the host. The army was able to cross the Apurimac River without a contest, filing unmolested across the famous suspension bridge slung over the gorge 120 feet above the tumbling waters.

This bridge has earned its right to be classed among the wonders of the world. It was certainly Pachacuti who had organized its upkeep, its biennial renewal, and the necessary tunneling to the approaches. Formed of spans of cabuya fiber that dipped in the winds constantly pouring down the canyon, it now pitched and vibrated under the weight of the first of those great Inca armies which were to move north in the years to come. It was the most strategic 250 feet to be found on the length of the great sierra road. Every Spaniard who crossed it remarked upon it in tones of awe, and they were indeed a folk not accustomed to that feeling.

There was stiff fighting with the hard core of Chanca warriors gathered in Andahuaylas, finally brought to an end when Hastu Huaraca and another Chanca leader submitted at last to the Inca *raj* and were placed under tribute. Part of this tribute was a levy of Chanca warriors, who were soon to be dispatched southwards against Collao to soften that area for eventual Inca attack. If this group should perish in the attempt, such an event would in no way have been unacceptable to Pachacuti, who feared the Chancas as he feared no other Peruvian people. It seems that this preliminary Collao enterprise was to go on somewhat simultaneously with his present Vilcas campaign—if so, its purpose is plain enough, for it would radically weaken the remnants of the Chancas by dividing their remaining young braves into two widely separated contingents, one in the Titicaca Basin, and one north of the Apurimac crossing.

Kingly leisure interspersed with memorable sieges and battles was the tempo of this campaign. From beginning to end it may well have consumed as much as four or five years, though Pachacuti appears to have left the last stages of it to his captains. The Chancas had been brought to heel in a victory at Corampa, a smelting center for the rich ores of the region; behind them stood the Sora Indians. True to his hunger for the "teardrops of the Sun," Pachacuti now swung his army down the road against these tribes, for it was they who controlled the flow of this metal out of the canyons of the Cordillera Occidental. What followed was a most signal passage-at-arms in Inca annals.

A pitched battle was precipitated as the Soras sought to block the passages into their valleys against the Incas, and heavy casualties resulted for both armies. Defeated there, the Soras fled to the *pucara* of Challcomarca, a flat-topped Gibraltar brooding over the river and well supplied with stone dwellings, springs, and caves; its only entry was by means of a single ladder. While this noose was being tightened Pachacuti was arranging a preliminary organization of the new province, accepting surrenders, and preparing to send out side parties, one of which no doubt was Capac Yupanqui's raid on the Chinchas of the coast. To Challcomarca, the the great rock of refuge, there now flowed a turbid river of do-or-die elements from all the regions around, including even the important Huamangas, and before long the rock had become impregnable to direct assault. It flanked the passage of all future Inca armies passing to the north.

It was attacked and because the attack was unsuccessful it had to be invested. To the Soras this was to become indeed their Starving Rock. A two-year siege began, displaying both the determination of the Inca and the desperation of the Soras, at the end of which only a few living skeletons remained to surrender and be slaughtered. With this accomplished and with the voluntary submission of the Rucanas (Finger People), a group farther up near the passes, an extensive new area had been welded into the Inca state, and the backbone of the toughest resistance in the sierra south of Ecuador was broken. This lesson also was not lost on the world.

The important center of Vilcashuaman had now fallen into Pachacuti's hands. He gave orders to refashion it into a great provincial center, an emporium in fine stone and a bustling capital second only to Cuzco itself. It would soon boast of seven hundred warehouses and a stepped temple with forty porters guarding the sacred precincts.

A triumphal return of the charismatic emperor and his army into Cuzco was staged to display to the sierra world his now irresistible power. In all the somber leisure of contrived pomp the long procession wound its way down the Chinchaysuyo road to flow in among the barrios of the crowded city of Cuzco. The mellow bleating of conch shells, the rattle of drumming, and the varied shrilling of flutes bore the current of feet into the sacred square. The leading captains filed in first, chanting a paean especially composed by Pachacuti himself and celebrating his historic *res gestae* up to that point. The captured *sinchis* were dragged in next, along with the most beautiful and well-born of the captured women. After them came the lines of carriers, with a rich selection of the spoils of the war displayed on their backs and in their hands. Next a battalion of soldiers, each with a head spitted on his lance. And only after this did the Caesar himself appear, almost an old man now but most majestic, borne along in his golden litter. Around him surged that part of the imperial nobility concerned in the governing of the new lands, the greatest of them cast as humble bearers of the litter. The Indians of Cuzco never forgot that day nor the appearance of its author; he is described for us as sitting quietly and somewhat hunched in his litter surveying the scene about him with "a face of granite" and "the cruel eyes of a tiger." The rest of the army, leaping, wheeling, howling, and boasting, cracking their slings and holding aloft their war clubs, exulted openly and enthusiastically behind him.

The procession wound around the plaza to display itself ceremoniously to the gods, who had been summoned out of Coricancha to look upon their favorite's handiwork, after which the leading prisoners were thrown down on their faces for Pachacuti and his nobles to trample solemnly underfoot, the ancient Peruvian seal of victory. On the following day began the long series of fiestas.

《 4 》

PACHACUTI WAS NOW AT THE PEAK of his active career and certainly at the height of his powers, a tall, full-faced Indian with eyes that blazed, martial still in spirit and excessively masculine, the "beau ideal" of the American Indian brave.

He had sired one daughter and at least four sons on his *coya* Mama Anahuarque. Of the sons his preference had long fallen on Amaru Inca (Dragon Inca), whom he appears to have idolized. At some period in the emperor's life—possibly indeed at these festivals of rejoicing which followed the Vilcas successes—he had announced a coregency with this son. In this he was to be grievously disappointed, for Amaru Inca is reported to us as that rarity in a highly masculinized society, a gentleman. Whether this be accurate or not—and what facts we do have support it—he preferred the retirements and domestic amenities of his country villas to the bivouac. As a war leader he was found to be ineffectual. Nevertheless the character of Amaru Inca made a lasting impression on his age, as the following may illustrate.

A protracted drought of several years' duration was to grip the sierra during the latter part of Pachacuti's reign. Starvation was widespread, and but for the system of state warehouses already instituted by Pachacuti, the whole Inca edifice of rule would have toppled incontinently. It was rumored that though Viracocha withheld his life-giving waters from the greater part of the empire, fat clouds that poured down their burdens at night could always be seen draped over the green *chacras* of Amaru Inca. From his bursting bins of maize and potatoes and *quinoa* he fed the people round about and only with difficulty prevented them from worshipping him as a living avatar of Viracocha. He had a large following among the humble folk on his manors, and his warm personality made him beloved by the great as well. Even after his deposition his father continued to honor him, and we know that the brother who superseded him utilized his special talents. He lived in peace on his estates and was to die a venerable old man in the same year as his younger brother the next emperor. His only failure was to lack those qualities of decision and ruthlessness which were essential to the guidance of a semibarbaric empire.

We saw that while he was in Vilcas, Pachacuti had ordered a sizeable Chanca force sent down into Collao, an area long linked to Cuzco in a sequence of uneasy skirmishes and treaty alliances. It was an area as *sui generis* in its way as was the smaller world of the Huatanay, and certainly with far older traditions behind it. Granting the new dynamics of Cuzco, the two were bound to contend with each other in some way. What the preliminary Chanca raid was able to accomplish is uncertain, but it seems at least to have precipitated the situation.

The old emperor rested from his Vilcas labors only for the rainy season, and then marched his veterans down the road towards the enemy. He first encountered that buffer people, the Canas, whose lands and pueblos lay athwart the watershed separating the Vilcañota from the Titicaca drainage, and who were now flouting the Inca power to which they had formerly been allied. To them be-

longed the strategic Pass of La Raya and its marshy summit, while
well beyond them tensely waited the real enemy, the Collas. There is
some evidence that Amaru Inca, the coregent, tried out his martial
skills as leader here, but was saved from disaster only by the valor
of his brothers. As the fighting mounted in intensity, Pachacuti had
to take personal command of the army in the field.

Ayavire was the pueblo where the Canas chose to make their
stand. Strategically it was a sound decision, for help could siphon in
to them here from two directions. Ayavire was positioned squarely
across that branching of the sierra road that split around both shores
of the lake. And just ahead, straight down the western branch, was
the Colla pueblo and refuge of Pucara (The Fortress), the eyrie of
an enemy even stronger than the Canas, a veritable Behistun astride
the road.

Ayavire turned out to be a disaster for the Canas. The Incas felt
that they had defected from a former understanding, and their purpose was therefore to exact full vengeance for that crime. When all
was over, that province was so decimated that settlers had to be
introduced from the outside to rebuild it. It became then an important site as an Inca station. It was never again to be a pueblo of
the Canas.

Passing over the smouldering ruins, Pachacuti's main force turned
down the left fork of the road to bring to heel the settlements in
that area; they hastened to offer their surrender. The purpose of
this deflected campaign may be seen in the advance made by that
army group which Pachacuti detached and sent north into the Carabaya (the Sack) country, beyond which were the Passes of the Nudo
de Quenamari and the wild montaña. The placer sands of Carabaya
produced gold in even more fabulous quantities than those of the
Vilcabamba streams. A road-building campaign was straightway
initiated to facilitate entry into the montaña at this point, and the
province was roughly carved out and organized around the placer
camps. Once again Pachacuti's foresight had created an organization
which over the years carried Inca mining and metallurgy farther
and farther into the remoteness of the east.

Either as an extension of Pachacuti's Ayavire campaign, or perhaps as a later and separate campaign entirely, came the final and

long-expected showdown with the tough core of Colla power. Well down the road from Ayavire was Hatun-Colla (Great Colla), the chief place of Colla power and the center of its loose hegemony in the area. Chuchi Capac, the leader of this coalition, was defeated and the northern Puno collapsed into the conqueror's hand. The decisive battle itself seems to have been fought at Pucara. In the triumph which took place upon the conqueror's return the loot from these Collao campaigns was presented to Inti, the *Sol Invictus* of the state, while Chuchi Capac was solemnly sacrificed to him in Coricancha.

This was to be Pachacuti's last personal appearance in the field. He was no longer physically able, and he had other absorbing interests. He had succeeded in eliminating the last organized power able to threaten him directly. He had created a durable state, secure on all its borders. All of the necessary groundwork had now been laid for a rapid expansion of Tahuantinsuyo, if such were to be desired. What was now to follow—the great raid which knocked out the kingdom of Cajamarca—is one of the dramatic advances in Inca history. But before this Amaru Inca was to be deposed.

Amaru Inca's coregency with his father had lasted five or six years, if we can so interpret the statement by Las Casas that Pachacuti fruitlessly tried to train his nominee in the arts of government and generalship for that period of years. When the last of the victorious Inca contingents had been drawn in from Collao, the strong feeling in the army concerning the younger man's ineptitude in war forced Pachacuti to summon a closed gathering of the leading Inca magnates. Tense and serious, Pachacuti's sons and brothers listened to the old man harangue them concerning his own deeds and those of the ancestors, finally ending with the weak plea that he had selected his third son, Amaru Inca, as the infante not because he loved him most but because of his prudence. When the magnates failed to take fire at his words, the emperor perforce accepted their mute decision. Weeping bitterly, he turned to his beloved Amaru Inca and informed him that in him there was no fault, but that it was their common father Inti who had withdrawn from him his favor. This moving spectacle of a father's mingled love and grief was climaxed when the emperor retired Amaru Inca into inactive status by appointing him

captain of the Capac Ayllu, the *panaca* that was now set up to support
and further the next heir—whenever he should be selected. Amaru
Inca received the announcement of his deposition with the dignity
of a great man, kissed his father's hands, and then turned back to sit
down among the other magnates among whom he was now to be
counted. Pachacuti wept aloud in his sorrow. It was obvious that the
army would soon demand another and a more acceptable heir apparent.

« 5 »

UNDER PACHACUTI'S CARE the Inca army had become a capable instrument of war. In particular it possessed one most amazing feature,
for, contrary to modern logistics, it tended to snowball in size the
farther it removed from its base. The first stipulation laid upon a
newly conquered province was the immediate harnessing of that
province's military man power in the continued outward march of
empire. This not only weakened that province's capacity to rise in
rebellion behind the army's back, but presented to the next province
marked down for subjection an idea of the advantages to be gained
by falling in step with the expanding Inca *politique*, perhaps even in
sharing in its prestige and loot. The contingents from those provinces
most recently conquered, however, were assigned to march and camp
on the fringes of the host, safely removed from the emperor's person. An able-bodied man was classified as an *auca* or warrior between
the ages of twenty-five and fifty, though with need the age limit
might be extended to sixty.

The Inca war cadres were in theory coterminous with the peace-
time organization of the provinces (which was based on the decimal
system wherever possible)—squads, platoons, and so on up. Those
provinces peculiarly selected to pay their tribute in warriors over the
years were organized in loose militia groupings under their own traditional *curacas*. The province of Chucuito, which included most
of the communities on the west side of Lake Titicaca, for instance,
was generally assessed at three thousand warriors, though one extraordinary levy in the last days of the empire of six thousand men
was imposed upon her, of whom only one thousand finally returned

to their homes. But the Inca rulers were not content to rely solely on scratch levies from the fields, for in some cases they appointed Inca captains in the provinces who were especially designated to exercise and train certain of these militia units. Thus without interrupting the local authority, the Incas had perfected their own complementary chain of command and introduced a greater professionalism in arms.

There was imposed on the march and in battle a type of discipline, made possible by the magnificent commissariat, that it unique in American Indian warfare. As the army moved outward, the peoples of each province would transport the army's provisions from one end of that province to the other, passing them on to their neighbors in the adjoining province. Foraging and looting were unnecessary and strictly forbidden, for every large center passed through opened up its warehouses, dispensing sandals, slings, war clubs, cloaks, maize, and *chuño* upon receipt of the imperial rescript. Provincial life was thus molested as little as possible. When the army went across the imperial border, of course, it became a different story.

Consultation and careful planning preceded these campaigns, and the ranking officers were specially appointed by the emperor for the task in hand. As a rule two Inca generals were appointed, corresponding to the two moeities of the city, Upper and Lower Cuzco, though how they shared their command is not stated. The taking of oracles, sympathetic magic performed to weaken the enemy *huacas* even before the army moved, and the usual sacrifices were additionally required to ensure the army's success.

Each tribal levy of proven loyalty carried its own *huaca* into battle and on the march, but the standard of the army as a whole was the national *huaca* of the Inca caste, the stone of Huanacauri. Victory was certain with this ancestral talisman in the midst of the army. Huanacauri was escorted by the famous "Old Guard" of Inca *orejones*, a dependable body of shock troops dedicated to the aggrandizement of the state in a way unknown and impossible to the local levies.

The provincial *curacas*, the ranking captains, and the regiment of *orejones* went richly dressed for war, startling in their occasional war paint, their helmets, feathered bonnets, and ornate parrying shields. The progress of an attack was well organized, with the slingers first firing their volleys from a distance, after which, if there were archers with the army, such as the Chunchos with their deadly black bows of chontawood, the army pressed in behind flights of arrows and entangling bolas, following which there ensued hand-to-hand combat with javelins, spears, war clubs, and two-edged chonta swords. Each squadron fought with its preferred weapon. The techniques of siege were well understood. Most grueling of the feats performed by these sierra armies was the storming of a defended *pucara*, high up among its crevasses and rocks and usually defended by the narrowest of approaches. This type of assault was an Inca specialty and was led by groups of about twenty braves holding over their heads as they moved up to the walls a giant testudo.

It is well known that primitive warfare in no wise resembles that of more sophisticated civilizations. This is certainly true of most American Indian warfare, which had a rigorous style and a strong ceremonial handed down from the past, where the soldier had not yet evolved out of the brave, and where warfare served as a way to sort out an individual's value—war was an arena in which to win personal acclaim, even though it was a tribally organized situation. But the Inca armies had already begun to evolve into grim and relentless instruments of an overriding *politique*. This would soon eventuate in the creation of an incipient officer class, professionally trained and inspired.

But Pachacuti's empire was not only the product of military power and of the swift and skillful organization of the conquered people; it rested as well on terror, division, and espionage. Terror was continually threatened or, if need be, exerted upon the newly acquired parts of the empire until time could glue them firmly together. Cobo says that the Incas ruled by a ferocity so vulpine and so devastating that the memory of their many atrocities was still fresh among the Indians of his day:

> The yoke which these wretched Indians bore was so heavy, that I have no doubt but that, if all the people in the world should join efforts in conceiving a worse type of tyranny and oppression, they could not do so.

Indeed when one considers the separatist and quarrelsome tribal life which preceded the Inca rise to power, and the multiplicity of raids and skirmishes up and down the length of the sierra, one can see no other technique strong enough to compel docility and compliance over a vast empire. The bitterness of the many revolts which broke out in the hundred years of Tahuantinsuyo speaks to the same effect. Cieza says that by the time the empire came to its end, the power of the emperor was so unquestioned that the very idea of rebellion was inconceivable. This is probably true, if he limits rebellion here to subject peoples and excludes Incas.

The *mitimaes* system (a Spanish corruption from *mitmac,* "one newly arrived in a region"), carried to its perfection by Pachacuti and his son about this time, is so well known as to need no extended discussion. Dissident elements in a newly reduced province, or those chosen at whim to be an example, were sometimes moved to older and more settled areas where the Inca yoke had been accepted. This institution of tribal extirpation was also used as a substitute for normal commerce between contrasting regions. The example of the Lupacas of the province of Chucuito beside Lake Titicaca comes to mind. *Mitmacs* from this highland area were settled at lower altitudes both in the coastal valleys and the eastern montaña; from these areas they would send back to their former kinsmen coca, feathers, maize, dried fish, and the like, while receiving from them the *quinoa* and *chuño* which was their native diet. This curious system had the advantage of enriching the general welfare of the province without allowing trade as such ever to become interprovincial. A province thus scattered and broken up remained always a unit, for the deracinated *mitmacs* were never allowed any interchange of goods with the foreign groups among whom they lived. Social control was thus not jeopardized by an expansion of the economy.

Often this curious coin was reversed. Skilled and loyal groups from well-integrated areas—always including some Incas from the Cuzco region—were uprooted from their homes, given gifts and women, and sent with their *huacas,* their genealogies, their tribal costumes, and all their traditions into the new area, where they were assigned good lands and set down as a higher contrasting moeity, a social level superior to those just conquered. In unsettled areas they functioned as garrison troops.

The function of the *mitmacs* was to serve as a deterrent to any unified tribal reaction in the new province which might be detrimental to the emperor's designs—in short they were resident spies among the local folk. To this system of delation Tahuantinsuyo was to owe much of its future security, for we learn of specific cases where treason among certain provincials was discovered and reported by the jealous and hostile *mitmacs* settled among them. Just as significantly this group also served as teachers of Inca civilization. They brought with them approved skills in weaving, patterning, metal-working, priest-craft, as well as knowledge of Inca claims and outlook. Fundamental in the passage of this culture was Quechua, the Inca tongue, taught far and wide by the missionary *mitmacs*. This wholesale and ruthless pedagogy created a great Andean *lingua franca*, without which Tahuantinsuyo could neither have been built nor have survived. Just as the masonry of the Incas has survived the long vandalism of time and the Spaniard, so has Quechua. It is today a living tongue, and the area it claims is retreating little if at all.

Pachacuti had moved *mitmac* settlers into Ayavire after he had absorbed that pueblo, and previous to this he had moved some defeated Indians to Huamanga. Sarmiento says the system however was not truly evolved until after the Chinchaysuyo campaign, to which we must now turn our attention.

« 6 »

WITH THE DEFEAT OF THE COLLAS, limitless horizons for imperial expansion beckoned in every direction. Pachacuti could have pressed on south of the Collas to secure possession of the entire littoral of the lake. He had as much of the montaña perhaps as he needed at present, having pierced it twice. He could move against the coastal valleys, so exotic and tempting. He could equally continue his push up the sierra, victory over the Soras having opened the way.

After the Sora victory it had been decided to send Pachacuti's younger brother and captain, Capac Inca Yupanqui, through the newly surrendered Rucana country to probe resistance down on the coast. As it turned out this venture of the emperor's was a signal failure. In the coastal area around the present town of Pisco lived the tough and resilient Chinchas, while just above them the uplands were held by the Rucanas. Through the Rucana gates the Chinchas had periodically in the past raided the sierra. The potentially most dangerous of these raids had extended even as far as Collao before Pachacuti's arrival upon the scene. A victory over the Chinchas would put a permanent end to this threat from the lowlands, though it is true that Pachacuti's victory over the Rucanas had effectively sealed off the passes in those areas.

Whatever the opposition met, whether equal skill in war or debilitating coastal fevers, the contingent under Capac Yupanqui was hurled back into the highlands. The heavy and cloying civilization of the coast could not be penetrated at this point. And this left, as the most available road to take in pursuing the imperial will-o'-the-wisp, the sierra route north into Chinchaysuyo.

Capac Yupanqui still stood in the good graces of the emperor, in spite of his reverses on the coast. He was assigned to the top command with two captains under him. At the same time a bit was placed in his mouth, for Pachacuti expressly enjoined upon him a limit beyond which he was not to proceed, the Yanamayo (Black River). When we consider the purposes behind this, we can perhaps deduce several reasons. As a rider of the imperial storm, knowledgeable in all its sharp ways and himself the result of a conspiracy, Pachacuti was far from giving any general his head completely, however useful his services. Empire (Capaccay) could be kept only by virtue of vigilance and suspicion. Again, Pachacuti was aware of the unstable conditions among the recently conquered Soras, who would be at the army's back after its advance north. Vilcas was still building, and the raw provincial administration of the area could not be trusted too far. It is possible that Capac Yupanqui may at the time have been the first Inca governor appointed over the Soras and the marches of Vilcas. If so his duties may have included the pacification and organization of those near parts of Chinchaysuyo lying just beyond his provincial responsibility and up to a definite point. Perhaps the Yanamayo has this reference, that it was the Rubicon to a potential Caesar.

As for the ever-present threat of Chanca resurgence, Pachacuti reduced it to reasonable proportions by requiring heavy levies of fighting men from them in this advance. Dragging the Inca war wagon behind them, their energies would be usefully siphoned off, and by employing them as shock troops the hope could always be indulged in of a spectacular disaster befalling them on the field of battle. The Chancas must naturally have been fully aware of this specter trailing them, for their blood had already been spilled for their Inca masters in like fashion in Collao.

On the road north the army under Capac Yupanqui found its way barred by a valiantly defended *pucara* near Parcos. In the sanguinary attack upon this fortress both the elite Inca *orejones* and the Chancas had to be thrown in. The victory which ensued, however, was the result rather of Chanca *élan* than of the martial qualities of the Incas, a humiliation to the Inca *raj* and one which bore sudden fruit in a dangerous unrest among the motley levies of the host. A crisis was preparing and there was no emperor on the spot.

Before any manifestation of this mutiny could take place, however, the army had moved ponderously on, northward past Acostambo and into the rich valley of Jauja. The opposition encountered here was swept aside, and the way forced open up to Tarma and Pumpu (Junín today), where far more bitter and successful resistance was to be encountered. This was the first ingress of the Inca warlords into these purlieus, and it was obviously meant to be a parade of power—probably only the most meager of provincial administration was left behind to consolidate Inca gains. In all of these places the Chancas performed notably, and the threat that their prestige would become a rallying point for disaffected elements in the ranks was correspondingly increased.

When reports of how the Chancas had saved the honor of the army and of all their subsequent successes reached Pachacuti in Cuzco, the old emperor decided that the time had come once and for all to emasculate this ancient enemy. He dispatched secret and urgent instructions to Capac Yupanqui ordering a general massacre of Ancoayllu (Tough Bolas), leader of the Chancas, and his men— a formidable task! This order arrived when the army was somewhere north of Junín.

The Inca generalissimo was either lax, overconfident, or disloyal. Certainly he botched the matter, the romantic reason adduced being that his light-o'-love in camp was Ancoayllu's own sister, a Chanca girl. She had overheard the midnight messenger delivering the grim rescript to Capac Yupanqui and gave prompt warning to her brother of what was in the making. Later under the pretense of a review Ancoayllu produced, in concert with his chieftains and some of the other *curacas* in the army, measures to avoid the trap.

Thus one midnight when the army was near Huánuco, at a preconcerted signal the Chanca faction, stripped for fast action, abandoned their campsites and fled, though not without casualties. The Chancas had seized the initiative and now intended to make the most of it.

On the flight north they looted the lovely Callejón de Huaylas to their heart's content, but the eventual appearance of the pursuing Inca vanguard finally turned them to the climax of their desperate venture. Gathering up what women they could from the area, they turned east and north to cross the two great Andean watersheds cleft by the trench of the Marañón. Capac Yupanqui's last sight from afar of these intrepid *serranos* was of their black antlike lines struggling in solemn agony over the snowy fields of the last passes. The Inca army gave up the pursuit. Eventually the Chancas were to fight their way into the land of the Chachapoyas and from there move out into the farthest confines of the wild montaña.

These Chancas were thus one of the very few Peruvian nations which refused to accept defeat at the hands of the Incas, and as such, safely ensconced in their far-distant and quarantined kingdom of the upper jungles, they became a name to conjure with. Honors perhaps were even—they could no longer do the Incas harm, yet no Inca ruler could ever effectively wipe that blemish of failure from his escutcheon.

The pursuit had taken the army across its Rubicon. This *fait accompli*, plus the removal of danger from within the army, presented Capac Yupanqui with an exceptional opportunity. Just next door to the north lay the compact state of Cajamarca, key to the entire northern sierra and ranking in wealth and strategic importance with such other provinces as Huánuco, Vilcas, and Cuzco. Its absorption would perhaps erase the stain of his inability to chastise the Chancas, and it would certainly push open the gates to limitless conquests beyond. He decided to move without delay. As a matter of fact necessity as well commanded this extension of the campaign, for as he lay thus extended after his exhausting chase, his rear and flanks were dangerously exposed to assaults from those newly overawed.

Shifting his forces to the north, he first subdued the Huamachucos. After this, in a stiff four months' campaign he totally broke the back of Cajamarca. This feat deserves to rank high in Inca military annals, considering the great distance involved, the previous dissensions which had racked the army, and the strength of the opposition. The latter must be particularly mentioned, for Cusmanco, the enemy leader, had called to his aid the allied coastal state of Chimor, itself rich, powerful, and explosively imperial. Chimor had sent relieving parties up to Cajamarca, but these had gone down in the same common debacle. Because Cajamarca played such a key role in the communications network, and because her full acquiescence rather than her hostility was desired for the near future, the house of Cusmanco was retained in power under this first makeshift Inca rule.

An issue had been joined and a challenge flung down. Cuzco now accepted the role of protagonist in what was to become a duel between the mightiest state of the sierra and the co-ordinated power of the entire northern coast of Peru. Capac Yupanqui's victory over Cajamarca had the effect of forcing a complete reorientation of Inca imperial policy, which up to this time was conceived among the peaks and *punas* of the highlands and reflected their stern limitations.

Capac Yupanqui left a dangerously exposed holding garrison in the conquered town and set out on the long way back, his army loaded down with women and loot. Such startling success as had finally been his may well have gone to his head. Whether a true cabal directed against the state was now formed under his reckless guidance, whether Pachacuti was jealous of keeping fame for himself and his heir, or whether it was indeed the open disobedience of his general which he insisted on punishing—whatever his reason, Pachacuti gave secret orders to his governor on the Apurimac line to have him killed. Capac Yupanqui and his fellow commander, Huayna Yupanqui (Honored Youth), both brothers of the emperor, were accordingly done away with at Limatambo (Oracle Lodge). The prince Apu Yanqui Yupanqui alone of the high command remained to lead the army back in its triumph to Cuzco. Pachacuti trod the loot and the captives underfoot as a sign of his possession.

Meanwhile all of the provinces of Chinchaysuyo, from the Quechua lands north to Cajamarca, through which Inca arms had just been carried, broke out into a chaotic melee of rebellion, undoing what little actual organization had been achieved. We may perhaps see some connection between this eruption and the general situation leading to the execution of the generals. The executions certainly made an indelible impression on the world of the day, and the Indians of the area where they occurred, even in the time of the viceroy Toledo, remembered them before all other historical facts. Though older now and physically enfeebled, the emperor could still surround himself with the aura of swift violence. But this purge, whatever else it may have meant, had brought an era to an end.

《 7 》

THE HIGH COMMAND of the northern army was swiftly reorganized and placed the next year under three other tested generals: Topa Capac (Royal Magnate), a bastard son of the emperor, and two half-brothers, Auqui Yupanqui (Honored Prince) and Tillca Yupanqui. And there also to learn his trade was the adolescent son now favored as the heir, Topa Inca (Royal Inca), who would in due course become the next emperor.

Pachacuti's vision had been expanded by the unexpected windfall from Cajamarca. Three necessities presented themselves. It was needful at the earliest possible moment to relieve the distant garrison, continually under attack by Chimor, and to strengthen it as a bastion in the north. It was even more necessary to subdue thoroughly and integrate the provinces that lay between Vilcas and Cajamarca, for Capac Yupanqui's previous campaign had been more in the nature of a massive raid than a mission of empire. And lastly, it having been unexpectedly proved that Chimor was at the moment incapable of matching Inca arms on the field, it was logical to prevent its further increment by continued pressure against it.

Matured by this greatest of Inca rulers in his old age, the conception of the campaign now to follow was the most inclusive of them all. A world view had appeared. From the confines of a closed Andean valley, Pachacuti had lifted Inca imperial policy, as if on the wings of a condor, into the empyrean. Harshly, cruelly, laboriously, and finally explosively, he had brought into being a memorable chapter in the story of empire. As a conqueror Pachacuti is the greatest American Indian in history.

SEVEN.
PACHACUTI
ORGANIZER OF THE STATE

By THIS TIME Pachacuti had given a recognizable form to the Empire of the Four Quarters. Inasmuch as the heart of the state was the imperial office itself, we shall begin our analysis with this.

We have previously stated that the Inca chieftain was basically a *sinchi*, which office had found its rationale in the border raids and massacres of the sierra tribes of the preceding age. The *sinchi*'s role was not only that of the braggart defender of the tribe; he was also expected to be brutally aggressive. This latter trait was encouraged by the custom whereby that tribe which he led in war presented him with honors and fiestas and with the choicest of the *chacras* and the young girls of the conquered people. Because he was not by usage allowed to impose tribute upon his own group, he showed a strong tendency to engineer raids against neighboring tribes in order to acquire these riches and honors. He must always be the most feared of warriors, and his boasting at the *chicha*-drinking had to be appropriately florid and heroic. To this end he drank toasts from the heads of his beaten enemies, trophies which had golden cups inserted into the skull and silver tubes for drinking between the teeth.

In regard to those pueblos which had resisted his threats, custom dictated a general massacre upon their defeat, though embassies of women with jars of *chicha* were accustomed to go out from the conquered pueblo to mitigate the blow if possible. For those who submitted without a fight, overcome by the mere prestige of the *sinchi*'s name, there was peace—with of course the degradation and servitude that go with defeat.

The *sinchi*'s son did not automatically inherit the father's office, for it was basically elective. Apparently it never rested upon any outright tyranny he could establish over his tribe, but solely on the good will and suffrage of the leading men. Nevertheless he was in the advantageous position of nurturing his own sons especially well in the skills of war. We therefore are aware of a pronounced tendency to shift the succession from election to blood inheritance.

> If a *sinchi* had two or three able and valiant sons, they were all elected to be *sinchis*. When they were not brave, others were elected. When these sons were very small, others were elected until they came of age, though if they were not brave they were not even elected then.

And we learn also—directly from testimony of the sierra Indians—that a bias also existed, though apparently not pronounced, to select the *sinchi*'s oldest son if he gave evidence of the required vigor.

The résumé above is of prime importance in understanding Inca imperial power as brought to its efflorescence under Pachacuti. Whatever startling innovations the Inca rulers from Viracocha Inca down to Atahualpa may have added—and many indeed were added—the office of the Capac Apu Inca (the emperor), was a pompous and ornate stucco laid over a most crude pre-Inca *pirca* below. Whatever else in his wisdom or policy he might contrive, the emperor was never allowed to forget that he was required to be a *sinchi* to his own group, a leader in war and a harvester of loot and honors.

This explains the curious problem presented by the conspiracy which had brought Pachacuti to the throne. Considered as a *sinchi*, Viracocha Inca had violated three of the usages of the office: he had not kept his captains busy, insisting instead on meddling with the cult and custom of the tribe; he had insisted on investing with the instruments of rule an unpopular and *unwarlike* son; and finally, in his desertion of the pueblo, he had personally failed of the hot courage always demanded of a *sinchi*. This is why his son could without contradiction brand him publicly as a woman. In a very real sense therefore Pachacuti was *elected* to defend Cuzco by those captains in whom burned the most ardent fires of the tribe. To use the term "conspiracy," as we have up to now, in describing the manner by which Pachacuti came to power is therefore only a convenience and a half-truth.

Once in the office Pachacuti raised his sons to be warriors, selecting at first an elder—perhaps the oldest—son as the leader to succeed. He was forced to relinquish this choice when the tribe failed to show its confidence in his selection. A younger son, Topa Inca, who had been more thoroughly trained in war was therefore selected by the coequal suffrage of the tribal magnates and the emperor, his father. All of this is surely a perfect description of the mechanics of the *sinchi*'s office though here acted out on an imperial scale.

《 2 》

THE INSTITUTION OF KINGSHIP was being rapidly elaborated all over Peru of the fifteenth century, with such expansive states as Cuzco, Chimor, Chucuito, Quito, and Chincha, all in various stages of perfecting the same. Whether in each of these cases we are entitled to derive this new and reinvigorated kingship from the common office of *sinchi* is arguable, noting as we must the richer antiquity of the coast and the vastly different problems imposed by contrasting terrain.

The imperial succession in Cuzco, however, can be elucidated only by deriving it from the procedures common to the *sinchi*'s office. The problem is mainly to discover what person or group had the right to bestow authority on the early Cuzqueño *sinchi*. In his lives of the earliest Inca rulers Sarmiento has shown them to have been nominated by their predecessors—who of course may not always have been their fathers—and confirmed by the "custodian *ayllus*," which are represented as bands of warriors, some of whom acted as personal liegemen pledged to the person of the heir. His picture is not wholly clear, and it may represent a stage intermediate between that of *sinchi* and emperor. Nor can we make out whether the "custodian *ayllus*" were those *allyus* most closely allied to the *sinchi* in blood and policy or whether they included members of the leading *ayllus* of all the farming groups in the community. No doubt it varied from time to time. In any case it is clear that some form of popular assent or election was necessary to the *sinchi*'s designation of his successor. It was therefore not simple election but a meshed procedure of nomination by the *sinchi* and consent by the ruling group.

The crisis of Pachacuti's accession wholly follows the pattern except that the gravity of the peril hanging over the state broke nomination and assent into two separate actions and reversed their order. The Inca war-lords assented first to Pachacuti as their new *sinchi* in the days of Cuzco's danger. His father and predecessor in the office did not nominate him until much later, when forced to on the actual day of the coronation.

In the withdrawal of Amaru Inca from the succession, we can see the retraction of tribal assent. The events in the later years of the reign of the emperor Huayna Capac reveal a split between ruler and magnates, which widened disastrously after his death into civil war—a dissension brought about over the problem of the succession. Following the fall of Tahuantinsuyo, when Francisco Pizarro nominated Manco Inca as Inca ruler, the Inca potentates still gathered to elect him, and the same custom apparently carried over into the refugee Inca state of Vilcabamba.

The first two emperors, Viracocha Inca and Pachacuti, perhaps because of the still unsettled state of the succession, passed their power on, while still alive, in the form of coregencies. The succeeding emperors broke this pattern and ruled alone up to the end, leaving their designation of a successor in a last will and testament. This was because they were not extremely aged at the time of their demise. But it is also evidence of the increasing independence of the emperor from the traditional controls exercised by the Inca magnates over their ruler. Coregency was thus the bridge by which the early state spanned the first chasms in the rocky ground of imperial succession.

The tendency of the emperors increasingly to dominate the whole system of the succession is apparent. We have no convincing evidence that primogeniture ever interested them as a rigid principle, whereas legitimacy did, this again being a reflection from earlier days. As far as we can see in the line of emperors, all were legitimate but only one, Huascar, was an eldest son.

<< 3 >>

LEGITIMACY WAS FURTHER PROTECTED by marriage with a full sister, an institution reversing the taboos generally enforced in societies against incestuous unions. We have seen the first appearance of this institution probably in the reign of Viracocha Inca, though Sarmiento attributes it to Pachacuti. It is at least coeval with the foundations of the empire. In a further bid to monopolize all access to the legitimacy Pachacuti established the custom of marrying all of his half-sisters as well.

The role of the *coya* in supporting the power of the state is evident, for if her royal brother was the son of the Sun, she herself was acclaimed "daughter of the sun and sole *coya*, kindly to the poor." Pachacuti appears to have made a definite attempt to suggest that the *coya* was also an embodiment of the more than earthly women of Manco Capac. His own *coya*, Mama Anahuarque, as well as the *coyas* of the following two emperors, all bore names found among the ancestral four of legend. Pachacuti, as a renewer of history, was thereby presenting his line as stemming from a rejuvenated Adamic pair. The *coya*'s major role in practice was a function of her fertility, for if she produced no sons, or incapable ones, a type of royal adoption came into play whereby the likeliest son of the emperor by another sister would be brought to her for her maternal acceptance.

The investiture and marriage of a *coya* was preferably an act in the coronation of her royal brother. Preparations for the ceremony seem to have included elements of the Peruvian *quicuchicoy* (feast of the first menstruation), the girl's puberty rites, when she discarded the headband of girlhood and combed back her hair in braids as evidence of her new womanliness; at this time also she received the name by which she would be known for the rest of her life.

The *quicuchicoy* was a communal event in the lives of the Incas. Several girls who had recently passed the milestone would be gathered in the public square with their thumbs bound tightly together (no doubt to symbolize their premenstrual state) and forced to undergo a cruel seven-day fast. Whenever they fainted or weakened their kinsfolk were at their side to lecture them on wifely duties and to exhort them to faithfulness and steadfastness. After this their thumbs were unbound and they were taken to the young braves, who presented them with sandals as tokens of their desire to have them for wives.

In her own special rites the prospective *coya* retired from the public view for a stated period and fasted. The sun-women then bathed her in the famous fountain in the garden close of Coricancha. This purification took place in the pale light before dawn and while the cold walls still radiated the chill of night. In a red and white wedding gown pinned with shining gold *tupus* or shawl pins, tinkling and glittering with bangles, she was escorted under the rising sun through the streets of Cuzco to her marriage. A mutual presentation of certain tokens took place, and the young husband presented her with golden sandals. Endowed with rich gifts and a retinue of women, she was then given her new throne name.

The royal seraglio was separated into divisions. The *coya*'s personal retinue was of course foremost and included the daughters of the most noble of the provincial *curacas*. Then came the smaller groups of the secondary wives—all half-sisters—each with lesser concubines assigned to them. In theory the emperor passed a week with each group, choosing whichever woman in that particular coterie who happened to please him at the time, and so on down the calendar until he returned to the *coya* and her women. We may imagine that the theory was more honored in the breach than in the observance. The emperor was served in his inner apartments in true Oriental fashion by that one of his many sister-wives and her women who were assigned to that eight-day stint. With them also, when pleasuring in an area of warm springs, he bathed. Spanish reports on the number of women in the royal harem vary erratically. We are perhaps safest with Cobo, who informs us that the seraglios of the late period contained two to three hundred women. Possessing this harem was of course an important road to the legitimacy, as we know from the fact that Atahualpa is said to have kept a part of the women of his deceased father. Because the daughters of the emperor alone carried the legitimacy, only the heir-apparent was allowed to marry his half-sisters; to all other princes of the blood these sisters were taboo.

The most important part of the ruler's varied regalia was the *mascapaycha*, the token of royalty which he generally wore affixed to the headband. It was an ornate, colored set of tassels which hung well down over the eyes, being inserted in the headband or llautu. This was his crown and was itself a powerful *huaca*. No one could become the Capac Apu Inca who did not wear it on his brows at the great occasions. To the headband was also attached a pompom with three feathers. Special honorific offices had been created in the court to care for these sacred items. For the feathered pompom mounted on a staff to appear in the hands of an officer making an arrest or delivering a royal order was in itself an incontestable warrant. The regalia was reputed to go back to Manco Capac, the first ruler.

The royal crest is of somewhat uncertain significance. Basically the royal blazon consisted of two snakes and a rainbow, to which were added the sun and moon. Inti, Mama Quilla, and Huanacauri the Rainbow are of course easy to identify here—the serpents are less easy. We have already seen, from one source, that a mythical serpent may lurk in the background of Inca cult, possibly a remote ancestor, for one version of Manco Capac's ancestry gives his mother as descended from a dragon or serpent, and his sire as a great serpent himself. Still to be seen by the traveler today, the serpent was commonly represented on Inca walls; it also appeared on the sides of the imperial litter. The cable carried by the Inca clan in their stately dance, which so excited the imagination of the Spaniards, was in reality a long woolen serpent made of many twisted strands and gold adjuncts and having an enlargement at the end to represent the head. Why, on the royal crest, the serpent is double we cannot say, unless we are in some such context as the twin serpents carried by the god of Tiahuanaco where they are meant to stand for the lightnings. Whatever its exact interpretation may be, it is evident that the Inca blazon was a visual statement of the claims of the royal house.

In addition to this dynastic coat of arms, each emperor carried his own personal blazon as a statement of his *sinchi*-ship. A ruler was thus not only the heir to the whole of the ancestral tradition, but also the architect of his own success as an elected war-leader, two basically opposed but mutually enriching conceptions. It was Pachacuti who solved this polarity when he defined and strengthened the royal *panaca*.

The *panaca* had undoubtedly been in existence before Pachacuti, possibly—in its incipient form—since the days of Inca Roca. Unlike the old and larger *ayllus*, with their inevitable connotations of both land and community, which had come together over the years to form the Inca population of Cuzco (whole pueblos or parts of them or bands of semi-migratory folk, Maras, Sañus, Tambos, Sutics, and others), the *panaca* was an artificial institution ordained by pronouncement of the living emperor. The word may be derived from *pana* (a man's sister). Sarmiento says its meaning is "descent."

The *panaca* consisted of certain living descendants designated by an emperor as being correct for the purpose, with the important exception of that son whom he had selected as the next ruler. This exception was necessary inasmuch as the heir would eventually have to organize his own distinct *panaca* once he was installed in power. The *panacas* of former emperors were kept filled by the assignment to them of bastard sons and daughters of the reigning monarch, even though one might have expected all to go to their royal father's group. The *panaca* was named after that son who had been appointed to be its head.

The emperor was the *genius* of his *panaca*; his death was treated simply as a ceremonial incident, for the royal mummy held exactly the same position as had his animated person—his *coya*, his wealth, his favorite women and servitors, all continued in his possession. In brief his estate was noninheritable and inalienable. The *panaca* was thus a special type of elective and ever-functioning family, the head of which never died, whose grip on his possessions never lapsed, and who was feted, entertained, and served *in perpetuum* in his palace. Only in its incidental features was it an ancestor-cult society, which of course implies death.

The emperor's *panaca* and those of his predecessors were organized into a loose dynastic cohesion by the common veneration of the Chima *panaca* of Manco Capac the founder. This overall structure we may confidently attribute to Pachacuti. And certainly it was he who turned it from a mere periodic cult practice to a theatrical production involved in a continuous rehearsal of activities. While all Incas by blood were members of one or another *ayllu*, all do not seem necessarily to have belonged to one of the imperial *panacas*. There is one meager statement from our sources that at the time of Pachacuti's death each *ayllu* in Cuzco could summon up about two hundred warriors. It is extremely doubtful if the *panacas* were this large, as they were conceived to be essentially integrated families.

Pachacuti confirmed the canon at ten *panacas*, dividing them between the two Cuzco moeities and appointing their captains. The first five were those of the rulers from Manco Capac down to and including Mayta Capac, forming Hurin (Lower) Cuzco. From there on down to the *panaca* already created for Topa Inca, Pachacuti's heir, the group made up Hanan (Upper) Cuzco. The names of the eleven *panacas*, from Manco Capac through Huayna Capac respectively, were: Chima (Red), Raurau (Fire), Hahuaynin (Grandchild), Apu Mayta (Captain Mayta), Usca Mayta (Beggar Mayta), Vicaquirau (Vica Cradle), Aucay Haylli (Song of Triumph), Sucso (Debility), Inaca (Head Covering, Mantle), Capac Ayllu (Magnificent Ayllu), and Tumipampa (Field of the Knife).

By the end of Pachacuti's reign, the imperial office was locked in a rigid protocol. On first presentation to the emperor, a subject—no matter how high his rank—entered the presence unshod and bearing a token burden on his back. On those impressive state occasions when the ruler appeared in state on the dais or *usno* in the great square of Cuzco, he sat on a golden stool while his most exalted servitors waved fly-whisks at him and held over his head the *achihua*, the feathered canopy of iridescent hues. The most intimate of his captains and courtiers clustered about him, elegant men with dark, heavy faces, while the butterfly colors among the pages of the court, the sons of the mightiest provincial *curacas*, each clad in his own tribal dress, gave to the occasion the full kaleidoscopic character of empire. The emperor was carried at a most stately pace when in his armorial litter, while liveried harbingers ran ahead to arouse the countryside to reverence; others swept all impediments and uncleanness clear of the road. The litter was surrounded by files of chosen warriors and moved in an appropriate hush through hills covered with those lowly folk who had come to hail "the sun child."

We have said that the royal power rested not only on the elective principle of merit but upon the inherited principle of family. A consideration of the latter involves an inspection of the Inca community.

《 4 》

THE INCAS ARE DESCRIBED as more tall than the average Indian of Peru; their women were handsome, in which respects they resembled the peoples farther up the sierra. As became their sublime mission in history they were also a sedate people, imbued with a sense of lordliness and the cold arrogance that goes with it. Pre-eminently a martial race, the stern drama of war satisfied both their passions and their sense of thunderous events, while what could be built out of conquest appealed to their sense of structure and control. Their family loyalties were deep and fiery, yet puritanical and rigid. Their search for a security consonant with their exposed social status is manifest in their prerogative of secret confession, for everywhere outside of Cuzco public confession was the rule. Their acquiescence in the emperor's authority was only reluctantly given, as we can see from the tumults and purges which periodically swept over Cuzco from the days of Viracocha Inca on. As a people they considered themselves always a body of "free knights," whose immunities from labor and other exactions had been divinely established and were thus sacred rights; this did not necessarily conflict in their minds with the belief that the emperor was the true son of the Sun and of the Moon, his consort. The culture they achieved was as brittle and as stately as the Andean peaks among which they had their being. They were a dour people and a great people.

In common with other tribal groups of the sierra the Incas celebrated puberty rites, by means of which their youths were endowed with the warrior's responsibilities and prerogatives. Not only because of the intrinsic interest in this most intimate of Inca ceremonies, but also because it was expanded and reshaped by Pachacuti out of the common stuff of Peruvian ritual to become the ceremonial heart of the new state, it is well worth commenting on. By means of this institution the Inca aristocracy received its badge of superiority. It was ascribed to Manco Capac, the fountain of all things Inca. The central *huaca* in the ceremonies was the war-fetish and ancestor, Huanacauri.

As elaborated, the ceremonies filled part of the month of December, which was known as Capac Raymi (the Great Festival). The specific rite and climax of the month's activities was known as the *huarachicoy* (the celebration of the breechcloth), a custom shared with other Andean tribes. Related to it and included in the same complex of ritual was the uniquely Inca rite of the *tocochicoy* (the celebration of ear-piercing) and the insertion of the earplugs. This took place when the boys were from twelve to fifteen years of age. When they had successfully undergone these austerities they became true Incas, *pakayoc* (earplug men), or *orejones* as the Spanish called them.

The ceremonies were both a coming to manhood and an extended test of the endurance, warlike spirit, and tribal learning of the young men. It began with a period of fasting and sexual continence during which the women of the households involved wove those special garments which the boys were to wear; to the girls was particularly assigned the weaving of the ornamented fringes of the boys' breechcloths. Beginning their harsh regime of semistarvation and relentless physical activity, the boys were sent up on the high slopes above Cuzco to gather grass for the plaiting of their sandals and the making of seats for the tribesmen in the coming days.

The ceremonies officially began when the candidates for induction were assembled in the square on the fifth day to be introduced to the emperor, to the *huacas* who had been brought out of the temple, and to the mummified ancestors. Here facing the lads in solemn pomp were the pantheon and the entire history of the tribe. Into this world they would step if they proved worthy.

After this they were escorted to the foot of Huanacauri, the sacred mountain. Prominently displayed in this procession was the famous white llama, the mascot or prosperity of the Incas, who personified the first such animal to appear after the flood. He was accompanied by his own two *mamaconas* carrying on their backs *chicha*-jars from which he had been trained to drink and coca for him to chew. That night the boys slept exposed on the frosty slopes near or on the ancestral grounds of Matahua, and there they prayed to the *huaca* for valor and for his aid in the coming ordeals. This exposure may have lasted three days and nights. At any rate on the tenth day they entered the presence of "their father" Huanacauri and were there given by him, through his priesthood, the leather or woolen slings which were the characteristic weapons of the Inca braves. The priests and the older men who served as mentors to the young squires then proceeded to whip them with these slings to impart directly to their bodies the death-dealing virtues of the weapons.

Back in Cuzco the boys demonstrated their special dance in the plaza and again were violently whipped on arms and legs by their unbending kinsmen. All of such trials, wherein psychological tension was compounded by physical pain and a half-starved body, the youths were constrained to accept with composure. He who winced or lost spirit disgraced his kinsmen and the *huacas*.

On the fourteenth day the boys put on special costumes and, now accompanied by the nubile girls of the tribe carrying jars of *chicha*, moved to the slopes of Mount Anahuarque. After an all-night vigil both sexes made the ascent to the top, where the appropriate rites were conducted. The girls then fled down to certain designated stations near the bottom, from which they enticed the boys with various calls and promises of *chicha*. Hereupon ensued the most punishing test of all for the lads, a headlong race down the long broken slopes in which loss of life and permanent crippling were far from unknown. The first one in to taste the girls' *chicha* was the most highly honored. This now led to the lads' induction into the manly tradition of *chicha*-drinking, served by the women of the tribe. We would assume from the previous complexion of the race that they were encouraged by the older men in the extreme forms of sexual license expected to accompany orgiastic drinking.

Two other mountains were ascended before the rites were concluded, Sahuaraura (Bound Flame) and Yahuira (the leading *huaca* of the Maras clans). Thus four mountains in all were involved, and one can suspect from the fourfold division of Tahuantinsuyo that each one of these mountains represented one of these imperial quarters, and that they may therefore be sought for around Cuzco at roughly the expected point of the compass as oriented from the Plaza de Armas. This would not necessarily deny that these mountains were also the particular *huacas* of the traditional four Ayar brothers. Anahuarque was southeast of the city. Huanacauri of course is identified and must be understood to symbolize the cardinal quarter, that wherein Pacaritambo, the cradle of the Inca race, first appeared.

On the twenty-first day the lads purified themselves in the spring of Callispuquio just behind Sacsahuaman. On Mount Yahuira they were dressed in the most splendid accouterments of war. Here they had their ears slit in preparation for the later insertion of the ear-plugs, and just as the girls had been given their real names on completion of their menstruation rites, so now the boys received theirs.

Adult men at last and members of the noble caste of Inca knights, the lads wound down the steep road to Cuzco where, on the twenty-second day, each one was invested in the plaza with his weapons of war, the gift of an uncle. Other kinsmen produced rich offerings and with each gift a heavy blow followed by a final admonition to courage and loyalty. The emperor in person bestowed the golden and silver earplugs.

A purgation of the city followed. Four Inca judges, sitting each in dignity at one of the exits from Haucaypata, condemned in varying degrees those brought before them by the headmen of the *ayllus* for offenses perpetrated during the year. Pachacuti and his family presided ceremonially in the center of the square while the city was thus being cleansed of its accumulated moral rubbish.

The last performance was a savage war dance by the youths dressed in puma- and jaguar-skins and feathered war bonnets. Divided into their two moeities, the dancers exhibited their future ferocity in mock battle.

A four-day *taqui* or fiesta of singing, dancing, and *chicha*-drinking followed, in which only the clans of Incas of the blood took part. Unlike the war dance of the braves, the unique dance of the Inca folk as a whole was decorius and solemn, measured, even dull, the true expression of a taut and restrained people. It began processionally from Coricancha, moving thence down the narrow streets to the great square. Dancing their peculiar step, the people carried the decorated woolen cable invented by Pachacuti, the men on one side, the women on the other. Once the file had debouched into the square, it began a progress around the four sides. Throughout the proceedings the emperor was the focus of action. He sat elevated on his royal stool in the middle of the square watching the dancers circle about him carrying at their head his royal insignia. The songs which were chanted recounted his valorous deeds and those of the royal ancestors. The culmination of the dance was reached when the performers spiraling in had become tightly wound about the emperor in a visual symbolism of support and centrality and the woolen serpent was laid down thus coiled, on the ground about the dais.

From the beginning of the Capac Raymi and up through the twenty-sixth day all traffic in and out of Cuzco was interdicted. At the four toll gates on the hills above Cuzco, and in the tambos along the ways, there had been gathering from the empire at large the most prominent *curacas* and provincial officials. These were now allowed to enter the city, whereupon the Capac Raymi ended with a four-day fiesta stressing imperial rather than tribal allegiance. Inclusive oaths of fidelity to the emperor were taken by the magnates, and so the month closed.

The symbolism in the Capac Raymi is vastly impressive. Though unclear in most particulars, because of our lack of knowledge, each detail masks a meaning. It is unquestionable that a mind of great imaginative power lies behind it. This mind was Pachacuti's. He utilized of course Inca rites long precedent to him such as the *huarachicoy*, the *tocochicoy*, and the *huayyaya* (the tribal dance of the Incas). He enshrined and formulated in the events of this month the full spirit of the tribe in its two parts, that pertaining to Incas of the blood and that to Incas by adoption. He changed the emphasis of the rites by tying together the concepts of tribe and emperor so that allegiance to the first—which had been primary—was coterminous with loyalty to the other. In this ceremonial wizardry Pachacuti gave the aristocracy an open book in which to read of its past, its duties, its mission, and its prerogatives. Surely no young brave who had once opened those bold and pompous pages would ever forget the lessons written therein.

« 5 »

The state which Pachacuti had made anew, with its superb integration around the office of the Capac Apu Inca, was a core area set up as the patrimony of the Inca nobility. Geographically it included only the Huatanay world and its close environs; administratively it encompassed both levels of the Inca aristocracy. Its territorial boundaries were identical with those of the Quechua tongue, extending from Abancay to the middle Vilcañota Valley, and including an almost equal extent of area to the north and south of Cuzco. Beyond this and extending out like the spokes of a wheel into the farthest recesses of the provinces were the lately conquered tribes under their *curacas*. Tahuatinsuyo may therefore be described as a compact caste state surrounded by a constantly expanding field of organized tribute. Emperor, aristocracy, and subject respectively were reflected in the ceremonial center of Cuzco itself, the small core state, and the entirety of empire as it was finally to exist from Quito into Tucumán and Chile.

The highest order of chivalry, the Incas by blood, were grouped artificially into *ayllus* in the two moieties of Cuzco. They resided in the sacred city by right although they additionally possessed extensive villas and *chacras* in the near-by country. Incas by adoption seem to have held their *curaca*-ships mainly in the pueblos of the core state. These were the men who were granted special quasi-feudal immunities by Pachacuti, in return for which they formed the most dependable cadres of his armies and leaders of the *mitmacs*. More distant *curacas* were brought into the ambient of the throne by providing them with full-blooded Inca women, whom they could divorce only upon cause of adultery and only after petition to the emperor. Their issue joined the ranks of the *orejones*, thereby creating in the next generation a wider world of adjunct Incas. Possibly included in this social rank also were the sons of those of the ruler's concubines who were not Incas, for we know that while these lesser princes did not hold offices in the provincial hierarchy they were still utilized as field officers in the armies. Any child sired by a member of the Inca nobility but whose mother was not of the highest *curaca* caste in Cuzco was held in low esteem; back in his mother's community however he might be accounted as one of the *orejones*. The orders of nobility could be distinguished by their mode of transportation; a privileged one or two were carried in kingly litters, others in hammocks, while the lesser knights went on foot.

The upper nobility Pachacuti had inherited. The second order he had practically created anew, as when he granted the earplugs to the Cotapampas and the Cotaneras in gratitude for their aid during the Chanca war, though it is true that the blueprint for adoption had been drawn up under previous Inca rulers. Nevertheless it was Pachacuti's thorough overhaul of the state and the vast compass of his plans that permitted a rapid expansion of the Inca caste.

« 6 »

IT IS INSTRUCTIVE TO FOLLOW PACHACUTI in his work of organizing this state. After those first swift and appalling campaigns following the Chanca war, the greater Cuzco area was turned into an unprecedented beehive of construction. The strong sun of Pachacuti's personality blazed over the land, forcing an incomparable pace of movement and industry out of the lethargy of centuries. A space of five years was allotted to bringing the new state into operation. These early years of Pachacuti's reign must have been among the most stirring in all Peruvian history.

The Chanca war and his own punitive measures had profoundly unsettled the Quechua-speaking populations of the greater Cuzco area. Pachacuti seized the occasion to erode further what particularism and local allegiances were left here. In a bid to unify the people Pachacuti's inspectors were sent into the many pueblos of the core state with instructions to move the nubile population widely about, marrying off the lads of one pueblo to the girls of another. Implicit in this was not only the creation of a new patriotism but also the need to augment rapidly the villages so recently devastated round about Cuzco. Pachacuti himself personally supervised the mass mar-

riage, on a mixed community basis, of the bachelors and virgins of
that area comprised within a five-mile circuit of Cuzco. Such forced
marriages in the empire were part of a vast breeding program designed eventually to fill the hungry cadres of the Inca armies as they
moved busily over the land.

Whole communities of commoners in the environs were uprooted
and assigned as *"repartimientos"* to the Inca nobility of the blood
who lived on the usufruct of their labor. Some filled domestic posts
and others worked on the large country estates acquired by the nobility, where they erected stone and thatch manor houses, reserved
apartments, pleasure houses, and hunting lodges, imitating thus on a
very minor scale the country properties of the emperor. When
grouped in several conjoined *canchas*, the largest of them were imposing baronial seats indeed, while the smallest were at least comfortable. Pachacuti kept as his personal lands the best parts of the
Yucay country, some of which as we have seen, his father had
formerly claimed.

Enriched by all this royal largesse, the Incas of the upper nobility
could be expected to identify their interests henceforth with those
of the imperial office, whatever they may have thought of the incumbent in person. Nevertheless we must not forget that their true
stations were in the city of Cuzco, where their town palaces were
being erected on Pachacuti's orders. A true *noblesse de l'épée*, they
were nevertheless cast also in the role of a *noblesse de robe*.

Pachacuti gave to the second order of Inca nobility the difficult
task of directly managing the new core state. He began with a census.
All the *curacas* and captains whose services during the Chanca danger
he had rewarded with the earplugs, or to whom he had assigned
curaca-ships in new and reconditioned communities, received the
peremptory order for a count of all heads, age groups, and llama
herds within their jurisdictions.

When the population of the core state had been somewhat sta-
bilized, Pachacuti initiated the second part of his program. He called
in all the *curacas* and at a notable fiesta in Cuzco outlined for each
his responsibility. There was produced a topographical clay map or
model of the whole area with each valley and grassed *puna* clearly
marked. On this map he pointed out for each *curaca* exactly what

were to be the limits of his pueblo, his *chacras*, and his grazing lands. There could be no cavil at this royal partition; all border squabbles, all contentions over water rights, all invasions of pasture lands were to cease forever in terms of this clarification by the crown. Overnight Pachacuti wiped out the long confused night of the pre-Inca past.

Leaving this impressive convocation, the *curacas* then moved out to their respective jurisdictions to set up the necessary boundary markers under the eagle eyes of the Cuzco inspectors. This done, they were then ready to initiate that outstanding expansion in the tribute which, on the basis of the census and his future plans, Pachacuti had imposed on them. Onerous it must have been, and a depressed serf-like existence was from now on to be the lot of those Indians who labored in the ditches or turned the earth. The *curacas* were harshly warned against allowing any idleness, and if the fields did not demand the care of the husbandman at a particular moment, the menfolk were to be assembled and exercised in martial skills. Large, stone-lined irrigation channels were to be constructed, llama flocks built up and inspected, and vast new *chacras* planted. Terraces were to be started on the slopes, which would both extend the tilth and prevent erosion into the flatlands.

Pachacuti drove his people to the limit of their endurance in these early stages of state-building. This afforded him the radically increased production needed for his plans while at the same time providing a strong depressant to the appearance of any challenge to his recently acquired power. Dawn-to-dusk absorption in the grinding work of supervision, with total responsibility involved, would allow no *curaca* the leisure to conspire.

Incas of the blood were used in the general oversight of this program in the field, but Pachacuti filled his own time in a traveling inspection of its progress. The mere announcement of the approach of the conqueror's litter must have stimulated these new landed officials into feverish activity. It was Pachacuti's own sense of planning, of supervision, and of inspection which made this perhaps the greatest period of administrative success in pre-Columbian history.

With his five-year plan well in hand, Pachacuti summoned the *curacas* back to Cuzco and, as a reward to the faithful ones who had filled his granaries and warehouses to overflowing, he assigned to each—according to his rank—a girl of his own lineage to be the legitimate wife. The children of these unions were to become Incas of the blood. At one stroke was thus created a loyal landed barony on the peripheries of Cuzco whose future was tied to the royal house and whose descendants were to be of the blood royal. Other rich gifts were given to these men by the emperor, but none of them had the same splendid meaning as the dowry of prestige brought by their new wives.

We may question our chronicler Betanzos that these works all formed successive parts of a five-year plan, but certainly within that time they were successfully begun. Nor could it have been the flawless project that Betanzos presents. But that it was a daring experiment in administration and that it imposed almost overnight a new tempo of living in the sierra—these cannot be doubted.

EIGHT.
CUZCO
THE LION IN THE MOUNTAIN

《　I　》

WHEN PACHACUTI CAME TO POWER Cuzco was already in its *floruit*. Its old adobe *canchas* and hamlets had been receiving the increment of Viracocha Inca's far-ranging imposts and tribute, and the city had grown until the intervening fields between the clusters of habitations had all but disappeared. But it was at that time still a disparate and jarring collection of lineages—each claiming its own *huacas*, its own *chacras*, and its own waters—it had no singleness of character as such. And, with some exceptions, it was still a town of *pirca*, mud, and thatch.

Pachacuti changed all this as thoroughly as he did every other sphere of Inca life. In one grandiose and integrated plan he aimed at razing wide areas of old Cuzco and reclaiming marshlands; he contemplated the erection on the new sites of town palaces in stone for the *panacas*, the building of a spectacular andesite palace for himself, and the complete remodeling of the sacred shrine of Inticancha in stone and precious materials—the whole city to be the *logos*, the Word, in stone of a new and supreme Inca dispensation.

With careful logic he had first provided for the establishment of a series of warehouses on the hillsides overlooking the city. These early began to fill up with the maize, *quinoa*, *chuño*, hot peppers, cordage, and clothing necessary to sustain both the dwellers of the city and those gangs levied from the outside who were to wrench an imperial city out of the soil and water and rock of the land.

The drainage problem had to be faced first. The two streams which traced between them the interfluvial triangle which was Cuzco proper eroded their gravelly banks rapidly in the many freshets, constantly drowning parts of their channels in quagmire. It was necessary to straighten and contain them in masonry flumes down to their junction; then for an additional dozen miles to Muina the Huatanay was to be shored and controlled against choking. One of the important parts of the immense hydraulic project concerned the mud flats at the Huatanay crossing, which was the hub of the whole area and a depression into which drained a spring under Collcampata. This task of channeling the two streams went along with the far-flung reorganization of the core state and was indeed just one of the projects of those busy years. It was completed in a record four years.

Pachacuti had the swamp filled, artificial banks constructed, and at the point where the ancient ford had existed, the whole stream was finally cased over with wide slabs of stone. This had the effect of joining the wide area newly provided on the north side of the stream with those old open market grounds on the south side of the crossing.

The northern section was to become known to history as Haucaypata, today the Plaza de Armas. The south half was Cusipata, the spot where from time immemorial travelers from the north and west had set down their goods beside the river crossing. Today the Plaza de Armas is as vital a part of the life Cuzco as it was in the days of Tahuantinsuyo, and indeed has almost exactly the same dimensions. Cusipata however has been utilized for building sites, the best known today being the present Government Hotel. One small piece of it only has been preserved, the present Plaza de Regocijos (Joy Square) next to the hotel, which still faithfully continues in Spanish translation its original Quechua name.

Haucaypata was the heart of Cuzco. Its very soil was sacred. In the years to come ground would be taken up from it and carried away into parts of the empire where Incas lived and governed, so that these expatriates could hold their *taquis* and worship their father the Sun on native soil sprinkled in distant plazas which mimicked the true and only Haucaypata. In the center of the great square Pachacuti planted the *capac usno* (great dais), on which the ruler sat for state occasions. This was a shaped stone set in the earth, contact with which gave the ruler power to invoke the gods successfully. Near by was the famous sugar-loaf stone which he had had splendidly sheathed in gold leaf. This stone had a perforation in it into which the sacred *chicha* of the Sun was poured when that god wished to drink toasts with his children at their fiestas.

Pachacuti insisted upon a clear-cut distinction between the two parts of the square, and this may well have been visibly maintained by some artificial demarcation cutting it in two along the line of the buried Huatanay. As a rule Haucaypata was reserved for festivals while Cusipata, the Inca *Champs de Mars*, sounded to the shouts and clatter of military parades. What was behind this division was the concept of the city of Cuzco as a peculiarly sacred *huaca*, with the two rivers of the Huatanay and the Tullu marking indelibly the outlines of that taboo. This is why, when Pachacuti required the attendance of provincial representatives of the empire in the state festivals, he still stamped upon the scene the privileges and superiority of the masters of Cuzco by segregating the two audiences, true Incas in Haucaypata, Incas by adoption in Cusipata, separate yet conjoined. The sanctity of Cuzco could not have been more explicitly stated, nor its close ties with Tahuantinsuyo better delineated.

But the remarkable concentration of Pachacuti's symbolism on the site was still not exhausted. The empire was known collectively as Tahuantinsuyo (The Four Quarters). From Haucaypata and Cusipata four arterial roads were born, each leading out to one of the theoretical divisions of the empire. By definition then the Plaza was the core of the world, and the glittering *usno* in the center of the square was even more the intense focus of the empire's efforts and the point from which radiated all authority and vitality into the land.

《 2 》

I recall having seen with my own eyes certain old Indians who, when they came in sight of Cuzco, gazed deeply and uttered great cries and wept tears of sadness; they contemplated past and present and they could remember that city which was ruled, in the years of their youth, by rulers of their own blood who in dominion and generosity offered what Spaniards did not.

So wrote Cieza de León, a conquistador with that rare thing, a heart. Movingly and most aptly he captured in those words the hold which the city had upon the people of Tahuantinsuyo. The very spot on the Chinchaysuyo road where the traveler first looked down upon the city was a famous *huaca*. Where the tourist sees today below him red roofs of Spanish tile, Inca Cuzco showed instead gray and yellow *ichu* thatches, matlike and soft and laid in the most cunning patterns. The various shades of these thatches both weathered and new must have afforded a pleasing variety to the scene when observed from the rim of the valley.

By the end of Pachacuti's reign and increasingly so in the succeeding reigns, Cuzco was a microcosm of the empire. An incessant stream of llama herds and human traffic flowed in and out of its environs: Inca officials on business; *chasquis* (post runners) bearing urgent advices and reports from remote parts of the empire or perhaps fresh fish caught the day before in distant lake Titicaca for the ruler's table; *curacas* called in to answer charges or to escort the Indians bearing their annual tribute; heavily guarded files of *acllas*, those girls chosen from every tribe or tributary state as the most beautiful and nobly born, destined for state apportionment as wives, concubines, vestals, or blood sacrifices; a file of a hundred chanting Lupaca Indians bearing the first fruits of their *quinoa* harvest to lay at the emperor's feet; pilgrims and holy men come to accrue the merit of worship at the fabulous *huacas* of Cuzco; sullen gangs of the subordinate or newly trampled peoples to labor on the building schemes of the Incas, to clean and clear the streets and perform other necessary tasks; contingents of warriors moving to their appointed bivouacs or to the distant reinforcement of some man-hungry Inca army out on the far frontier.

All of this traffic was rigorously controlled at designated checkpoints outside of Cuzco. One of these guard-stations still stands today, in all the neatness of its excellent masonry, just beyond the ruins of Pikillacta—this being the port of entry which enforced Topa Inca's later security measure restricting the number of Colla Indians in Cuzco at any one time. Everyone passing through these gates was closely interrogated. This was to prevent the illegal smuggling of weapons into Cuzco for purposes of treachery, as well as, on the exit, to see that no gold left Cuzco without due authorization.

In the city and its suburban areas there resided peoples from all over the empire, many of them brought in as *mitmacs* with special skills. These folk were required always to identify themselves by their national mode of dress or hair style. After Topa Inca's conquest of the coastal kingdom of Chimor, we find a ward of highly skilled craftsmen from those parts settled in Cuzco and working under the requirements of the state. Fifteen thousand Cañar Indians from what is today Ecuador were settled in the suburbs by Topa Inca, and in the palmy days there were finally *mitmacs* from all over the empire resident in greater Cuzco; Huancas, Chachapoyas from the northern montaña, Collas from the Titicaca Basin, even Araucanians from Chile, each group segregated in their separate suburban barrio and all regulated by a special *ius gentium*—drawn up, of course, in the interests of the Incas. According to Betanzos, Pachacuti had instituted a "dole" on every fourth day to these potentially dangerous groups in greater Cuzco consisting, where needed, of food and clothing. It is evidence of a stringent paternalism on the part of the state, however, and not idleness on the part of a city mob. This dole lasted down to the coming of the Spaniards. The working population was homogeneous insofar as it relied on state maintenance and also, by virtue of being drowned in such a cosmopolitan isolation, incapable of discovering again any of its old racial allegiances.

Counting in this motley Peruvian population, plus the regional *curacas* who lived in the city, plus finally the establishments of the Inca nobility and the ruler, it would perhaps not be rash to accept the estimate of Cristóbal de Molina de Santiago that greater Cuzco, extending out about six miles in all directions, had forty thousand householders. Even if the figure of forty thousand is exaggerated, we can still see a very high concentration of people at the upper end of the Huatanay Valley.

As ROME HAD DRAWN ABOUT HERSELF A SACRED FURROW, the pomerium, within which all things belonged to the civil gods, so the rivers drew a pomerium around Cuzco, the open base of the triangle being sealed by the heights of Sacsahuaman. It was this area alone which Pachacuti broke into an Upper and Lower Cuzco, the division between them being represented today by the street of the Triunfo. We can only guess at the number of pure-blooded Incas in the triangle. An isolated remark in our sources allows us to guess that by the time Pachacuti died there were on the average about two hundred fighting men in each of the ten *ayllus* which, on rough computation, gives a little less than one thousand souls for each one; this would then bring the Inca population of inner Cuzco to about nine thousand souls.

In the emperor's mind this city, awakening at the touch of his genius, was a symbolic puma. He himself was its head, and its noble inhabitants were the various members. The ward at the confluence of the two rivers therefore he named Pumapchupan (Lion's Tail), a designation still used, while the warlike heights at the other end, armed with the tusked ramparts of Cuzco's fortress, he likened to the muzzle of the beast.

This was no mere whimsy but a parable of his intentions and a mystique of noble proportions. The concept of Cuzco as a lion-body made actual in the communal life of its inhabitants is somewhat analogous to the Christian doctrine of the church as the body of Christ. Pachacuti carried the symbol to its conclusion when he designated the highest habitable piece of land on the head of the lion as the special preserve of the dynasty's founder, Manco Capac. And logically his own manor was next below this, extending all the way down to the plaza.

Along with the aforementioned drainage project went an equally bold enterprise: the remodeling of the entire sacred area to fit it for its new role. There had been some building in fine stone in Cuzco in the preceding reign, but the city was still in great part a jumble of ill-assorted adobe structures. Byways and thoroughfares wandered carelessly over the gravelly ridge and past the more humid areas without pattern. It was vigorous, busy, and crowded for a remote highland center, but it was neither logical nor magnificent. Like Augustus, Pachacuti was thus to find his city of mud and leave it of stone. This rebuilding began around or just after 1440 A.D.

For the work new quarries—some about fifteen miles away—were opened, Pachacuti himself selecting the first stones. Calls were put out for quantities of rope for hauling and the opening of additional clay pits. After a characteristic outburst, in which Pachacuti accused both himself and his magnates of lethargy, he decided on the size and apportionments of the city-to-be. This decision was then communicated to the Inca *ayllus* and the favored *curacas* in a ceremony inaugurating the work. On a clay model of the ideal city Pachacuti pointed out to each their future habitations and himself then drew the first surveyor's cord. Crews which had been levied were then given their tasks, hauling stones, leveling land, mixing clay, casting adobes, razing the older edifices, and erecting, plastering, painting, and thatching the new. The emperor's foresight in having first provided full warehouses to support this concentrated work can be appreciated.

Pachacuti ordered all Incas temporarily out of the triangle while the work went on. Even across this space of time we may still conjure up the mixed pride and resentment of the *ayllus* as, bivouacked on the far sides of the streams, they watched the inexorable destruction of their ancestral plots and the rise of more stately substitutes. The Alcavizas, that stubborn people who had from the earliest days inhabited Pucamarca, the crossroads hamlet in the Huatanay crossing, were however not allowed back. They had continued to exist as Cuzqueños and Incas simply because they were too tenacious to be fully dominated, but now they could be demoted once and for all. They would continue thenceforth an existence of dwindling importance in Cayaocachi, a village center suburban to Cuzco, today the parish of Belén. Thus ingloriously ended a minor Andean history that might have been vastly different had fate so cast the die.

To do justice to this renovated Cuzco, we shall describe it not as it was at this time but as it finally became in the reign of Huascar, last of the imperial line.

《 4 》

THE FIRST EUROPEANS ever to see Cuzco reported back to Pizarro that the city was not as large as they had been given to understand, that part of it was level, and that the streets were paved and well laid out. The city was certainly more sanitary and better provided with amenities than in the days of the Spaniards who inherited it, as we can see from Lizarraga's unflattering portrait of it in early colonial times. The most explicit written description of Cuzco, and the one that is basic to any reconstruction of the city, is Garcilaso's plan, an interesting clockwise description of the whole layout. We shall find it more to the point, however, to depict it as Pachacuti did—in the guise of a mountain lion.

Seen from above, the lion's body lies on its right side with its muzzle, the heights of Sacsahuaman, pointing northwest. Rump and tail are the tapering end of the triangle where the streams join, the barrio of Pumapchupan. The outline of its back is the Tullu River and of its belly the Huatanay; the spine is the street San Augustine. The massive thorax (Hanan Cuzco) was separated from the belly (Hurin Cuzco) by the diaphragm, the Antisuyo road, today the street of the Triunfo. Haucaypata, the Plaza, is the great beast's heart.

Here in the mountains the lion crouched watching that ominous horizon to the north and west from which its astounding death was finally to come. Today the traveler finds in every street and passageway the dark andesite bones of the imperial beast, left over as if from an obscene feasting of Spanish kites and vultures.

Ten barrios, or major *cancha*-blocks, made up the Cuzco of Pachacuti, five for the upper part and five for the lower—this at least was the theory. Each one was the city palace of a *panaca* and was presided over by its leading male member. Though the *panacas* of the first five Inca rulers belonged to the lower moiety, this was not reflected consistently in the topography, for the palace of Manco Capac lay in the upper part of the city.

These Cuzco *canchas*, of which there might be as many as four to a city block, were generally rectangular and enlarged versions in masonry of the ancient *cancha* of adobe and *pirca*. Narrow and straight streets separated their outer walls, so narrow that the over-

Northern and Central Parts of Tahuantinsuyo

hanging and richly shingled thatches almost shut out the light of day. The walls were severe, blank, rich in the effect of their batter, and oppressive in their dignity; many were washed in brilliant paints. Generally only one entrance offered admittance. Inside were as many as six or more masonry apartments, clustered against the yard walls and leaving an open space in the center for gatherings of the members within.

Nearest to the lion's head, under Sacsahuaman, that is, was situated that terraced barrio accorded historical primacy by the Incas, Coll-campata, the first clod of earth possessed by the founder Manco Capac. On the field leveled here was performed yearly by all the Inca magnates the harvesting of the holy *chacra*. The staring aper-tures of one wall of an edifice are plainly in evidence today at the back of this open terrace; these ruins are all that is left of the last palace of Huascar, who had usurped the site, a monument to the chasm that yawned between him and his Inca kin in the city below.

The barrios assigned to the descendants of the rulers from Sinchi Roca to Yahuar Huacac have not been and will probably never be identified. Beginning with Viracocha Inca, the sites are more or less well attested, all grouped like vital organs around Haucaypata, the central square. First here stood Condorcancha (Enclosure of the Condor), the dual palace of Pachacuti in sections of Cuzco popu-larly referred to as Casana and Coracora; the latter was appropriate-ly named "The Weed-Patch" for it stood on partially reclaimed ground.

Condorcancha was a *huaca* of extraordinary power. In one of its doorways was a niche where sacrifices were made to prevent turbu-lent winds—for it was to be expected that the demonic energy of this emperor would impress people equally as a power of destruction or a force for quelling tumult and evil. Choice of the site of Casana had been dictated by the presence on the slope at the back of a spring of sweet water called Ticcicocha (Foundation Water), which Pachacuti piped to a tank inside the palace. Sacrifices were made to this holy source, and from it drinking and bath water for the royal household were drawn off, all within the walls of the *cancha*. A narrow street which follows the course of the old Incaic runnel is still today called Teccecocha. Probably no other *cancha* in Cuzco, with the exception of Coricancha, possessed such a supply of running water.

Behind these joined palaces, both of which fronted on the square, and in some way closely attached to them, Pachacuti constructed Yachahuasi, the Inca university. Thus the whole area from the pres-ent street Amargura down to the Plaza was a vast and formidable complex from which—in Pachacuti's day—emanated not only all executive action but all legal, historical, and religious formulations. From here scunded the slow thunder of the lion's heart.

On the site of the present cathedral stood Hatuncancha (The Great Enclosure), the palace of Viracocha Inca, presenting to the square a façade with only a single entrance. Bitter and restless currents swarmed about its walls in those days when empire appeared and a new god with it. Here Pachacuti had been raised as a youth, here he had learned his alphabet of intrigue and diplomacy and his manual of arms, within its walls he had organized latent loyalties for the Chanca war, and just outside he had reviewed his first musters. Here, too, within the prisonlike walls and under the heavy thatches, the Spaniards were to stand siege in the most courageous single exploit of the conquest, emerging from it as masters of a new dispensation. The visitor can still see a corner angle of this palace on the present Cuesta del Almirante. Ironically the church of the Triunfo, Cuzco's cathedral of the sixteenth and seventeenth centuries and the first symbol of conquering Christianity, has usurped the foundations of Viracocha's shrine adjoining Hatuncancha.

This annexed shrine of the Creator was called Quishuarcancha and must have been built by the god's first great convert, the emperor Viracocha Inca, though it is Pachacuti who is credited with its expansion and enrichment. Its inner walls were adorned with tapestries, and on the altar—on the spot where Mary was to stand—glittered the image of the Creator with right arm elevated and fist shut except for an extended thumb and index finger.

In later reigns other palaces were added. Little is known of these except that all had entry on Haucaypata. Topa Inca pre-empted Pucamarca on the east corner of the Square, the site of the historic Alcaviza settlement. His successor Huayna Capac appears to have terraced up the slope below this leading down to the Huatanay and there erected his palace, Amarucancha (Dragon Enclosure). The Church of the Compañia and the old university possess the site today. Huascar, last of the emperors, in order to stay in the area at all would have had to commandeer or cut away part of one of the four earlier palaces. His domicile may have been squeezed in between the palaces of Topa Inca and Huayna Capac or even usurped from one of them, but he also resided in a palace in Collcampata.

All the palaces, being thus north of the Huatanay, were within the sacred pomerium, and all had contact with the great square. On those three sides of the square and masking parts of the stone façades were large thatched sheds within which, in the inclement season, business or fiesta could be carried on without interruption. Cusipata, the adjoining square, was reserved for the periodic markets and the participation of non-Incas in the city ceremonies.

« 5 »

JUST EAST OF HUAYNA CAPAC'S RESIDENCE stood the Acllahuasi (The House of the Chosen Women). Part of the site today is occupied by the Dominican nuns of Santa Catalina—a not too unexpected residual effect of history. This famous compound was the apex of a highly organized state monopoly in women. Needless to say, it fascinated the virile Spaniard and continues to impress the modern historian with its barbaric efficiency. It must be noted that the Spaniards generally confused an *acllahuasi* and its inmates with a god's establishment served by *mamaconas*, Inca nuns, in short. Here we will consider only the former.

Desirable girls had always made up a conspicuous part of the loot taken in the early Andean world. It is therefore easy to posit some method of dispensing these women in Viracocha Inca's day, but it was probably Pachacuti who changed the system from one involving intermittent loot to one supplying the Cuzco *acllahuasi* with a continuous stream of the selected women from all the provinces of the empire. Formerly tribute, they now acquired the bitter dignity of a tax. Each province was assigned a specific tax in nubile girls of seven to twelve years of age, depending on their availability in that district and the needs of Cuzco at the time. They had to possess virginity, high birth, and legitimacy as well as beauty. From them the Inca governor selected the most desirable and deposited them under seal and guard in the provincial *acllahuasi*, which might contain anywhere from two to six hundred girls. Here in groups of ten they were intensively trained for three years by a "*mama*" in quality weaving, the manufacturing of *chicha*, and various religious duties. Packed in cells as cheerless and solemn as their lives must have been, the *acllas* learned to produce those miracles of the loom which hang in our museums today. What additional out of their lives they were able to add to the soundless eddies of Andean history we do not know.

On completion of a three-year novitiate at fourteen or fifteen years of age they underwent the final winnowing. Corresponding to that year's assessment from Cuzco, a number were selected for the honor of this higher service. The tribes laid upon most heavily were the Chachapoyas and the Huancas, both noted for the beauty of their women. Girls from the coastal regions were at times introduced into Cuzco, but the unaccustomed altitude rendered them fragile items at best.

Escorted along the Andes in vigilantly guarded convoys, these choice girls were brought annually into Cuzco and turned over to the mother superior in charge of the central *acllahuasi*. They were brought before the emperor, who divided them into three groups, one for his own harem, one for the service of religion either as nuns or as sacrificial victims, and the third to be kept as a state treasury out of which they could be drawn at a later time as rewards for his captains and favorites. There may have been as many as three thousand of these women in Cuzco.

Besides its employment as a warehouse of women, the *acllahuasi* had other uses. For one thing it seems to have functioned as a convent school where the daughters of the magnates could be trained before their marriages. A use totally at variance with this may have been confined only to the provincial *acclahuasi*, where some girls were trained in singing and piping and serving as state geishas or temporary concubines when army divisions, embassies, or high officials came through.

« 6 »

THE BARRIO OF PUMAPCHUPAN was reserved for the close kin of Pachacuti and possessed a lovely park of trees until the Spaniard destroyed it. Here, just under the lordly Coricancha, there appears to have been a shrine of Mama Quilla in which, on those festival days when the emperor was at his religious devoirs above, the *coya* performed hers accompanied by the noblest and most elegantly attired of her ladies, the *pallas*, and the favored ones among the *ñustas*, princesses of the household. While aviaries of parrots and other exotic birds, perches for monkeys, and quiet fishponds were to be found in the imperial *canchas*, every nobleman's home seems to have had also some sort of flower garden to delight his womenfolk.

Outside the pomerium was the *sankahuaci*, the dungeon of ordeal and execution. Used by Mayta Capac in the cruel tortures inflicted upon the Alcaviza leaders who failed to admit his claim to Cuzco, it had from that time on become a permanent part of Inca polity. Its name was a thing of terror, and doubly so now that it had become institutionalized in the popular mind as a subterranean snake-pit and a den of jaguars. This Tartarian horror was reserved for those *curacas* who had dared—unsuccessfully, of course—to pit their forces against the Inca *raj*. After being displayed in triumph they were thrown into these holes lined with razor-like flints and sealed up. If found alive after a stated time, it was presumptive evidence that they desired to become loyal servants of the empire and they were released. Pachacuti is supposed to have built three prisons, one for torture and interrogation, two of them for lifetime detention. Bimbilla, one of these latter, about a mile and a half away, was a fortress prison used for the detention of the most dangerous class of state criminals, false prophets, poisoners, and practitioners of black magic. The place of common execution, however, was at Arahua (The Gallows) just south of the city where thieves, adulterers, and other common lawbreakers were hanged by the feet until dead. The need to immunize the sacred area of Cuzco from the taint of blood and death dictated the removal of these gruesome places to areas outside, which contrasts vividly with the Spanish habit of erecting the public gibbet in the main square.

The environs of Cuzco offered in panorama a most unusual sight. In the bowl at the head of the valley, the suburban pueblos of Carmenca (present Santa Ana), Tococachi (San Blas), Cayaocachi (Belén), Chaquillchaca (San Pedro), and others pressed in on the city along the various routes of approach. Tococachi, for instance, boasted a shrine built there by Pachacuti for his personal talisman or *huaoqui*, named after Illapa the thunder-god. Between these pueblos and behind them, laid well back up the slopes, were the giant steps of the terraces, broad, flat, and comfortable in the lower courses, dwindling to dizzy ledges at the top. It was Pachacuti who ordered most of these into existence. In the growing season these *patas*, as they were called, were veritable hanging gardens over the city, and in whatever direction one looked their satisfying and varied geometry filled the eye. Today none of them remain; the need of the Spaniards to maneuver their cavalry during the great siege brought about their destruction. The barrenness of these slopes today is one of the least desirable parts of the Spanish heritage.

« 7 »

MIGHTIEST OF ALL THE CITY'S OUTWORKS and one mentioned by every early Spanish writer with infinite respect was Sacsahuaman (Royal Eagle), at once Cuzco's *pucara* and the head of Pachacuti's lion. From its towers and walls one could peer down into the intimate inner apartments and patios of the city or, gazing eastward, contemplate the remote bulk of Ausangate in the cobalt sky. On the esplanades of Sacsahuaman over the years there walked representatives of all the varied classes and peoples of the empire: sun-women waiting in the dawn for their divine consort to appear, treasurers checking the vast inventories of the stores assigned to them, Inca prelates from the city below on fiesta, young captains on their first stations come to review the five hundred Cañar and Chachapoya sentinels who manned the walls, or heavy-faced and cringing *curacas* on embassy to the emperor or to his regent. Only at the very end of the imperial century with the coming of the Spaniards was it necessary to close the three narrow sally ports of Sacsahuaman against an enemy.

The site had been utilized in pre-Inca times as one of those common hilltop settlements into which a valley settlement could withdraw for safety. The spring near by appears to have given the *pucara* the name by which it was early known, Callispuquio. This was the spring in which the young Incas bathed at the ceremony of knighting to acquire for themselves the full flower of valor—martial magic in keeping with the warlike structures on the site.

That there was a fortress there in the days of Viracocha Inca may be taken for granted. Nevertheless it was Pachacuti who undertook totally to redesign the structure. Three and possibly four reigns in all were required to complete it, and the intermittent labor of twenty

thousand tributary Indians constantly employed in quarrying, hauling, and construction. So notable was the project that the names and
succession of the four architect-engineers who carried it to completion
over the years have been preserved—the first and greatest of them
being Huallpa Rimachi Inca (Cock Intercessor Inca). It was this
man, imbued with the grandiosity of Pachacuti's spirit, who conceived
for him the scope of the work and initiated it. In recompense he was
elevated to the highest rank.

Sacsahuaman had many uses. In one sense it was a hilltop city in
its own right, an elevated Cuzco as it were, a distillation of it on a
higher plane. And for the reason that it was a hilltop refuge city, it
was fortified. Again it was a strategic castle commanding the northern
approaches to Cuzco, which concept was a consequence of the Chanca
war and will have been no doubt the motive which impelled its re-
designing. As the powers of the north were hurled back, however, to
a point where they ceased to be a danger, the castle became a mere
passive arsenal, a state depository, a chateau where the court diverted
itself and where at need ten thousand inhabitants could dwell, and
always a temple of the Sun. Last and not least it was a palace annex,
as we can see from the fact that Pachacuti named its massive and
superimposed walls after his, his father's, and his heir's royal *canchas*
in the square below. City, fortress, Sun-castle, chateau, and palace—
no other structure in the Inca empire was comparable to it.

What its appearance was before the Spaniards so thoroughly mined
it must remain conjectural. Its apartments and ceremonial buildings,
placed on two levels up the smoothly rounded hill crest, were gained
by stepped ascents, the whole interspersed by paved open areas. Three
enigmatic towers, one circular, rose impressively above all this construction well back of the walls. The great walls, spiked in plan, are
breath-taking in their grandiosity.

Sacsahuaman fronted on Chuquipampa (Field of Lances), a bare
field today as flat and featureless as the sea. Directly across this open
space is seen a cluster of rounded echeloned rocks like a school of
porpoises dipping through the stillness—a simile brought to life when
the rain wets them into the glisten of watery backs. This curious stone
outcrop stimulated the religious sensibilities of the Indians. They saw
it as a *huaca*, and they carved it out in places into flat steps where

offerings were placed. Together with field and fortress adjoining it
formed a vast and notable locus of storage, ceremony, and strength.

« 8 »

THE PECULIAR SANCTITY OF CUZCO, the fact that it was "the house
and dwelling of the gods" and a museum of idols, *muchaderos*, and
shrines cannot be overstressed. An Andean pueblo always swam in a
vague mist of *huaca* anyway, but when—as in the case of Cuzco—
there was added to it the superior power evidenced by empire, holiness then broke over that city like a thunderstorm.

Pachacuti's reign emphasized this. Victory over the Chancas was
memorialized by Pachacuti in the myth of the *pururaucas*, the spirit-
helpers sent him from heaven. Touring the battlesite afterwards, he
had designated various detached rocks and stones which he recognized as the now congealed persons of those spirits. Brought down
to Cuzco with awe and rejoicing, these *huacas* were placed in niches
in the walls lining the squares and streets, where like the wayside
crosses of the Christians, they were publicly worshipped. Many of
them were placed in the outer walls of Coricancha. Near Coricancha
also there stood a reliquary within which were deposited the weapons
that the god had given to Pachacuti for the performance of the great
feat of deliverance.

Other *huacas* of Cuzco are known. A certain shrine contained the
oracular effigy of a serpent. There was a trophy house where the heads
of Pachacuti's powerful enemies were displayed, the *huaca* in them
now in the service of the state. And there was a shrine of Pirhua,
deity of the corn bin. But indeed almost all things of moment in the
life of the city and its environs were *huaca*.

These *huacas* were all linked together and provided with a common rationale in the amazingly ingenious and artificial *ceque*-system.
From Coricancha as a center 40 *ceques* or invisible "lines" of force
beamed in all directions out to a vague circumference some 12 miles
in radius. It is evident that these rays, emanating as they did from the
home of the Sun-god, represented a symbol in a solar theology. Along
them were plotted the *huacas* of Cuzco to the number of about 350.
Each *ceque* had an Inca family or group assigned to it and charged

with the care of maintaining the various ceremonial usages all along the line. The emperor and his *panaca* by definition carried on the worship of the Sun in the center, the focal *huaca* of them all.

A partial listing of these *huacas* is instructive. Typically they were rocks, springs, or summits, but others there were also: the house where Pachacuti died; a cave where the hail lived; Chuquipampa, the open area in front of Sacsahuaman; a spot where Viracocha Inca used to sit; a quarry; a place where Sleep lived; a rock controlling the emperor's wrath; Haucaypata, the plaza, and more specifically the place where the north road entered it; an ever-renewing *quinoa* root from which since the earliest days Cuzco had derived nourishment; the wives and concubines of Viracocha now turned to stone; the origination cave of the Hualla Indians; the emperor's hunting lodge; a valley where the wind lived; and a tomb where the Inca dead periodically assembled.

« 9 »

THE PARAMOUNT SHRINE OF THEM ALL, the holy of holies, the primate church of the Incas, was Coricancha. Known up to that time as Inticancha, its peculiar sanctity had prevented it from undergoing any notable enlargement. The site was one of the two original locations in the triangle, roughly straddling the ridge down which the taper in the triangle began. Its southwest side was covered by the steep bluffs of the Huatanay. To the northwest it looked up the hump of the ridge along the highway; in the opposite direction the road slipped past and down to the gathering place and crossing of the Tullu (the plaza of Limac Pampa today), a stone's throw away.

Tradition had it that in the earliest *cancha* on the location, or in a small hut or shrine adjoining, the four sister-wives of Manco Capac had dwelt on first coming to Cuzco. Here also the ancestors had huddled in fear of the Alcaviza settlement of Pucamarca up on the other crossing. Mayta Capac had brought prestige to the site, but it was the act of Inca Roca in moving his residence elsewhere and leaving Inti, the family *lar*, as the sole proprietor, which allowed the name Inticancha thenceforth to become its popular designation. All this was to expand and radically alter at Pachacuti's coming.

No project was more focal than Coricancha in the emperor's re-modeling scheme. Not only had old foundations to be respected, possibly even the small decayed naos of the beginning incorporated and preserved, but new glory added. So it was that in the presence of his full retinue and with his own hands Pachacuti had pointed out the first stones to be taken from the quarry of Sallu and then had drawn the measuring cord at Coricancha.

The work was pressed with special vigor, being brought to completion on the emperor's return from the Collao campaign. The excessive donations of gold, silver, and semiprecious stones gave rise at this time to the name by which the enlarged temple was thenceforth to be known, Coricancha (The Golden Enclosure). The installation ceremonies of the temple culminated in the placing of its final piece of furniture. This was a new image of the Sun-god which Pachacuti had ordered cast in solid gold. The spiritually charged work of fashioning the item had proceeded under the hands of the most skilled Andean goldsmiths available, and within the enclosure itself—for the god could not be made on other than his own sacred soil. This statue had a small cavity in it, serving as a coffer, within which later was poured a mingled dust of gold and the ashes of the hearts of emperors, symbolic of the return of the sons to the father.

Meanwhile the god's household had been assigned, a celebate priesthood clad in the traditional white robes, a harem of five hundred of the most lovely women serving under the high priestess of the Moon, a major-domo, *chacras*, llama flocks, and two hundred young farmers and herdsmen. The housewarming was celebrated by drawing lines of blood across the faces of the god's new family and along the walls, and burying in secret receptacles under the floors the extravagant offerings of gold and silver. This was both a consecration and a fattening. Llamas and priceless vestments were burned in sacrifice, and children selected for their bloom were buried alive on the spot in Coricancha where the image, when completed, was to rest. All of the Inca *ayllus* were then ushered in to greet their new father, to offer him gifts, and to receive the blood-line on their faces. During the manufacture of the golden statue, continence and the strictest fasting had been mandatory upon them, while within Coricancha the flames of the sacred hearth were fed by the *mamaconas* night and day.

Approximately a month was consumed by the smiths in producing the naked, child-sized image of the Sun. A decorated wooden box, resplendent under a fan of feathers, was used as its naos. Then, as the beloved son and only direct earthly heir of Inti, Pachacuti personally carried both god and container across the threshold. In front of the image a brazier burned, and on it Pachacuti—again with his own hands—cast the offerings of llama meat and *chicha*. The other kinsmen humbly waited outside with their less spectacular offerings.

Thus was the curtain of history raised on the most important religious building in all the Americas, important not only for its meaning as an archepiscopal church but as a vivid expression of an empire that would continue while royal palaces filled and emptied. In size Coricancha appeared utterly provincial beside the colossal terraced temples of the more elegant coastal civilizations, and indeed, whatever its wealth, it was never truly a temple with a religious architectural tradition behind it, but only a family house in a yard. The tightness and severity of this concept gave it unprecedented power as a symbol.

From the outside Coricancha presented a normal Cuzco façade of finely cut andesite, plastered over and painted. No elaboration and no playfulness were suggested in its lines. Squat, hefty, heavy-browed, immobile, Coricancha satisfied the Inca soul. Today its walls and broken rooms form the shell and foundation of the Dominican monastery.

The entrance to Coricancha was on Intipampa, probably on the spot where the side door of the church exists today. Just inside was a restricted court of lesser sanctity, an antechamber where the unqualified magnates awaited the results of the solemn rituals within. From here one then passed into the central patio, around which were grouped the gods, a great clan, each in his own house placed in the usual way up against the inner sides of the *cancha* wall. The thatched roofs of these houses were steeply pitched and almost pyramidal in shape. The house of the Sun, plated with gold, must have taken up most of the space along one wall. Flanking it were other sacred buildings, housing gods, priests, and *mamaconas*. In the houses on the side facing the northeast were two niches, wholly plated inside with gold and crusted with gems. Here, waiting for the solar father to awaken beyond the hills, sat his Inca son when participating in those rituals where the first rays fell on the emperor's countenance to bless it and lighten it for his people.

Inti possessed his symbolic *chacra*, a sacred garden, beside these walls. This was irrigated from a fountain piped in with great skill by Pachacuti's engineers. Here were lovingly planted and hand-tended the god's fruits, and when the first clod-breaking or the first harvesting took place the emperor in person led the work. On such occasions heavy-eared maize modeled in gold was inserted in the garden, along with other symbols of joy and plenty, also in gold and silver—llamas, herdsmen, and birds. Grain pits of silver stored the harvested ears of corn, and the special *chicha* fermented from this was offered to the god in a great octagonal, gold-sheathed stone jar or basin, closed with a golden lid.

Because Coricancha was an imperial cathedral as well as a family chapel, it housed not only the gods and *lares* of the latter, but on occasion the *huacas* of the former. These provincial *huacas* occupied the numerous niches let into the walls. For this latter reason—if for no other—Coricancha was the final place of piety for those thousands of Andean Indians who went on pilgrimage to Cuzco.

The house of the Sun was the largest single building within Coricancha. None of the walls existing in the Dominican cloisters today can be identified as proved relics of it. According to Rowe, however, it may have stood approximately on the space that is now the Salón de Entrada and its apron outside. Within the arcane interior of this dwelling stood the gold effigy of Inti, while round about were grouped figures, made in bundled woolens, of other hypostases of him.

Flanking it on right and left were the houses of Viracocha and of Chuqui Illa (Shining Lance), the Lightning. The Moon, wife of the Sun, also had her shrine here as did Mama Ocllo, semi-divine first resident of the site, her effigy in gold having been dedicated by Pachacuti. In this Mama Ocllo we can see the Inca version of Pachamama, that earth that suffered Coricancha to rest so heavily on her bosom.

In one of the walls facing east, perhaps within a shrine, there was inset a circular plate of gold enclosed in an aureole of rays; this was called Punchao (The Day). Whereas the image in gold ordered by

Pachacuti represented Inti anthropomorphically as he was in Inca legend, this latter was a straightforward depiction of the physical sun-disc itself. It was so placed as to respond to the first efforts of the morning sun like a shimmering cymbal. Similar golden sun-discs were standard iconographic items in the larger provincial temples of Tahuantinsuyo.

In distinction to the great state ceremonies, Inti's daily rites were essentially domestic and differed in their splendor alone from what took place in the most barren Andean hut. Setting the fire, cooking, *chicha*-manufacturing, cohabitation, retirement, and rising—all of these found ornate echo in Inti's daily round. The thought behind this service was twofold: to profess Inca gratitude to the divinity for his light, and to imbue him with the force to continue his station in the sky.

Having arisen before dawn, the *mamaconas* presented the god his collation, intoning, "Eat, O Sun, this which your wives have prepared for you." Part of the breakfast was sent on a spirit journey to the god by being thrown into the fire, or poured out into the offering basin. The rest was consumed by the priests and *mamaconas*. Each day a red llama swathed in a red blanket was sacrificed to him. "Eat this, Apu Inti," murmured the priests, "as acknowledgement that we are your children."

As one triumph after another carried the Inca empire out to its limits, immense portions of the spoils were poured in upon this primate see, once the stone and daub home of unknown *sinchis*. In plated bullion, idols, and cult objects, Coricancha probably ranked as the richest single edifice of its size in history. But compared to the intangible mystique with which Pachacuti endowed it, all that wealth was the merest patina.

NINE.
PACHACUTI
CREATOR OF
THE IMPERIAL MYSTIQUE

« I »

CORICANCHA WAS PRIMARILY THE DOMICILE OF INTI. The other gods were therefore resident within its walls through no right of proprietorship but only because of their participation in a common undertaking—the enhancement of the Inca clans over all other peoples of the earth. These gods we must describe.

Inti was the primordial mascot of the Incas, Manco Capac's own "spirit-brother," the first *lar*. He had been that sacred falcon called "Inti" which the first Inca had brought in an ark of rushes out of Pacaritambo. By imperial times this fetish had become an effulgent male god, generally young, who gave oracles of greatness to his people but who in cult was otherwise the actual sun-disc called Punchao. Corresponding to the three diurnal stages of the sun, the priesthood had broken Inti up into a trinity of father, son, and brother, represented by three images made of tightly packed woolen blankets and named respectively Apu Inti (Chief Inti), Churi Inti (Inti the Son), and Inti Huaoqui (Inti the Brother). It was Apu Inti whose *coya* was the Moon and whose virginal daughters were the stars. When these three hypostases of Inti were brought into Haucaypata for the fiestas, Apu Inti was enthroned while the remaining two of the trinity flanked him at attention with golden lances and other pieces of regalia in their hands. Set up thus, Inti displayed clearly the essential characteristics of a conqueror. When an Inca army marched, it was believed that he had sent them forth for one purpose only: to spread his greatness and his cult. And when a recalcitrant province had bent finally under the Inca knout, the first duty imposed upon it was the erection in their capital city of a house for him. Yet in spite of his fusion with the Sun and in spite of his wide conquests Inti remained always narrowly Inca, for he was the bodily father of the clans. Beyond the confines of their particular achievements Inti was uninterested, inactive, silent, evasive, indeed nonexistent. He might conquer a world outside, but it still remained a usurpation.

The storm-god of the Incas was Illapa, a deity who had closer affinities to the Peruvian norms of heaven than did Inti. The mere fact that it had been the Sun and not the Thunder who had been elected to become the father of the clans kept Illapa's pan-Peruvian citizenship purer. Thus, except for a possible appearance as one of the four Ayar brothers, he plays no noticeable role in the expansion of the Inca *raj*. He stood in the Inca pantheon simply because no Andean tribe could do without a personalization of the lurid atmospheric powers to which they were subject. We have already described him aloft on the keenest peaks, wielding his mace and sling, a Peruvian Zeus, and as such master of all things in the sky: rain, hail, thunderbolts, rainbows, whirlwinds, and lightning.

In Coricancha he was one of the high gods, being lesser only than the Creator and the Sun, and like them he too was theologized into a trinity. As such his names were Chuqui Illa, Catu Illa, and Inti Illapa, each avatar being modeled in woolen blankets. Pachacuti had given him an additional shrine outside the sacred triangle where he was represented as an image of gold. This image was the one apparently taken by Pachacuti as his patron saint or "spirit-brother," and went with him to the wars.

Mama Quilla (Lady Moon) does not appear in the Inca legends, but she too was pervasively Peruvian. Theologically it had been inevitable that she should become Inti's *coya* in Coricancha, and in consonance with this on feast days the mummies of the deceased *coyas* were placed, like ladies in waiting, around her in niches in her apartment in Coricancha. Her Dianesque cult there was tabooed to the male ministry; sacrifices to her in the great fiestas were made by the empress, and her idol could be carried about only on the shoulders of her own *mamaconas*. In Coricancha, Titicaca, and Vilcas, as elsewhere, she was always of sufficient dignity to possess a separate shrine in which she was adored as a silver image.

The stars were grouped as retainers or princesses in this heavenly court. By royal statute an order of precedence was established for them. First came the Pleiades, Collca, who because of the mysterious fountains of nourishment which gushed from them were also called "the Mothers." Then came the constellation Lyra, Urcochillay, thought of as a parti-colored male llama in whose virility lay the secret of those vastly important economic assets to the empire, its llama herds. "The Radiant Star with the Flowing Hair," Venus, dispensed also an exceptional *huaca* because of her beauty and her kinship with the Sun. Then followed the Hyades, known as "the Stag's Jawbone," the rank and file of the other stars, and Cuychic, "the Rainbow."

《　2　》

WE HAVE AVOIDED A CONSIDERATION of the Creator in the Inca pantheon until now, as he cannot be understood without a preliminary statement on that remarkable convocation summoned by Pachacuti, which we shall denominate the Council of Coricancha.

If one considers closely the Christian councils of the fourth century, one sees, rising out of their combined decisions, a massive theology, a hierarchy of heaven, purposeful, eminently useful, compressed, inclusive, enduring, splendid, a recasting of old religious molds to receive the molten metal of a new spirit. Within limits, this is what in Inca history the Council of Coricancha was and did. A major difference between Nicaea and Coricancha is that, while in both cases ruthless imperial masters summoned them and enforced the final agreement—Constantine on the one hand, Pachacuti on the other—it was the Peruvian alone who possessed the spiritual power to detail what these formulations were to be.

The bishops at Nicaea had formed a body autonomous in doctrinal matters. The Council of Coricancha on the contrary was a gathering of Inca magnates and priests to accept a dogma already defined by the growing imperial situation. At this point the increasingly successful drive of the Inca clans to world domination seemed not too far from its glorious climax. As a glacier locked in the chill of the high Andean air melts slowly at first but more copiously as summer lengthens, so the necessity to control and formalize belief, which had been implicit but frozen in the earliest levels of Inca history, now liquified under the hot sun of empire and carried all before it. But all would have been mere flood and stale drownings had not the torrents of that necessity flowed between superbly constructed levees, dykes thrown up by an emperor who was also a notable religious innovator. It was obvious that, as the fullness of his empire approached, a hierarchy of the Inca deities had to be established lest doctrinal chaos on earth be reflected in the heavens.

When the Council assembled, Pachacuti began by pouring out his scorn upon the provincial *huacas* and their purile claims to power. Their only role now was to serve their master Inti. After an initial fiat to this effect, Pachacuti moved into the theological phase of the Council by propounding for the wise men assembled those doubts he had concerning not Inti's power but his supremacy and perfection.

In thus reviving the schism of the days of his father, Pachacuti was accepting a real risk, though one perhaps not so great considering that he in person had been designated as heaven's champion. Certainly the susceptibilities of both the Incas and those subject to them must have been insulted in thus calling for a definition of the Sun-god's status. For the latter, if Inti was not omnipotent, then they were fools to serve him; for the former, if he was not perfect, then he was not their true father in heaven.

Pachacuti is reported to have promulgated his doubts in three "Sentences":

1. Inti cannot be universal if, while giving light to some, he withholds it from others.
2. He cannot be perfect if he can never remain at ease, resting.
3. Nor can he be all-powerful when the smallest cloud may cover his face.

This heresy from the throne demanded an answer—an answer at once swift and cogent. Pachacuti drew to the attention of the Council the certainty that there must exist a god greater in all respects than the Sun, and he left it to them to nominate that deity. All were aware of the answer implicit in the question, and together they acclaimed the Creator Ticci Viracocha Pachayachachic as the sole supreme god of the universe.

So did Pachacuti bind together the Inca gods and the gods of the provinces in a clear order of authority. The local *huacas* acknowledged Inti, whereas Inti himself—seen from below as a warrior and a conqueror—was only the major-domo, the intercessor in the house of the Creator. The historian today can conceive of no credo by which both Inca and non-Inca could have been more securely harnessed to the exigent chariot of empire. But it is also evident that noble advances in religious insight and religious diplomacy were made at the same time. When Cobo makes the observation that the Incas changed their religious idea to conform to their ideas of empire he is, of course, referring to such events in Inca history. To seal this new dispensation Pachacuti ordered the embellishment of Quishuarcancha, the Creator's shrine.

Taking up more concrete matters next, the Council considered the problem of imposing acceptance of this divine *stasis* upon the Four Quarters. New provinces were henceforth to be required to maintain their native cults in low-lying areas and without too obvious embellishment. The Inca temple, placed on a high site above the capital city of the region, from its elevation would thus visually remind all peoples of the superiority of the Inca heaven. Throughout Tahuantinsuyo there were at least one hundred of these elevated Sun-temples by the time of the entry of the Spaniards, and they were probably as potent a means of control as the most alert garrison could be. The cults of the gods worshipped in these centers naturally formed an Inca monopoly. Only a full-blooded Inca could officiate as high priest, and woe to the unauthorized local *curaca* who had the temerity himself to "speak to the Sun" or to the other gods.

The Council went even farther. In various ways it immunized or proscribed those local *huacas* hostile to the Incas. A part of this program of humiliation was the probationary imprisonment of the *huacas* of recently subjected areas and their confinement in Coricancha where their conduct could be minutely scrutinized. To administer the Council's decisions in the matter of these provincial cults, Pachacuti sent out two of his sons as plenipotentiaries at large.

« 3 »

ALL THIS IS NECESSARY to the understanding of the position of the supreme god. As delineated by the Council of Coricancha, Illa Ticca Viracocha is one of mankind's more exalted visions of God, and the conception of him is proof of the muscular clarity of Inca thought.

We have learned that just at the moment when the Incas stumbled upon empire they became aware of a creator-god, worshipped as Viracocha, "The Lord," in the upper Vilcañota Valley, and we have seen that the ruler who magnified his cult in Cuzco took that deity's name as his own. But Inti, the family god, was jealous of this invasion of his prerogative, and bitter hostility resulted. It was Pachacuti who, without altering the basic jurisdictions of the two great gods, calmed this hostility by the theological expedient we have just seen. In the ensuing discussion, however, we must bear in mind that an inherited Viracocha of cult—to whom would cling many vulgar tags—will never have been wholly replaced in Inca thought by the rarefied Viracocha of theology.

The attributes of this theological creator are inspiring. He is ancient, remote, supreme, and uncreated. Nor does he need the gross satisfaction of a consort. He manifests himself as a trinity when he wishes, though otherwise only heavenly warriors and archangels surround his loneliness. He created all peoples by his "Word," as well as all *huacas*. He is man's Fortunus, ordaining his years and nourishing him. He is indeed the very principle of life, for he warms the folk through his created son, Punchao. He is a bringer of peace and an orderer. He is in his own being blessed and has pity on men's wretchedness. He alone judges and absolves them and enables them to combat their evil tendencies.

Inevitably confusion appeared between Inti and Viracocha. This was unavoidable considering that a late-coming high god had been suddenly foisted on top of an earlier paternalistic *huaca*. The texts show a tendency to present Inti as the founder of the Inca state, the god who brought it glory and led its armies, whereas Viracocha is depicted as the god of empire and the sanction of victory. Inti therefore seems to have been more the arrogant and victorious general whereas Viracocha was a pacifying force, a statesman.

Nor did the Spanish chroniclers ever clear up the confusion concerning the identity of Cuzco's divine patron—was it Inti or Viracocha? Both statements are in fact true, and this involves no charge of ignorance against their Inca informants. Cuzco was Inti's first conquest and acquisition; it therefore belonged to him. In the broader context of empire it just as obviously was under the aegis of Viracocha. We can only guess at Pachacuti's personal position regarding the identity of the god who had appeared to him during the Chanca war with the presage of victory for Cuzco. It was certainly no derogation of Viracocha's later suzerainty that Inti, the actual father of the Incas, should have been first on the scene to protect his beloved city.

In résumé, it would be an exaggeration to state that our data fully support the theory that Inti was the god of all the Incas (including the emperor as an Inca), but that Viracocha belonged to the emperor qua emperor alone. Nor could the Incas themselves have accepted such a bald and crude statement. Nevertheless such an emphasis is present, elusive but all pervasive, in Inca history.

What mattered to Pachacuti of course was that the world should be explained and its dependence upon the organizing genius of his people made manifest. We find traces of his thinking in those fragmentary hymns and prayers which have drifted to our shores through the Spanish storms of yesterday.

As the Old Testamental Psalms are attributed to David, so are the Viracocha hymns attributed to Pachacuti—with perhaps an equal amount of truth and error. They are documents remarkable in the anxious quality of their wording and in the spaciousness and economy of their concepts. The following two prayers show respectively the Inca Creator's universal immanence on the one hand and on the other his role as a cultural orderer and sustainer of the empire. They should be set beside the Biblical Psalms 13 and 50. The first prayer, which is a series of querulous castings-about for the ear of the Almighty, may be very old—possibly standard in certain other Peruvian Creator cults.

Oh ancient Lord, remote Lord, most excellent Lord, who createth and establisheth, saying: "Let there be man; let there be woman"; molder, maker; because thou hast made me and established mankind, may I live peacefully and safely.

Where art thou? Without? Within? In the clouds? In the shadows? Hear me, respond and consent! For ever and ever give me life, taking me in thine arms, lead me by thy hand; receive this my offering wherever thou art, oh Lord.

§   §   §

Oh Lord, happy, fortunate, victorious Lord, who hath compassion on men and showeth affection for them, let the people, those who serve, the poor, thine unfortunates, whom thou hast made and established, endure in peace and safety with their children, with their sons; walking in the straight road, let them not think on temptation; long years let them live; without interruption, without breaking, let them continue to eat, let them continue to drink.

When Viracocha Inca first found his god in Cacha, he did not take him over without bringing out elements of his liturgical practices as well. It reminds one of the religion practiced in Exodus, Judges, and Chronicles. In Viracocha's scheme of things his son Punchao very roughly fills the role of a Saviour. One might think of Christian analogies, but Punchao was either the physical sun-disc that banished the damps of night or he was, as Inti, a bloodthirsty Inca idol interested solely in his kith and kin and in no others. It is God the Father here who is the late-comer, the compassionate friend to all, and not the Son. So the roles are reversed.

Concerning Viracocha's cult among the Incas, little is known. The god's original seats in the upper Vilcañota Valley were famous pilgrimage centers, and the multi-stage temple built there at Racchi— the scene of the god's first revelation—continued no doubt to remain the Jerusalem of this church whose Rome was Cuzco. But the cult in Cuzco had known other earlier and more popular practices. These can be detected in such crude *huacas* in and around Cuzco as the god's faithless wives who had been changed to stone, or the Creator's own "spirit-brother."

The reasons for the paucity of material bearing on Viracocha's cult are twofold: the first is the concentration in the Viracocha religion on theological sanction as opposed to ceremonial observance; the second was the overriding floridity of Inti's rites. The first we have already discussed. The second can be appreciated by noting that the Inca calendar provided no specific festival for the Creator such as the Inti Raymi which celebrated the Sun. Thus the new sacrifices and psalms which Viracocha Inca and Pachacuti established for the Creator had to be tacked on to the fiestas of the other gods. They were additive, not basic in the canon of cult. At coronations, as was to be expected, the Creator was appealed to as the giver of wisdom to the new ruler, and received the first sacrifices. In the main, however, he cut a rather shabby figure compared to Inti, and his priesthood appears to have been small, though this was masked somewhat by the theory given out that all sacrifices to the gods were by them then presented to Viracocha.

Thus Pachacuti's passion for structure which had produced a new and monolithic earth ended by producing a similar heaven. Though the trinitarian idea was known to the Incas, the simple Olympian authority exercised by Viracocha kept him from such a radical division within unity as is seen in the Christian trinity. This simplicity as well as the brevity of Inca religious history prevented warring gods from rising in time to assault the gates of heaven—contrary to that common mythical pattern where there is always a Lucifer to threaten Yahweh, a Baal who unsettles the older El, or a Zeus to challenge the power of Cronus.

Pachamama alone (like the Greek Demeter who was at the most only vaguely present on Olympus) did not truly march in Viracocha's divine *ayllu*. This vast, recumbent, resistless, chthonic being had her own law and her own Tartarian version of the world of *huaca*. She had no need to oppose to Viracocha's dogma another one of her own. Though these Incas might train their thoughts on the stars and even on invisible spheres of light, Pachamama knew that in the end she would gather all of them in, and huddle them down in her own black bosom.

TO CARRY ON THE WORSHIP OF THESE GODS, Pachacuti redesigned the Inca ecclesia. We know very little about the priesthood—probably, as Las Casas suggests, because the pagan gods, temples, and priests were among the first targets of Spanish zeal and greed. One thing before all was of interest to Pachacuti: the sterilization of this ecclesia. No doubt in the Inca past priestly leadership had loomed more impressively. In successfully harnessing these tendencies, Pachacuti showed himself willing to have an archbishop but not a pope.

Each Inca deity had a priestly household. The metropolitan of all these churches was always the high priest of Inti's service, and lived in Coricancha. He was the villac-umu (announcing sorcerer), and his office was Levitical in one of the Inca families. The *mamaconas* assigned to Inti's harem were under a mother superior who, as the earthly person of Inti's spouse, was therefore also high priestess. All of these women were under the rule of the Villac-umu. A college of ten Inca bishops (*hatun villac*) was founded to handle the needs of the state cult in the provinces. Under them were the *yana-villacs* (servant sorcerers), or common priests. Outside this state system, but licensed by it, were the numerous native sorcerers, shamans, and *huaca*-priests which we have adverted to in a previous chapter.

It is difficult for us to realize the fear which the local Peruvian *huacas* inspired in the Incas. When Cobo says "The sanction of religion was one of the most significant which they used in conquering other people," he is also implying its reverse—that resistance to the Inca *raj* could always be apprised first in the oracles and influence of a local cult. What the Baalim and the Ashtaroth were to Yahweh, what the medieval devil or the witch's cult was to the Roman church, these *huacas* could become to Inti and his priesthood. It was for this reason that many of them underwent a period of captivity in Cuzco. In one of the city festivals, in fact, it was customary for *huacas* to be tested for duplicity in their annual oracles, and those found guilty were punished by exposure on the glacial heights. Control extended even further. The mummies of the great Inca conquerors, when ritually installed in Coricancha, had in their entourage the *huacas* of those peoples and lands they had brought into the empire. The highest status to which a duly co-operative provincial *huaca* might aspire was that of an intercessor for his people before Inti.

Inca history speaks loudly of this animosity to other gods. Manco Capac came in, as it were, under the aegis of a blindingly jealous god. One of the tales treasured from the days of Capac Yupanqui, the fifth ruler, related with relish a stunning victory over a local *huaca*. The venomous hatred between Inti and the non-Inca *huacas* of the valley in the reign of Mayta Capac has been related. The picture under Viracocha Inca is unclear but probably runs in the same direction. Pachacuti's mockery of the *huacas* in the Council of Coricancha we have noted. Topa Inca found it necessary to exterminate numbers of *huacas*, and we have the record of Atahualpa's revenge upon the high priest of Pachacamac for the treason of his god. When Manco Inca of the Vilcabamba line raided among the Huancas, his first care was to hang their tribal *huaca* by a rope, after which, having killed the priests, he disposed of it in a river. In the instances where the Incas found it impossible to cow a great *huaca*, they either stole its mythology, as in the case of Titicaca, or came to terms, as with Pachacamac.

The potential evil in these sullen and intransigent *huacas* was dramatically focused in Supay, a pan-Peruvian concept translated as "the Devil" by the Spaniards. Somewhat distinct from a *huaca* in specific stone and wood, Supay seems to have been more in the nature of a universal demonic principle whose domain was injury. The Viracocha myths enshrine him—or at least the principle—in the figure of that evil son who constantly perverted the order and beauty established by the Creator and who was cast down but never died. Concretely the name Supay could be applied to any or all of the *huacas*, if the intent at that moment was to stress their treason against the majesty of the empire. When pluralized and placed in the setting of an underworld, Supay became those grim and swarming hordes of fiends appropriate to it. Cobo and others state that Supay had a class of sorcerers as his henchmen. This makes it seem probable that he came from a most ancient level of religious practice, neither chthonic nor stellar but shamanistic. The difficulties of policing his *chicha*-maddened sorcerers rendered him always an object of concern to the Incas. When Manco Inca, emperor under the Pizarros, referred as naturally to Supay as to Viracocha the Creator he was merely expounding a force which his dynasty had long known and combatted.

Thus was the mysterious presence of evil accounted for and placed on a ground of authority almost as sure as that of the Creator's. But evil is lonely and unplaced, whereas the supreme god maintains a moral hierarchy of stellar deities, spirit warriors, and canonized emperors, just as the god of the late Roman empire had his archangels, his missionary Spiritus, Mary Theotokos, and the ranking saints.

《 5 》

PACHACUTI WAS THE AUTHOR OF INCA CEREMONIALISM at its most theatrical. Without his peculiar genius for inventing idioms in visual and formalistic language, the work performed by his armies would have been inadequate. As it was, after his captains and secret police had created an exhausted peace among a people, at that point the grandeur of his spectacles, the continual ritual display of a heavenly order to which the Inca world was securely linked, worked to continue that peace by conviction.

And as in all other fields, Pachacuti's plans here were conceived broadly. The whole Inca calendar was strictly redesigned to present an intelligible order of rites and religious obligations. It is clear that his interest was less in the perfecting of abstruse time calculations and stellar observations than in the dramatization of the spiritual life of his people.

Betanzos graphically enlivens our vision of Andean history at this point. He catches Pachacuti at the very moment of outlining to the nobles the novel pattern he has projected for their rustic and time-honored rites. Every aspect of rite, whether banquet, precedence, dance form, priestly gesture, or costume was displayed under the searchlight of his imagination and amplified with additional meaning. Deeply impressed, the magnates then requested that he set a prescribed annual order for these festivals, whereupon he promulgated a canonical list which seems not to have been changed by later emperors. To bring about a closer coincidence between the solar year (whose beginning he shifted back from January to December) and the lunar year of twelve months, he ordered certain sun towers erected on the high skyline above Cuzco. Observations of the rising sun were taken by means of these from the center point in Haucay-pata. These pillars, called *sucancas*, became notable *huacas* to the Indians of Tahuantinsuyo, enshrining as they did the magic of a mind familiar and easy with empire.

So deeply was Pachacuti imbued with a sense of the sacred, and so keenly did he feel the need to give concrete form to it, that two special-purpose ceremonies outside the mensual order of fiestas received his attention, the *capacocha* and the *itu*.

The *capacocha* was a petition presented by the whole empire to the totality of *huacas* everywhere, Inca and provincial. The occasion could be the illness of the emperor, a coronation, or the launching of a campaign—in any case a nonperiodic event. And man's placatory gifts to the gods of necessity had here to be his most cherished possessions, his children. If the bloody rites on the small knob just above modern San Sebastián where these children's hearts were torn out for Viracocha's pleasure were somber indeed, how much more appalling were those toiling processions of the young sent out from Cuzco, not by the roads but in a direct line over all obstacles to the limits of Tahuantinsuyo, where the suffocating embraces of the great provincial *huacas* awaited them. No eyes beside their route ever dared to profane these holy lines of girls and boys and smaller ones at the breast, nor in their passing through the settlements did their quiet shuffling echo against anything but empty walls.

The *itu* was a mourning and a supplication, though it was a cry from the hearts of the Incas only—the empire was not involved. Drought, disaster in war, plague, earthquake—these could be the occasion for an *itu*. All non-Incas were expelled from Cuzco, and absolute silence was imposed on those remaining, who sat or moved about with mantles pulled over their bent heads. The culmination was the appearance of the young nobles grimacing silently, rapping their drums hollowly, and performing a peculiar and interminable dance circuit of Haucaypata. It was only natural, after the coming of the Spaniards, for the people of Cuzco to surreptitiously insert a decayed version of this eerie spectacle into the Corpus Christi processions.

As for the periodic fiestas, Pachacuti expanded them into a vast ritual colloquy between heaven and earth. We will mention only six of these. They begin with the December Capac Raymi which we have analyzed elsewhere and which Pachacuti placed logically at the inception of his calendar, as it meant for the Incas the replenishment of their ranks of warriors—upon which all else depended.

Pachacuti's calendar had two New Year's fiestas, pointing to the simultaneous use of an astral and an agricultural year respectively. The first one, the Mayocati (River Procession), solstitial in intent, came at a time close to ours (if we consider ours as an extended one composed of Christmas, New Year's, and Epiphany). The other one, the Situa, was in September and marked the sowing of maize and therefore the start of the agricultural cycle. Both Mayocati and Situa are reminiscent of ceremonies created by nonliterate, nontechnological peoples all over the world, but both still bear the additional stamp of Pachacuti's invention.

The January Mayocati saw all the sacrificial ashes in the city, which had been saved over the year, thrown at evening into the Huatanay at the apex of the triangle. A commendation to the river spirit to carry this spiritually charged and contaminated load down to the sea and to Viracocha for his final disposal accompanied the rite. In the darkness that followed Indians equipped with flaring straw torches moved out along both riverbanks. With special poles they pushed off the river's edges any of the impurities being washed down, while their torches both gave them light and spread a purifying magic over these spots. In this way they preserved the spiritual cleanliness of the river. This dramatic decontamination squad then followed the refuse all the way down to Ollantaytambo, where, the gorge holding up their further progress, they halted with appropriate sacrifices. So did the city of Cuzco symbolically in ashes remove its accumulated soilure.

In May was celebrated the Inca harvest-home, the Aymoray. As might be expected, that holy *chacra* devoted to the cult of Mama Huaco, the local Earth Mother, was reaped first. Even the most splendid grandees of the clans bent their backs to the labor here, with the emperor himself wielding a golden plow-stick. The fields of the other gods followed in their hierarchical order.

There followed the Inti Raymi in June, month of the summer solstice. This festival was created—or re-created—by Pachacuti as a memorial of the divine aid which gave him victory over the Chancas.

Attendance at these moving and solemn celebrations was restricted to the Sun's immediate family, his children the Incas, all elaborately dressed. In a meadow on Mount Manturcalla (Crimson Cliff) the tents of the emperor, his *coya*, his kinsfolk, and the mummies of the ancestors were pitched along a broad avenue. The silence before dawn under these dark awnings must have been singularly oppressive. It served to set off the deep joy of the event as the emperor rose quietly from his throne to begin the chant of welcome which, harmoniously with the rising of the Sun out of Mount Ausangate and swelled by the addition of many throats, broke finally into a sonorous paean. Step by step with the course of the Sun the hymn grew to its climax at noon and dwindled off into loving farewells at dusk. Solstitial bonfires were lit on the hills, and gaily bedecked wooden figures burned in them to the accompaniment of dancing. One of the impressive scenes in this ritual was the appearance of the women of the Sun dressed in red and white mantles and carrying on their backs jars of the sacred *chicha*, coming up like tiny dolls from Cuzco to serve their solar husband. The feast ended with a joyous return to Haucaypata, which had been strewn for the event with red *cantut*-flowers and lovely feathers.

In September the bulk of the crop was in. At this time the renewal rites of the Situa were celebrated. Pachacuti divided the main part of the Situa into three acts, each one strictly Inca: purging of evil, communion, and a saturnalia. To these he added, as imperial and extra-Inca necessities, three final acts: fealty, the fixing of destinies, and largesse. His genius for reworking traditional elements into a dramatic new amalgam created here a complex of rites corresponding to our Lent and Easter. To begin with, all non-Incas, all foreign *huacas*, all cripples, all dogs whose howling might profane the abeyant holiness in Cuzco, were banished to beyond a six-mile limit. Meanwhile the magnates, assisted by a picked lot of young braves, waited at Coricancha for that divine moment when the new moon should send them into action. Mother Moon presided at the threshold of the agricultural year, and the month itself was dedicated specifically to her.

The first act began when a warrior, taking the part of an angelic messenger, came racing down from Sacsahuaman to burst into Haucaypata where the young braves were stationed, now divided into four parties. Touching his lance to theirs, he passed on to them Inti's

Macchu Picchu, City in the Montaña

Tambo Machay

Inca Doorway

A *Huaca*

Ruins of Viracocha Inca's Villa at Pisac

Temple Entrance at Vilcashuaman

Terracing over the Urubamba

Gate at Sacsahuaman

Kenko

Ruins of Topa's Palace at Chincheros

A Corner of Coricancha

Cuzco Today

Lower left is a corner of the Plaza, and *en face*, the site of Pachacuti's palace. Extreme lower right are the steps of the Cathedral on the site of Viracocha Inca's palace. Just to the right of the steeple of San Cristobal, upper center, can be seen a long wall of Collcampata, the residence of Huascar. Above on the heights are the outworks of Sacsahuaman.

commission to expel all evil, all disease, all wickedness from Cuzco and its province. Shrieking and brandishing their weapons, the warriors thereupon poured out of the four exits of the Square, their cry of "Evil, depart!" to be taken up by other relays in the outer pueblos who in turn rushed along the great highways sweeping the evil-charged atmosphere ahead of them with their strokes and forcing pollution out. The last teams finally bathed themselves and their weapons in those distant rivers which marked the limits of the province, and thus the hostility and stain attendant upon that combat was dissolved. In Cuzco and along the routes people stood in their doorways and in the plaza exits shaking out their mantles. When night fell great and humble alike performed the *pancunco* (fire-tumult), a popular melee where the participants struck at each other with straw torches, brandishing them or hurling them through the air—a fumigation and a terror to evils of every sort. At the next dawning the whole populace, including the mummies, went out to bathe in sacred waters, each Cuzco *ayllu* in a spring or river on its assigned *ceque*.

An impressive communion followed. This was the partaking by all of the *yahuar sanco*, the sacred "blood-porridge" prepared by the women of the Sun, a mixture of corn flour and the blood of llamas. The entry of this purified food into the bodies of the Incas and the smearing of it over the idols recemented the bond between the Sun and his children.

With evil removed and the gap between heaven and earth bridged over, the saturnalia could begin. The city's poor and withdrawn, the unlucky, the crippled, and the despised were brought out to feast abundantly. Neither quarreling nor sharp words were allowed to infect the new purity. Only the most resplendent finery was worn; pipes, trumpets, feathered headgear, cleverness, and charm were prominently displayed. Sexual license was allowed even beyond the normal usage as a token of the happiness and prosperity which awaited the world, while the gods and the dead rulers blandly looked on at the glorious orgy.

At the end of four days of this Cuzco was reopened to foreigners, and the Situa became a celebration representing all of Tahuantinsuyo. The *curacas* present received the communion meal as earnests of their loyalty, while porters were sent to each of the great provincial *huacas* to see that this forced feeding was performed upon them as well. The fixing of destinies was done by augurs who inquired of the gods what the coming year had in store for the empire. With the glad tidings which they voiced of prosperity and health for the emperor, all uncertainties could be erased. These foreigners, clad in their native costumes, performed their dances by gracious permission of the emperor, who thereupon dispensed gifts to them. So ended the Situa.

« 6 »

BUT BESIDES CREATING A LANGUAGE IN CULT between heaven and earth, Pachacuti had also to create one between his new state and the people if a full rapport all along the line were to be established. This second language was the organization and proper display of Inca history.

Pachacuti, it was said, "was curious to learn of past things." He had made a special pilgrimage to Pacaritambo as a curtain raiser to his recoloring of the history of his people. Here he had entered the famous cave of origination, that earthly womb from which had issued the ancestors, and he had ordered religious edifices to be built for the *pacarina*, including one with a door in gold leaf. He finally set up an oracular cult on the site. By these gestures he personally appropriated the sources of Inca history.

Up to this time short heroic lays had been the genre in which the deeds of the tribe, fateful or otherwise, had been recorded. We recall that Pachacuti himself had ordered a eulogistic lay to celebrate his Sora victory; and Huayna Capac, his grandson, was to take note of treachery off the island of Puná in a famous dirge. Nevertheless these snatches of Inca history had floated about without any coherence, each clan, each family hymning its own ancestors exclusively. Because some of those scattered chapters of history could be dangerous to Pachacuti's pretensions—for we cannot imagine that he was without opposition from other *ayllus* in the state—he ordered a general overhaul of this corpus of epic lore, suppressing some of it totally, muting parts referring to weak predecessors, and further elaborating those pieces that referred to rulers of energy or to heavenly sanctions supporting his house. A canon of past rulers and their *coyas* was thereby set up, and from this orthodoxy it would henceforth be treason to depart. At the risk of repetition, it is of interest to make a résumé of it here as a reflection of Pachacuti's tastes and aims.

The new revised historical gospel was in its whole and its parts the story of the mission of the Incas to subjugate the world. It began with Creation; explained the appearance of the sun-god and his election of the Inca clans; moved outward in the Pacaritambo wandering; stressed the Inca right to Cuzco but obscured the length of time they had needed to effect its full occupation; presented Manco Capac as both the Moses and the Numa of the group, Mayta Capac as the epitome of vigor and ruthlessness, and Inca Roca as the father of martial sons; stressed the legitimacy of the passage of power from Viracocha Inca to Pachacuti, while at the same time underlining the cowardice of the former and therefore Pachacuti's right to take over; omitted Urcon; presented the Chanca war as a renewal of the sun-god's original commitment to the Incas through his favorite, Pachacuti; and in brief presented Pachacuti as a second Manco Capac, the renovator of Inca glory. The artificiality of this construct is at once obvious, as are also the strength of its logic and the vitality of its meaning. In itself this falsified Pachacutean view of history is a historical fact of major importance, for it served to steer the course of future events.

According to Sarmiento, Pachacuti set about his task characteristically:

> He summoned a great gathering of the oldest and wisest men of Cuzco and elsewhere, and with excessive diligence he sought out and inspected the ancient histories of the area, principally those of his Inca ancestors, and he commanded that it be put in pictures—as well as conserved in the system we have already referred to (i.e., the quipus).

The pictures referred to were placed under the care of special librarians living in a holy annex of the great temple, situated just outside the city on the hill of Puquín, sacred to the noonday sun. Access to these records, which were deposited in an archive called Puquín Cancha, was forbidden to all but the emperor and those designated by him. Having himself stolen parts of many people's traditions to create this universal history, he had no intention that the monopoly should be broken into by any other thief.

If Puquín Cancha was the archives, the Yachahuasi (House of Learning), just back of Pachacuti's palace, was the university. Totally revamped by Pachacuti, it was staffed by *amautas* (Wise Men) appointed by the high priest. In their care were the oral traditions of Inca history as well as its entire hymnology. Placed under the tutelage of these men were sons not only of Inca magnates but those of conquered *curacas*; to these youths they taught the correct view of Inca history, and to the latter in particular the arts of the Quechua language so that when they should be elevated to important offices in their native provinces, they might go well indoctrinated in loyalty, refinement, and proper speech. It is no wonder, as Cobo remarks, that the Incas had their traditions "sculptured in their bones."

The *amautas* preserved their records by two methods: by the *quipu*, the variously knotted cord series (which gave them the order, number, and category of what they had memorized); and by the short lays already mentioned which concerned deeds, treaties, and fiats. These bardic lays were committed to memory and passed unchanged down through their sons. Those specializing in them were set apart as a different, more druidic order of *amauta*.

That this history had by now been totally taken over as a royal prerogative can be seen from the fact that, upon his coronation, an emperor nominated three or four of these bards as his official historians who were to compose and record in lay form each great action of his reign as it occurred. These eulogies, heard at most of the state fiestas, were under the emperor's copyright and could not be sung outside of his presence without his permission. On his death, his successor ordered the totality sung to him and had those he approved added to the canon. Popular history, probably in prose form, there must have been, contradicting in many ways the glorified state presentation, but these were of course driven underground and were only partially to rise to the surface again under the Spaniards' probing, carrying with them a melancholy load of information on Inca deceit, arrogance, and cruelty.

State history was also officially and visually presented in processional dramas enacted by the *panacas* at many of the aforementioned ceremonies. Here the ancestral mummies were chronologically paraded through Cuzco, each with their own deeds chanted and roughly enacted. This is a true emergent theater and owes something to Pachacuti's genius. As each *panaca* moved along, its men and women linked arm in arm, drumming and chanting drunkenly, certain of them mimed the historical deeds. Recitative by the *panaca* leader and antiphonal response by the family gave a form to the proceedings. This was the *purucalla*. Their national history was unrolled before the Incas in these celebrations, and the past for that moment became present in the timeless glory of Tahuantinsuyo.

« 7 »

FOR ONE CLOSELY RELATED AREA OF LIFE Pachacuti did not establish an orthodoxy—this was the world beyond the grave. The reason would seem evident: his theatrical need was the opposite, for he had to treat the ancestral dynasts as being *still alive* and supporting his throne by their combined acclamation and prestige. These ancestors lived not only in the dance-dramas just described, but in the *panacas* as mummies who carried on a daily domestic life in their Cuzco palaces; they attended all the tribal fiestas, they went calling on both living and dead, and, vicariously through their attendants, they spoke, ate, asked questions, drank, worshipped, urinated, and indeed performed sexual acts. When the first Spaniards burst in upon the establishment of the deceased Huayna Capac in Cuzco, the overpowering realism and solemnity of this house of the living-dead caused them to remove their footgear out of respect like any other menials. They found that most of the retainers in this house of the dead were women and that one woman, superior to the rest and wearing a golden face-mask, stood behind the mummies of the emperor and his *coya* whisking flies away from their blank features. So ornate was the service that even the clay jars in which the daily *chicha* was stored were covered in gold leaf.

Such mummies had been once merely family possessions and good-luck charms. It was Pachacuti who formed the *panaca*, that unique corporation in which the royal mummy was considered as a still living paterfamilias. In these corporations the unburied dead were to become the irresponsible owners of vast aggregations of tribute and the unpoliced protectors of numerous retainers, many of whom had been

179

attracted from the outside to volunteer their adherence to these luxurious and vicious organizations. Thus upon the death of an emperor, his personal wealth ceased to be available to the imperial line and went banqueting instead in the blind halls of the dead. Though they formed centers of intrigue and immorality, because of their sacred origins they were completely untouchable. The last legitimate emperor, for all his own extremism, correctly advocated the proper action to be taken against them when he threatened to bury all the mummies and seize their wealth. Yet even he found himself impotent against the weight of such vested interests.

Herein Pachacuti's ceremonial genius had overreached itself. He failed to subordinate the ancestors to the living authority of the empire. The later inability of Tahuantinsuyo to defend itself against Atahaulpa's rebellion must have been in part the result of the divided councils of these islands of self-interest in Cuzco. They began as a lurid echo of Pachacuti's grandiose desire to remain in possession of his own vast wealth, his family, his pleasures, his sovereignty, and his person—even though dead. Their final effects produced only a morbidity in the body politic. It was not until the viceregal reign of Francisco de Toledo that the mummies were at last searched out and done away with.

An Inca royal funeral was a ceremonial masterpiece, obsequies without a tomb. The less great were mourned and feasted in their homes for a month before being consigned to the tomb. The imperial mummies were not referred to by the common word for corpse, *aya*, but were specially canonized as *illapa*, which we can translate as "blessed," a more heavenly and spiritualized concept to accord with the semidivine status they had attained as rulers. It was possible for the *illapa* to desert the mummy after death, however, as punishment for treason against Inti. For the royal dead the pan-Peruvian practice of the suttee was standard. Specially designated spots were provided with nooses, heavy rocks, and other instruments where those wives, retainers, and friends who wished might seek destruction for a greater end in store. As in all societies, women were the professional mourners, keening the dead ruler, moving restlessly through his apartments to the tapping of their tambourines, visiting the sites where he was in the habit of enjoying himself, calling on his name, and chanting his deeds. Grass girdles were worn by them as a sign of mourning. The rites attending the death of an emperor lasted a full year and involved the whole population of Tahuantinsuyo.

Our statements here concern only the Inca crown and nobility; we know nothing of the common Indian. An Inca possessed a *huaoqui* (brother), normally resident in some exterior fetish, which was in his possession and which after his death descended in his family as a simulacrum almost as important as his mummy. A man could choose his own spirit-brother—as when Pachacuti chose an image of the god of lightning—of any size or material. The spirit-brother of Manco Capac, as might be expected, was the Inti-bird. That of Sinchi Roca was a stone thought to be a dragon. The *huaoqui* of a person was his "luck," his vicar in case of the disappearance of his mummy, his friendly companion, the repository of his special talents, his oracular mouthpiece after he was dead, and his patron saint and intercessor— in brief a double of the human spirit, endowed with great powers of *huaca* and dedicated mainly to the preservation and aggrandizement of the fleshly twin—reminding one rather vaguely of the Roman emperor's genius. The personal immortality implied in the possession of a *huaoqui*, confined originally to the very highest royal rank, was at length usurped by the noble class below.

« 8 »

Totally unconnected with this aristocratic immortality were the speculations concerning Upamarca (City of the Dumb), the destination of souls. With his fierce reliance on cult to achieve his ends, Pachacuti himself had little care for these matters, yet we know that the Incas divided the afterlife into a heaven and a hell. *Ucupacha* was "the Underworld"—otherwise known as *Supaypa huasi*, "House of the Devil." This underground region was reached after a horrifying journey wherein souls crossed deep chasms on bridges of hairs, etc. This was the road taken by evil or unworthy people—which meant non-Incas. The pitiful phantasm that had once been a man here endured cold, thirst, hunger, loneliness, and great fatigue. Only grave offerings from the world of the living could lighten this torment. Monsters or devils forced into his ghostly craw food made up of toads, excrement, putrid water, and other filth. The dead sometimes appeared on earth as heads or wraiths to prophesy ill.

Heaven was *Hanan Pacha* (The Upper World), destination of the proud, the wealthy, and the victorious—Incas, of course. Here were the seats of Viracocha and Inti, and here food, *chicha*, and women were plenteously enjoyed. This eternal enjoyment was what was subsumed under the concept of the dead Inca ruler as an *illapa*, mentioned above.

The Incas entertained those variant ideas of an Armageddon or final cataclysm common to all Peruvians, wherein the Creator would overturn his world, blotting out sun, moon, and stars and sending a torrid and final drought. After that, it seems, the dead would be revived and the world—or a world—would presumably begin again. On the evidence of the women keening Atahualpa after his execution, who insisted to the Spaniards that he would return to them, we know that the spirit of an Inca ruler was supposed to rejoin its body at some time after death; whether this belief was contained in the Viracocha resurrection of the dead cannot be stated.

As a corollary of their historical mission, the Incas had claimed a status as "more than human." It is clear that they so impressed others, for the subject peoples were found worshipping the ruler as the equal of the sun-god—a phenomenon quite analogous to the early divinization of the Roman emperors by the peoples of their Eastern provinces. Yet the Inca rulers never actually usurped full divinity, if we can argue from the fact they could—and did—commit sin, which had to be confessed to heaven. These royal confessions were made directly and without priestly intermediaries, however, which would equate the status of emperor with that of a supreme pontiff. We may state then that Pachacuti considered himself a mortal, but one endowed with a superior *huaca* of rule.

This rule was supported by those angelic demigods, the *pururaucas*, visible only to his eyes. We recall that he had toured the battlefield of his Chanca victory, and one by one had pointed them out, lying scattered about in frozen attitudes of stone. These had been joyously escorted back to Cuzco, where as the saintly *huaca* host we have already seen that they were much reverenced. Each had its name and observances, and official cicerones were there to guide pilgrims and ambassadors from one to the other. They continued to fight with his armies throughout his reign, always assuring victory. Thus was this greatest of Inca emperors surrounded with a stately and unsleeping army of sentinels, and few indeed were the desperate ones who would have dared break through such a cordon.

Cobo was of the opinion that the Incas were geniuses in the organization of religion, and we may be sure that much that is attributed to Pachacuti belongs to the whole corpus of the tribal history instead. But the mystique which he certainly created, when analyzed, brings out the inner lineaments of Tahuantinsuyo in too individual and too logical a fashion to be merely an accumulation from the past. It is a measure of Pachacuti's capacity that he built armies and successfully led them and still could see the concomitant necessity of explaining his creation in architectural, ritual, and theological terms.

PART THREE
CAESAR'S HOUSE

TEN.
TOPA INCA
CHIMOR AND THE NORTH

―――――――

《　I　》

Topa Inca Yupanqui, probably the youngest of all the legitimate princes, was born to Pachacuti about 1448. His royal mother, either real or adopted, was the timid Mama Anahuarque. The curious attraction which the *huaca* of Titicaca was later to have for Topa Inca as emperor makes it not improbable that he had been born in Collao during his father's campaign in the region.

When the prince was born, Pachacuti was well past middle age and already approaching his hoary December; he greeted the occasion with that April thaw of affection always felt by an aging father for a last son. He celebrated a great *capacocha* in honor of the event and himself devoted the child at dawn to his resplendent father the Sun.

Topa Inca was considered as a possible infante almost from the time when his older brother had been demoted from that dignity; in the meanwhile the emperor had been exercising his most inventive arts, revamping and expanding the knighting ceremony to make it a more impressive instrument for the prince's initiation. In this ceremony the emperor was the first of either gods or men to offer the boy gifts, and it was he who led him sedately through the various stations of the Sun, finally to invest him with the earplugs, weapons,

187

and insignia appropriate to his new rank. He was crowned as heir and coruler and given in marriage his remarkable sister Mama Ocllo. At the time Topa Inca was about sixteen. Thus appeared upon the stage of history a man who was to equal his father in vigor and warlikeness, though not in his inventiveness or personal power, and who was to surpass him in the arts of imperial administration.

The raid on Cajamarca had taken place only a year or so previously; its erratic and brilliant leader Capac Yupanqui had been executed and the entire army command changed. The Inca garrison which had been left in Cajamarca, isolated by five hundred miles of seething tribal unrest and provincial rebellion from Cuzco, continued to hang on in anticipation of relief. And Chimor, a distant but dangerous enemy, had meanwhile swum into the ocean of Pachacuti's discontent. The accession of Topa Inca as coemperor is intimately connected with these events that were rocking the Inca state.

Topa Inca's coregency was to last from approximately 1463 to 1470 and was to be entirely taken up with the pacification and settlement of Chinchaysuyo, the northern quarter, both coast and sierra—an extended, varied, and remarkable series of conquests. The incidental drain on the empire's man power and the destruction wrought outside the province of Cuzco were to appear linked in later records with seven years of drought, cannibalism, widespread earthquakes, and volcanic desolation, while in Cuzco itself the strain of readjustment to the influx of new wealth, new ideas, and new peoples were to produce tumults and intrigue. In a sense it was the most crucial period which the state had had to face since the days of the Chanca war—even though it was brought about by success instead of by the imminence of disaster. The very name Pachacuti (Earth Upside Down) had as one of its meanings the sense of a vast and public calamity.

《 2 》

LIKE THE SPOTTED BUSHMASTER coiled in his leafy tangle, the aged emperor was still deadly. He quickly picked up the challenge flung down by Chimor and his own rebellious provinces to the north and west. A new army of ten thousand men was organized and placed under the skilled direction of three highly placed officers, men of Pachacuti's immediate family: Auqui Yupanqui, Tillca Yupanqui, and a bastard son Topa Capac. With them as both their lord and youthful apprentice in war went the new coregent accompanied by his *coya* and harem. This was not to be a raid but a campaign in full force, and the glory was to belong to Topa Inca. The eldest of the three generals, Topa Capac, was one day to revolt against his younger brother.

The first item was to crush the rebellious Quechuas who had for so long been locked in close alliance with the Inca state. How and why Cuzco felt impelled to this tragic necessity we do not know. The process by which early comrades-in-arms are transferred into bondsmen running beside the conqueror's chariot is a well-known, if unsavory, logic of empire. The defection of the Quechuas may have expressed the same despair we find in the reasons behind the Roman Social War.

On the way north Topa Inca stopped in Vilcas to push forward the building campaign instituted there by his father, which he did with such energy that he was thereafter remembered as the city's true founder. A marsh was filled in to provide space for what was to be the most spacious plaza in all the empire, capable of holding in all twenty thousand people. There were erected garrison accommodations for as many as thirty thousand troops. The whole was dominated by a temple complex in five ascending stages, topped with the two gold-sheathed stone seats reserved either for the emperor and his *coya* or for the images of the sun and the moon. Five hundred *mamaconas* served in this brilliant colonial church, though we may suspect that a part of their number were *acllas*.

Three hill forts had to be assaulted and taken near by, and the army then moved on past Vilcas to overawe the Angaraes of the Mantaro Basin. Against the Huancas of Jauja, Topa exercised the diplomatic sleights for which the Inca state was famous. Ostentatiously he pitched his camp among those settlements from which the natives had fled in seeking the shelter of the heights. He made no hostile move but simply waited, and it was not long before a mixture of awe, curiosity, and hunger inspired the local *sinchi*, accompanied by only ten braves, to appear in the camp. Topa Inca loaded him with gifts of drinking vessels and fine garments and sent him back to bring in the tribes. When all the Huancas had submitted to this display of generosity, their most able warriors were drafted on the spot both to swell the army as it moved north and to provide hostages. By the time the army of Tahuantinsuyo moved out, mighty in this bloodless victory, it left behind it an orderly bustle of building, surveying, and numbering—in short, the beginnings of government.

On the upper Marañón lay Huánuco where the famous mountain *huaca*, Yaro, was worshipped. The *curacas* who ruled in his name seem to have submitted peacefully to the Incas for Topa Inca gave an Inca princess to their chieftain. We know that the Yarovilca kinglets, Incas by title of this first injection of the blood, were to hold a privileged position in later Tahuantinsuyo.

The deep-set valley of Huaylas, full of the remains of more ancient civilizations, was added next, after which the army finally arrived before Cajamarca. To the relief of the generals, the embattled Inca garrison had succeeded in turning back all of Chimor's efforts to crush its resistance, and Topa Inca immediately set about transforming Cajamarca into a formidable Inca bastion, settling roundabout many Cuzco indians as *mitmacs*. So enduring was this instance of colonization that, even after the slaughter and disasters of the civil war between Huascar and Atahualpa, the city still claimed a solid population and numerous noble edifices.

Established now in Cajamarca, Topa Inca mounted a sweep down into the montaña country of the Chachapoyas. There were several reasons for this. Security demanded the decimation of these vigorous clans, whose organized brigandage at the Inca's back would be intolerable if allowed to go unchecked. Revenge also demanded their reduction, for it was through their country that the Chancas had escaped into the Moyobamba jungle. An added element was that the Chachapoya girls, almost white of skin, cleanly and pleasing in their ways, were considered by the Incas (and Spaniards later) as the most desirable of all the sierra women.

The country of the Chachapoyas lay across the Marañón. It seems to have been a piratical and loosely organized tribal republic afloat in the upper jungle, joined to the sierra by easily defensible bridges across the Marañón and well provided with fortified crags overhanging the dangerous trails. Sudden blizzards in the passes and several bloody engagements put the issue of the subjugation of these people long in doubt, but the main Chachapoya stronghold was finally successfully stormed and the native *sinchi* captured. Various pueblos were sacked and some of the folk scattered; even Moyobamba—almost one hundred miles due east—seems to have been entered by an Inca column. But whether all of this was the result of a single campaign is doubtful.

« 3 »

TOPA INCA'S MAIN EFFORT WAS DIRECTED—as could be expected—against the coastal kingdom of Chimor. Chimor may not have been the most dangerous enemy the Incas had ever met, but culturally she was by far the most sophisticated. What Greece, though vanquished, became to Rome, so in some sort was Chimor to become to Cuzco.

The earliest rulers of Chimor, like the Incas and the Chancas, had in the past been invaders; they had first appeared in the already ancient and heavily urbanized valley of Moche, having come in from the sea under a Homeric leader named Taycanamo. Whereas the Incas counted ten rulers through Topa Inca, there were nine in the line of Chimor down to and including Minchançaman, the one who would finally suffer defeat at the hands of Topa Inca. The two states were thus equally matched in experience and age, and at that moment in history Chimor had shown the same expansiveness along the coast as Cuzco did in the sierra. The capital of the kingdom was the vast adobe city of Chanchan, the ruins of which even today cover some eleven square miles and bear witness to the former presence of thousands of perpetually green and irrigated gardens, stone-walled tanks, gabled houses, pyramids, and tribal areas enclosed in extensive walls. Court ritual was elegant and elaborate to an extreme—so impressing the Incas that they were to take away with them for their own uses her best craftsmen and entertainers.

Though war had been a primary activity of Chimor, her princes seem to have had no creator god to lead them out of kingdom to true empire. Si, the moon goddess, was supreme. She controlled all avenues to fertility and prosperity, and seemingly—like many other

Great Mothers—received the king's embraces to these ends. If he should be unable to prove his potency, she announced her displeasure in flood and dearth, whereupon his subjects might sacrifice him by drowning.

Intricate forms of homosexualism and temple sodomy had long been entrenched in these coastal valleys, customs supposedly introduced by a race of giants who had long before landed on the northern shore unprovided with their own women. Indeed sexual aberrations of all varieties flowered rankly in the hothouse atmosphere of these cultures. The coastal harems were served by creatures so grotesque as scarcely to be believable, men who had not only been emasculated but had had their lips and noses slit away so as to cause in those women whom they guarded revulsion and horror. The impact upon the narrow and dedicated mind of the Inca conqueror of such modes of behavior may readily be imagined, for whatever contempt the typical *serrano* may have felt for the lowlanders in the realm of general hardihood, he still stood in awe of his finesse and luxury.

Only with the third king of the Taycanamo dynasty did Chimor take the first steps toward expansion, seizing the two valleys neighboring on the north and the two on the south. A century later Chimor was ready for her brilliant *floriut*. Minchançaman seems to have come to power around the year 1460, just in time to meet the first Inca raid under Capac Yupanqui. As we have seen, his reaction to this was weak, the reason being that he was involved in completing a far-flung conquest along the coast—no doubt initiated under earlier rulers—so that when the two great protagonists finally stood face to face, he was ruling from Tumbez in the north to Huarmey in the south. This quasi-feudal state was ruled by the Chimor Capac, as he was known in title to the Incas, through a system of governors. No doubt in matters administrative it closely resembled Tahuantinsuyo. Its glaring weakness was its comparative lack of a full and vigorously defined mystique. It had no lack of military ardor.

In attempting to penetrate the meaning of Chimor's inclusion of Huarmey in her plans, we can make the easy speculation that she was aiming at breaking the back of that coastal power centered in the Rímac Valley. The state on the Rímac may have been threatening an Inca alliance, or at least adopting an alarming posture to this effect.

Should such come about—and there is reason to believe it did—Chimor would see her southern flank exposed to overwhelming power.

This Rímac power, centrally located on the coast but not particularly militant, was the kingdom of Cuismancu. Having succeeded in halting Chimor's drive to the south, it now stood uneasily on its battered frontier, grateful for the near presence of the new power also hostile to Chimor, though no doubt fearful of both. It contained within its borders two renowned oracles and as such was the most theocratically oriented of the Peruvian states of which we have knowledge. In appearance it was a series of busy pueblos dotting a richly irrigated set of confluent valleys which appear today as the generally barren and dun-colored environs of Lima. The capital city founded here by Francisco Pizarro was certainly a pigmy compared to its native predecessors in the area.

The kingdom of Cuismancu thus had all of the importance which, in any rapidly fluctuating international situation, attaches to a weakly committed and richly endowed state. It consisted of three fluvial sections, of which the southernmost two, the Rímac and Lurín valleys, were united in one tongue, while the other valley, Carabayllo, spoke the language of the Chancay people. Back of Cuismancu stood the congested and terrible peaks of Pariacaca, land of the *soroche* sickness.

Earlier in their history the people of the Rímac had attempted to penetrate this Pariacaca barrier but had been prevented by the Yauyos. Halfway up the Rímac Canyon was situated one of the most notable *huacas* in Peru, undoubtedly that one which is so often referred to as simply Rímac, "the Oracle." Here the main branch of the stream, the Mama, was joined by the Chacalla, while sited at their confluence was Pachamama's great shrine attracting unending streams of pilgrims to her from far and wide. The Spaniards named the site San Pedro de Mama, and its situation may still be studied just a few miles above the resort town of Chosica.

The principal pueblo of the northern valley was Carabayllo; the Rímac area possessed two: Maranga was inland somewhat and in the middle of the valley, while Surco was placed on the inner face of that massive coastal *pucara* now called the Morro Solar just south of Lima. The Incas, when they came to form the area into one province, correspondingly divided it into three moeities, with Pachacamac receiving special and outside treatment. Surco was the grandest of all these Rímac cities and as such can claim to be the legitimate predecessor of the City of the Kings. Its vast ruins, sumptuous temples, rich apartments, and walls adorned with figures in brilliant color were there to impress the Limeños long after Pizarro. "They will last," they said, "for many centuries as a memorial to the days of Indian heathenism"—but the centuries have about reached their appointed time for modern edifices now clamber across the blackened feet of the rock.

With our sources contradictory at this point, the order of assaults against Chimor and even their number is impossible to ascertain. More than one however was required to dispose of such a vigorous state. The additional fact that Topa's army was operating in several columns each on their own schedules adds the final touch of complexity, with Topa in person generally with the highland group. It is as if the historian had to reconstruct a master chess game from its first and last moves alone. It may be that Inca arms first appeared in the Rímac Valley as a result of negotiation, for no evidence points to hostilities with Cuismancu. At any rate this state now flung out her banners behind those of Cuzco and proceeded north with her against the enemy.

Having passed the valley of Huaura the advance came to Patavilca (Sacred Terrace). Chimor had constructed near by a most formidable roadblock, the brick fortress of Paramunca, still amazingly intact today. Paramunca is a masterpiece of military architecture, and in its day, with its plastered walls painted a deep red and covered with great friezes of heraldic animals and birds, it must have been even more impressive. A bloody repulse for the Incas and their allies is recorded under these walls. With this prong of Inca power stalled, Topa Inca sent back from his highland headquarters an urgent request for reinforcements to shore up the collapsed front so that no drain need be made on his sierra armies, at that moment grinding slowly ahead. Here we leave this coastal group until their advance picks up again.

As adequate elbowroom had now been secured in the Cajamarca area, it was decided to make a strong frontal attack on Chimor down the mountain road from Huamachuco to Chanchan. Serious opposition was expected. The heaviest pressure was therefore exerted, and Topa's generals succeeded in breaking out of the canyon country sufficiently to invest the key fortress guarding the great city. But again the Incas were repulsed. In order to salvage something of their prestige, the frustrated Inca columns apparently raced north up the coast road to the valley of Jequetepeque, which they undoubtedly looted before hastening back to their base in the sierra. Thus while Minchançaman had again balked the predatory Inca, at least his kingdom had been deeply penetrated and insulted. Mighty boasts have rested on less than this. And certainly it was no mean achievement.

« 4 »

THE MAIN ARMY IN THE SIERRA was meanwhile rolling back the immediate northern frontier. As each tribal state was forced to submit, it was in turn subjected to the *Pax Incaica*. Cannibalism and sodomy where found were forbidden, tribute imposed, and the scattered groups were brought down from higher ground and settled in accessible pueblos—this latter policy of course all important to the success of Inca rule in the provinces. And matching these in importance was the immediate *corvée* levied among the people for carrying the Royal Road through the area. Where the Inca army advanced over narrow foot-trails and dangerous declivities, it returned over paved, stepped, and widened roads rendered safe from freshets by culverts and drainage. The road system of Tahuantinsuyo is one of the most startling engineering projects in human history.

The Palta Indians of Cusibamba (Happy Valley) and those on their approaches were subdued in a five months' campaign. The Cañars, redoubtable braves with olive skins and acquiline features, were absorbed and their capital, Tumibamba (Knife Valley), taken. This was as momentous a victory as the relief of Cajamarca, and its consequences were to be even more portentous. Vast numbers of the Cañars were hastily moved south, some of them to the valley of Jauja, with a further fifteen thousand sent beyond to settle around Cuzco.

At this point Topa Inca left the scene of action and returned to

Cuzco to celebrate a triumph under the dubious eyes of the aging Pachacuti. This first portion of the Chinchaysuyo campaign had already taken at least two years, so the triumph may be roughly dated to 1466. One suspects that the old emperor had in reality recalled the high command at this point simply to make sure that its ultimate control did not slip out of his grasp. He specified no more than another four years for the complete subjugation of the north.

Increasing in skill and confidence, the still youthful Topa Inca then returned to Tumibamba. Already it was becoming a notable Inca city, its palaces, apartments for the magnates, temples, forts, *acllahuasi*, public places, gardens, hot baths, caravansaries, and storehouses transforming the green pocket in the Andes into a civilized Eden for the conqueror and a relentless workhouse for the vanquished.

Not all the Cañars had submitted, and with the passing of the seasons Inca arms had probed farther up the sierra trails in search of them. Southern Ecuador had not been too difficult, but now a reckless struggle was finally precipitated under the great volcano Chimborazo against the remnants of the Cañars and the Puruháes, who had been drawn together in a coalition under the presidency of the kingdom of Quito. The Quitos clearly felt that the moving finger had at last come to rest on them. With these groups it was a "now-or-never" stand, and its effects staggered even the hardened Inca armies. For the Ecuadorans it was too desperate to be a heroic defeat, for the Incas too exigent to be accounted a glorious victory. The maturer power won—but barely—and the Incas set out to exact the direst penalties upon their captives. This battle uncovered the whole of the northern Ecuadoran sierra. The Inca army then crawled forward into the center of Quito—the prize—to lick its wounds and regroup.

It was during this storm of blood in the north that the lightnings of treason played also over the city of Cuzco. We only know that newfangled ideas had incited a certain group of *orejones* to plot against the state. Pachacuti is curiously not mentioned in the outcome; he may have been now in a full state of retirement. The governor of the holy city was the one who brought events under control with the expected "extreme reprisals." Topa did not find it necessary to return. Such a grimy little historical fragment cannot be defined further.

The most we can say is that the phenomenal growth of Tahuantin-suyo was producing nightmares of splendor and desire as well as of horror in the spirits of men. Whatever the tumults meant, they were undoubtedly spawned by the appetites and repressions of empire.

« 5 »

LIKE TUMIBAMBA, QUITO, astride the narrow backbone of the Andes, was to become a future springboard for continuing conquests into the north. At this juncture we have a picture of Topa Inca ruling alone as a mighty war-lord in Ecuador. At daybreak he ate and feasted heavily until the sun was high and enjoyed his women in the privacy of his royal apartments. After noon he sat in public judgment and heard complaints as well as communications from distant Cuzco and from his armies in the field. He ended the day with convivial *chicha* and the final banquet by the light of fragrant wood fires. It was either in Tumibamba or Quito—probably the former—that his heir and successor Huayna Capac some years after this was to be born. The enslavement of the Inca royal house to the Cañar and Quiteño fleshpots is vaguely foreshadowed at this time, if a ukase of Topa Inca's is correctly attributed: "Cuzco is on the one hand the center and chief refuge of my great empire; on the other hand is Quito." And to make this explicit he created for the region a specially power-ful governorship, an office which was in reality a viceroyalty and which was to promote in the days of his grandsons the collapse of his house.

Because the kingdom of Quito which Topa had incorporated into the body of Tahuantinsuyo was to play this malign part in later Inca history it therefore needs comment. Its history had begun, according to a somewhat uncertain tradition, with a group who wandered in from the sea and who called themselves the Caras. They first settled on the coast just north of Manta, but after some time they fought their way up to sierra via the Esmeraldas River. They soon brought their new neighbors on the south, the Panzaleos, into confederation, and the seal of this was the city of Quito which arose on the exact border between their original claims.

Thus a new people, the Quitos, appeared. From this point as a

197

nucleus, their writ spread northward into the Ibarra Basin, where an understanding was arrived at with the Caranguis, and southward to include the Puruhá people next door to Tumibamba. This latter advance had been accomplished by a famous marriage between a Quiteño princess and a Puruhá lord which produced the so-called Duchicela dynasty of four kings in Quito. Orienting itself to the south, the dynasty succeeded in forcing an alliance upon the Cañars of Tumibamba just as the Inca juggernaut began to roll northward. We have seen that Topa was able to shear away from Quito its Cañar shield. Hualcopo, the fourteenth *scyri* of the original line, had then fortified the province of Puruhá against the expected Inca pressure, with the results we have already seen.

But wonderful as these far lands were under the smoking volcanoes, lovely as were their women and potentially rich the fruits of their soil, Quito was not the accomplished goal. Topa's mortal enemy still lay down along the edges of the sea, viciously entrenched in every valley head, as dangerous as a rattlesnake under the cruel spines of the maguey. Topa had reached thus far north along the sierra road not for glory alone, but tactically to outreach his enemy, whose last tributary state, Tumbez, now lay behind him. By finding his way down to the coast above Tumbez, he could take Chimor on this flank while ordering at the same time a reopening of the stalled southern attack. Inasmuch as this is what seems to have happened—though the exact co-ordination of events is unclear—we must assume it was intended. The pincers were about to close. Whether this master-piece of strategy was Pachacuti's last contribution to the history of his people we cannot decide. It may equally well have been worked out by the capable generals on Topa's staff.

When all had been prepared, Topa turned over the administration of the Quito area to a trusted elder, Challco Mayta, conferring upon him such semiroyal privileges as the use of the litter and golden table-ware. From Quito he was to keep Topa in constant knowledge, through post runners, of the business of his office.

As was usual, envoys had been first dispatched to the lowland *curacas* demanding their submission. These had been slain out of hand as had also a flying column sent in to search for them, so greater and more menacing preparations were set in motion. The only route feasible for large groups dropping off the sierra and desiring to emerge just north of Tumbez was the Guayas River, and we may assume that Topa, having passed under the skirts of Chimborazo, reached that river somewhere near the modern Babahoyo. He must have then transferred his warriors, now beginning to feel the effects of the humid lowlands, onto balsa rafts prepared for them and launched them out on the glassy face of those waters. The savage Huancavelicas along the river were overawed sufficiently to allow the flotilla to pass along, until it finally formed camp near the estuary.

Ahead of them now lay a maze of low, steamy islands, the outermost and largest of all being the island of Puná, fronting the Pacific Ocean. Puná was a wealthy commercial and warlike state of several confederated pueblos. It was the barbaric Venice of these western waters, envied and feared by its neighbors and bitterly hostile to the city of Tumbez, some fifty miles down the coast. In any attempt upon the latter city, the aid of Puná was essential. A garbled folk tale, repeated and embellished by the credulous Spaniards, seems to refer to the fact that Topa and a part of his forces sailed out to the island state, remained there some time, and then returned with gifts and curios from its *curaca*. Fighting is not hinted at in the tale, so we can only imagine that it was a visit intended to cement an aggressive alliance against Tumbez. Farther up the Pacific coast lay Manta, a considerable settlement of some two thousand inhabitants. These people possessed a rich enough culture to attract the insatiable Incas, for Topa seems to have sent off a column to reduce them, though with unknown results.

Any success Topa had in the Ecuadoran lowlands could only have been temporary at best. We know that the garrisons and commissioners which he left behind were massacred at some time after his main forces had departed. Nevertheless the leverage momentarily achieved at Puná enabled the Incas by some unspecified means to take Tumbez.

As Pizarro was to discover some sixty years later, Tumbez was the gateway to Peru, the first of its great cities visible to mariners coasting down from the north. All maritime commerce put in here, and it was probably the main taker of those goods the merchants of Puná brought in from distant parts. It was a rich city with a type of polity found only here and in the area immediately south of it, for it was ruled by a female *curaca* called a *capullana*, polyandrous and highly revered. The meager remains of this once splendid and certainly unique Peruvian city lie today in the sand at San Pedro de los Incas.

The seizure of this city by the Incas spelled vast troubles for Chimor. Rapidly yoked to the Inca war machine, it was garrisoned, provided with the usual building program, a resident governor, and its warriors drafted into the ranks.

Confident that the plan was well under way, Topa himself now returned to the highlands by the Huancabamba road, leaving the major part of his forces to push south through the deserts under the two generals, Auqui Yupanqui and Tillca Yupanqui. The loss of Tumbez had so weakened Chimor that this army was now enabled to march unopposed through 250 miles of difficult and sterile country. On the approaches to Lambayeque a roadblock set up by Chimor was swept aside, and the enemy governor of that city forced to surrender his strategic valley.

Chimor was dying. Already the southern prong of Inca arms was in motion. North, east, and south—whichever way Chanchan, the frightened city, looked—there stood the Incas. Only in the heaving reaches of the Pacific were there none. But to the sea the rulers of Chimor could not return.

History has obscured the death agonies of this kingdom from us. Whether the northern or the southern armies reached Chanchan first we do not know. The southern group seems to have finally pushed past the fortress of Paramunca, and to have fought serious battles in two valleys to the north of it, Huarmey and Santa. In the latter, the defenders put up the fiercest resistance, using to their advantage but in the end fruitlessly that eight-foot-high wall of rough stone still in evidence today which runs up out of the waves of the Pacific and into the high hills for over forty miles. It was Chimor's last proper line of defense. State and city foundered in a holocaust of blood. This will have been about the year 1470, an *annus mirabilis* in the annals of Tahuantinsuyo.

Minchançaman was carried off to Cuzco, a heroic hostage, and a son moved into his seat of rule. Inca craft was never more apparent, however, than in their final disposition of the captive king, for he was given as wife one of Topa's daughters. Thus the new *curacas* installed in the valley of Moche, sons of Minchançaman, had always to keep in mind, for their good behavior, that up in the sierra there existed others of their line—and indeed ones that had become Inca by blood. As the event transpired, three more generations of the line of Chimor ruled as *curacas* of Moche in a direct descent under the Incas. The last one, baptized by the incoming Spaniards, was known as Don Martín Cajacimcim. There is evidence that most of the coast, with its dangling rosary of riverine cultures, received special treatment from the Incas, Tumbez for example being allowed to retain her female *curaca* down to the coming of the Spaniards. The prestige of the strange and baroque will have been one factor, but one equally as important was the difficulty an alpine people like the Incas had in keeping surveillance over lands eleven thousand feet below their natural habitat.

« 6 »

THE LOOT FROM CHIMOR was transported first up to Cajamarca for assembly, and from there it began the return journey. Immense lines of porters, captives, llama herds, and warriors filed south into stifling trenches at the bottoms of the gorges and across bleak *punas* where the shriveling winds at twelve or thirteen thousand feet and the hard nights of exposure took their customary toll of the lowlanders. So this mingled company of human splendor and misery wound its dreamlike way back through lands which only eight years before had rejected the Inca call to submit and now crouched in silence as the litters of the conqueror and his queen were borne slowly past.

Hovering over this cavalcade was the unblinking eye of Pachacuti. His suspicions never slept; and no doubt he had passed them on to his son and coemperor as a matter of common precaution. In the last eight years of warfare the three generals originally selected—sons and brothers of the old man—had proved their worth, but this fact did not damp the fires of Pachacuti's envy. Tillca Yupanqui, who had been with Topa at Puná and had been co-commander of the army group moving out of Tumbez, was the selected victim. Orders left Cuzco for his execution. The other field commander, Auqui Yupanqui, may also have been involved in this purge, though the top commander was spared. Topa Inca himself is reputed to have made frantic attempts to dissuade Pachacuti from his course and did succeed in somewhat blunting the full design. We can neither accept nor reject this. History has offered two and possibly three contradictory reasons for this characteristic and terrible denouement. None of them are conviving. Without deigning to explain why, at this point Clio, the muse of history, has just for an instant drawn aside a curtain to let us behold the dagger which always glittered beside the Inca mace.

Pachacuti went out as far as Vilcaconga with a personal army to meet his victorious son, and there the two retinues joined company for the road back. At Sacsahuaman, the heads of some of the *curacas* of the northern tribes were struck off and added to the procession, borne aloft on lances. The review and trampling of the captives took place in the double square under the eyes of Tahuantinsuyo's three greatest men, Pachacuti and his two sons, Amaru Inca and Topa Inca. In Coricancha the gods were thanked and assigned their portion of the loot; from the gold and silver amassed in Chimor, Pachacuti had statutes made of Viracocha, Inti, and Mama Ocllo, as well as that broad band of gold plates which the Spaniards later stripped from the walls of their shrines.

But the old emperor's unprecedented success had raised for him a host of troubles he could no longer meet. The previous revolts in Cuzco, the recent executions, and the growing power of his son's party bore heavily upon him—if we may guess from common analogies in history. Either he decided to resign or he was forced to. In a solemn and weary pronouncement to the magnates he formally stepped down from the sovereignty. Topa Inca was then crowned full emperor, and in a re-enactment of his previous marriage with his *coya*, he had her endowed with the dignities corresponding to her new role. Some thirty-three years of rule were ended, and Pachacuti had only a short while left to live. All of our sources stress his advanced age at the time.

A TRUE SCION OF HIS ENERGETIC HOUSE, Topa without resting turned his attention to the coastal area south of Cuismancu, the area that had only recently forced Capac Yupanqui to retreat. None of these valleys possessed such developed urban sites as Chimor or Cuismancu, and all of them were lost in howling wastes of driven sand. They had a certain family resemblance, however; they were ancient, hieratic, and rich in the wealth which fluvial irrigation confers.

The one folk who were expected to offer strong resistance were the Chinchas, organized under a tribal *curaca* who autocratically guided the exogamous *ayllus* subject to him. In those days the total population of the state of Chincha may have approached one hundred thousand. Their superiority lay in the diversity of their economy, for they relied equally upon farming, fishing, and commerce; their merchants in particular were widely traveled, appearing in regions as far off as the Titicaca Basin, bartering for the great quantities of silver they needed.

Topa dispatched his army through the province of the Rucanas to debouch on the coast through the canyon of the Acarí. Perhaps a display of strength was sufficient to bring to heel Acarí, Nazca, and Icá. Chincha, more obdurate, had assembled a large number of warriors, many of whom she pulled in from areas tributary to her; yet at the last moment, when approached by Topa's generous diplomacy, she seems not to have made the expected resistance. At any rate, the Inca settlement imposed on her was not burdensome for she was allowed to retain an unusual degree of autonomy. Hints appear in our sources that the lowland summer, then beginning, was taking a heavy toll of the highlanders in fevers and general debility, and this may have made such an equable settlement expedient for the Inca commanders.

Topa himself had gone farther up the sierra road to Jauja, where he turned off over the dizzy Pariacaca feeder road to emerge in the friendly kingdom of Cuismancu. His appearance here on the coast was to strengthen the bonds of loyalty which Cuismancu had so recently assumed; his action therefore took the dramatic form of a pilgrimage to the shrine of Pachacamac. We cannot doubt, however, that the presence of Inca armies here was additionally to face those yet unsubdued valleys to the south with that same military dilemma of encirclement as had brought about the collapse of Chimor.

Because of the peaceful submission of Cuismancu, its most important *huaca*, Pachacamac, was not hauled away for punishment in the mountains. But the Incas would have been tender of his feelings in any case, so wide was his influence and so cogent his oracles. We do know that from this time on this famous god became a staunch supporter of the legitimate Inca line and was in turn favorably considered by them. An intimate relationship was thus established between Cuzco and the Lima area which, though broken by the first entry of the Spaniards, was to be by them immediately re-established and which continued throughout most of the colonial period. It is not without interest that this same general relationship between the central coast and the southern Peruvian highland seems to be reflected in the archaeology in the pre-Inca period as well.

In the case of Pachacamac, Topa Inca rescinded certain regulations formerly passed by the Council of Coricancha in regard to provincial *huacas*, according to that shrine special privileges of tax collection along the coast—no doubt sanctioning or extending what had been a previous condition. However, to secure the *huaca* from totally escaping the Inca net, Topa insisted that new building begin on the site which would include an establishment for Inti and a house for his *mamaconas*. In the years which were to follow the Incas kept the *huaca* from straying by the use of *mitmacs* on the site, as is evidenced by certain near-by cemeteries which have produced quantities of pure Inca-style pottery. So important was Topa in establishing a solid pacification that folk tales of the coastal peoples soon sprang up in which he was the central figure—one of them, of some interest, stressing that after all Inti was only a somewhat subordinate brother of Pachacamac.

A totally unexpected reversal for the Inca army advancing up from the south brutally checked its progress. Seldom had the Incas met such stubborn and intelligent opposition. This was the small kingdom of Chuquimancu, comprising Cañete, the main valley, plus the two to the north, Malá and Chilca—the latter being cheek by jowl with the shrine of Pachacamac and thus a true frontier. The folk of the Cañete Valley had a martial tradition. Several fortifications scattered among their oasis pueblos near the mouth of the river attest this fact. One of these, known as Huarco, was perched on an overhang close to the Pacific and was formidable to a degree.

The Inca army succeeded in seizing the upper part of the Cañete Valley among the foothills, but were bloodily defeated under the walls of Huarco. Having by now paid his respects to Pachacamac, Topa moved south to join his commanders investing the fortress. Even though the full coastal summer was on them—sullen and deadly—Topa refused to allow any relaxation of their efforts. Eight months of futile assaults, added to the decimation of the lowland diseases, completed the Inca disaster. Topa withdrew.

This was something new in Tahuantinsuyo. Those coastal valleys which had given in without a contest, deeply amazed at this event, began to concert measures to revolt, and here and there began to fall away. Topa and the survivors of his army returned to Cuzco.

But the Huarcos in their fiery spirit had raised up an apocalyptic fury named vengeance. With that demonic presence in the ranks of the new warriors called up as levies from the length and breadth of Tahuantinsuyo, the future of the coastal people was inauspicious indeed. One of the mightiest empires of history had focused the full glare of its injured pride upon one small valley, one folk, one fortress by the sea.

Topa poured down off the highlands and back into the same area with dire threats directed against the waverers and with reprisals for those in rebellion. He knew that the stability of his own regime was tied up with the outcome of this venture. Therefore he took one of the most amazing shifts ever recorded in chronicle to ensure his success. In the canyon country behind Huarco, which he still possessed, he ordered the immediate erection, at all costs, of another Cuzco. Few decisions in history can equal this. Here, near modern Runahuana, a city sprang into being called New Cuzco, designed to be a symbolic facsimile of the sierra capital. The human misery entailed by the performance, in a limited time, of such a project staggers the imagination of the historian who would wish to recapture the fainting sighs of the past as well as its glories. It reveals—as little else does—the giantism with which the Inca soul was infected.

The ruins extend for over four square miles along the river bottom and up the precipitous slopes of the enclosing rock walls: immense storage areas, barracks, *acclahuasis*, ceremonial apartments, palaces, and an extensive plaza, recalling the dual squares of Cuzco, with even a base for an *usno* in the center. A paved road was driven back from it over the divide to hook on to the sierra road. The builders transferred intact the names of Cuzco's streets, barrios, plazas, and hills. To this new Cuzco, Topa now moved his whole government, court, servants, entertainers, and harem. Cuzco was now no more than fifteen miles away from Huarco, and the war might be pursued with dispatch and comfort. The fort of Huarco was immediately reinvested, but even so three more years were required to crush it; and in the process Topa had at least twice more to relieve his whole besieging force, for he drove them on despite depletion and disease. Come the summer heats, however, and Topa and his harem left the furnacelike canyon country and ascended into their cool native highlands. Few sieges have surpassed this one.

Four years from the beginning of hostilities, the Huarcos accepted Topa's pledges of fair treatment in return for their surrender. When the dreary files of haggard men and women emerged from the postern gate, a horrifying slaughter was begun which exterminated the leaders and the mass of the others, many being hung from the walls of their fortress to glut the gulls and condors. The fragments of human bodies left were denied burial and lay rotting where they had mercifully expired, a sign to all passers-by concerning the public intentions of Tahuantinsuyo. Extensive piles of bleached bones were still in evidence beneath the fortress in the days when Cieza rode down the coast some seventy-five years later. The impregnable citadel itself was totally remade by the Incas, who now transformed it from adobe to stone, for as masters of siegecraft they had tested it and found it worthy. It was to become an Inca stronghold second only to Sacsahuaman itself in splendor and probably superior in military advantages. Henceforth the inhabitants of the Cañete pueblos who had been spared were to be permanently subject to the cruel surveillance and bitter memories of their Inca lords. Finally as a contemptuous gesture of the casualness with which he viewed the whole affair, Topa ordered the abandonment of New Cuzco. It had served its purpose.

THE CHALLENGE FROM CHIMOR had led to astounding results. It had drawn the Inca armies by a necessary strategy up the long volcanic funnel of Ecuador. It had forced an understanding with the kingdom of Cuismancu and had faced the Incas with the higher sophistication of the coast. But once Chimor was subjugated and Cuismancu attached, the tidy mind of the Inca demanded that the remainder of the coast be included. Thus was made possible a world view, while the inevitability of Tahuantinsuyo as a life for all men could be read in the lesson of those Huarcos who to their sorrow had refused its gospel.

Topa was in the sierra when his father's life came to an end. The superb and frightening quality of Pachacuti's reign had so impressed the world that, at the mere rumor of his approaching demise, there was sensed that abeyant doom always associated with the passing of the very great. His reign was to be remembered by the humble as one during which a great bearded dragon with fangs had issued out of Pachatusan, the hill against which Cuzco slept, to wander eerily about until it plunged into a lake. And two dire comets had flared up from Mount Ausangate; Pachacuti himself was reported to have uttered the prophecy that, after him, Tahuantinsuyo might expect no more than two imperial reigns.

For years he had been building extensive pleasure areas in the lovely Yucay Valley, where, like his father before him, he repaired to take his ease. As a very special resort, however, he had erected for himself and for later sacrifices to his memory parks, baths, and a palace at Patallacta. While his *huaoqui* or spirit-twin had elsewhere its own place and service, here at Patallacta were prepared the rooms and courts where after death he could demand from his kinsmen and people the fullness of reverence. Until his latter days, however, he continued to live in Condorcancha, the palace facing on the great square of Cuzco.

His last illness found him within the rusticated walls of Patallacta. Topa Inca and his intimates were admitted to the scene, which for reasons of state was kept strictly secret. Thus caged away in his last moments and surveyed by the keen eyes of kinsmen who impatiently awaited the moment of his decease, Pachacuti is said to have sung a lament and a farewell to his own glory:

> *Like a lily in the garden was I born*
> *And thus I was created.*
> *When my age came, I grew old;*
> *And as I was to die*
> *So have I withered and so died.*

After which he turned away to die painlessly in his sleep.

《 9 》

THE MOMENT OF ACTION HAD ARRIVED—that moment always fraught with extreme danger to a monarchical state. Leaving the body with two trusted counselors, Topa and his group moved swiftly back to Cuzco and Coricancha. Surreptitiously the heads of the *ayllus* were routed out, along with the full complement of their warriors, all heavily armed. These latter guarded the entrance to Coricancha while within it Topa had himself secretly reinvested with the full regalia, the sun-god himself, through his high priest, handing it over to him. This preliminary step was extremely necessary, for without it all subsequent action might well be contested as illegitimate.

Surrounded by the excited and now vociferous warriors and priests, Topa and his party poured out of Coricancha and into Haucaypata where, as supreme head, he was elevated to the *usno. Orejones* of all factions, thus presented with a *fait accompli,* rushed back to their *canchas* to return with much of their wealth and pile it at Topa's feet. Foreigners in the city, menaced by club and spear, likewise hastened to deliver up to Topa their choicest possessions. Then, with this feverish homage accomplished, Topa allowed the news to be publicly conveyed to him that his father "rested," whereat—all things in the city now under his control—he felt free to mourn. Covering his head with his mantle, he made his pilgrimage to view the holy body of his father.

The mummy was rapidly prepared and took its honored place among the ancestors. The eyes were covered with gold film to convey the flashing vitality that had once appeared in that face, but the mummy's thin grey hair and the deep scar on the head from the blow he had received at the beginning of his reign spoke rather of his common mortality. Here in Patallacta, except for interludes with his *huaoqui,* the mummy was to remain. The palace became a *huaca* especially efficacious in guaranteeing to succeeding rulers both physical and imperial vigor.

So disappeared the most lucid, the most ambitious, receptive, and consuming mind in Inca history. Wedded as it was to the arrogance and ferocity of the ideal Inca brave, none had been able to withstand it. No known person in all pre-Columbian history ever created such a large structure as did he, and none so judiciously orchestrated the harmonies of both heaven and earth.

ELEVEN.
TOPA INCA
REBELLION AND THE SOUTH

WE HAVE PREVIOUSLY MENTIONED the fascination exerted upon the Incas by that limitless drop of montaña, jungle, and plain, which lay east of their mountain bastions. Anti was their name for it. Packed down under its perpetual canopy of haze or cloud, like a soft blanket of wool, that quiet, eerie world of raveled waters stretches farther than the eye can see. The Incas peopled it with bewitched serpents, creatures half-men–half-monkeys, beings with two faces, tribes of Amazons, and sleepy kingdoms of untold riches. These tales were not of their own spinning but were warp and woof of the mysterious montaña itself. The Incas credulously accepted the lore common then to the eastern foothills of the Andes running all the way from Colombia to Bolivia. The Spaniards later inherited this farrago of gilded speculations and embroidered them further. The great unknown is history's most prolific teller of tales.

This is why, once freed of the heavy incubus of the preceding reign, Topa looked first in that direction. Gold, glory, adventure, and women—perhaps even in that order—must have been his motives for invading the eastern jungles. His trans-Andean campaign was not dictated by preceding events but represented a bold disconnection in the whole stream of Inca history, an unprecedented luxury for the emperor in that he was not compelled to make it. That it called up, however, a whole new series of events filling most of the rest of the reign will be seen in the sequel.

At the annual festival all the governors were informed of the plan and assessed their quotas of men and goods. When finally gathered, the levy was split three ways for the Incas, as skilled mountain fighters, knew they must have manageable bodies of men in penetrating the passes and thick river country. Topa Inca himself headed the main column, giving the others to close kinsmen, Otorongo Achachi and Challco Yupanqui. The name Otorongo Achachi means "Grandfather Jaguar" and was probably given to this redoubtable warrior because of his exploits at this time. Later years were to endow him with the characteristics of a folk-hero and to see him as a jaguar-headed lord of that green and romantic montaña.

As his viceroy and governor in the city, Topa had appointed his ever dependable brother Amaru Inca. Staging his columns at Paucartambo (Colorful Lodge), he finally sortied via three passes down into the headwaters of the Amarumayo (Anaconda River), today the Madre de Dios. Each army then began its passage down the river assigned to it, their projected meeting being on the upper Amarumayo at the confluences. Though the country was previously known to the Incas, and though Topa had taken the precaution to send out advance scouts, nevertheless he was still entering an intractable land. Jungle trails—dense ambushes for disease and poisoned arrows—had to be hewn out of the undergrowth by hand for the bulk of the forces. The columns often wandered uncertain of their bearings or stifled in torrential rains, and while four villages were picked up en route, the gain was infinitesimal. The Machiganga people made elusive targets in such a tangle.

The columns finally reached the territory of Manopampa where the present Manu River joins the Madre de Dios. Though decimated they continued to struggle on, lured by a whole set of garbled reports concerning the land of the Mojos far down in the gallery forests of the Beni. These people possessed palisaded villages, wide farm lands, drainage ditches, and roadways, but supplemented their vegetable diet with the hunt. They were widely famed for their jaguar cult and erected special shrines to this deity. There is no doubt their culture was superior to their Amazonian neighbors, for it possessed many features borrowed from the sierra. Whether or not any of the depleted Inca groups succeeded in crossing the mired river country to reach the land of the Mojos we do not know, but considering its

Southern Tahuantinsuyo

distance from where the Incas first debouched into the montaña, it is improbable. Nevertheless from the fact that Mojo nobles later appeared on a friendly mission in Topa's court, we may judge that some contact was at this time established.

The situation of Inca arms down on the Madre de Dios was unenviable, and discontent soon appeared in the Colla levy. Here the Colla leader was the son of that Chuchi Capac who had been the last independent ruler of Collao before Pachacuti had destroyed both him and his rule. This wily officer now seized the opportunity to slip away unobserved and take the trail back. When he reappeared in his native land it was with the electrifying news that Topa Inca had disappeared forever in the fastnesses of Amazonia; Collao was thereby easily incited to declare her independence. And inasmuch as Pachacuti himself was just dead, this Colla *curaca* himself assumed the mighty name "Pachacuti Inca," becoming thereby the great man's avatar and the would-be assassin of his glory.

The defection was not at the time known to Topa's group in their jungle base. From a Collao aflame the news was first reported by runners back to Cuzco, whereupon Amaru Inca promptly relayed the message down to his brother in the jungle. Topa's reaction was immediate. He took half of the army with him and set out on the return journey by forced marches. The other half of the army he assigned to Otorongo Achachi with the charge of continuing the subjugation of the area down river and of returning upon its completion via the Pilcopata Pass to await further orders in Paucartambo. On no account was he to enter Cuzco ahead of his brother and sovereign. Rebellion, Topa knew, was catching—even brothers were not exempt from its contagion—and the sacred city was the greatest prize in Tahuantinsuyo.

These plans of Topa Inca's—not to let the suppression of dangerous rebellion interfere with the conquest of Amazonia—are of interest to the historian in revealing the false conception which the sierra rulers always held concerning the montaña. As for the reduced forces which remained under Otorongo, despite the loyalty and assiduous campaigning of the renowned general, they were further milked owing to the increasing seriousness of the situation in Collao. By the end of three years the entire middle Madre de Dios region had slipped from his grasp. The Paititi River had been reached only to be abandoned by the depleted columns. For a short while on its mute banks stood one of the proud monuments that marked the frontiers of Tahuantinsuyo. And then the green serpent that was the montaña arose from the slime and consumed it.

《 2 》

İT WAS OBVIOUS that great errors sown in the past had been accumulating an evil harvest. As so often in history, the reign of a great man extending too far into his senility had exacerbated or obscured problems of state. Sarmiento explicitly reminds us of this when he relates how Pachacuti, to push his grandiose building designs in the Yucay Valley, especially at Ollantaytambo, had saddled the Colla *corvée* with intolerable labor exactions, amounting to an unmitigated slavery. The venom in Pachacuti's early subjugation of the Collas will be recalled, and he may well have treated these wretched ones with special rigor. We know they were a people of whom the Incas were always particularly suspicious.

On Pachacuti's decease these toiling labor gangs broke away from their masters, streaming out over the countryside. There is no reason to doubt that this upheaval was tied in closely with the desertion of the Colla captain, for many of the fugitives seem to have made their way without opposition back to the Bolivian Altiplano. While it had been the blind obduracy of the old emperor which had created this situation, it had been encouraged by Topa Inca who had evolved the whimsical campaign on the Madre de Dios which, in turning Tahuantinsuyo's back to her enemies within, had invited the dagger of treachery.

Soon the whole of the land south of the Vilcañota watershed had fallen away from Inca rule. On his way back Topa had dispatched an urgent order to Amaru Inca for new troops, and that reliable prince had succeeded in moving some down from Chimor and Cajamarca, areas so distant that they had not as yet been affected by the poisons of disintegration coursing through the veins of empire. Though the situation was most desperate, Topa still had to move slowly, delicately combining in the right proportion pressure against the rebels with reorganization of his own sadly depleted montaña army. And to assure the aid of all the thunders of heaven, he ordered a most splendid *capacocha* to be performed back in Cuzco with rich human sacrifices—recalling a similar drastic action by the Roman Republic in the dark days of the Second Punic War.

Cuzco now faced a full confederation of disaffected peoples, led by the Colla captain Coaquiri as well as by another son of Chuchi Capac. The great *curacas* of the northern Puno had leagued together, pledging their efforts in a ceremonial cup of *chicha*, which they had then deposited under supernatural seal in one of their shrines as a sign of their determination to persist until they had thrown off the Inca yoke.

Initially all of the tribes of the northern lake basin had risen and in a blood bath had slaughtered all Inca *mitmacs* resident among them as well as all Inca officials and the garrisons of the four strategic forts in the basin. This Mithradatic horror was swiftly followed by an advance up to the headwaters of the Vilcañota. Most luckily for Topa the Canas and Canchis had held firm on this line, for otherwise his only point of entry into the valley shielding Cuzco would have been impossible.

For an appreciable time—several months at least—Topa had to be content with merely holding the line above Urcos while reinforcements were coming in and his high command was being set up. So pressing was this crisis that he could find no time to return to Cuzco, only a few miles in his rear.

We know little of the reconquest except that it took several years and was of unprecedented bitterness. After a while the Inca army was able to advance out of the Vilcañota Valley and point the engines of its ire against the walls of the *pucara* at Llallagua. The siege seems to have lasted almost three years. When the end came, the Collas summoned up their last reserves and poured out in a berserker sortie, thus completing their tale of ruin. Their leading *curaca* was snatched out of the carnage, grossly reviled, and then returned to Cuzco to await his fate at the appropriate time when he and his brother were to be skinned and made into drums for Topa's carousals. Similarly the Colla *huacas* were dragged out of their shrines, treated to unthinkable and obscene indignities, and hurled into the deep lake at Urcos, never again to reappear.

Consequent upon this disaster dissident groups in the Titicaca Basin who had been in any way associated with the Colla rebellion poured south in panic along the shores of the great lake, goaded by the specter of Inca reprisals. While Topa still had to mop up the other *pucaras* holding out in the north of the basin and to rebuild their garrisons, ultimate victory was nevertheless now certain. It does not take much imagination to feel, out of that past, the chill of terror which was creating barren deserts, starved corpses, and silent pueblos on the route ahead of his advance. Cowed by the terrible collapse of the Collas, normally their enemies, the Lupacas submitted without a serious contest. A last and futile stand of the rebel bands was made on the reedy banks of the Desaguadero River which drains the lake at its southern tip. Those who survived fled even farther south. The war was over. By the armies of Topa and Otorongo the ensuing triumph in Cuzco was sumptuously celebrated, with Mama Ocllo, Topa's *coya*, ordering brilliant fiestas of her own as a part of the general rejoicing.

Topa's reorganization of Collao, announced at a gathering of the defeated at Chucuito, involved a much more thorough occupation of the territory than previously, rearrangement of the native settlers, and the repopulation of deserted pueblos by transplanted groups, plus a new arrangement of the tribute. Only the uncouth Urus, a people numbering perhaps some 4,000 who lived isolated among the totora reeds of the lake, were exempted from the all-important obedience to the cult of the Inca gods. Collas, however, were now forever marked as untrustworthy; they were to enter Cuzco only with permission and in small isolated groups, and their numbers were to be carefully controlled at the toll gates guarding the approaches to the city. Should the count of Collas in the city be found at any one time to exceed the permitted number, they were to be instantly destroyed.

The province of Chucuito, inhabited by the Lupacas, was undoubtedly also repopulated, for we hear later of specific settlements of *mitmacs* at Pomata and Juli. In the last census ever taken under Huascar this valuable province was able to number 20,270 tributary men available for army service, not counting the Urus. Judging this to mean a total population in the last days of Tahuantinsuyo of something over 100,000, it is apparent that Topa's stern reorganization laid the groundwork for a full resuscitation of the area.

This event showed that wherever the Inca writ ran, reorganization was a pressing need. Affairs had drifted badly in the latter days of Pachacuti, and changes were long overdue. Immediately upon his breath-taking victory, therefore, Topa dispatched *visitadores* into Contisuyo and Antisuyo to feel the pulse of the people and to report on the competence of their Inca governors. A tendency had also been reported toward the assumption of a hereditary posture by the provincial *curacas* in regard to their offices, and this also had to be checked

and regulated. At this point we give, therefore, a summary view of
the Inca administration, as it was Topa Inca who informed it at this
time with whatever coherence it was eventually to display.

« 3 »

IN THE PROVINCES there were both general and special imperial
officials, each group somewhat hostile to the other. The *tocricoc* was
the regularly appointed resident governor, an Inca, with general
supervisory powers over the province. The province itself was divided
into an upper and a lower moiety (with sometimes a third), a situation designed to create and perpetuate a natural enmity among the
subject people, for the Incas had long since learned the maxim
"divide and rule." The governor's powers were potentially tyrannical
in his limited sphere—at least until the dreaded *visita*. On a call from
Cuzco he levied and dispatched troops; he confirmed in the ruler's
name a *curaca*'s nomination of his successor; as a royal favor he selected and bestowed upon the *curaca* a virgin from the *acllahuasi*; he
bore the responsibility for delivering his province's tribute to Cuzco
at the annual Capac Raymi; he had a special supervisory responsibility over the lands and herds assigned to Inti and to the emperor. He
had jurisdiction and could inflict penalties, including death.

The *micho* was the governor's lieutenant. He was stationed in the
principal pueblo of the province and kept the governor intimately
informed of every event and attitude of interest in that community.
There could be several of these officers in a large province. In conjunction with the *curaca*, he aided in the settlement of small feuds or
quarrels over landmarks or water rights; larger issues he carried up
to the governor. When an Indian died without an heir the *micho*
sequestered his property and sent an assessment of it to the governor,
who ordered what its disposition was to be. The *micho* in brief moved
fluidly from level to level, listening, eliciting possible signs of discontent or rebellion, and informing. Thus, besides being an important
executive officer on the lowest level, he was the basic spy in the all-
pervasive espionage system set up by the masters.

Being the true representative of Inca power in the province, the governor bore full responsibility. His compensation seems to have been ample. The produce or service of one per cent of the Indians in his district belonged to him as maintenance. This did not include forced labor on his *chacras* and herds in the province. For the maintenance of his dignity he went everywhere accompanied by a bodyguard of *orejones*. In theory his office was nonhereditary but exceptions are known.

Under the governor were four possible grades of native *curacas* echeloned in an artificially imposed decurial system, the institution of which is attributed to Topa Inca. Every one hundred men had a *curaca*, every five hundred, every thousand, and finally, at the peak, every ten thousand. These *curaca*-ships were generally hereditary after confirmation. The larger *curaca*-ships appear to have been passed on preferentially first to the brother, while the sons were being fully indoctrinated at the court in Cuzco in warfare, policy, or even espionage, so that the succession in the province, when they should assume it, might be reliable. From this reign onward none of these local leaders were ever again to be dignified as *sinchi*—a title reminiscent of the savage independence of pre-Inca days. Their domestication in the house of empire was complete.

Such a simplified pyramid of *curacas* allowed a rapid and logical passage downward of imperial demands as well as a sure osmosis upward of information and produce. For purposes of work control and efficient tribute distribution all natives from cradle to the grave were ordered in the twelve famous age classes, a consideration of which reveals both the contempt that was so basic an ingredient of the Inca view of the world and the clarity and rigor to which they could reduce that world.

Periodically special officials were sent out from Cuzco on circuit charged with various responsibilities. They supervised requisitions of *acllas* and other tribute, inspected the extent of land reclamation, looked into the warehousing of goods, reimposed new census counts, advised on the road *corvée*, rectified injuries, and dispensed special judgments and punishments.

They appear also to have participated in the administration of the imperial mass marriage, which otherwise belonged to the governor's sphere. In this periodic institution, decreed by the state to insure steady propagation, the *visitador* had all the nubile men and women of a pueblo (who because they had just come of age or for some other reason lacked a spouse) lined up before him in rows opposing, each age group opposite its counterpart. Then beginning with the highest ranking—*curacas* if there were any represented—he chose for them the mate he considered most appropriate to their condition. The eugenic effects of this amazing program must have been stupendous.

One of the special Inca officials was the ominous *tocoyricoc* (he who sees all). His was not a true bureaucratic function but a personal assignment from the emperor, and the token of this high commission was that, like the emperor, he rode in a litter. If he came on an errand of punishment, he wore sewn on his right shoulder a red fringe; if to perform lamentations in a time of disaster, a black fringe; and if upon an auspicious occasion, a white one. Whenever present in a province, his power overruled that of the governor. Probably all types of *visitadores* had inquisitorial duties which could make them dangerous to the governor after they had reported back, but the *tocoyricoc* was specifically an informer whose business it was to probe the zeal and loyalty of the governor. An adverse report sent to Cuzco—which naturally did not pass through the governor—produced swift and dire effects. Huaman Poma mentions the evil aura clinging around various classes of spies sent out from Cuzco, and some of this must refer to the *tocoyricoc*. These officials were thought to corrupt the emperor with their malicious or exaggerated reports, at the same time advancing their own careers behind the black weeds of delation. When one of these inspectors appeared in a province, both provincials and resident Incas there exercised the most extreme caution.

Awards of merit in the field of administration, as in that of war, could be made only by the ruler or his deputy. There existed an ascending tariff of recognitions by the state: a bag of coca and a mantle of the finest weave (*cumpi*) as a minor favor; for a greater, the diversion of the tax labor of a gang of provincials in the lower decimal system to be added to the fortunate person's income; for a ranking *curaca* who had signally proved his competence, the personal service of many Indians either as permanent field hands, herdsmen, or *yanaconas* (domestics). The award prized above all was of course a woman. Insofar as these awards went to the *curaca* class and not to the Incas, they represent simply promotions to a loftier grade in the hierarchy.

Provincial administration thus had two functions, each quite separate from the other: regulation designed for the subject peoples and espionage directed against the Incas. Two governments ran side by side: the first was bureaucratic government set up to support Inca rule; the second was the emperor's personal government designed to maintain him alone.

The links between the provinces and the central government were the four *suyus*, or quarters, of the empire. Over all the provincial governors in each one of the quarters was a prefect resident in Cuzco, who had a generalized responsibility for his area and for keeping informed about its situation. These prefects were the *apuconas*, and the inner council on which they sat was the *hunu* (junta).

Outside of the permanent secretary, one member of the council seems to have acted as president in its discussions and decisions when the emperor was away. We do not know whether he was one of the four prefects or whether he may rather have been the viceroy and governor of the city during royal absences. A curious identity in the names of the four generals selected by Topa Inca to serve under him in Collao—close kinsmen—with those of the four members of the council under Huayna Capac makes it likely that, during the dangerous minority of Huayna Capac, the council was acting as sole regent and as such was holding the empire together by collegiate effort—no mean tribute to its loyalty and efficiency. We can be sure, however, that the number four was not sacred. Certainly the council was in some way involved in that regency of seven or eight magnates which was initially to rule Tahuantinsuyo under terms of Huayna Capac's will.

We are as ill informed about this body as about any other item of Inca polity. One feels that it came into true prominence only following Topa Inca's death during the minority and finally the extended absences of Huayna Capac from the imperial city. If this is true then its role will have been vicarious, and its authority will have fluctuated with the emperor's comings and goings and his immersion in other interests. How far it could have evolved without challenging the emperor's power we do not know.

The advices, deliberations, and actions taken by this council were set before the emperor or sent on to him. Final decision—therefore true government—stood above the council in the exclusive organs of the imperial household. Herein were the ruler's personal secretary, his deputy and "second person" through whose mouth he conversed on all state occasions, his treasurer, and his major-domo or governor of the city. His eyes and ears were those special officials and agents already mentioned who ransacked Tahuantinsuyo for information and reported to him alone.

A certain event attendant upon Topa Inca's reorganization well illustrated why delation and espionage were necessary and separate arms of the state. The emperor had appointed his older brother Topa Capac to a full viceregal status to institute and supervise throughout all the provinces the changes thought necessary to produce that government described above. In return for his labors he was to remunerate himself with the services and tribute of as many Indian subjects as he saw fit. Topa Capac was an outstanding general and had long been singled out by the *coya* as her favorite brother; thus he had built up a strong faction of supporters even within the imperial household. Already he possessed vast holdings in the Four Quarters.

On his progress through the lands he abused his powers by adding outrageously to these holdings, and he succeeded in suborning the allegiance of some of the important *curacas*. Then, seizing a time when Topa Inca was absent from Cuzco, he re-entered the city with an ominously swollen retinue. Topa Inca was at the moment in Paca-ritambo celebrating the knighting ceremonies of one of his sons, Topa Ayar Manco, and it was to this place that there came to him the urgent information that, on the evidence of his arrogant demeanor, his brother was preparing to seize the rule.

No puma padding down from the heights could have exceeded in guile the stealth and swiftness of Topa's return. Treason was speedily served, and the severed head of the principal malefactor displayed. Whereupon, as was tragically usual in such cases, Topa's headsmen moved rapidly up and down the narrow streets of Cuzco to leave their mutilated memorials behind them. The purge sought out even the most remote nooks of empire; Topa Inca in person carried his vengeance out into that province which the rebel had made peculiarly his own. Here an unprecedented slaughter was let loose upon the defenseless peoples, guilty and innocent alike, which our source says was brought to an end only at the frenzied pleadings of the bereaved Mama Ocllo. Another brother, Apu Achachi (possibly the great Otorongo) took the rebel's place and carried out the uncompleted task with success and loyalty.

<< 4 >>

AN UNUSUAL AMOUNT of new law was required to support the imperial reorganization. Topa's later renown was to rest as much on this legal codification as upon his conquests. If he was not the Justinian of Tahuantinsuyo, he was at least its Theodosius. Pachacuti's work, rough hewn in many ways, received some radical alterations here, though we fail in any case to see a highly developed system. In Quechua there was no single word for "law" but only "the word of the chief," *apup simin*.

The forms of Inca justice were simple enough. Out in the provinces a native was often arraigned on the evidence of one of the confessors, a group whose ability to elicit damaging testimony was notorious. The defendant stood among his accusers, who squatted in a circle about him. If the case were of major importance the governor himself or his lieutenant heard the evidence, and when necessary they could demand more information from the *curaca*. Decision then followed swiftly. Women and very low-caste persons could not testify. As is well known, money produces great flexibility in the severity of penalties, and because Tahuantinsuyo lacked this form of economy, its punishments tended to be rigorous: torture, banishment to the mines or coca fields, hanging by the feet till dead, the dropping of a heavy rock on the culprit's back, or incarceration in Cuzco's infamous dungeons—these were the norm. In some cases first, second, and third offenses were defined.

For the Incas of Cuzco there was, on the appellate level, a special judiciary. Two panels of six judges each—representing Upper and Lower Cuzco, respectively—heard civil and criminal cases which involved members of their moeities. Either court could call upon the legal learning of a clerk who sat with them and carried in his memory and on his *quipus* and colored tablets a tariff of crimes and their punishments. These, when required to do so, he chanted in the form of a song or lay. Over these judges, one of higher rank selected such of the cases as should be brought before the emperor personally. In preparation for the important purification of the city during the Camay festival of January, these panels acted as courts of presentment, for on the last day of the old year four of the judges sat in Haucaypata—one for each of the four quarters and in a place corresponding—to decide the residue of cases which had accumulated, and by their decisions to purify the holy city from all taint of crime. The emperor himself sat enthroned in the center of the plaza, the symbol of the awesomeness and the personal quality of Inca justice.

The main feature of the tariff of punishments was the more humane treatment accorded to the Inca aristocracy. Inca magnates could receive sentence only from the ruler or the court of Twelve. When the death sentence was imposed on an Inca, he was beheaded in the square; if it were a noblewoman in question, she was not subject to public hanging, but was executed privately. This double standard of justice is of course to be expected in an empire that represents—from one point of view—the garnered loot of a favored few. Bitter memories of the excessive penalties inflicted on them were to be retained by the subject peoples long after the collapse of the empire.

We can distinguish at least five areas of imperial law in Topa's work. There was first the impossibly vast corpus of local usages all over the empire, such as that concerning irrigation rights, and these areas were left untouched except as the state acted to preserve the peace.

Then there was the law of the province which was administered by the *tocricocs*. In most cases this was set procedure and subsumed such legislation as the imposition of the Quechua tongue, native obligation to wear local costume and to remain and marry only in the pueblo, the prohibition against idleness and leisure, and the duty of taking one's place in the training ranks of the militia. It was to check on the implementation of this administrative law that the *visitadores* were sent into the provinces.

We can group together in a third category those usages and laws designed to support the monopolistic practices of the Incas. Stringent prohibitions upheld that most striking of all the monopolies, that in women. In discussing the *acllahuasi* we have seen the mechanics of the system that siphoned off the loveliest girls from every province, but the monopoly in women was in theory broader even than this as we can understand from that periodic act of grace when the emperor gave up his rights to all the women in Tahuantinsuyo and bestowed them, in mass marriages, on selected mates. From this latter property right were to spring injunctions against adultery.

No complete monopoly over all the llama herds of the empire can be proved, but the well-being of the subject peoples brought about royal ordinances prohibiting the killing of female llamas and protecting the state pastures on which grazed the wool-bearing guanacos and vicuñas.

The production of coca in the montaña was a full state monopoly, as were its use and distribution in the sierra. Just as the auriferous parts of the montaña were tapped by feeder roads, so the coca terraces and drying patios of the lower Urubamba were seemingly served by a paved Inca road, a miracle in that jungle and one expressive of the value placed on the monopoly. Topa Inca had introduced the widespread chewing of this narcotic leaf among the Incas and among the higher *curacas*. In the succeeding reign it was to become the common minor vice among the nobility, but it was still far too much a luxury item among men and gods to find its way into popular use.

The tightest monopoly was that in the precious metals. So important was the extraction industry that the Incas built some of their most imposing roads into the mining country: witness as an example that road, still partially intact, that crept over the fifteen-thousand-foot pass between Carabaya and the montaña gold fields beyond. With strong lungs and stronger nerves the traveler today may try it. We have seen that all bullion produced was drawn as by a magnet to the city of Cuzco. Once it had passed one of the four toll gates into the city, there it remained except as, under royal patent, it was dispensed for temple-building in the provinces or for the rewarding of higher nobility. Every person leaving Cuzco, subject or Inca, was searched. Immediate death followed the discovery in his effects of any unauthorized metal, whether bullion or shaped.

A fourth category concerned crimes of trespass, sex, and violence.

Included here were the expected commandments against banditry, murder, poisoning, rape, abortion, incest, sodomy and bestiality, adultery, fornication, prostitution, and procuring. By insisting that homicide was a crime against the state, Tahuantinsuyo claimed the right to punish it. This is logical when we call to mind the Inca's insistence on ruthlessly denaturing the social levels under them. The prominence of sex in the legislation is a common feature of civilizations at this level. Adultery in the ruling class was theft compounded with soilure. What could be stolen was Inca blood or lineage, which had to be preserved as the supreme monopoly, and what could be soiled was the receptacle in which Inca blood was stored. The laws against sodomy were different. Here the shocked attitude of the highland Inca in the face of the epicene practices of the coast led to severe penalties.

Lastly were the laws of treason and *lèse majesté*. Because these regulations most immediately protected the person of the emperor, they were codified with care. They covered lack of respect for the emperor or for the state cults; assumption of divine honors by individuals (this law was reissued twice in succeeding reigns); worshipping *huacas* which had been officially banned; disobedience to commands of the state, whether issued through the *curaca*, the governor, the *hatun villac* (bishop) or villac-umu (metropolitan), or through the emperor; participation in sorcery or omens aimed against the state; and conspiracy and rebellion.

This last category touched upon the most immediately sensitive spot in the Inca body politic: its psychopathic dread of those peoples it had ground down into the Andean dust. The power of a single world-vision could create an empire, but only iron vigilance and commensurate punishments could maintain it. Yet among the Incas themselves treason seems to have been a family possession. Sons and brothers, with their privileged status, their arrogant, masculine appetites, and their intimate view of the treasures of luxury and pride which belonged to the emperor, circled his effulgence with agitated wings. The periodic purges so common in Pachacuti's reign appear to have been designed to provide the laws of treason with victims—to produce exemplars, so it would seem, of the ineluctable rigor of the throne.

In the corpus of crimes against the emperor are many charged against the *huacas* or those who used the *huacas* cabalistically. Topa Inca had a reputation for hostility to the provincial *huacas*, and in the implementation of these laws he is said to have burned or destroyed a large number of them, even salting the ground whereon they stood. Certainly he tightened up the laws in this regard, hoping thereby to reduce the incidence of rebellion. On the coast Pachacamac however had always been a special case. Basically unassailable, this *huaca* was made an honored ally in heaven, not a subject.

« 5 »

BUT ANOTHER SPECIAL CASE was now about to emerge, where the usual laws governing the provincial *huacas* had no application. After its pacification, we have seen that Collao presented for Topa Inca an eminently serious problem in reorganization, for it had been this land which had concocted the witch's brew of rebellion from which most of the empire had drunk. It is no wonder that Topa's solution to the Collao problem, in terms of control of its cultus, should be exceptional.

Under the open eye of heaven at 12,500 feet lies Lake Titicaca, cobalt blue and piercingly cold. It is a treacherously beautiful body of water, whipped by waterspouts or arched with ineffable rainbows. Its northern and western shores and the adjacent countryside supported numerous Aymará-speaking communities which somehow grubbed a livelihood from the soil of this grave Altiplano. Potatoes and the hardy cereal *quinoa* were their staples. The northern part of the basin was the ancestral land of the Collas, while the entire southwestern shore belonged to their sworn enemies, the Lupacas. At the extreme southern tip of the lake the plain whereon lay the ruins of Tiahuanaco was held by the Pacasas. Across the lake and under the great peaks were less important groups.

We cannot understand Topa's actions here unless we realize the peculiar venerability which this land possessed. The pre-Inca ruins which we see today from Pucara in the north to Tiahuanaco in the south were not then in such a state of disrepair. Relics of the cults of which they were the tongue-tied witnesses must still have haunted

226

the reeds of the lake, the rocks of the shore, and the rosy snows of Illampu. Regardless of what the Pacasas may have told Topa Inca concerning their total ignorance about the builders of Tiahuanaco, we simply cannot believe that some of the patterns of their beliefs were not known to the area three hundred years later (if that is a fairly just approximation of the Tiahuanaco chronology)—however differently they may have been reinterpreted in the interim. The well-attested virility and aggressiveness of the Collas and Lupacas were not the outcome alone of poor soil and thin air—they were also the heirs of a mammoth oral tradition which Inca history finally succeeding in sweeping away.

In this pre-Inca cultic tradition the island of Titicaca (The Rock of the Cat) was the central *huaca* of regional significance; we may guess that on that rock there was venerated a male deity whose worship differed somewhat from the god on the monolithic gateway in nearby Tiahuanaco. The island itself was the Earth Mother of the Collas, while there was thought to be a heroic guardian serpent coiled about her in infinite embrace who was the personification of the waters of the lake, the fluid principle of impregnation. When the people wished to worship her, they adorned her flinty slopes with garments of *cumpi* so that her queenliness might be visually manifest. From her womb had sprung the great god who periodically appeared upon the rock as a shining cat lost in a blinding nimbus of rays. Before the time of Topa Inca, the Collas had possessed a temple on the island with a full complement of priests and priestesses of the rock. Here if anywhere were to be found the mainsprings of Colla beliefs: therefore the means for the control of these folk could best be exercised here.

Topa commandeered the holy island and incorporated its myth into Inca theology in a thoroughgoing reinterpretation. All of the original clans who had lived on the island and some who lived on the approaches to it—later called the Yunguyos—were expelled, and only a small number of sacerdotal persons were retained to pass on their cult traditions to the incoming Inca incumbents. Topa poured *mitmacs* into the area, settling most of them in the provincial capital of Copacabana close by. We are told that these settlers represented forty-two nations gathered from the highland areas ranging from northern Ecuador to southern Bolivia; thus they were consciously intended to be a microcosm of Tahuantinsuyo. Along with the natives left, it was an unhappy and unwieldy population, except for the pure-blooded Incas. It was broken into the usual two moieties, upper and lower, with the added third of the brutish and incoherent Urus. The governor appointed was a grandson of Viracocha Inca, Apu Inca Sucso (Discolored Chief Inca), a tested officer. In later days his descendants were still rooted here where they seem to have strongly absorbed the underlying separatism of the area, as witness the common cause they made later with the Spaniards against Manco Inca.

Copacabana, newly elevated to the status of provincial capital, was the gateway to the sacred island and possessed only a slightly lesser holiness, even in pre-Inca days. This aura of *huaca* permeating the region was if anything to increase under the Spaniards, for here, under the rock where victims and rebels were formerly destroyed, resides the Virgin of Copacabana, the most efficacious saint in all highland South America. This Virgin stepped into the place of an Aymará Earth Mother who had been manifest in the gray rock of Copacabana. She is more gracious now, but her children seem no different.

A curious tale was told intending to make more palatable Topa Inca's theft and reinterpretation of the cult of the island. The high priest of Titicaca, a Colla sage, once made the uncomfortable journey to Cuzco to convince Topa Inca to take the site under his protection. Stressing the antiquity of the cult and its miracles, he finally revealed that it had in actuality been Inti, the paternal *huaca* of the Incas, who had been the one to emerge so effulgently from the rock in ancient times. Naturally Topa was eager to go to this newly discovered Jerusalem, this Trojan homeland, and do it reverence, but his captains, hearing of his desire through the usual grapevine in the royal seraglio, tried vigorously to dissuade him. Their reasons were his pressing imperial and reorganizational commitments elsewhere. But Topa was a master of diplomacy and won them over.

This anecdote carried of course the official line. Yet by probing we may discover some gleanings. In it there is suggested that the Incas were merely taking up another's burdens, that there was in reality nothing ruthless or dispossessive about Topa's actions, because the Collas wished it so, even initiating the action themselves. Another point made was that thereafter no one was ever to mention the shining cat of the Aymarás as the god whom the rock gave up—rather it was to be Inti. Because of this the Inca ruler's proprietary rights to the island through Manco Capac of Pacaritambo could not come into question, for Inti had been his father. Topa's wisdom in teaching the reluctant magnates in the story the necessity of this crusade was added as an official imprimatur. The prestige and venerability of the site was transferred lock, stock, and barrel to the Incas by means of this tale, and its former deities were forever erased or recast in favor of the Inca theology.

We have no corresponding license, however, to insist that Topa was insincere in all this. He may have considered this something like a second beginning of Inca history, a re-creation in fact. We have already mentioned that about this time he gave to one of his sons the name Topa Ayar Manco, the name of the first ancestor, and that in his entourage was another son named Sinchi Roca after the second.

« 6 »

HAVING ASCERTAINED THE GENERAL LIMITS of this rape of heaven, there remains to delineate its details which clearly display the cere-monial imagination of the ruling line. The reformed Titicaca cult now possessed the full Inca pantheon, including Viracocha, Inti, the Illapa trinity, and the Great Mother of the Incas.

With this latter deity we come to the heart of Topa's reformula-tion. The Aymarás had conceived the island of Titicaca as the chthonic and parturient Great Mother. Topa moved this concept of female-ness to Coati, a smaller island some four miles down the lake, and recast the rock of Titicaca in the masculine gender, more congenial to the warrior's spirit. Thus Titicaca could become Inti, while Coati was his Inca consort Mama Quilla, Moon Woman and mother of the Incas. Nevertheless a confusion always persisted in the popular understanding, for some said that Titicaca was the true mother of the Incas. Surviving shamans today on the island (who do not, how-ever, represent a continuous oral tradition) state that the mother rock out of which the Incas emerged was not named Titicaca but rather Mama Ocllo.

Topa arranged for the bodily union of the two islands, god and goddess. On the lesser island resided, at least for ceremonial occasions, that Inca *ñusta* chosen to be the high priestess and earthly vessel of the Mother. Here was erected an arabesque two-storied temple of Mama Quilla fronting on a view across the lake whose sweep and majesty defy description. Within was placed that precious statue of the goddess given by Topa—a female figure with the lower parts of gold and the breasts of silver. Periodically at each new moon Inti sent the goddess his invitation to a *taqui* or orgiastic *chicha*-drinking. Then the priestess as the impersonator of shining Moon Woman ordered her *mamaconas* and retainers into their decorated balsa barks beached in the coves for the slow coasting up the glassy lake to Inti's island. On disembarking it was her theatrical role to greet and caress the priest of Inti, requesting him with all the cajolery and blandishments of a wife to pour forth his fertilizing beams over the land, banishing frowns from his broad and healthy face and continuing the ruling Inca in length of years and contentment. When her women had poured out of their jars enough *chicha*, he would finally indulge in expansive assurances and thus the dramatic dialogue was closed, though the fiesta and the license that went with it continued. These visits could be returned, with Inti's fleet dimpling the reflecting waters in the reverse direction.

The role of Mama Quilla in this cult drama is of interest. In this lunar form of hers the Great Mother is an intercessor, a pleader for mercies to be showered on Tahuantinsuyo. The corollary is that Inti is conceived as whimsical, somewhat irresponsible, animistic in short —an all-powerful actor god without a pattern of action. Mama Quilla on the contrary shows the way dimly to a divine law: that of continual mercies and benefits for the Incas and their lesser subjects, and of a *consistency* in these things. This is the aspect of religion which one begins to find generally at this level of civilization, but it is well to point it out in the case of the Incas.

When the priests of Inti brought out the high priestess for the people of Copacabana to behold, splendidly robed and glittering with silver medallions, her jet-black braids adorned with luxury and crowned with a diadem—at that moment she was very little different from her mild, saintly, and equally rich sister of today, the Virgin of

Copacabana. The Inca concept of Mama Quilla may indeed stand midway between the uncouth Aymará Mother and that Augustinian Mary whose first holy image was carved some forty-five years after the conquest by a Copacabana Indian. These are speculations; whether or not they truly clarify the present, they plainly indicate the past.

In pursuance of his policy of claiming this holy land for Inti, Topa worked to expand it as a pilgrimage center vast enough to outrank Pachacamac's demesne on the coast. People who wished to acquire merit and embassies dispatched to consult its oracle were soon to come from the most distant parts of the empire to behold the miracle in the waters—even as they do today who wish to bask in Mary's compassion, and as they did before the time of Tahuantinsuyo. An important incidental increment to the Incas from this pilgrimage was the forced collection of intelligence from all areas of the empire by means of the rigorous confessional established on the approaches to Titicaca.

The pilgrim normally reached the peninsular area down the road skirting the west side of the lake, with the lunar landscape of Puno, sullen, abraided, and unsmiling on his right, the reedy shores on his left. Loutish Uru Indians and squabbling grebes fished together in these thick canes rooted in the icy mud below. The view over the lake was vast, backed only by the bright snowfields of the eastern Andes. At the narrowest point of the isthmus, beyond which was the holy land populated with Incas and Quechua-speaking *mitmacs*, was a wall and a guard station where the pilgrim underwent his preliminary check. Attached was a confessional where fasting or self-mortification delayed the pilgrim. Farther down the cliffside road and sunning itself on one of the few genial bays along the lake was the crowded pueblo of Copacabana, an Inca provincial capital equipped with all appropriate buildings. The environs of the site had been planted with parks of alder trees, and in one of them was the Inca temple fronting a square named of course Haucaypata so that the gods might feel at home. Most unusually, this temple had five doors which might possibly—analogous to the three doors of the Catholic cathedral—represent the portals reserved for each of the *huacas* who had rights within. Mama Quilla, however, had a special shrine apart from this greater Inca pantheon. Two thousand specially selected *mitmacs* settled near by paid their tribute to the empire in personal service at the two great island *huacas* and that of Copacabana. No Colla Indians were allowed in the vicinity.

Copacabana was the second station on this *Via Crucis*. There was a *corpahuasi* (guesthouse) here for the traveler's relief, and here again he confessed, worshipping for a day or two at the doorway of Topa's palace which was fronted with four efficacious stone *huacas*, two pumas and two condors. After this the pilgrim moved on.

The road swung on past the pleasant bay heading north and west, finally to move out along that narrow finger of land that pointed toward the insular god. Another settlement of *mitmacs* was passed on this neck before the pilgrim came down to the point of embarkation, from which he could look across the narrow channel to Titicaca, greener then with occasional alder and *molle* parks which Topa had encouraged in the folds and recesses of the island.

Ferried across in a balsa, the pilgrim ascended the path that led past bucolic terraces and down the sparsely grassed spine to the island's farther end, seven miles out. From this island roof the pilgrim could sweep the entire horizon with his gaze. Over there was lordly Illampu, a king of the Andes, dozing in the turquoise air with a court of lesser but still majestic peaks around him, and below him lay the lake patched with darker islands. The shore waters directly under the pilgrim's feet were clothed, in the shallow places, with totora thickets clamorous with cormorants, herons, wild geese, flamingos, and divers; in the racing winds above glided the gray eagle and an occasional condor. For the gods this island bloomed like a garden.

Nearing the end, the pilgrim came to Intipuncu (Sun Gate), which marked off the area of dangerous *huaca* from the rest of the sacred island. It was at this spot that Topa Inca, master of half the world, had humbly descended from his litter and, unshod, had moved into the divine presences. This famous entry was itself trinitarian, being composed of three portals, no doubt one for each of the three Inca gods worshipped there, Sun, Thunder, and Lightning. At each gate the pilgrim confessed again. Thus these three final stages of examination and penitential purification assured the *huacas* that no uncleanness whatsoever could enter the arcane paradise where they disported themselves. The first gate was Pumapuncu (Lion Gate). Kentipuncu was next, adorned with feathered hangings made from the breast of the hummingbird, from which little creature it took its name. Lastly was Pillcopunco, similarly adorned with the rich feathers of the iridescent bird of the montaña, the *pillco*.

Close to Intipuncu but within the *temenos* the priests and *mamaconas* had their dwellings. They were charged with accepting gifts from the pilgrims, without which no approach to the *huacas* was allowed. This inner area overlooked a subdued cove, where there was a quiet alder park and well-constructed baths fed by a small spring. Here the god bathed alone with his favorite women whenever the whim took him. Inti's wealth, garnered at the gate, was stored in a large complex of storerooms whose tumbled ruins are called today the Chingana (Labyrinth).

The holy of holies was the rock itself, a sandstone outcrop fissured and vertical on one face, standing some twenty-five feet high. It was otherwise unpretentious. A level space stood before it, around two sides of which were built the masonry shrines or houses of the gods. The inner wall of one of the shallow natural cavities in the lower part of the rock was plated in gold, and a resplendent *chicha* basin and offering stone fronted it. This was the golden womb of the Earth Mother from which she had produced the Sun. Every new moon four or five unblemished virgins, male or female, were sacrificed here and their bodies crammed into the crannies of the rock or buried round about.

Here, if anywhere, Tahuantinsuyo could behold its *pacarina*. Pacaritambo was after all only the place of origination of the Inca folk and had no meaning to others in the empire. The sun who shone or raged alternately across every land of the empire had from this spot first launched forth his laughing light. This Calypso island, so enchantingly locked in its icy sea, had at one time trembled in iron parturition to bring this god forth. This portentous event was here annually celebrated with especially theatrical splendor. Leaping bonfires were built on the higher scarps of Titicaca, repeating the light of that first birth, and from the many islands in the lake far and near, other fires sprang up under the night sky in a most holy antiphony of sparkling lights.

《 7 》

VICTORY OVER THE COLLAS was richly acclaimed in Cuzco, while the imperial reorganization, with the new Titicaca policy as its sanction, rumbled ahead. It must have been with some amazement that Topa Inca accepted the full implications of his victory. The new cult lay on a dangerously exposed border; beyond were the Colla *émigrés* certain to be stirring up trouble among the Charcas to the south. It was obvious that the conquest of the entire Bolivian Antiplano would never be as easy now. Furthermore the cult could be adequately protected only by another advance of empire.

So we shortly thereafter see Topa with an army of perhaps twenty thousand poised in this area. They passed through the ruins of Tiahuanaco, which the emperor visited with as little enlightenment as the modern researcher, and the army was then broken into three southward-oriented corps, each having a specific assignment, one to advance on the east, one in the west, and one down the center—thus recalling, though in reverse direction, the triple journey of Viracocha in myth. These campaigns were as much a gigantic metal-prospecting as they were advances of conquest and bringers of an Inca civilization. Certainly the vast provinces they joined to the empire never added appreciable contingents of men to future Inca armies, nor are Quechua-speaking *mitmacs* prominently reported in the areas. The story is little known and therefore soon told.

Cutting easily through the Pacasa people south of the lake, Topa drove headlong into the Charcas, semicivilized and hardy dwellers of the plateau clustered about the flanks of the Cordillera Central. The siege of one particularly resistant knot of Charcas was memorable because of the stratagem used by Topa to wedge open the gates of their *pucara*. Under its walls and just out of slingshot every night a portion of the Inca army was ordered to indulge in open and extravagant orgies, displaying every form of excess known, whether of eating, drinking, or sexual abandon. The effects of this aphrodisiac warfare on the short-rationed guards defending the walls may easily be imagined.

Sizable Inca columns from this center corps probably penetrated below the territory of the Chicha Indians. The important pueblo of Tucumán, some six hundred miles south of this general area, was impressed enough by the Inca advance to send gifts to the emperor, but we have the impression that Inca arms represented to it not a present cataclysm but only a distant threat which would soon disappear. Topa did however appoint a resident commissioner to the Argentine pueblo, dispatching him to his new post with some *mitmacs* in his train, no doubt all garrison troops. We do not hear of them again.

The center corps ransacked the Altiplano for metals, locating rich deposits in the Porco mines of the Cordillera de los Frailes. That the Incas were unerring in their ability to ferret out the metallic secrets of Mother Earth is quite evident in this passage for not far away was to spring up some time later the fabulous Spanish city of Potosí, built at the foot of a mountain of silver. The opening of these silver lodes by the Incas and the immediate introduction of Lupaca Indians to mine them helped to provide the greatly increased luxury of the succeeding reign.

The montaña venture was a disaster. Previous scouting had warned of the difficulties to be expected. Nevertheless some ten thousand warriors, half of them *orejones*, were sent out below the "eyebrow" of the montaña. Two heartbreaking years down there eventuated only in constant calls for reinforcements and supplies, but it proved difficult to get these relief parties through to their objectives. The main body had meanwhile met one of the cannibalistic Guaraní groups known as the Chiriguanas. These Indans had for some time been pressing in through Amazonia toward the Andean massif, moved by an uncanny urge to seek out a hypothetical Eden, a spiritual homeland, the so-called Land of the Grandfather. From this time on contacts were to become more frequent between Incas and invading Chiriguanas, and one of them was to be prophetic of final disaster.

The western or Chilean campaign carried Inca arms to its last frontier along the far shores of the South Pacific. Topa himself did not accompany this advance, which had been preceded by Inca spies penetrating as far south as Copiapó; instead he appointed his son Sinchi Roca as commander and placed under him ten thousand warriors. These were broken into a vanguard and a supporting column for more unimpeded movement. Ahead of them lay the Atacama, a land of volcano, high desert, and salt swales. The usual logistical skills of the Incas proved able to drive the spearhead through and down to Copiapó, where it was stalled by attacks from the Diaguita Indians. Not until succored by the second regiment could it continue the advance. At Coquimbo the rocky road south turns out to the coast. This was the strategic key to the great Central Valley that lay beyond, and here the joined armies were forced to fight again. When they were finally able to move on they left the point strongly garrisoned. This was indeed no easy campaign; Garcilaso says that from beginning to end it took six years and called for incessant reinjections of men—in all, using up fifty thousand men. Almost certainly he lumps it in with the entire Charcas and montaña advances in arriving at such high figures, but the fact remains that it was costly.

The Central Valley belonged to the heroic Araucanians, most noble of all the adversaries met later by the Spaniards. Movement through their northern tribes was relatively easy, and some Inca influence may have been effected here in the years to come. But when the Inca armies, now much attenuated, had ground on farther down past stately Aconcagua, the most princely crest of the southern Andes, and past the site of the Spanish capital-to-be, Santiago, they arrived at their end, the Maule River. Here was precipitated a fierce three-day battle which the Incas were unable to sustain, and they drew back from the area to consolidate as well as their limited strength would allow. The line of the Maule is commonly stated to have been the southern frontier of Tahuantinsuyo, but effective rule—which meant the extraction of gold from the natives as tribute—could have been felt only well to the north of this. Coquimbo was probably the last garrison town of consequence, though outposts or factories surely existed in the Santiago area.

Thus in a matter of some forty or forty-five years the empire of Tahuantinsuyo had been created, an Andean colossus whose head rested among the fiery volcanoes of Ecuador and whose austral feet were cooled in the flowing streams of Aconcagua.

THE LAST ACT IN TOPA'S REIGN was an august progress through the empire. Here, in a sense, he was his last great *visitador*, reviewing with his own eyes the effects of his reorganization, noting and punishing derelictions and insufficiency. For four autumnal years he, along with his court and harem, poured in cluttered splendor over the roads of Tahuantinsuyo, campaigning a bit perhaps among the always difficult Chachapoyas, and reaching as far north as Quito, which had recently—incited by the Colla example—revolted. In the flourishing northern capital of Tumibamba was born to him the legitimate prince who was to succeed him as emperor.

Because it produced no startling or warlike deeds, being simply a grand concourse, history is reticent about the details of this royal progress, but because it was Topa's final expression of imperial responsibility it is worthy of mention. He could now rest assured that the system which he and his father had created was working adequately. His grandfather had dreamed of that imperial home. His father had been its architect. He had been its contractor. His son would have the pleasure of simply inhabiting it. It was not to be until the fifth generation that the heirs should fall to quarreling over title to it, and in the quarreling leave the door unbarred to trespassers.

Like his father Topa devoted the remainder of his rule to the completion of many luxurious building projects already instituted and undertaking new ones. Palaces begun by Pachacuti in Ollantaytambo were enlarged or completed among others in the Yucay country. But of all his monuments the most grandiose was Sacsahuaman, for he now carried it vigorously forward to completion.

In 1493, the year when Columbus sailed back to Spain to report to Isabella his discovery of the fringes of Cathay, the emperor Topa Inca was taken ill and died. His labors and constant cares, especially the Collao problem, had worn him out physically. At the time of his death he was residing in one of his favorite retreats just outside Cuzco, the great villa complex of Chinchero, thick walled and stepped with noble terracing. Few historic places out of Inca history touch one as intimately as this does. It is located at an altitude higher by over a thousand feet than Cuzco. The air is appreciably thinner and the visitor, when he looks up from the past at his feet, feels himself placed as it were along the rolling roof of the world, for out beyond the llama pastures of the ancient kings which stretch bleakly over the *punas* there is only the jeweled horizon sparkling with the snows of Verónica, Salcantay, and Soray.

Topa's mummy took its place in the ancestral retinue. It was to be deliberately burned by his illegitimate grandson Atahualpa some forty years later.

TWELVE.
HUAYNA CAPAC
ABSENTEE EMPEROR

《 I 》

Out of the Oriental involutions of court life under Topa Inca there comes a tale illustrating the dangers which would face the new heir.

Topa Inca had possessed a concubine, striking to look on, whom he loved ardently and too openly. To their son he transferred much of his affection. On all state occasions mother and son were to be seen with him, thereby providing a ready shield behind which any faction intent upon exploring the fierce precipices of power might advance. The party of legitimacy, centering in the Council, naturally opposed the emperor when he wished to endow the young prince with an important governorship, that of Urcosuyo. To achieve his purpose, therefore, Topa had to resort to deception; he celebrated a great *chicha*-drinking where, in the unrestrained gambling which ensued, he managed to lose that very province in a wager with the prince.

This is indicative. With the empire now almost fully formed, Cuzco was rocked by violent palace storms. And it was always possible that when a king died the windbreaks erected against these gusts blew down. This was now to happen.

The name of the prince who succeeded was Tito Cusi Hualpa, but history then and now called him by his coronation name, Huayna

Capac (Young Ruler). His mother Mama Ocllo had borne him in Tumibamba, the second of two legitimate princes. His elder brother was Auqui Topa Inca (Princely Royal Inca), a person of solid dependability; at least seventy bastard half-brothers completed the roster of his close kinsmen. Huayna Capac seems to have been about five years of age as the events of this chapter begin.

Among the harem intrigues in the latter days of Topa's reign, none smoldered as insidiously as that centering about the then favorite concubine, Chiqui Ocllo (Pure Parakeet), whose little son Capac Huari was to become the pawn in a most devious game. There seems no reason to doubt that Topa Inca intended legitimacy to prevail in his succession, but the proverbial spy was hovering beside him as he lay within the close walls of Chinchero approaching his end. Timing it carefully, a kinswoman of Chiqui Ocllo slipped away and sped toward Cuzco with the certain tidings of the royal demise which would send the conspirators into action. Manufactured rumors promptly flooded the city, and in the initial paralysis of action, neither the party of legitimacy nor the party of the bastard was able to secure the necessary advantage. The latter group had spread the story that the emperor on his deathbed specifically nominated the son of Chiqui Ocllo as his successor, and it was not until a countervailing rumor was put out to the effect that Chiqui Ocllo was a witch and had poisoned the emperor that the deadlock could be broken. The legitimate party thereupon seized the decisive moment. The offending Chiqui Ocllo and her kinswoman were done away with—no doubt with all the refinements of cruelty—and their support fell into sudden ruin. For some unknown reason, the focus of the whole conspiracy, the young Capac Huari, was suffered to live. Instead of being clubbed to death, he was exiled to Chinchero apparently to serve out alone a menial life, a living embodiment of the sin committed against the great man, his father, who had died there and whose shade brooded like the skimming cloud shadows over its terraces and open places.

《 2 》

MAMA OCLLO, THE QUEEN MOTHER, had played a stellar role in these events, for it had been she who had turned the tide in favor of the party supporting her. Though she was to die shortly after this, her son never forgot that he owed the throne to her, and he soon decreed to her memory and her cult exceptional honors. Her villa on Picchu (Sparrow) was declared a *huaca*, which was all the more easily venerated by the people in that she merged, via identity of names, into the mythical mother of all the Incas and indeed a form of the Great Mother.

Huaman Poma depicts her as a dumpy figure, jealous of her great husband and "desirous for wealth." More than the average *coya* her stratagems were feared and admired and her influence was long remembered. One court tale of her youth, relating to the conquest of the northern stretches of Chimor, tells how Topa Inca had once dispatched a brother of his to require the submission of one of the princely coastal cities (probably Tumbez) ruled by a woman. When the report of his embassy's costly failure reached him, Topa took the matter jokingly for nothing was allowed to disturb the royal aplomb; nevertheless it was a serious reverse. Hereupon Mama Ocllo offered to subdue the *capullana* without loss of a single warrior. Allowed to indulge herself in this whim, she returned the embassy with the message to the *capullana* that she could now consider herself and her realm safe from further attack, for her courage had won the day. A request was added that the bearer of that happy news be accorded a good-will boon, a thanksgiving fete to the *huacas* of the sea to be offered by the *capullana*'s city. When the city was festively afloat in its balsas well beyond the gray breakers of the Pacific, the Inca warriors broke from their concealment in the hills and stormed in. The *capullana* became the personal captive of Mama Ocllo.

The passing away of this queen so soon after the death of her husband marks a watershed in the history of Tahuantinsuyo. Bereft thus young of parental care, the prince was put under the protection of a regent named Hualpaya, a cousin of his father. The choice to fill this delicate post is curious, if there is any truth in the report that he was a son of that brilliant and restless Capac Yupanqui executed some years before by Pachacuti for insubordination.

A long-range conspiracy was evolved to substitute the regent's own son for the legitimate prince at the time of his formal accession and coronation, and to this end certain of the provinces north and west of

Cuzco were suborned of their loyalty. But the regent had failed to reckon with the narrow-eyed vigilance of the imperial Council. The prefect of Chinchaysuyo represented on that body was Huaman Achachi, the boy prince's uncle. This tough servant of the state had been for some time receiving intelligence of a disturbing nature from his quarter of the empire, and he finally laid his suspicions before that body. Soon after, the discovery of supporting evidence completed the picture. Certain bags of dried coca leaves, just up from the montaña and on their way via the Royal Road to Cuzco, had been inadvertently opened at the Inca way station, Limatambo. Hidden among the densely packed leaves were weapons to be smuggled past the check points of the city into the hands of Hualpaya's partisans. The *curacas* who were bringing this deadly freight into Cuzco were immediately put to the torture in Limatambo by the agents of the Council and confessed their part in the plot.

Hualpaya became aware of these happenings on the approaches of the city and was thereby forced by such premature disclosure to move swiftly into action. It is a matter of interest to the historian that this man, able to make single and unopposed decisions and enjoying almost supreme power, should have been in the end overwhelmed by the collegiate principle of the old *ayllus*—a testimony to the cohesiveness of the Inca clans even under extremes of stress.

The boy Huayna Capac was at the moment rusticating in near-by Quispicancha (Crystal Enclosure), where a prolonged *chicha*-drinking was taking place. Two parties, rebels and loyalists, raced down the Huatanay Valley to secure possession of his person. The warriors selected as the prince's bodyguard had only enough warning of the approach of danger to push him to momentary safety through a window, whereupon, uttering their hoarse shouts of war, they turned to defend themselves and their charge to the death. But Huaman Achachi arrived at that moment with five hundred *orejones* loyal to the throne, and the prince was snatched from immediate danger. The last act, however, had to be played out in Cuzco, where Hualpaya had remained to guide events. Encouraged by the addition of new loyalist forces, Huaman Achachi's men, with the prince heavily guarded in their midst and displaying in their van the awe-inspiring imperial standard, bore down upon the *cancha* of the regent, formerly the dwelling compound in Cuzco of his notorious father Capac Yupanqui. Realizing his failure too late, Hualpaya appeared framed within the narrow stone portal for one breathless instant before the standard, which he had staked his life to gain, moved in upon him and forced him back. Then began inside these walls the bloody, methodical work of torture, extraction of information, mutilation, and finally death, ignoble and sans rites—save such as the dogs gave. All the adherents to the conspiracy were tracked down and along with their leader disposed of.

« 3 »

THE DRASTIC NATURE of these events made it imperative that Huayna Capac, though a boy, assume the rule immediately. As his counselor and coadjutor in government he designated his distinguished elder brother. The coronation followed the usual pattern, an integral part of the ceremony being the royal nuptials between the new emperor and his legitimate sister Cusi Rimay (Good Luck Speaker). Nuggets of gold, good auguries, were strewn along the streets the new pair would take, while the *cancha* walls of the city were hung with glowing textiles and arras of hummingbird feathers. The prince emerged from the palace of Pachacuti while his bride-to-be and her entourage debouched from that of Topa Inca across the great square, each borne in the state litter belonging to the respective royal *panaca*. A sedate press of dignitaries pushed silently along the narrow street that led to Coricancha, where the high priest bound golden sandals on the feet of the royal couple and invested the prince with the imperial regalia.

Thus began Tahuantinsuyo's most elegant reign. Folk memory spoke of this emperor as the possessor of untold wealth, riding in priceless litters, and endowed with a splendid and gargantuan capacity for *chicha*, though never drunk. He was somewhat short in stature, thick-set, grave, and of an unchanging countenance. In accord with the dignity of his office, he spoke little and sententiously. It was he who brought to its peak that Byzantine tendency to surround the royal power with a nimbus of remoteness and luxury. We can well believe the report that he was to become prey to the lies and intrigues of the saccarine time-servers who settled like flies thickly upon him.

In the court and harem the atmosphere was stifling, shifting and humid with danger—the unwary might awaken to find too late the braided sling of some Peruvian Sejanus already tightened about their throats.

Consonant with this was a move in the direction of divinizing the reigning emperor. While still young Huayna Capac had specifically degraded the office of high priest, creating over it a Caesaro-papist office called the Shepherd of the Sun which he himself filled. The implications of this are unclear, but it was probably the source of that claim found in our sources that he was on a more divine plane than any of the emperors who had preceded him. How far this dogma of the divine king on earth was pushed, we cannot say; we are permitted to feel that it did not go all the way when we call to mind the later mutiny of the Inca *orejones*.

The pace with which events had moved in the first perilous days of the new reign had not allowed the full obsequies to be celebrated for Topa Inca and his more recently deceased *coya*, Mama Ocllo. Customarily these ceremonial lamentations demanded pilgrimages to the spots once frequented or conquered by the great ancestor. Consequently a grandiose imperial mourning was now ordered. In Cuzco many human lives were sacrificed to the dead and the suttee performed by such of the loyal retainers and women left as desired that special form of immortality. *Chasquis* carried the message everywhere into the empire to institute similar sacrifices. This mourning lasted a whole year, during which time Indian women of many tribes cut their braids and wore about their hips the grass skirt or girdle traditional for female keening. That the two deceased spirits might accrue further merit, the royal pardon emptied the prisons while alms over and above the dole were distributed to the lowly of Cuzco. Images of Topa Inca and Mama Ocllo, charged with their *huaca*, were made accessible in public places for the people to worship. And if Huayna Capac is to be considered as claiming partial divinity, this excessive apotheosis of the parental spirits was certainly a corollary to it and indeed a necessity.

While in Cuzco, Huayna Capac had been residing in a temporary palace, probably the great *cancha* of Pachacuti. When he set forth on his pilgrimage he left Sinchi Roca, that older illegitimate brother who had handled his father's Chilean campaign, as governor of the city, and he charged him with the construction of his own palace there. Then with a funereal pace and to the accompaniment of the shrieks of the women who lined the route, the royal procession moved away at last toward Cajamarca. Here the young emperor dutifully visited the spots memorialized by his parents, fasted in filial silence, mourned the lost presences, and then returned. On his return he installed himself in the *cancha* completed for him on Haucaypata and ordered a year of festival and merrymaking to replace the preceding gloom. His more intimate pleasures, however, were taken in the Yucay Valley, where his brother had additionally carried on an extensive and ingenious building campaign for his delectation; this included the slabbing and straightening of the Vilcañota River which can still be seen today at Pisac.

So began Huayna Capac's early adolescence, and for several years we now find him dividing his time among the surrounding pleasure spots.

The *coya* Cusi Rimay had by now produced her one and only son, Ninan Cuyochi (Fire Shaker). Traditionally therefore this prince, though only about ten years younger than his father, was the legitimate heir. But there seems to have been some flaw in his claim which we cannot precisely assess.

A second son, Atahualpa, had been born to the adolescent emperor near the turn of the century. His mother, a noble girl of one of the Lower Cuzco *panacas*, Tocto Coca (Tender Coca) by name, was shortly to die. Both of these sons were specially favored and were to accompany the emperor in his later campaign to the north, where they would acquire the arts of war.

A third son, born in this studding period, first saw the light of day among the orderly villas above the sapphire waters of Lake Lucre. History was to know him as Huascar; his mother was not the *coya*, but a younger full sister, Rahua Ocllo. The uncertainty which surrounded Ninan Cuyochi's claim may perhaps be invoked here to explain the celebration, which is reputed to have taken place some time later, of the event of Huascar's birth, as if indeed this latter were already considered to be the true infante. On the highland rim of hills over Cuzco, there was an ancient *huaca* of the Incas today called

Kenko which, with its piercing, expectant monolith and its hollowed adjoining rock, can only be an evocation in stone of such overpowering genesis as the Earth controls and dispenses. The whole area of these curious formations was enclosed theatrically in a semicircle of splendid masonry cut with niches, and in it was held that convocation of gods and tribal magnates who published the birth of Huascar. All three of the princes we have mentioned above were later to inherit, wear, or usurp the imperial fringe.

In view of Huayna Capac's alarmingly precocious activity—as is evidenced by this full quiver of sons already produced as he himself was in his early adolescence—it is not hard to understand a new danger to which the state, floating almost rudderless across these Halcyon seas of peace and indolence, was now subjected. This was the tendency for the magnates to surreptitiously aggrandize power during the youth of the emperor, allowing old alignments in Cuzco society to harden into cabals and new ones to arise. We will catch faint echoes of these things as we move along in the reign. Heretofore emperors had come to power fully able and matured.

《 4 》

BY THE TIME the emperor was approaching twenty it was considered desirable to institute a complete survey of Tahuantinsuyo. Twelve or more years of inaction had intervened since Topa's death, and in that time the hinges and locks of the empire were admitted to have sprung and grown rusty. Accordingly Huaman Achachi, elder statesman and war leader, was designated to make a viceregal progress north as far as Quito, while his nephew the emperor carried his progress simultaneously into the Collao area. Both were to take the *residencias* of the various governors and *curacas*, remove or punish them where fitting, and order works for which the need had become evident. A review of what the emperor found wanting on his southern progress is of interest as providing evidence of the state of the empire's health.

First of all he poured more *mitmacs* into the Cochabamba (Lake Valley) area, rearranging and strengthening the provincial boundaries in this eastern Bolivian fringe. He forced the Charcas and other tribes to submit to more stringent ordinances regarding the production of silver bullion from the mines as well as gold from the montaña washing fields. These actions plainly stem from two allied policies: the need to expand the production of precious metals on the Altiplano, and to build a correspondingly strong protective screen between that area and its Amazonian outlands. To further this latter end a punitive expedition was sent down against the raiding and cannibalistic Chiriguanas, for it is probable that by this time their increasing activity had cut those gossamer ties which bound Tucumán into the empire. In Chile an administrative reorganization was similarly ordered.

As his father had done, Huayna Capac performed his obeisances to the *huacas* of Tiahuanaco and Titicaca. The latter indeed was moved up a notch in the hierarchy of imperial shrines when the emperor appointed one of his own daughters to become there the resident high priestess and earthly consort of Inti. To enrich her power he ordered a new establishment for her *mamaconas* to be built on the island of Coati. In other ways also he attempted to expand the Inca religion in the Titicaca area, even designating other islands in the lake as official *huacas*.

But now there came disquieting news. The *visita* of Huaman Achachi had been incontinently halted by a general uprising in Ecuador and northern Peru. This was the evil in the north against which too late Tahuantinsuyo had instituted inquiry and search. It was the empire's good luck that Collao and the lands south were patched and mended in time to utilize them in the desperate struggle ahead.

Huayna Capac summoned a solemn parley of Colla and Lupaca *curacas* at Chucuito on the shores of the lake and informed them of the massive contribution they would have to make to imperial defense, spicing the undesirable news with the possibilities of fabulous rewards in loot and women. They must have known nevertheless what his decision implied—it was an old trick in his house. He not only needed their warriors but he needed the safeguard of peace at his back. By calling every one of their available contingents into his service, he emasculated the Altiplano of all vitality and propensity for unrest at home. Collao had become familiar with itself as a tired land of women, where the beautiful fiestas of old were increasingly neglected or only weakly celebrated for lack of men, where the young boys to be joyfully inducted into their manhood had no fathers to emulate, and where the girls in from the potato fields stood sorrowing together in the dusk wondering who there might be for their husbands.

When the contingents had assembled, a spectacular review was held. Huayna Capac increased the pomp of the occasion by divulging his ultimate purpose of overleaping his father's conquests in the north. The emperor's elder brother Auqui Topa Inca was placed in superior command of this army, sharing it with Michi (Shepherd), an almost equally famous personage. Because of the weight of the enterprise, a special announcement was concomitantly made that the prince Huascar was henceforth heir apparent, though whether this went as far as a coregency and investiture is uncertain. With the emperor himself so young and so virgin of warlike prestige, the act would have had no precedent in Inca history. Huaman Achachi was installed as governor of Cuzco and thus given full responsibility for the safety of the state while the army was in the north.

The two oldest princes, Ninan Cuyochi and Atahualpa, were to go north with the army to be molded into useful men of war. Huascar, aged about eleven, was of necessity left in Cuzco. Two other boy princes were similarly left behind. Their names are of interest because like the three above, they too became Inca emperors, though puppets of the Spaniards. The first was Manco Inca, who became in time the brigand lord of the neo-Inca state of Vilcabamba. He was a child at this time, having just been born while his father was down in Collao. The other was Paullu, known to history better by his later Christian name, Don Cristóbal Paullu Inca, a dignified, passive, and devout man.

All of this was in or close to the year 1511, just about the time when Vasco Núñez de Balboa, still in the Caribbean, was listening raptly to the first rumors of golden Peru. The emperor Huayna Capac was then about twenty-three years old.

《 5 》

THIS NORTHERING MASS of warriors, nobles, women, imperial servants, and bearers of baggage—perhaps the greatest ever to have been seen along the giant passageways of Chinchaysuyo—looked more like the removal of a whole civilization than an army routing to the scene of a rebellion. At Vilcas the caravan was joined by the Inca's war idol Huanacauri, an earnest of the successes to come; it was to remain in the north as long as the emperor lived for its place was always in the heart of the carnage.

At Cajamarca the first campaigns were mounted against the perennially difficult Chachapoyas, and after some initial failures the province was brought back to its allegiance. A short stab into the jungles of the Bracamoros in pursuit of the usual renegades as well as that will-o'-the-wisp, a Utopia in the Amazon, harvested only naked savages and baleful death and so was hastily withdrawn. Perhaps it was in this first phase that another army corps was dropped down into the northern coast to take action against the lowlanders there. We will mention this later.

So far so good. Tumibamba had been held by its garrison as an all-necessary springboard against the great rebellion, and in this Cuzco in the north the ponderous host now settled down to chew and munch and engulf the labors of the Cañar tribes round about. But for the warriors there was to be no bucolic period of digestion, for they were now to be tested in such hot fires as had not burned since Chanca days or the Collao revolt. Thus opened the Carangui war.

The Carangui people lived in what is today northern Ecuador from the central Quito Basin up to and perhaps beyond the headwaters of the Mira (Increase) River. They had already cut off and perhaps destroyed most of the Inca garrisons here, and they straitly menaced Quito itself, now a beleaguered and exposed bastion. Huayna Capac's first duty being apparent, he moved his army north to clear the passes leading out of the Quito Basin to the lost forts beyond.

At the outset there were difficulties of command at the top. A fierce rivalry had developed between the leaders of the Colla contingents and those of Contisuyo over assignment of the first command, and this, flaring into the open with possibly disastrous consequences for all concerned, demanded the emperor's personal intervention. It was agreed after consultation that leadership on the field-officer level would be divided between them, two generals from each levy, while the customary regimental core of two thousand *orejones* stiffened the whole. This first reconnaissance in force met the disaster its weakened command had marked out for it, for it was allowed to penetrate well in Carangui territory and there ambushed while carousing one night under the cold glitter of the Andean stars. The Collas sustained the most severe losses, and the vestiges of this rash group staggered back along the hard road they had come, the regiments of *orejones* guiding their retreat. Quick relief was forthcoming. On receipt of the news, a holding column—commanded by the two princes Ninan Cuyochi and Atahualpa—moved up the trail to their support to make a joint stand where practicable. The unscathed Caranguis now possessed in force the *pucara* of Cayambe, key to the northern exit from the Quito Basin.

Huayna Capac was reported overcome with rage at this humiliation, and his actions no doubt corresponded. But with other Ecuadoran tribes beginning to take heart at this Inca reverse, the rod of terror had first to be applied to them lest they stab the great army in the back. All this took time, as did the filling of the ranks by new recruits called up again from far Collao. Possibly as much as two years transpired in this interval. When ready the reinforced army was led out of Quito by Huayna Capac in person.

But the cup of Inca gall was far from drained. Two enemy strongholds, Cochisque (identical with the *pucara* of the Cayambes) and Huachala, opposed him south of the Carangui centers, and each had to be assaulted in turn. The first was a victory for which the Incas paid in Pyrrhic coin; the other was finally added. They were strongly regarrisoned, and the advance continued over the passes into the narrow homeland of the Caranguis. Here under Mount Cotocachi (Salt Heap), custodian of a thin terrain, stood the defiant *pucara* of the Caranguis, guarding the ascent from the Mira Valley on the Royal Road just north of modern Ibarra. To properly isolate it, however, from neighboring allies on whom it might call, its investiture was accompanied by the strafings of a detached Inca group which roved about the vicinity at need, bent on harassment and dislocation of the enemy.

It was known that when the signal for the final assault was given, sustained fighting would be necessary to take the fortress, but no one was prepared for the unexpected enemy sally which fell like a thunderbolt on the heavily committed Inca forces. In the confusion a swift stream of Carangui braves pierced the solid ranks of those *orejones* clustered about the emperor's palanquin and momentarily broke them up. In the wild melee the royal litter was heaved about like the plumy top of a chonta-palm in a montaña storm until it came crashing incontinently to the ground and the emperor was spilled out into the dust of battle. Some of the more resolute *orejones* who had held their ranks were barely able to drag the suffocating ruler out from under the enemy lances. The only cause for comfort on that sour day was the last-minute rally at dusk by the *orejones* who grimly forced the Caranguis back within their protecting walls. A later tale had it that the emperor returned over the long road to Tumibamba on foot and carrying his lance in his hand, a walking apparition of humiliation to his own people who had so miserably failed him.

Again shoring up the Inca garrisons still in the Mira area, and ordering a continuation of the siege along with a scorched-earth policy round about to foreshadow the full terror to come, the emperor returned to his headquarters with a host of new and harsh problems to solve. The loss of life among the *orejones* had been especially grievous, and for a while at least the situation was as bad as it could possibly be—short of total disaster. The Inca garrisons in the area were barely able to hold on where they were, locked helplessly in forts while a now exultant and mocking enemy swirled about under their walls at will. With Quito lost, Tumibamba would be greatly menaced, and Tumibamba was too greatly prized by the Incas for them to allow such a situation to occur. However, it should be noted that a deeper injury than that to the territorial integrity of the empire had been inflicted, and this was to its ruler's personal dignity.

An urgent call now went out to Cuzco to replace the losses among the *orejones*. We have seen that these invaluable troops, the flower and treasure of the empire, few in number, were always either Inca by blood or by adoption and were presumed to carry the irreplaceable ethos of that self-centered people. Here for the first time they had openly and shamefully failed in their duty—nor would the subject peoples of the empire fail to note this wonderful fact. In Tumibamba an alarming crisis, born of this disaster, now appeared.

Singularly embittered and feeling himself widely alienated from his people, Huayna Capac pointedly omitted the Inca captains from the series of recuperative fiestas which he now instituted. He even ordered that the daily rations of all the *orejones* implicated in his recent humiliation be cut to the barest subsistence. Public opprobrium could have gone no farther.

But the emperor was indeed most ill advised to cast this torch of studied insult into the accumulation of Inca grievances, a tinder pile that had long been set, as can be seen from the suddenness of the explosion which ensued. The mutiny of these troops was from no anemic or transient reason, for the causes had been long in the making, perhaps from the very time when Pachacuti had first harnessed the proud Incas to his apocalyptic vision.

« 6 »

HUAYNA CAPAC HAD COME TO THE THRONE in his infancy. Twice both his inheritance and his life had been threatened in plots of Inca origin. Father and mother had been early taken from him, and we may suspect on indirect evidence that glozing advisers and hardy sycophants other than Incas occasionally succeeded in reaching the ear of the young prince. We know also that it was customary for ranking provincial *curacas*, their ambassadors, and their sons to reside for extended periods in Cuzco, forming exotic islands of interest in the imperial court, and with the completion of Topa's sweeping conquests these citizen-strangers must have become far more numerous and important. A straw pointing in the direction of our surmise is the wrangling to which assignment of the first Carangui penetration gave rise, a contention between captains of provincial levies that was to affect the upper levels of policy—to that extent purely Inca councils must have been considerably eroded by this time. And there were growing numbers of provincial captains both loyal and able in war, while the Incas by birth remained a static few and therefore increasingly defensive of their prerogative. This was the tinder. The emperor's deliberate and open humiliation of his people provided the spark.

Michi, the co-commander, with three other leading *orejones*, prepared the mutiny. They secretly summoned a tribal junta of all dissident Incas and assembled them about the glowing campfires out in the cold fields of their exile. In his exordium to the braves about him Michi made two points: first, that the collapse of the royal litter had been an accident and not a sign of panic or defection; secondly, that while he himself stood high in the emperor's estimation, he could not forget that those present in the darkness were his brothers and kinsmen. The action he proposed was that they move that night upon Tumibamba fully accoutered and assemble in their ranks at daybreak in the square, prepared either to fight or march, preferably the latter. In any case, they were to take possession of the *huaca* of war kept in the sacred area—for with Huanacauri they would repossess the author of their being and their ancient dignity as men of Manco. With this emblem in their midst they would take the long road back to Cuzco like a cloud rack bearing the star of their being to its home in another part of the heavens. This was the plan of the mutineers. Alexander's Macedonians in the Land of the Five Rivers would have appreciated the emotions which prompted it.

When the next day's sun rose, three thousand silent Inca troops were standing in the half-light facing Mollecancha, the temple. They stood there unbending while three separate commands came from the deeply disturbed emperor demanding an explanation. After his last message was curtly answered to the effect that they were being driven out by hunger, exposure, and his contempt, Michi and the three leaders entered the sanctuary, to reappear a short time later with the beloved *huaca* of their people. A great shout of reverence and released emotion greeted the event, dangerous, morbid, triumphant, and sonorous. Thus, at the very moment when their stellar father arose to light the land, did the Incas reclaim their earthly progenitor certain that as the former banished the shadows from the earth so must the latter banish the night of their misease.

Huayna Capac came at last in person into the square and disregarding the protocol which had for so long been sundering him from his people, took Michi's arm as a brother and expostulated with him, the two of them meanwhile walking slowly back and forth in sight of all. Michi proudly reiterated that inasmuch as they, the *orejones*, were Huanacauri's appointed bodyguard, so they were now rightfully possessing themselves of him. But the emperor's long parley did not placate his lesser kinsmen drawn up in their files and brooding over their javelins, and word came to him that their example was encouraging a similar spirit among the provincial regiments. With the Inca *huaca* in their custody the rebels controlled the god of victory. The Pachacutean state was trembling.

Dropping Michi's arm, Huayna Capac hurriedly summoned the priestly hierarchy and charged them to inform the other gods within Mollecancha of the event. While this was being performed time elapsed and still the *orejones* stood.

At last, to the furious bellowing of conch shells, the remaining gods, clad in the habiliments of mourning, defiled in slow procession out of Mollecancha. Leading the way was the goddess Mama Ocllo, whose high priestess and oracular mouthpiece here was a stately Cañar girl. This great female *huaca* approached the awe-struck ranks of the *orejones* and began, through her priestess, to plead with them. She reminded them gravely that she was their true mother and therefore claimed their love; finally, in a melting maternal peroration, she said that, being her sons, they could not set forth on their journey until she herself had properly sandaled and clothed them.

"Surely you are our Mother," said Michi, for he and the rest were deeply moved by the appeal. In token of greater transigence, though not of any intent to abandon his claims, Michi therefore announced to her that they would delay their departure a bit. The *huaca* was then taken back into the custody of the priesthood, and all the gods—never greater than on that day—turned and re-entered their sanctuary. The actual terms of the settlement which followed were discussed in the royal apartments, with only Huayna Capac and the leaders of the revolt present. That night a great fiesta was called. The emperor ordered the plaza filled with treasures of many varieties, and all the *orejones* in their ranks downward dipped into the piles for whatever suited their fancies. This gigantic largesse was extended into a series of brilliant *taquis* in the succeeding nights, with the loveliest girls culled out of the *acllahuasi* and from among the prisoners to be paraded before the Inca captains and lavishly handed over. The orgies that ensued satisfied every soldierly heart.

Here appears to have been a clear-cut victory of the Incas over their emperor, however tactfully it may have been handled by him. Nevertheless, our interpretation of the results is perforce based on superficials. The *orejones* had succeeded in gaining what they considered theirs by virtue of hereditary right and hard campaigning— the choice of the loot—and this may have been sufficient. As for that feeling which we believe more truly sparked their actions—a progressive alienation from the imperial center—we are not informed whether they did succeed in redressing that imbalance for the remainder of Huayna Capac's rule. The following reign was to reveal such a deep cleavage among the Incas that we cannot be far wrong in feeling that the fountain of unrest may have continued to flow in spite of Huayna Capac's accommodation. And similarly, because we cannot certify whether the royal litter had been overturned out of annoyance, weakening discipline, or pure inadvertence, so we cannot decide whether the formidable Inca warriors had there at last, like the Spartan hoplites on Sphakteria, finally discovered their mortal limitations.

《 7 》

Auqui Toma (Encirclement Prince), another of the emperor's brothers, was selected to lead the army, at long last placated and rejuvenated by new recruits from the far corners of Tahuantinsuyo. This was now probably the mightiest force ever held under one command in these northern marches. Two of the three advanced Inca fortresses in enemy territory were still holding out, but Auqui Toma withdrew even their garrisons as he surged past on the road back. The last encampment was made under the outermost of the five concentric walls of the Carangui *pucara*, a mountain stream forming a screen across the Inca rear. Inasmuch as the emperor was not here in person, as last time, to immobilize the *orejon* regiments into a purely custodian function, those warriors could now display their fighting *élan* to its fullest.

Which indeed, under the inspired personal leadership of Auqui Toma, they did. The assault lasted for days. By disregarding his appalling losses the Inca general breached one wall after another until the innermost one was reached. In the shocking melee that accompanied the final penetration, with the end plainly in sight, a great stone which had been rolled down from above incontinently found Auqui Toma and crushed him. The key was already in the lock, when the one who could turn it was thus suddenly removed. Nevertheless the surviving *orejones* and the levies continued the Homeric fight until, exhausted and with weapons broken, they stood on the piles of dead and fought with their bare hands.

But the assault broke at last and the shattered relics of the attack were harried slowly back over the remaining walls and down to the torrent which from a protection was now to become an open sarcophagus. Many were slaughtered, pressed up against the bank, while others weltered and were swept away below. Only a reduced force was able to gain and hold the other side. As the Caranguis then returned to their *pucara* to restock it and repair its walls, the defeated dispatched runners with the first official report of the battle.

In Tumibamba the imperial aplomb held as Huayna Capac, merely passing the comment that men were food for war, proceeded to take vigorous personal command. An Inca lord in such a situation was clearly at his most dangerous, as the event shows. Certainly few episodes in the annals of these people reveal as strikingly as this the skeletal stratum that lay just under the surface of the imperial office, that of the tribal *sinchi*, fierce, irresponsible, unconquerable, and relentless.

Cunning planning now evolved a stratagem to replace the necessity of a frontal assault on the *pucara*. Once back in the vicinity of the enemy, a large column under Michi pushed rapidly on past the *pucara* as if on its way north to reinforce the lone Inca group still entrenched up at Rumichaca (Stone Bridge). Under the emperor's command the main body again took up assault positions under the walls, and a third column moved off in an opposite direction, apparently to the relief of another Inca post.

The attack was swiftly and heavily delivered and continued on a prearranged and sanguinary schedule for several days. On the appointed day the attack arose to a crescendo, and then slowly buckled. Loss of zeal flared first into panic and then into headlong retreat. For a while the emperor could be seen on foot, brandishing his lance and wildly endeavoring to stem the flight. Then he too mounted his litter and was carried swiftly away in the pandemonium. The Caranguis, unable to resist such a lure, poured out of their sanctuary in hot pursuit. But at this juncture the two other Inca columns, which had skillfully redoubled on their tracks and had concealed themselves by night in the neighboring ravines, swept out onto the vacant battleground and entered the defenseless fortress. Ascending columns of thick smoke at their back showed the Caranguis their fatal error.

At this moment Huayna Capac and his well-briefed officers turned the fleeing army about and struck their confused opponents with the full weight of their long-frustrated wrath. Hereupon was offered up, under the unfeeling flanks of Mount Cotocachi, a holocaust intended to seal up forever those pages of history. A marsh of reeds and thicket near by provided the Caranguis only momentary protection. No quarter was offered, nor did despair ask it. Forced deeper into the marsh, they were either drowned or cut down in huddled batches. Two of the enemy *sinchis* took refuge in some willow growth but were knocked out of the trees with a veritable hail of slingstones. Only one of them, Pinta, was able to escape in company with a thousand of his Cañar allies. By imperial order the remainder were totally exterminated where they floundered about in the reeds, leaving the waters tinted with eddies and streamers of Carangui blood. The spot was remembered ever afterward as Yahuarcocha (Blood Lake). And of all the male Caranguis only small boys were left to the women.

Pinta led his band into the montaña, home of all fugitives. Ensconced on the heights over the Chillo Valley, he soon took to raiding and rapine in the Quito Basin. With temporary headquarters in Quito, Huayna Capac superintended the immediate introduction of *mitmacs* into the devastated Carangui area and then dispatched a special column to pry Pinta off his crags. Success was difficult to come by in such an undertaking, as Spaniards would later discover in that type of terrain, but all exits from the valley were finally sealed off and the capture made. Brought into the emperor's presence, Pinta refused with contemptuous silence a knightly offer of pardon. He was therefore killed and made into a drum, which was sent back to Cuzco to tell in syllables of thunder the story of his defeat. The great Carangui war was over. The date was 1522 or close to it.

There remained only the grand parade to advertise the momentous breakthrough. The pueblo of the Carangui was now reconstructed to become an important Inca provincial center, the largest one this far north, and the uncontested Mira was crossed. A fortress was easily liquidated en route and the imperial insignia moved north until it came to the famous natural bridge of Rumichaca over the Anca-smayo (Blue River). Here was established the uttermost frontier of Tahuantinsuyo. That it was supposed to be only temporary, however, can be seen from the later probing advance beyond it into the country of the Pastos, today southern Columbia.

It was in the midst of the grandiose celebrations held at the conclusion of the Carangui war that the first ominous raindrop that was to swell into the dreadful Hispanic storm splashed down upon the face of the empire. But the report came to Huayna Capac well disguised; it spoke only of the irruption of certain "vagabond" Chiri-guanas into the Bolivian province of Charcas and the failure of the Inca frontier posts to stem their advance. In their push across the Altiplano to the very environs of the provincial capital, these savages needed only one short leap beyond to have carried them into the midst of the rich silver mines. What the report could not have told the emperor was that the bearded war leader of these Chiriguanas was a Portuguese well versed in the Guaraní tongue and that his name was Aleixo García.

This mercurial European who had been cast up on the Brazilian coast had heard of a land to the west called by the Guaranís *Cara-caraes*, in which remote paradise was said to be a great white king and a silver mountain. Harbinger of the later breed of conquerors of New Castile, this man had succeeded at the head of some Chiriguanas in forcing his way into the Inca Empire, but he had no muskets and his steel-corseted horsemen were stealthy savages whose only armor was the ambuscade.

Huayna Capac dispatched one of his most capable lieutenants post-haste to handle the menace. This officer left without troops but picked up levies en route. With this scratch group he retook and refitted the broken garrisons in Charcas and expelled the last of the jungle men. The poor quality of the recruits under this southern command may be evident from the somewhat dangerous latitude allowed them in rallying about their own tribal *huacas* in the affair. They were however successful and returned to Cuzco for mustering out. As for Aleixo García, he returned through the Gran Chaco to be murdered near Asunción by his own Indians.

« 8 »

THE CARANGUI WAR in all its vicissitudes had lasted some dozen years. It had been a raging furnace indeed, and in it had perished not only vast numbers of the enemy and of subject peoples but of the flower of Inca knighthood as well. It had caused such a stripping of frontier garrisons in every part of the empire as encouraged the Chiriguana thrust. It had created or at least brought into the open the serious breach between the emperor and his kinsmen. Finally it had produced a real professionalism among such as had fought and survived, captains tenacious in assault, skilled in subterfuge, and, because of the twelve years spent in Ecuador at the emperor's side, little knowing or little respecting the role of Cuzco as the seat of empire. To these veterans Tumibamba was Cuzco, as appears from the fact that here, beyond the confines of the holy city, was held for the first time the preview of an imperial triumph. As for the gains from the war: the northern revolt had been crushed and the land recovered as a springboard for further advances.

Though composed of more than three hundred disparate lands and provinces, Tahuantinsuyo still had no region quite so apart as Ecuador, for Huayna Capac re-established it as a co-ordinate kingdom and as a quasi-appanage within the empire. A string of Inca cities from Carangui to Tumibamba hung exotically like a filament of pearls down the breast of the land. The elegance of the city of Tumibamba especially was astounding: warm springs cunningly piped, apartments and barracks for the captains, an *acllahuasi* of two hundred Cañar girls, a central square with the *usno* raised in the center, and the extensive palace and temple complex known as Mollecancha. In Mollecancha's chapels the niches were jewel encrusted and the garden of the gods glittered with golden birds and llamas. Here, as we have seen, resided the gods in domiciles modeled on those in Coricancha. Of particular note was the gold-plated royal chapel devoted by Huayna Capac to the cult of Mama Ocllo, Mother of the Incas, as

259

well as in proxy his own deceased earthly mother. Her statue was of gold with a hollow in the belly which contained Huayna Capac's placenta. Tumibamba had been the emperor's birthplace and the scene of his marriage to his second *coya*, Mama Rahua, mother of Huascar. Armies once bled out of the veins of Tahuantinsuyo into this receptacle were never returned—when their work was done they were settled on the emptied lands and given local women as wives. Their allegiance was here and so seemingly was the emperor's.

At some earlier time Huayna Capac had sluiced an army group down among the coastal cities of northern Peru to punish those who had caught the earlier contagion of rebellion. Near Piura twenty pueblos at least had been crushed and left with the dead in their streets. Tumbez had remained loyal, perhaps because of a population of *mitmacs* which had been inserted into the city under the nominal rule of the *capullana*.

Puná, however, always the mortal enemy of the people of Tumbez, had joined the rebellion. Upon its arrival in the environs the Inca army had been invited out by that island *curaca* to accept his formal surrender. No treachery was suspected. When out of sight of land and securely riding the vast swells of the Pacific, the Puná mariners who guided the first large flotilla at a preconcerted signal turned on their unsuspecting passengers and spilled them into the waters, after which they sailed murderously and methodically among them with clubs and javelins. After delaying the appropriate length of time they returned and shipped their second load of Inca officers and troops to repeat the massacre. Puná for the time being was safe.

But now that the Caranguis had been removed, Huayna Capac could turn his attention to lowland Ecuador. It was about the year 1524 when Huayna Capac took off from the sierra with a large army into those western bottoms where heat, miasma, starvation, and fevers were soon felling his veteran troops in large numbers. At one point on the grueling march the situation was almost irreparably lost when the hitherto elusive Indians suddenly rose up around the desperate Inca army as it emerged onto the sandy barrens. In these straits Huayna Capac was barely able to save his army and move on to Puná.

While this was transpiring another conqueror on that same coast was extending his jungle-blackened hands solemnly and relentlessly southward in search of Huayna Capac and his empire. This was Francisco Pizarro, one of those *compañeros* of eleven years before to stand upon "a peak in Darien," now on his first voyage south from Panama, for the great Balboa was dead. Reports of this apparition in the Pacific, profoundly unsettling, were soon in the emperor's possession and prompted him to send gifts to the strangers. No direct contact was made, however, inasmuch as Pizarro had returned unsuccessful to the Isthmus.

How the thorny island of Puná was subdued by Huayna Capac—whether by negotiation or invasion—is unknown. It is certain however that Tumbala, the hideous god of war of those people, whose rites demanded the opened bodies of prisoners captured in battle, sat fettered in his windowless shrine a prisoner of the Incas for the second time. The emperor was reported to have been splendidly regaled there with all of his ten thousand troops in a series of fiestas. An Inca governor backed with a garrison was left on the island while the bulk of the army went on to finish the pacification of the Huancavelicas. To open the area to closer control from the sierra, the emperor ordered a paved feeder road built through the hotlands up to the Royal Road. We may doubt whether all of this grandiose project was completed.

At some point toward the end of his lowland sojourn Huayna Capac was apprised of an overwhelming disaster which had befallen his empire. During the decade of the Carangui war, a fulminating disease introduced by the Spaniards had been gestating along the reefs and rotting beaches of the Caribbean; perhaps it was that illness, similar to both typhus and bubonic plague, which had been brought into Darien during August, 1514, by the armada of Pedrarias. It had flared and smoldered its way over the Isthmus and down along the mangrove coast of Columbia, bartered unwittingly by native traders. It flashed inward wherever there was a road, a trail, or any passage through the thicket. No skirmishers could have been more cunningly insinuated—like hooded heralds they flew silent and unseen ahead of the bearded men, their captains, and few were their poisoned darts that missed the mark.

The news of the pest abroad in his empire was so astounding that

Huayna Capac ordered a direct and immediate advance through the bush back to Tumibamba, regardless of the cost to the army. The troops crossed the Guayas River and straggled blindly through the back country up to the Ecuadoran capital, where already frightened *chasquis* were pouring in from Cuzco and surrendering *quipus* sent only seven days previously, each one compounding the losses. What perhaps Huayna Capac did not know at that moment was that the invisible death was now roaming among subject peoples of the coastal areas he had just left; and that doubtless his returning troops had carried it with them in their baggage, in their bundles of javelins and bags of slingstones. The news from Cuzco was repetitious and brief: great numbers of the Inca nobility had been violently swept away by the epidemic. Two close kinsmen of the emperor whom he had appointed as joint governors of Cuzco had perished. The locks of his harem in that city too had been forced by the invisible intruder, and many of his women had died; his sister Mama Coca, abbess of the prized Cuzco *acllahuasi*, was one of them. Government in the sacred city indeed was almost at a standstill. For the first time since the Chanca war an enemy, more silent than the Chiriguanas and more bellicose than the Caranguis, was within the jurisdiction of the city, yet this enemy showed no part of him against which to strike, and he left as evidence of his passage only the impure bodies of his victims. While the emperor commanded an imperial lamentation and penance to be performed, an all-inclusive therapeusis of holocausts, there seems to have been no thought in his mind of hastening to the aid of his stricken capital. Whether his actions speak of demoralization, or whether sixteen years of absenteeism had become ingrained, we cannot judge. Certainly the last we are to see of him is not on the road posthaste to Cuzco but in Quito, the farthest pole away.

« 9 »

BUT THIS WAS NOT the sum of misfortune. The matter of the bearded beings—whether they were gods or men—was now pressing in upon Tahuantinsuyo. Clear oracles regarding this were hard to come by; of all the *huacas* consulted, only Pariacaca dared an answer, though we do not know its purport. Everywhere men were beginning to mutter that there might indeed be a twelfth ruler over Tahuantin-suyo but there would be no more. This unrest was caused by reports now arriving that the bearded ones were again drifting down the Ecuadoran coast in a "house in the sea" that gleamed like white bones in the sun. This was Pizarro's second expedition and the year was 1526. The emperor Huayna Capac was then nearing forty years of age; the thin, bearded man sailing inexorably into his ken was some fifteen years his senior.

Huayna Capac's equanimity had been thoroughly shattered by this visitation from an unknown people and their plague. So much so that in person he interrogated special messengers sent up from the coast—an unprecedented lowering of the royal dignity. The powerful science of the omen-takers whom he consulted failed them here, and they were callously sent from the presence, as were finally the great mag-nates themselves. Unbelief, foreboding, curiosity, and irritation on the part of the emperor made him ever more insatiable for news of the Spaniards, but though more and more details were produced re-garding their progress, no clarification resulted. His only action was to pour out a destructive wrath on certain of the priesthoods whose *huacas* he suspected of being treacherously in league with the new-comers. The order went out to exterminate those priests and to de-stroy and utterly uproot their *huacas*. Thus the emperor himself helped to spread abroad a net of terror, especially in those provinces that worshipped the erring idols.

The questions to which Huayna Capac demanded answers are manifest. Were the bearded beings mere mortals to be dealt with like any other invaders? After all, they had shown understandable lusts, and on one count they appeared indeed to be spying out the land, for they had incessantly asked after him, the emperor, his resi-dence, and his state. Or were they angelic dispensers of the thunder, masters of shining metals, and walkers on the waves in their wooden *pucara*? A venerable prophecy had long existed that the Viracochas who had once disappeared in the northern ocean off Ecuador would some day return with a new dispensation, a cosmic renewal. What part then would the empire play? Had its historic mission already been fulfilled and would it now suffer demotion and be forced to step down from the stage of history to make room for the gods? Or was it to be punished for hidden sins? Whether it revealed the lineaments of heaven or hell, such a near prospect of the divine was not pleasant to contemplate.

The last scene in this melancholy picture of widespread disaster and imperial vacillation came with the suddenness of a thunderclap. While the bearded ones were still hovering off the coast that ally of theirs, the disease, had appeared in Quito. Like a colossal figure, it squatted in the center square flicking its invisible darts into every corner of the city, coughing and spewing forth contagions. Sacrifices were instantly ordered and severe penances undertaken, and the emperor retired into the farthest gloom of his apartments for a prescribed fasting and period of continence. But soon two hundred thousand men and women lay dead and untended in Ecuador, and the powers were still not appeased!

One apocalyptic night before the terror began, so ran the tale, Huayna Capac was accosted by a messenger in a somber cloak. Making due and mute obeisance, this apparition handed the emperor a small box and vanished. Unable to restrain his curiosity, the emperor lifted the lid whereupon out fluttered unending swarms of wispy, mothlike creatures to disappear soundlessly into the corners of the night. Two days later the epidemic appeared in the court. The messenger had come from Viracocha and the gift was the plague.

A glaze of dream, portent, fact, and rumor thickened over Quito. Michi, the outspoken protagonist of the old Inca way of life and the general holding highest rank, expired and soon there were added many others of noble status. The emperor was known to have dreamed that three uncanny dwarfs came to summon him. They vanished when he screamed for help, and his serving women found him alone, badly shaken and feverish. He announced that he was going to die.

Pachacamac, the greatest coastal *huaca*, was immediately informed and an answer urgently required. But the emperor's time was rapidly drawing on. He thereupon called in the magnates and in their presence dictated his legacy, announcing his final belief concerning the Spaniards, that they were people of Viracocha, for they it must be who were sending him and his people this terrible death. He feared them and he cautioned Tahuantinsuyo to placate them if necessary.

As concerned the state, he made clear his desire to have the special political status of Ecuador continued. He did not create a gap between Quito and Cuzco by any specific division of the empire into two parts as commonly stated, but simply defined the area from Quito north as a hammerhead of empire, in short a viceregal border march to be equipped with its own forces. Tumibamba was to fall back into the mass of well accultured provinces and was to be, at his death, peacefully administered from Cuzco.

Secondly—and most inadvisedly—he partially reversed the already settled succession. We cannot follow clearly this tortuous thread of history. Only one thing seems certain: some distrust of the infante in Cuzco, a young man now, existed, and correspondingly the standing of the eldest of Huayna Capac's legitimate sons, the enigmatic Ninan Cuyochi, had increased. This person had had the advantage of being with his father all through the Carangui war and was presently down in Tumibamba filling a position of trust. In short Ninan Cuyochi was appointed heir and Huascar was dispossessed. There was however an important proviso attached to this shattering last-minute change, a codicil dictated by the known anger of the gods toward the empire. The omens were to be taken and if unfavorable, the original succession should be maintained. Thus the uncertainty concerning the passage of the royal power, as displayed at least in the mind of the dying Huayna Capac, had its origin in the disastrous signs and events connected with the advent of the Spaniards.

A final requirement was that the emperor's mummy was to be returned to Cuzco not in a funeral cortege alone but in an imperial triumph, a vast display of the loot, victims, and victories which sixteen years had given to him but which his untimely death, now upon him, did not allow him to celebrate. He still meant to return in glory. The will was mnemonically recorded on a wand in various colors by the royal *quipucamayoc*, its items being committed to memory as they fell from the dying lips of the emperor.

As he lay *in extremis* word came that Pachacamac had consented to restore him. The oracle ordered that the sick man be taken at once into the presence of his father Inti. Inasmuch as a royal demise was customarily a dark and secret affair, this constituted a radical cure indeed, but even as the solemn group laid down their unconscious charge before the idol and under the living light of the sun, he passed away.

The reign had lasted some thirty-five years. At its inception it had been marked by intrigue and drift. It had erupted into volcanic war at a vast remove from the center which had drained away great human reserves from the empire. The allegiance of the old Inca *ayllus* had eroded as the makeweight of military professionalism had appeared. In being tragically appointed by history to greet the vanguard of the Spaniards and to suffer the shock of their diseases, the reign had ineluctably run onto the shoals of fate. It had boasted an emperor who possessed the virtues of a *sinchi* but who neglected the nicer duties of government by administration. Huayna Capac had been an absentee emperor, and from that fact was to flow the most dire of consequences.

THIRTEEN.
HUASCAR
TWELFTH EMPEROR

THE YEAR 1527 opened on an uncertain and conditional succession—
and neither the heir designate, Nina Cuyochi, nor his alternate,
Huascar, were present in Quito where the executors of the imperial
will were sitting.

That Ninan Cuyochi had a faction there strong enough to win
the first cast of the dice is evident. When Inti's high priest in Quito
took the solemn *calpa* (strength) omens, they upheld the candidacy
of this prince, and accordingly an embassy was sent south to invest
him with the royal fringe. But fate was otherwise minded, for as the
mission arrived in Tumibamba it was met by the news that Ninan
Cuyochi had just expired of the pest. The high priest and his party
therefore returned to Quito. This regrettably thrust the executors
of the will back in the limelight, and an increasingly dangerous interregnum dragged on, even as advices were arriving that in Cuzco
action had already been precipitated by Huascar on his own.

We are totally unable to judge of the passage of time here; many
months indeed may have elapsed, for by now Huayna Capac's remains had been mummified, the heart deposited in the Inca temple
that looked down from its eminence above Quito, and appropriate
lamentations performed. Years later it was still reported that this

king's *huaca* had been so exceptional that the shrieks of mourning arising from all parts of the empire knocked the birds out of the skies! The widowed *coya*, Rahua Ocllo, was sent south with a splendid entourage, while the royal mummy which was carried over the cold paramos on the shoulders of sons and brothers and accompanied by many gods and their mourning priests followed more sedately. A pause of an entire month was made in Tumibamba for extraordinary fiestas of mourning, while in every provincial capital on the way south the cortege was joined by local grandees as well as the *acllas* chosen for the holocaust destined to take place in Cuzco—of the *acllas* sent up from the coast, not all survived the rarefied heights and many predeceased their fate.

An event of importance occurred as the funeral party left Tumibamba. While some troops had been assigned to the new governor installed in Tumibamba (one of Huayna Capac's sons) the majority of the veterans had been left in Quito under command of Atahualpa, who must have been thus the legally appointed governor or viceroy of that northern province. Atahualpa came as far south as Tumibamba whence, after bidding a mournful farewell to his mummified progenitor, he returned into his province. The charge leveled at him later was that this constituted an act of filial desertion.

In Quito, Atahualpa was bedeviled by the revenants that had so unsettled his father's last days. Awesome advices from the sea were rolling in on a flowing tide of panic, telling that the drifting "seahouse" of the Spaniards which had come to rest in the roadstead by Tumbez had then gone on. The event had been prepared against; the Inca governor had welcomed the strangers, but the strangers were curious and passionate beings and sent one of their company into the city to bring thunder and storm down with a sorcerer's stick. They continued coasting southward well past Chan Chan. Along the way they had been given women, llamas, and bits of gold by the *curacas* of the various subject cities on the coast; these had been hesitation gifts, probably unauthorized by an empire sickening between two reigns. One fact of ill omen was that the strangers had stopped by the Chira River and kidnapped some natives of the region to train them in their tongue for use at a later time. On their return, two of the bearded people had been left ashore at Tumbez and the "sea-house" had then drifted away to the north whence it had come.

((2))

WELL BEFORE THESE EVENTS—in fact upon the first receipt of the news of the death of his father—Huascar had seized power in Cuzco. He was thus openly ignoring the executors appointed by his father in Quito. Nor had he paid any attention to Ninan Cuyochi's candidacy. Though the high priest of Inti—who alone could perform the coronation—was still in Quito, Huascar had elevated to that eminence two priests attached to his party, and these had invested him with the imperial office. This action amounted of course to the deposition of the high priest in Quito who had been his father's appointee. This was followed by peremptory orders that Quito at once return his father's harem and household—always a necessary step in the full assumption of a prince's inheritance. It was this command which brought back ahead of the cortege his mother, her women, and particularly his full-sister through whom alone he could command a pure line of legitimacy.

The swiftness with which Huascar had created a situation dangerous for the government of the interregnum and for all those even remotely associated with the terms of his father's will was alarming. Lavishly he now dispensed gold, offices, and women to bind important magnates, including forty-odd sons of his father, to his dispensation. From these magnates he selected three to become additional counselors, and thus overnight he had in operation a fully formed state—at the very moment when the government of the interregnum was drawing closer to Cuzco, wrapped in the weeds of mourning. Huayna Capac's last-minute rejection of Huascar's legitimate candidacy in favor of a more warlike son had not added to the prestige of this prince, and one could reasonably predict that injured pride would exact a toll.

But other spiders were spinning webs also. Huascar had dispatched a distinguished group of brothers and other kinsmen up the Chinchaysuyo road to greet his mother and her retinue. At a *chicha-*

drinking en route an ill-founded and poorly timed plot was hatched to kill first the queen mother and then the unpopular Huascar and his partisans—the brother chosen for the dubious honor of stepping into Huascar's place being a certain Cusi Atauchi, popular with all. Cusi Atauchi, however, was not informed of the conspiracy. The ringleader, Chuqui Huaman (Lance Hawk), had fomented this plot by design; he was in fact an *agent provocateur*, and when the affair was well on foot he stole back to Cuzco with a full muster of the plotters to divulge to Huascar. The traitors met the usual excruciating ends, and the innocent Cusi Atauchi was cut down as he came in the dawn to offer the accustomed homage at the imperial levee. Chuqui Huaman became from that time on one of Huascar's intimates and received as his reward one of the two generalships against the rebellious Chachapoyas soon after. His final reward was to come from that enemy—a sudden death in a drunken sleep.

Under such an inauspicious star did the queen mother's party arrive in Cuzco. Behind it the funeral party was already approaching the Apurimac bridge when Huascar's orders unexpectedly came for the executors to leave the royal mummy and hasten on ahead. It can be understood how this message appalled these elders, whose only protection was the silent person of the dead emperor. With Colla Topa at their head they were arrested at the station of Limatambo, tortured, and then brutally slaughtered. On such a hapless shore was finally flung that wave that had begun as an indecisive ripple stirred by a dying man in Quito. The great concourse of people who had escorted the emperor's mummy, and who now stood waiting farther back on the road, were struck by the news as by a hurricane and scattered—some of them—far and wide. Many of the provincials as well as some of the *orejones* turned and fled into the north where either Quito or the Chachapoyas offered asylum.

These two related acts, the conspiracy of the brothers and the murder of the executors, are the keys that unlock the secret of Huascar's hostility toward Atahualpa. From the Ninan Cuyochi candidacy we can assess the danger for Huascar in the existence of any kinsmen who could advance the shadow of a claim to the royal fringe; this danger produced the proscription of the brothers. But one brother, Atahualpa—and he already a renowned war-lord owing

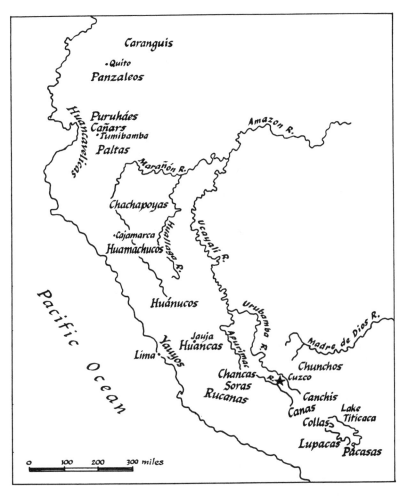

Highland Tribes of Tahuantinsuyo

to the part he had played in the Carangui war—sat securely in far-away Quito endowed with a great army. The funeral cavalcade could even be considered, by Huascar's dark and involuted mind, as an army murderously advancing upon a sleeping Cuzco; this at least was straightway to become the official line which explained the affair of the executions. The inquisitorial question which had been put to the trapped men at Limatambo had been designed to discover why Atahualpa had chosen to remain in Ecuador instead of accom-

panying the cortege south as most of the other Incas had done—the
implication being that he did so in order to prepare revolt at a distance and at his leisure. The executors confessed to nothing, from
which we may presume that there was no such treacherous plan in
Atahualpa's mind at the time. But Huascar was making inevitable the
very thing he feared, for already he had begun to fill the infamous
torture pits and hanging places of Cuzco with victims. The harem
did not escape. One of his prized females incurred the lethal suspicion
of Huascar and, for her reputed sexual irregularities, he ordered her
buried alive. His younger brother Paullo, involved in the same
offense, was cast into the terrible dungeons reserved for Incas of the
blood and systematically starved. His real crime may have been that
he was thought to belong to the pro-Atahualpa faction. Inasmuch as
Atahualpa belonged to the Upper Moeity of Cuzco, it was that half
of the Inca nation which found itself increasingly spied on by
Huascar's informers and isolated from the imperial presence.

The relict Huayna Capac at last was allowed to make his triumphal entry into Cuzco. There followed a grandiose display, to which
was added Huascar's formal coronation and wedding. But an un-
toward hitch in Huascar's plans had first to be unsnarled. It appears
to have been customary, when a bride was desired, to request her
of her mother. The girl in this instance was Huascar's full-sister,
Chuqui Huipa, but contrary to all imperial protocol the queen
mother refused her assent when Huascar's emissaries approached
her, so deeply had she been embittered by the wanton killing of her
late husband's executors. No amount of pressure was successful, so, in
a most undignified and unprecedented concession, Huascar had
finally to go in person to his mother's palace and put his unwilling
suit. This also she adamantly refused. Huascar was thus suddenly
plunged into a most alarming and indeed unheard-of position: without the sanction of a legitimate queen and the blessings of his legitimate predecessors, he could not complete his investiture—an open
invitation for those to rise who wished him ill. A solution was found
only after Huascar had ordered Viracocha and the full complement
of Inca gods out of Coricancha to assemble before his unhappy mother
presenting the request to her in the irresistible accents of heaven. Out
of fear of treason to her own gods, Rahua Ocllo could in no wise

refuse this and with a weary heart she handed her daughter over to the son whom she hated.

The coronation and wedding took place and Topa Cusi Hualpa (Royal Fortunate Cock), better known as Huascar, became the twelfth emperor, duly seated. He ordered commemorative buildings erected at the site of his birth and in the Cuzco ward of Amarucancha. As a reward to his toady Chuqui Huaman he sent him forth to raid the turbulent Chachapoyas and to find in that commission a graceless death.

《 3 》

Atahualpa had not been in attendance at the coronation. However he had sent his congratulations and made due homage through emissaries, requesting at the same time formal permission from Huascar to remain at his post as viceroy in Quito. Because for the moment he could not do otherwise, the young emperor had grudgingly though perhaps only tacitly allowed him the title of *Incap ranti* (legate), which had almost certainly been his by confirmation of the previous reign and of the interregnum that followed. Whatever we may think of Atahualpa's motives, his request was *pro forma* and can be interpreted without recourse to the theory of a treachery set on foot at this time. Ancient Inca protocol however usually thought of full homage as an act in person; in this sense he was summoned and did not comply.

It would be naïve to assume that Atahualpa was unaware of the thickening mists rising about him and his friends or that he was inactive in the face of the threat. About this time people in his confidence who had been sent to Cuzco contrived to visit the *coya* and her mother with gifts and words of friendship. These two women—the most important in the realm—were a potential focus, however innocently, of anti-Huascar sentiment, and in consequence the emperor was instantly suspicious. He is reported to have burst in upon the two women after Atahualpa's spokesmen had left and to have viciously berated his mother particularly with being Atahualpa's prime adviser and the instigator of his concealment in the north. This was almost tantamount to a direct accusation of treachery. The denials of the two queens failed to convince Huascar, and he under-

took to subject them from this time on to a round of furious accusations, for which however he was never able to adduce positive proof.
Out of the murk of his mind he contrived to cast the two queens into
a situation of many austerities, of grief and cruel harassment. Rumor
had it that the *coya*, in utter terror of her brother-husband and of the
spies he introduced about her, refused all food during the day, eating
only once at midnight, as if to conceal even this innocent activity from
her suborned retainers. Lost to happiness, she took incessantly to
the narcotic euphoria of coca and even asleep was not without its
solace. The city of Cuzco was aware of these happenings and though
to the outward eye its placid and chill streets, its soft thatches and
painted walls seemed the same, terror was not far off.

We must suppose that Atahualpa's motives in the move he now
made were proper, having no evidence to the contrary. Huascar had
refused in the long run either to define or specifically to order the
continuance of Atahualpa's office in Ecuador—which was a *sine qua
non* for the prestige of the incumbent in that province. Accordingly
Atahualpa made a serious effort to arrive at an understanding: he
dispatched an embassy dignified by the presence of a mutual half-
brother. The mission was to reiterate his loyalty and to request the
final confirmation of his viceregal office as ordered by the government of the interregnum. Attached to this group was Quilaco Yupanqui, a son of the distinguished council member Auqui Topa Yupanqui,
who had died in the plague. This young nobleman had been reared
almost as a son in the household of Rahua Ocllo in Ecuador, and it
was expected therefore that he would be able accurately to sound
out the sentiment supporting Atahualpa in Cuzco, for Rahua Ocllo,
while not a Quiteño partisan, certainly did not favor the party of
her son. This embassy was to be the most fateful in the history of
Tahuantinsuyo for its ultimate issue was to be the collapse of legitimate rule.

Near Anta the ambassadors were approached by a messenger
from the two queens. Parenthetically, it is at this point where there
begins the love story of Quilaco and Cori Cuillor (Golden Star),
the reputed but rejected daughter of Huascar, a tale of constant love
lit up in the lurid glare of espionage, war, and intrigue. The lovely
Golden Star, as well as the older woman in whose villa she lived,

seem to have been utilized by the pro-Atahualpa party as informants. Golden Star indeed was one of the girls who served those male parties traveling along the Chinchaysuyo road which stopped at this tambo, and if we read between the faded lines of the romance, we may possibly see her as one of the *acllas* used for sexual solace and entertainment and her "aunt" as the mother superior of the girls.

Huascar was in Calca at the time, so five members of the embassy humbly presented to him there the rich gifts brought from Quito. His response was immediate and devastating. The gifts were hurled into the fire to a volley of accusations of treachery against Atahualpa, while the ambassadors were sneered at as exposed spies. Carrying on further in this vein, and spurred by a prominent sycophant in his entourage as well as by his own flair for the unforgettably wrong, Huascar commanded the immediate execution of four of the group while those waiting in Cuzco were to be stripped of their clothes and appareled as women for the return to Quito.

Back in Cuzco, Quilaco, as the sole member of consequence left of that embassy, stood himself in the shadows of death. He immediately got in touch with the two queens as well as with Golden Star, whose sympathies were now even more with him and his cause. He was finally permitted to return with a peremptory command for Atahualpa to come instantly to Cuzco for an accounting. As he went on his way into the now ominous north, he stopped off surreptitiously to give assurances to his beloved that the years would see him back with her. They were not to meet again until the battle was upon them.

It may have been at this juncture that Atahualpa, in order to claim Ecuador by the prescriptive right of inheritance, allowed his partisans to give him a fictitious parentage, for it was to become a common rumor that his mother had been a legitimate princess and "queen" of Quito. Needless to say, there was no truth in this.

《 4 》

WE MUST HERE MAKE SOME ATTEMPT to account for Huascar's character, as it cannot be doubted that the end of a great empire was inscribed in the covert calligraphy of his heart. The naïve Huaman Poma blackens even his exterior, describing him as swarthy, ugly, and uncouth in his actions. Cobo, who assessed much of the surviving evidence, concluded that he was tactless with his subjects and the object of their profound dislike. Some of the Indians inhabiting Cuzco referred to him as immature and willful, while one excellent source attributes to him the most shocking public indecencies. He is also said to have ordered the slaughter of all the males and pregnant women in two pueblos close to Cuzco. In short he was believed to be irresponsible, almost half-mad, and to have provoked his own condign destruction. Huaman Poma makes finally the revealing statement that the hatred for him in Cuzco and the resulting disunity was so great that the city did not later defend itself adequately from the intruding Spaniards. Cieza alone of the primary sources makes him more presentable, though this is by contrast with the later Atahualpa and because of the unquestioned legitimacy of his rule. When in the year 1610 the descendents of the Incas happened to be parading their history through the streets of Cuzco under the eyes of the Spaniards, they mimed only eleven emperors—Huascar was missing. It is thus permissable for us at least to characterize the actions of this emperor as divisive in all their effects.

Since his adolescence, his court had evinced a peculiarly feverish atmosphere. One of his favorite concubines from the coast, found unexpectedly dead one day in the harem, was thought to have been poisoned by some of the other wives who were jockeying for a place in the hot sun of his affections. In a wider ambient, the Quilaco episode reveals an involved court situation with highly placed women manipulating the springs of action and with the imperial post road under the vigilance of spies of opposing factions But what most fostered suspicion and at the same time made it difficult for the central government to have full access to knowledge was the by now gigantic wealth and influence radiating out of the establishments of the dead but still sovereign emperors. Their immunities made them perfect little clubs and sounding boards for revolutionaries and begetters of unrest. Huascar's displeasure at the Hanan Cuzco group is in part to be explained this way, a fear of the silent and the unwatched. As a matter of fact Huascar did proceed violently against certain of the *panacas*, claiming that vices of all kinds were being encouraged behind their windowless walls, but here he was flying in the face of the most sacred Inca tradition. The feeling aroused by his measures against "the ancestors" must have made its contribution to his downfall. Huascar's police were everywhere, but the specter of Atahualpa was not thereby put down.

In his early years Huascar appears to have lived on the southeast side of Haucaypata in a palace adjunct to Amarucancha, the royal edifice erected by his father. After his coronation, however, as if to show his contempt of tradition, he removed to Collcampata—a spot hitherto sacrosanct in Inca history. Since the days of Viracocha Inca, all the emperors had resided on the square, and now all the available space fronting it was taken up. Still it was a radical step to commandeer Manco Capac's first *chacra* and the supposed site of his first stay. Severely beautiful today—even in ruins—Huascar's palace at Collcampata like the stony eye of suspicion looked down upon his subjects safe from their whisperings and discontent only at this remove.

« 5 »

ATAHUALPA WAS IN TUMIBAMBA when the shattered and humiliated remnants of his embassy appeared before him. That the insult could not be borne by a great Inca war-lord was obvious, as indeed it was equally obvious that for him to appear in Cuzco without an army would be his end.

This was about the middle of the year 1529. For Quito it was a time of considerable danger inasmuch as the old *curaca* of the Cañars in Tumibamba, consistently favorable to Atahualpa's cause, had just died. His successor listened to the pleas of his lesser chiefs and turned to Huascar for the confirmation of his new office, thus precipitating the first direct clash between the jurisdictions of the two brothers. Both Atahualpa and Huascar fully realized that the Cañars would form the strategic anchor in their respective plans, so competition for their allegiance was intense. If the Cañars were to defect to Quito, then Huascar's influence would automatically be thrown back upon Cajamarca, an unhappy frontier at best with the undependable Chachapoyas on its flank. If on the contrary they remained fully loyal to Tahuantinsuyo, then Atahualpa's secession would be limited to the far north of Ecuador.

Atahualpa hereupon put forward a claim to all territory as far south as Paita on the coast and at the same time began ostentatiously to build a royal palace for himself in Tumibamba. He confidently underlined these actions by ordering all those petty Cañar chiefs who had misled the new *curaca* to be impaled. But at this juncture Atoc (Fox) appeared in Tumibamba, an ambassador publicly sent by Huascar to Atahualpa but bearing in addition secret instructions to undermine the Cañars' respect for Atahualpa and to persuade the *orejones* in Quito's army to return immediately to Cuzco. Atahualpa seems to have thoroughly underestimated that person's craft, for Atoc succeeded in planting Huascar's banner again in Tumibamba.

The affair erupted in the midst of some festivities in that city at which Atahualpa was incautiously present, believing himself master of the situation. Without warning, Atoc and the Cañars whom he had brought into his intrigue rose and attempted the person of Atahualpa. With a few troops Atahualpa incontinently fled from the city but was captured and brought back unarmed.

Atahualpa was thus in Huascar's power before he had even adopted a strategy. Pending advices from Cuzco he was incarcerated in a solitary room in Tumibamba, though as it eventuated it was not to be for long. A friendly Indian girl smuggled a copper bar in to him, and with it he broke open a hole through the thick adobe wall to perform a daring and famous midnight escape. In Quito the official version of the story was that his divine father, the Sun, had appeared to him in his duress and had foretold a certain victory over Huascar; hereupon he had been changed into a snake and had glided to safety through a minute hole in the cell. Thus at the very end of Inca history a miraculous tale served as the same kind of patriotic catalyst as had the famous revelation to Pachacuti in its early days.

Committed irrevocably to war, Atahualpa was now acclaimed as the full and sovereign potentate of Ecuador, though a year was to elapse before he could complete his preparations for war. The local Indians were finally organized into auxiliary formation and in a military review held for the purpose, Challcochima, the chosen spokesman for the *orejones*, addressed the new throne and offered it the loyalty of every member of Huayna Capac's "world-girdling army," whereat the great northern drums spoke out in thunder and the heavy Panpipes of war moaned of coming things; the morose sound of that challenge bore swiftly down the Andes to the ears of Huascar.

Though it had been he who had precipitated events, nevertheless the reception of this news fell on the emperor with the fury of a storm. For days no one dared approach him; the flood of his wrath and terror rose in its tide to suck down those persons who had had even the remotest connection with his father's funeral party. The *coya* and her mother barely escaped with their lives. The council advised that one should maneuver for time, perhaps by temporarily placating Atahualpa, but Huascar rejected this out of hand and dispatched the above-mentioned Atoc, a brother, to levy troops among the Paltas and Cañars with those preliminary results we have already seen.

Behind the appearances Atahualpa's situation was unenviable. Though he appears not to have fully claimed Inca power yet in its entirety, he had still set up a viable sovereignty out of what had been Tahuantinsuyo's most active march. Furthermore, those tribes recently subjected by his father could well be expected, at his first reverse, to swarm like venomous reptiles out of every chink and hollow at his back, and indeed the Huancavelicas in their dismal lowlands had already done so. Besides this everyone knew that since the days of Pachacuti no contender had succeeded in toppling the might of Tahuantinsuyo. Offsetting this was his one undoubted superiority, the possession of the veteran core of that empire's army, a group of men and officers whose homes, women, possessions, and honors were in Quito and not in Cuzco.

The scars of this army had been fraternally achieved, but the bitter factionalism of the moment plagued it. On the death of Huayna Capac a prominent group of captains had arisen advocating quick action against Huascar. This had deepened into something very like a conspiracy and had forced the opposition group to take to their heels southward to fill the air of Cuzco with the noise of their parleys and alarums. Atahualpa had felt himself irresistibly drawn into the orbit of the anti-Huascar party though he still attempted some accommodation with Cuzco, as we have seen. When forced into the open, his policy, a blend of revolt and caution, reflected both the legal weakness of his own position and the boldness of the anti-Huascar party. His was to be at first the part of the wronged prince who, to protect his undoubted rights to the appanage, had felt himself reluctantly forced to secede.

Atahualpa was now a *sinchi*, elected in the ancient highland manner by the magnates of Ecuador and carrying the onerous military expectations of that office on his shoulders. Undoubtedly the exposed position of Ecuador contributed to the influence which the generals at first seem to have exercised over his actions. Taken collectively these generals were more like the sons of the sixth emperor Inca Roca than, for instance, the officers whom Pachacuti had selected to command his armies. Pachacuti had had to use grandees of acknowledged social status whose designs could thus always be suspect, whereas one feels in the lieutenants of Atahualpa a narrow professionalism, a cruel collegiality, a rigid military ardor which was probably the result of their greater social distance from the throne. Atahualpa perhaps did not feel the nagging of incipient rivals as much as did Huascar.

« 6 »

THE CONFLICT WHICH NOW BROKE OUT was the final Inca masterpiece in their chosen art of war. The records say that one hundred thousand combatants were destroyed in the engagements, a not improbable number if we include massacres. We know that three thousand able-bodied men from the province of Chucuito alone were thrown into the struggle and died. This conflict was to extirpate the principle of Cuzqueño legitimacy and to topple that city forever from its Jovian pedestal. Sullan proscriptions were to thrust the state back into the gladiatorial days of Mayta Capac and the Alcavizas, and destiny would raise up no native Augustus to allay them.

A serious matter for both sides at the beginning of hostilities was the question of the allegiance of the coast, particularly its northern half. Embers of the recent revolt against Tahuantinsuyo still glowed in the cities and reed-thatched villages by the sea. Tumbez and Puná could of course be expected to translate their normal quarrels into terms of Huascar or Atahualpa, and we do have knowledge that in the former city the two factions were indeed present, with the loyalists at first in control. Piura and Lambayeque, like Tumbez, were solidly with Cuzco at first, but Atahualpa's policy of arousing latent coastal enmities was not difficult to put into action, as witness the stirring up of an old and vituperative hatred between Jayanca and certain of her neighbors who were traditionally in the camp of Chimor. Promoted by Atahualpa's agents, the *Pax Incaica* on the coast thus disappeared in a welter of intercity warfare, and it was not long before Atahualpa's agents were followed by a detachment of his troops, with himself at the head. Possessing himself of Tumbez, Atahualpa proposed to clear his rear with a heavy naval attack upon Puná, still strongly held by Huascar's governor, Atauchi. In this battle of the balsas he was not only unsuccessful, losing as captives seven hundred men, but he was personally wounded in the thigh by an arrow. He retired rapidly to Cajamarca to recover, leaving a governor and a holding garrison in Tumbez. It was not long before Huascar's governor in Puná launched a counterstroke across the Gulf of Guayaquil and put Tumbez to the sack, though he was unable to occupy it for his imperial master. Atahualpa's attempts to engineer a complete and massive defection on his vulnerable right flank had thus failed. That this did not deter him from continuing his determined struggle against Huascar in the highlands was a token of the desperation of the struggle. It was also a sign of the difficulty, always to be reckoned with, of integrating effects and movements between the sierra and the coast. Puná, in the glassy reaches of her gulf, had successfully defied him, but in any real sense she offered little immediate threat.

In Tumibamba, Atoc had organized the two thousand *orejones* sent up from Cuzco and added them to his loyal Cañars. Atahualpa was forced to thrust some of his formations into action against Atoc before they were ready, and this haste of his brought on a disastrous skirmish in Mocha territory south of Ambato bridge. His main strength was moving south out of Quito, however, and met his fleeing contingents just to the north of Latacunga. A glance at the map will show his plight. North of the paramo he had just left behind him was the basin of Quito itself—if he should lose here, there would probably be no second chance. When Atoc's pursuing army broke into view somewhere near Ambato, the two armies met in full conflict.

The battle of Molle Ambato saw operating together for the first time Atahualpa's two generals Challcochima and Quizquiz (Small Bird), a marriage of utterly efficient human predators that was soon to cleave the Inca world apart. Holding to their orders of no retreat they succeeded in winning a pronounced victory and in capturing Atoc and the Cañar *curaca*, both of whom were promptly hauled back to Quito for suitable refinements of torture. Atahualpa had not forgotten the slight upon him when Huascar had destroyed his ambassadors, and he proceeded to exact horrible vengeance upon the person of this half-brother of theirs. When the miserable life of Atoc was at last extinguished, his skull, rimmed with genial gold, was transformed into a drinking goblet. This was a new and gruesome departure from custom—to practice such barbarities against one's kinsmen—for up to now the practice had been reserved only for foreign enemies of the state. Cieza, who years later saw the bones that still littered the field of Molle Ambato, estimated that some fifteen thousand had been killed there.

Tumibamba was tactically exposed by this victory, and the Cañars had to look now not only to the defense of their distant master in Cuzco but of their own homes and fields as well. These perilous happenings, exaggerated by rumor, had been immediately flashed by *chasqui* and by fire signals into the far corners of Tahuantinsuyo to shake the empire like the first pangs of an oncoming mortality. Impelled to action, Huascar appointed a brother named Huanca Auqui (Field-Guardian Prince) with almost plenary powers of command and provided him with a staff of *orejones* and some additional levies hastily brought in from the provinces. As this army sped north, they were provided with some auxiliaries picked up en route. The result was unlooked for.

Huanca Auqui, upon whose back the fate of the empire had now been shifted, is variously characterized in the sources. He was said to be a competent and loyal officer; he was said to be dogged but not perhaps of the sternest stuff; some believed he was treacherous; others again held him to be simply unlucky. His competence is hard to assess, but his unbroken string of defeats is not easily explained away. The charge of treachery, however, is quickly disposed of by the tenacity and courage which he was to display in the struggles ahead. The assertion that the dark star of unluck followed him seems particularly revealing; like Nicias at Syracuse, one feels that he was fated for tragedy for he was matched against the two greatest generals of his age. In short he appears to be that most forlorn of figures, a commander cracked relentlessly between an indomitable enemy in front and the cabals and plots of a Neronian court at his back.

Huanca Auqui was forced to fight just outside Tumibamba, outnumbered by about sixteen thousand effectives. The contest opened with a tense struggle for passageway across the river. Singularly protracted, it seemed to be favoring the cause of Huanca Auqui until a well-timed downhill charge out of the mists of the second morning hurled him back into the city with his forces near panic. Stopping only for a brief reorganization of their cadres, Atahualpa's officers flung their army forward. Huanca Auqui moved out to meet this attack head on, and a titanic struggle ensued in the very gates of the city. Fought in such fashion, it could not last long, and Cuzco gave way step by step until her forces broke. In the flight southward out of the city some were drowned. Huanca Auqui rallied those remaining to take stock of his situation, but decided that the event was serious enough to make further control of the basin impossible. His dejected columns therefore swiftly made their way down to Cusibamba, hoping to dig in there. But the relinquishment of Tumibamba was bigger than the loss of an important city; it was the denigration of a symbol as well.

Atahualpa knew how to intrude further upon the dignity of that symbol. His subsequent action was motivated by that abiding personal hatred he cherished for the tribe which had not long since held him captive. The defeated Cañars now had nothing left but to shuffle out of the surrounding hills and the passageways of their lost city, garlanded for peace and weeping for mercy. When the helpless mass of humanity had assembled in front of him to plead, shrieking and sobbing, for their lives, Atahualpa gave the order for a general massacre, and when the long hours of bloody work were completed, all the adult males and all pregnant women had been destroyed on the field of their submission. The ornate city of Tumibamba was leveled almost to its foundations, and fire and sword were visited upon the Cañar villages round about, Atahualpa hoping thereby to bring that race to an end. Word of this vindictive act of genocide spoke in Delphic tones to all who would hear. In Cuzco, Huascar ordered the *itu*, reserved for dire calamities, to be performed. So ended the Cañar phase of the War of the Two Brothers, a strategic and propaganda victory for Quito of the highest significance.

Atahualpa's forces were soon replenished in the pause which followed, and his captains were quick to grasp the fact that a more aggressive policy was now feasible. Where before Quito had been defending its rights by means of a pro-Ecuadoran policy solely, the possibility now suddenly appeared of capturing the whole of Tahuantinsuyo. As Tacitus had said, reviewing a similar situation, "A secret of empire was revealed that an emperor could be made elsewhere than at Rome." The new *élan* released by this knowledge among the generals may well be conceived, and their actions were fully sanctioned by Atahualpa. When the army was unleashed—forty thousand strong it was said—it moved out and ahead with all the effortless ferocity of a school of sharks headed toward teeming atolls in the south. The men who led it were celebrated and feared greatly during their short day in the sun: Challcochima, Quizquiz, Rumiñaui (Stone Face), Ucumari (Bear), and others.

Huanca Auqui had attempted to throw Atahualpa off balance by a lightning raid on Tumibamba during the build-up, but Cusibamba was no proper base from which to operate and the move failed. Furthermore, in a most curious diversion of his energies, Huanca Auqui had gotten himself partially involved with the Pacamoros. Though this side campaign in the montaña was probably taken to reduce new troops to Huascar's persuasion, it ended in spectacular defeats. In cruel derision at his ill luck, Huascar sent to him and to his beaten captains those symbols of the familiar Inca affront: combs, cosmetics, and women's wearing apparel. Yet a revealing sign of the paralysis of decision in Cuzco was that, though its commanding general was thus gratuitously insulted and his prestige practically nullified, he still was not removed. Huanca Auqui was easily forced out of Cusibamba in the next hopeless encounter.

At Cajamarca some new groups heavily spliced with Chachapoyas had been gathered to support the cause. Leaving only a skeleton garrison in the city, Huanca Auqui heroically moved north to meet Atahualpa's generals on the Royal Road between Huambos and Huancabamba. But the northerner's assessment of the tactical situation was impeccable. It was suspected that the Chachapoya levies raised under duress were Huanca Auqui's, weakest link. Like a thunderbolt therefore Quizquiz launched himself against that wing and continued his hammering until the corps collapsed and fled. Of ten thousand Chachapoyas engaged, eight thousand were left dead on the field. This battle of Cochahuaylas (Lake Meadow) opened all of northern Peru to Atahualpa. Cajamarca was relinquished.

Atahualpa, just up from his local defeat on the Gulf of Guayaquil, now moved his court from Quito to this northern bastion. Success of course fed on itself. Every foot of territory gained had given to him new recruits, and his army, veteran at its core, had tripled in size from the first days of the war. Concomitantly Huascar's troops were more raw and less sure of the quality of their cause.

But the greatest of the provincial *huacas* of central Peru still held out against him, for the famous shrine of Catiquilla as well as that of Pachacamac had remained in the loyalist camp. Against the latter Atahualpa was to save up his spleen until his last days. On the former idol, caught in *flagrante delicto* of an unsatisfactory oracle, he wreaked true Inca vengeance, overturning and smashing it and rolling the broken head into the river below. The entire area of the shrine with its attached pueblos was systematically destroyed by burning. The high priest, while clad still in the ankle-length robe of office adorned with sea shells, was beheaded in front of the altar and a purge instituted among the Huamachucos of the province to convince them of their political error.

But there was probably another and more sinister reason for this vicious attack upon the Huamachucos and their *huaca*. During the hostilities around Cusibamba word had come to both Huascar and Atahualpa that the Spanish ships had reappeared at Puná, where their crews had achieved a notable victory over the islanders. Few historians have attempted to assess the impact of this appalling news upon the respective strategies of the two brothers. On the one hand Atahualpa significantly stepped up the pace of the advance; on the other Huascar seems to have shown a dawning but still confused sense of the realities of his plight. It is tempting to see here a new fear on Atahualpa's part countered by a new hope on the part of Huascar. Atahualpa's personal move to Cajamarca is to be interpreted in part as covering a suspected Spanish advance on Cuzco; we know that at any rate he now recognized the "bearded ones" to be men and not gods. Huascar's more tenuous communications with the north Peruvian coast on the contrary fostered in him the dubious luxury of thinking of the Spaniards as heavenly henchmen of Viracocha sent to support his house.

« 7 »

As the last of Tahuantinsuyo's levies were being called up, it was decided that Jauja was to be the core of Inca resistance in central Peru with Junín to the north as the frontier. The stubbornness of the fighting in this area was not surpassed in the entire campaign.

Huanca Auqui had his position carefully chosen to guard the approaches to the upper Mantaro bridge. Here the army of Quito came upon him and a seesaw battle began, lasting well beyond the first day. At great cost Atahualpa's generals drove through to finally force the passage, pushing Huanca Auqui back past the shores of Lake Junín and down into Jauja. Ten thousand casualties are claimed on both sides.

Late imperial levies to the number of six thousand now arrived to reinforce the line, a last pathetic attempt to build a wall of men around Cuzco. The news of the disastrous loss of the Mantaro crossing had almost driven Huascar insane, and all people connected with him felt the onslaught of his unbalanced personality. The two queens especially were in unremitting fear of death at his hands as he sought out scapegoats for his troubles, now here, now there. It was at this juncture that he summoned a meeting of the magnates to announce that he had appointed Mayca Yupanqui as the new generalissimo and correspondingly invested him with plenary powers to salvage the situation. All men in and around the city were immediately to place themselves at the disposal of this new Caesar. This order was a signifi-cant departure from tradition inasmuch as it reduced the pure-blooded Inca residents to the ranks of common subjects, liable to any draft upon their resources, energies, or lives.

Mayca Yupanqui arrived in Jauja barely in time to take up his com-mand against an enemy who had learned the value of unrelenting pressure. As he relieved Huanca Auqui of his supreme position he is reported to have carelessly injected the invective and divisivness of the capital city into an already deteriorating situation by abusing his predecessor almost to the extent of directly accusing him of com-plicity with Atahualpa. Whatever his talents as a commander, Huanca Auqui as least did not lack fight and a full awareness of the difficulties. His reply was brief and ominous.

Mayca Yupanqui marched the army north out of Jauja about five or six miles to take up favorable positions along a small stream named the Yanamarca (Black Town). Here the enemy struggling down from the pass between Tarma and Jauja must meet him. On this unmarked field began that struggle which was to seal the fate of Tahuantinsuyo. From dawn to dusk it was fought with tre-mendous *brio*, a battle where the dead entangled the feet of the living and the wounded crawled through the press to continue the fight. In the end Mayca Yupanqui abandoned the field.

A small and curious footnote to history is appended here, for among those who fell seriously wounded on the field was Quilaco Yupanqui, Atahualpa's commander of the reserves, whose entry into the fray must have had a decisive effect upon the tide of battle. By this time he had somehow contrived to have his inamorata, Golden Star, join him, and it was she who, according to the tender story, drew him half-conscious out of the piles of dead, extracted the javelin from his body, and nursed him in hiding back to health. He was to live only about three years after this, being christened before he died after his patron the great Hernando de Soto. Thus he be-came Don Hernando Quilaco while Golden Star as his wife became Doña Leonor Coricuillor. She was later to become by De Soto the mother of a daughter who, in time, was to marry a Spaniard and produce a long line of mestizo De Sotos who lived in colonial Cuzco.

From now on the retreat was hardly different from a rout. Jauja was abandoned and ravaged by Challcochima. His exultant army, fat with spoils, raced on down to the Ancayaco (Eagle Water) crossing on the approaches to the Huamanga (Ayacucho) Basin, where Mayca Yupanqui's shattered forces stood on the hither side of the river. They held for two days on the lip of the gorge, then fled, burning the suspension bridge behind them. But some of Challcochima's advance units descended into the canyon and plunged into the seething waters to rig a temporary crossing, and the hot pursuit continued almost without a pause.

Huascar's courage collapsed at this news, and he would have destroyed himself, Cieza reports, had not the sterner councils of his kinsmen demanded a last scratching up of reserves from the south and in particular a diplomatic *démarche* requesting aid from the Viracochas who had just come into the land. As a result of their solicitations on this latter point an embassy was dispatched to make contact with Pizarro, who was then at Tangarara (San Miguel), but the contact, though the reply was not unfavorable, proved too thin and the time too late. Huascar however was no longer looking to the sons of earth to succor him and his city. He had turned wholly to the heavens for his help. The year 1531 was rapidly on the wane when the distraught emperor held a last ironic synod of all the notable *huacas* of Tahuantinsuyo. For those provincial *huacas* considered doubtful he had nothing but curses and threats. To his own *huacas*, especially Huanacauri, he appealed humbly that they might intercede for him before the august Viracocha, whose unaccountable wrath was thus destroying the empire. Huascar was oracularly informed that he would recover the charisma if and when he led the last battle array in person.

With Vilcas gone, Huanca Auqui had returned to Cuzco to give a personal assessment of the situation. By some personal alchemy he had recovered his fallen prestige with Huascar and was swiftly dispatched to his earlier post. He ordered the army drawn back to the heights covering the Royal Road between Andahuaylas and the Pachachaca (Earth Bridge) River. Strategically this area was most significant because from it branched lateral roads to the south which the enemy might use to threaten Cuzco on two fronts—though in either case the Apurimac River would still have to be crossed. The inauspicious action was fought at Pincos. Huanca Auqui's army fled over the river to Abancay. Turned by their amazing and enigmatic leader, the defeated troops then fought another fierce and no less fruitless delaying action in front of the famous Apurimac crossing at Corahuasi (Weed House). It was recognized by both sides that Cuzco stood or fell on the line of the Apurimac.

With Atahualpa's forces now in possession of more than one approach to their objective, Cuzco's riposte was obvious: to plug up the defensible crossing at Corahuasi from the Cuzco side and to be in the field in front of the other crossing with the main body of its troops in time to choose the advantage. This other crossing, upriver, was the Cotapampa bridge just south of the basin of Anta. Here in the extremely rugged country contained within the triangle made by the Apurimac with its strong northward-flowing tributary the stage was set for the valedictory battle of Cotapampa.

An extraordinary turn of the wheel now favored Huascar. A formidable captain of his, here heard of for the first and last time, in leading an important reconnaissance in force met the enemy's strong advance guard moving toward Cotapampa, caught it off guard, and with negligible losses to himself delivered a devastating blow. One of Atahualpa's most redoubtable captains, Tumarimay (Devious Speaker), fell among the ruins of his force.

Meanwhile the bulk of Huascar's army, now south of the Apurimac, had moved up into the Pass of Cotapampa, bearing with it their mercurial emperor. On chosen ground and fighting an enemy already blunted, Huascar had disposed his men for a dawn attack. The battle lasted all day and fortune seemed to be still his, as indeed the gods had predicted. By nightfall Challcochima and Quizquiz, badly ravaged and with units scattered and isolated, had been flung back in confusion across the Cotapampa River onto the bare heights beyond. Many of them took refuge in the long reaches of *ichu*-grass that waved on the slopes and along the ridge tops. But Huascar's captains had fire laid to the dry lower courses which eventually drove the disconnected bands above into the open either to be cut down in the pall of smoke or hurled back into the rolling flames.

With the forces of Atahualpa now in serious trouble, Huascar's time had come. He had only to show one-tenth of the leadership of

Pachacuti, of the skill of Topa, or the determination of Huayna Capac to compel fortune into his camp once and for all. Instead he ordered the attack withdrawn at this point, and under cover of advancing night Challcochima and Quizquiz had time to reorganize their units for a show of force at dawn.

During the night Huascar had given his consent to a plan for dividing up his forces with the intention of slipping in under the enemy's wing for an easy final blow. But with the guile of a serpent the enemy had foreseen this, and when, in the first moments of dawn, a flanking party moved silently up a long draw they were detected and annihilated. Huascar's general, badly wounded, was tortured to divulge Cuzco's further plans. Challcochima and Quizquiz now set their final trap, splitting their troops for the purpose.

Huascar, surrounded by eight hundred picked warriors, was seen following upon his general's tracks, confident that he had been properly preceded and the way cleared. Then the signal to spring the trap was given at that moment when he and his men were staring down horrified upon the corpses of their forerunners. Quizquiz struck his van at the same instant that Challcochima closed on his rear. The massacre was appalling. The bodyguard of picked *orejones* fell blindly around Huascar in the last martial dignity the Incas were ever to know. Here on the slopes of a mountain called Chontacaxas, Huascar had given away his last throw of the dice.

The wiles of Quito were inexhaustible, for the captured imperial litter, properly escorted, was sent as a decoy back down the road in the direction of Huascar's camp while the rumor was at the same time spread by spies that Huascar was dead. The bulk of Huascar's army was still intact at its base camp south of the Apurimac and waiting for further orders. By the time the victors were upon them, however, rumor had already broken their ranks and they were in disorganized flight back to the safety of the Cotapampa crossing. Great slaughter was made among them on the road, and the suspension-bridge passage over the mighty river saw the most terrible deed of all: hundreds in their frenzy spilling through the frail cabuya rails into the gorge below. Taken intact, this bridge gave Challcochima his long desired break-through. In record time he had a strong build-up on the other side, and followed this by moving through the

Plain of Anta to bivouac at Quihuipay, near El Arco. Sixteen years later Gonzalo Pizarro, the Spanish rebel and pretender to the crown of New Castile, was to defend the city of Cuzco at the Cotapampa crossing and in his overconfidence to lose, like Huascar, both his kingly city and his life. The Apurimac, however majestic the deep line it traced in the Peruvian earth, was never the barrier that Cuzco in her fantasies conceived it to be.

Huanca Auqui's force holding the major crossing down river, with its left flank now turned, must have begun a precipitate retreat toward Anta, where it hoped no doubt to rejoin the remnants of Huascar's army. The news of Huascar's death or capture at Cotapampa probably came to it too late, for we last hear of savage fighting on this line at Limatambo. Characteristically, Challcochima had not overlooked this important mopping-up operation at his rear before turning his full attention to Cuzco. The Apurimac line had collapsed. Now the question appeared: would the imperial city defend herself at the gates as she had in the intrepid days of Pachacuti? Or could she be lured into an easy surrender?

« 8 »

QUIZQUIZ HAD FORESEEN THE POSSIBILITY that Cuzco might rediscover her ancient soul in a desperate stand under a new *sinchi*, and he attempted to prevent it by holding out the false possibility of Huascar's return. To this end he forced or tricked Huascar into personally ordering the surrender of his remaining imperial forces around Cuzco on the promise that a favorable adjustment could be made. There seemed at the time to be a distinct possibility that Huanca Auqui might muster his remaining veterans for an all-out attempt to recapture the lost ruler. This was frustrated when Challcochima sent a message reassuring the city of his peaceful intentions and of the good treatment being extended to Huascar, while requiring of the Inca magnates and noblewomen of Cuzco only that they come out to his camp to do obeisance to the fetish of Atahualpa which had accompanied the army on its strenuous campaign. Thereafter a *modus vivendi* would be arranged.

For the last time Cuzco was given the chance to debate its future.

The Inca lords who were left there solemnly agitated the matter even as the vultures of Atahualpa were gazing down upon them from the lips of Mount Yahuira. All must have known how little to be trusted was the mercy of the destroyer of Tumibamba, yet Huascar's orders to them—even if issued under duress—compounded of the inertia of defeat, won the day. Terrible indeed was the final decision to give up their birthright—even more terrible was to be the sequel.

In their *ayllus*, in the dusty dawn of their decision, the captains and magnates came up the steep pitch of the Chinchaysuyo road and over El Arco to hear the terms prepared for them, to bow to the image, and then to sit squatting in orderly rows—all in complete silence. When they were settled three files of warriors closed in and sealed off any avenues of escape. First Huanca Auqui, who had succeeded in making his way back from the futile Apurimac assignment, was yanked out of the rows along with all the officers who had fought under him. Then followed the two ranking priests of Inti whom Atahualpa had not forgiven because of the sanction they lent to the coronation of Huascar. They were condemned to be punished as common criminals. In the sight of all, heavy rocks were dropped on their backs. Badly mauled but apparently still alive, they were put aside for further uses.

Quizquiz then ordered that the defeated perform the *mocha* of reverence, the plucking of eyebrows, in the direction of Cajamarca, and the offering of blessings to the new lord Atahualpa. Thus was the surrender and homage accomplished. Too late was it borne in upon the defeated that this was no parley but rather the setting of their final humiliation.

Huascar was now brought out, bound to a stretcher, and mockingly installed among his captured counselors as if in the act of presiding. To this burlesque council of state was added the *coya* and the queen mother. Having thus convoked Huascar's discredited government, Quizquiz had the battered and bloody Huanca Auqui and his officers revived, shouting at them to reveal the name of the priest primarily responsible for the illicit crowning of Huascar, at the same time accusing the queen mother of having been not a legitimate queen but an unprincipled concubine and worse. This imputation of Huascar's illegitimacy brought the queen mother to her feet, distraught and raving. Rushing up to her wretched son, she reviled him in the bitterest and most violent language—testimony to the indignities she had suffered so long at his hands. In tones that may still appall with their tragic intensity she reminded him of all his misdeeds, including the murder of Atahualpa's ambassadors, of the fact that Viracocha's vengeance never slept, and most particularly, that while he, her son, rightfully deserved everything he was suffering, he had involved them all in his own ruin, recklessly and without cause. The rows of squatting Incas hung their heads in shame while the victors, jovial at this proof of the enemy's guilt from within his own camp, mocked Huascar with their fingers. In the fierceness of her frustration Mama Rahua rushed up to the tightly swaddled emperor and struck him across the face.

Huascar spurned his mother's accusations and ordered Challco Yupanqui, the priest who had invested him, to give his reply to Quizquiz. The priest iterated that Huascar was the true son of the queen mother, he himself having crowned him. On Challcochima's interruption that he was a liar, Huascar haughtily stated that, inasmuch as he, Challcochima, was a mere subject, the matter in dispute concerned only him and his half-brother Atahualpa.

After this lamentable scene had been played out, the generals dispatched an urgent message to Atahualpa in Cajamarca, requesting orders on what dispositions to make of these people now that Cuzco was helpless and its surrender fully confirmed. While awaiting the reply, the fortress Sacsahuaman was taken over and additional troops sent down into the city to hold it for its new master. Quizquiz himself appeared in the streets of Cuzco, says Cabello Balboa, "where even the mute stones felt the agony of his presence."

Atahualpa needed little time to reflect on a policy toward the imperial city. He ordered that, without exception, all of Huascar's kin and supporters be killed, and to ensure its performance, he sent Cusi Yupanqui, his own appointed high priest of Inti, to oversee the work. Already on his way, this new inquisitor was borne in his hammock down the Royal Road like the cold shadow of a speeding storm. On his arrival all the prisoners were turned over to him for his disposition.

Most of the Cañar Indians captured had been previously slaughtered as a matter of military precaution, so on the day set for the massacre only Huascar's kinfolk, women, and retainers were summoned. Huascar was set up like a puppet in Haucaypata to witness the affair, which was to include over eighty of his children and all of his concubines who were pregnant or already mothers. His sisters Miro and Chimpu Cisa, favorites of the harem, led the parade of victims, the former leading one child and carrying another at the breast. At intervals during the ghastly work Huascar was heard to cry out to Viracocha that he visit these horrors upon their author. The broken bodies of the victims were left sprawled overnight in the square to be a sign to the conquered. Afterwards they were impaled on stakes lining the road out to Jaquijahuana, the unborn children ripped out of the corpses of the mothers and fixed pathetically in their arms. No more than four of Huascar's many women are known to have escaped.

Then began the door-to-door canvass. Some thirty of Huascar's brothers were ferreted out and along with any and all known supporters of the regime were similarly impaled, with Huascar a constant witness. The *coya* with her two legitimate children, the queen mother, Huascar himself and his counselors were saved for a later spectacle to be witnessed by Atahualpa in person.

It was known that Huascar's power had centered particularly in the household of the deceased Topa Inca, his grandfather. The members of that establishment were therefore hanged and the palace of the dead monarch invaded and looted of its wealth. The mummy of the great Topa Inca was unceremoniously dragged through the streets to the place of burning, while all of those *orejones* who followed, daring to mourn as the bedraggled bundle of cloth and bones bumped along on its strange journey, were cut down in the streets and left where they fell. In all, some fifteen hundred Incas of the blood were exterminated; Atahualpa's grip on the city could no longer be put in doubt. His specific orders to extinguish the legitimate branch of the Inca race had been almost totally achieved. The high Andes and the farthest parts of the Titicaca Basin sheltered the cowering remnants of the line.

Under the presidency of Atahualpa's high priest, Quizquiz instituted a reign of terror for the lesser inhabitants of the city. Incredible tortures were ordered by him during his brief military rule in Cuzco. Within a fifteen-mile circumference communities were decimated in a calculated and relentless fashion—some had every fifth person killed, others every third. All of Huascar's official records, *quipus*, etc., were burned in order to sweep clean for the new era about to begin under Atahualpa. So many of the state archivists and historians were killed that the curious Spaniards were later able to round up only four. Thus beaten, threatened, and outraged daily, the people of Cuzco muffled themselves in their cloaks and gave way to stolid grief, their only recourse being to call upon Viracocha for succor in solemn rites and in an agony of supplication.

While Cuzco mourned the collapse of its greatness, part of Atahualpa's army was dispatched down the Collasuyo road, not only to break up any loyalist parties there before they could form but to crush the expected provincial rebellions. A not-unexpected national uprising along the shores of the lake had involved the Yunguyos, some Lupacas, and the Pacasas, the intent being to regain for its original possessors the sacred site of Titicaca and to restore the independence of the area. This revolt was cruelly punished, the ringleaders being hurled to their deaths from the rock of Copacabana, but time had run out for the conquerors as well and they had to be swiftly withdrawn.

FOURTEEN.
THE ADVENT
OF THE BEARDED MEN

《 I 》

WHILE ATAHUALPA WAS IN HUAMACHUCO celebrating the extra-ordinary victory of Cotapampa, the news of the bearded men—up to now deeply engaged in Puná—had taken an ominous turn. They had succeeded in reducing that island and had captured the *curaca*. This was in the spring of 1532. Hearing of these doings in the north, fainting Cuzco began to take some heart in the conviction that Vira-cocha had at long last heard its pleas.

Much of Atahualpa's drive south had been a desperate gamble, for there was nothing to insure that he would not be caught between two opposing fires should legitimacy and invasion decide to throw in their lot together. His sustained push through the rainy season at the end is eloquent of his feeling of urgency. For a number of reasons he now decided to pull his headquarters back to the city of Cajamarca, where he was closer to the Spaniards. Perhaps he had at the very first, as Sarmiento says, believed in the divinity of the Spaniards, but by now he held a far more pragmatic opinion. His training had inclined him to realism.

Between Atahualpa and his now captive brother the contrast is striking. Everything about Atahualpa bespoke the great Inca *sinchi*. Like Pachacuti he had been thoroughly trained in field and bivouac;

in stratagem he was versed, in terror he was a master. That he was proven brave and hardy is evidenced by the fact that he was the darling of the army, especially among the older officers. He had almost recreated the Pachacutean personal legend when he turned the initial disaster of his captivity among the Cañars into a heavenly revelation supporting the rightness of his cause. Faced with a serious cleavage of factions in Ecuador, he had skillfully weathered it and remained master in his own house. His orgies of vengeance, while fearful, were still a part of a studied Inca policy and were not just the promptings of an injured pride. His *huaoqui*, always carried by the army, was the Ticci Capac (Foundation Ruler), and its name referred to his grasp of those qualities which anciently had built Tahuantinsuyo; until his fall, his generals considered him the beginning of a new era for the empire. In personal appearance he was fastidiously clean, of moderate stature, becoming a bit heavy, though still in his early middle age. His eyes were noticeably bloodshot, his aspect fierce but handsome, and when he spoke, it was with acuity and dignity.

《 2 》

ATAHUALPA HAD HAD HIS FIRST POSTS of Pizarro as far back as the battle of Cusipampa. Between April and September, 1531, the Spaniards had successfully conquered and looted the coastal region of Coaque and then had moved south to insert themselves into the island of Puná at a time when it was engaged in difficulties with Tumbez. Previously during his war with Huascar, as we have seen, Atahualpa had sailed against the island in a strong flotilla of balsas, but had been defeated with the capture of seven or eight hundred troops. Pizarro, in search of a policy, had freed these prisoners and had returned them with a conciliatory and exploratory message to Atahualpa's governor in Tumbez, for he was only at this time becoming fully cognizant of Huascar's importance in the picture. Still heavily engaged with Cuzco, Atahualpa had returned a cautiously worded embassy. It ill behooved him to act rashly for the additional news was brought to him that, having savagely put down the heroic islanders of Puná, the Spaniards then had crossed the Gulf of Guaya-

297

quil and had taken Tumbez by fire and sword. Tahuantinsuyo's northern gates had groaned and opened.

About the time Pizarro was appearing in Tumbez, Atahualpa had captured Huascar and thus abruptly ended the War of the Two Brothers. Relieved of this task, he could therefore pay more attention to the reports of his spies and top officials on the coast. The tenor of these reports had become generally contemptuous for it was known that some Spaniards and a horse had been slain in the fighting on Puná. Spanish swords, for instance, were said to be as harmless as women's weaving battens, their horses were likened to large dogs, and the ridiculously few Spaniards there were said to be exhausted. When to these advices were added the lists of goods looted by them from the government warehouses and the women taken from the *acllahuasi*, it became absolutely certain that these were not Viracochas but mortals and very little different in their activities from the Chiriguanas. The general mood of bravado among Atahualpa's inner set at Cajamarca can be seen from the words of one of them, Mayca Velica, *curaca* of the Pohechos, who while reeling nobly in his *chicha* boasted that with 4,000 or 5,000 *orejones* he could easily bag every one of the 170 Spaniards. The more cautious advices of those captains who had been in the fortress of Tumbez when the Spaniards had attacked and taken the city at night, warriors who had actually tried their skills against Spanish arms, did not prevail.

Supported by his new sense of victory, Atahualpa decided on a somewhat more warlike attitude toward the invaders, and for this he had the oracular support of Pachacamac on the coast, now of course friendly to his cause. Rumiñaui was accordingly dispatched to Tumbez with the demand that the Spaniards return at once to their own shores, promising them gold and silver if they complied. Several young virgins were handed over to the bearded captains by him as earnest of the commitment. From this dubious interview Rumiñaui, that captain whose very name was a terror, brought back only the unsettling news that the Spaniards intended in any case to seek out the court in Cajamarca. With the failure of this embassy stern orders therefore went out to the populous towns around Tumbez calling up their last warriors, both to prevent their defection and to build up the expanding army in Cajamarca. This action was a part of a scorched-earth policy to strip the country in the path of the Spaniards of its man power; that it was successful may be seen from the fact that, unlike Cortez who came to Montezuma with Indian allies in arms behind him, Pizarro arrived at his goal commanding Spaniards alone. Unaccountably however, the warehouses and *acclahuasi* in the path of the Spaniards were not emptied.

Tumbez had been too sadly depleted by the previous plague and the last eight years of unrest and destruction to detain Pizarro, though while there he had received the embassy of Huaman Mallqui (Hawk Scion), Huascar's Incapranti or personal viceroy. He had therefore moved south to found San Miguel, his first Spanish *cabildo*, at Tangarara in the Chira Valley, and here the *curacas* roundabout in their hatred of Atahualpa had with dispatch thrown in their lot with him. Nevertheless, to Atahualpa's mind the full intent of the bearded men seemed still obscure, whether reconnaissance, petty looting, or full-scale war he could not guess—he decided therefore to remain in the highlands until the situation jelled. What was particularly disquieting was the fact that the loyalty of Chan Chan, the old Chimor capital, could not be counted on. It was known in Cajamarca that Pizarro had entered into friendly correspondence with this former enemy, and indeed it was not to be long before the *curaca* of Chan Chan had also bound himself in an understanding with the strangers. Atahualpa's hold on the coast was apparently slipping, and it was therefore the better part of valor for him to await developments in the sierra, his chosen territory.

In those days Cajamarca was a city of two thousand families, with two bridges guarding its approaches. Many of its houses had three floors; some were of tapia or ordinary rammed earth, but the public buildings and those around the capacious square were of Inca masonry and were supplied with running water. Overlooking the plaza was an elevation and castled on top of this an Inca fortress. Not far off were the famous warm springs of Cunú where the emperors had built a tank, with steps leading down into the deeper sections, whose temperature could be raised or lowered by opening and blending the proper channels. This establishment was royal property and was set in the center of a high-walled *cancha*; here the ruler and his harem were accommodated in four thatched houses set up around the patio, the interiors being painted in reds, whites, and other colors for pleasing variety.

Though Atahualpa knew well how to play on these luxurious Lydian pipes, he did not neglect his immediate problem. Several reasons can be glimpsed behind his decision to hold his armies in the sierras instead of meeting the Spaniards on the coast below. The instability of Chan Chan has already been mentioned, as has Atahualpa's inability to place the Spaniards in any well-accepted category of Inca warfare. Another was the person of Huascar, whom Atahualpa was keeping to grace his trimuph, but whose continued existence nevertheless had the effect of keeping the Spanish picture out of focus. Another was the whiff of dubiety which still enveloped the diplomatic intentions of the bearded people, who had already begun to appeal to the sentiments of the Huascar group on the coast while they were at the same time sending assurances of amity up to Cajamarca.

At last it was learned that with less than two hundred men Pizarro was on the move and headed for the passes. To reveal to Pizarro the hopelessness of any possible adherence to Huascar's cause, Atahualpa hereupon sent him an embassy meant to disconcert him and possibly turn him back, for it bore the news that Huascar was a captive and that the whole land belonged now to Atahualpa—but Pizarro had of course been aware of that for some time. Events now moved fast, for the Spaniards advanced at unexpected speed into the cordillera. Either Atahualpa had withdrawn the bulk of his garrisons from the pass guarding the Spaniards' route or he had been late on the field. If the former, it was an act of insane overconfidence. More possibly it was taken in response to a local situation, for these were areas just recently ravaged by Atahualpa's men of war and consequently still unfriendly. Nevertheless the passes could easily have been held against any odds if a firm policy had been set. When it was known that the Spaniards were approaching a tambo called Cajas on the Royal Road, ruined and depopulated from the recent war but well stocked with food and women, Atahualpa adopted an ambivalent attitude whereby he could still receive the bearded men if it seemed expedient to do so; this is evident from the curious embassy he sent to Pizarro in Cajas, though the ultimate hostility of his intentions admits of no doubt. When the Spaniards were only two days to the north on the Royal Road, a plan was drawn up to throw Rumiñaui with a thousand men secretly behind the Spaniards, thus locking the enemy between two forces.

« 3 »

ON NOVEMBER 15, Atahualpa, in his painted chambers at the warm springs, heard that the Spaniards had come into Cajamarca, most of them walking and weary, some riding. According to Atahualpa's spies no leader could be discerned among them marked out by his panoply, for like brothers they all dressed alike, spoke alike, and looked alike. Out of their dark faces their teeth and eyes shone white like those of feral animals—and yet they were so very few! The years of Peruvian history have echoed to the sullen sound of that entry, which has cast a spell of gloom, of blood, of deceit, and of extortion over every passage of Peruvian life since.

In the army camped around the royal establishment at Cunú there existed an uneasiness that was not reflected in the composure of the new emperor. With Inca guile he had ordered an overwhelming display of tents, stacked lances, and men-at-arms for the visitors he was about to receive, and the general effect was indeed to cast awe and something like abject fear into the hearts of the Spaniards that memorable night. Hernando de Soto and Francisco's brother Hernando Pizarro had been selected with a guard of fifteen mounted men to make the initial approach to the emperor. A file of silent *orejones* in full military parade showed these riders the way through the gleaming tents and up to the royal baths. Sedately and speaking in low tones, Atahualpa finally came through the narrow doorway, followed by his women. He then sat down on his golden stool with his women ranged behind him standing in close order and his magnates, including the rich lord of Chincha, beside him. Lowering his eyes that he might not be considered vulgar or curious, he gave the sign for the interview to open. Surely little that the Quechua interpreter, who rode on the crupper of Hernando Pizarro's horse, could have said would have been impressive to a man who had just conquered his own world. Atahualpa told the Spaniards that he knew

301

of their thefts and torts against his property and that they would be required to return every piece stolen. He added that he would come to Cajamarca in person the next day to see to the matter. The Spaniards were not accustomed to such contempt from the Indians of the New World, and in a bravura attempt to recover their damaged prestige, Hernando de Soto, a famous horseman, put his mount through his most exciting paces, curvets and sudden starts and stops, ending with a head-on charge into the royal party climaxed by a rain of flying gravel. The rearing forefeet of his horse pawed so close to Atahualpa as almost to fluff up the heavy woolen fringe covering that saturnine face. Some in the front ranks of the courtiers wretchedly shrank back and cowered under the flying hooves, yet all through it the emperor showed the utmost composure, never flicking an eyelash though several times in imminent peril of being trampled on.

After the embassy had left, the delinquent court had reason to fear the worst, for Atahualpa's wrath was rapidly unloosed. With silent ferocity he singled out those—among them some of his own sons and concubines—who had flinched, ordering their immediate execution as cowards and traitors to their glorious heredity; they were promptly hauled off and killed.

The terrible impact of this event on the court, coming hard on the heels of the news of the bearded men, threw the grandees into a paralysis of indecision and excessive caution. Atahualpa took notice of this by lecturing them on the purpose and extent of the responsibilities of their caste. At the end of this harangue intended to inspirit his people, he set in motion his plan to entrap the Spaniards by dispatching Rumiñaui, now with five thousand men, on an overnight circuit north around Cajamarca to block the city from that direction. His intent was to capture the malfactors alive and sacrifice them to his *huacas*. He announced his own entry into the city next day to take place as the sun would be sinking, for he had information that the Spanish horses, when unsaddled for the night, were useless as weapons of war.

Around noon the next day, November 16, 1532, Atahualpa ordered the move. His spies had already told him that the bearded men were all ensconced inside the buildings about the center square.

Atahualpa interpreted this not as an ambush but as the action of craven men. He left in a magnificent entourage properly timed so that the climactic arrival would occur at sunset as planned.

The city was ominously empty as the four hundred Indian fore-runners of the litter in bright checkered livery moved into the square sweeping all uncleanness away from the head of the crowding column of men behind. The main concourse of magnates, armed guards, and attendants—perhaps five thousand people—followed. Finally the emperor's litter arrived as if borne on a smooth-running stream and took its station in the very center of the square. Atahualpa waited for the confrontation. When there appeared to him only one bearded Spaniard unarmed and in a black gown accompanied by the inter-preter, it became apparent to Atahualpa that the invaders were in-deed an abject people. This particular Spaniard, a friar, had come out from under the heavy thatch overhanging one of the many door-ways piercing the long masonry fronts, but no others revealed them-selves. When he spoke, his words contained references to an emperor, a *capac* greater than Atahualpa, who was now demanding his sub-mission. Atahualpa replied with contempt, merely saying that he had come to receive back his stolen property, after which he would take care of the Spaniards in a manner fitting. Hereat the gowned Spaniard seemed to compound his lunacy by informing the emperor that the Spaniards' god was the only one in the heavens; Atahualpa was to accept this strange god and destroy all of his own *huacas*, and to this end the friar produced a small black book, a breviary. Ata-hualpa demanded to see it and it was handed over for his inspection. It could be seen to be indeed curious for it looked as if made of pressed coca leaves, but at best it was a tawdry *huaca*. Atahualpa had destroyed many idols nobler and more inscrutable than this—and with militant tribes behind them. Derisively he flung the book down in the dust. The Spaniard retrieved it and floundered back into the gloom of the silent houses, crying out loudly in his native tongue as he went.

Atahualpa then rose up in his litter and briefly addressed the court, informing them that the bearded men had already capitulated and that condign retribution must fall on them. He ordered as a first step the eviction of those sacrilegious ones who had ensconced themselves in the temple tower overlooking the square, wherein the gods had their seat. In the midst of his words, a crash of thunder seemed to burst from that very tower accompanied by rolling clouds and lightning, and hollow heavy voices burst out from every direction with the war-cry, "Santiago! Santiago!" This was followed by the eruption of mounted and running Spaniards out of some sixty of the black apertures under the thatch. An amazement absolute in its effect fell upon the Inca host. Was it perhaps to be another demonstration like the equestrian feats of Hernando de Soto? Because Atahualpa had not gotten around to issuing specific commands or ordering a general posture, the mass of Indians crowded backward from the hurtling horses and the upraised swords, and when the charge struck they were flung aside by its fury. The swords thrusting and cutting, rising and falling like Illapa's lightning, had all the horrid splendor of an Andean storm. The tumult became deafening as the tower above continued to shower death below, mingling its heavy coughing with the distracted voice of the crowd below.

Into the midst of the now thoroughly demoralized mob of Indians sprang two Spaniards, wreaking havoc against the defenseless litter-bearers huddling together under the emperor. Panic had snapped the chain of authority; Atahualpa's shouted commands fell like pebbles in a raging sea, unheard and unheeded. One of the two Spaniards, tall and gray, had methodically hewed his way up to the litter and now extending his arm yanked the emperor out onto the ground. He then stood over him fending off the eager swords of his other companions, for the living person of the emperor meant a great deal to him. This soldier was the leader of the Spaniards, and this was the supreme moment of his indomitable career. Meanwhile the bearded men had sealed off all the exits from the square and stood in the passages pointing their thunder-sticks. Corralled in this slaughter-pen the crowd surged about in an agony of fear, trampling the wounded and crushing many up against the walls. One of these walls, about six feet high, was of tamped earth. Some tried to scale it; more died of suffocation at its base. Finally under the intense pressure it gave way like a rotten dam, bursting outward in a cloud of dust. Through this breach then streamed what was left of the upper echelon of the Inca world. Night had now completely closed in.

Between 2,000 and 2,800 souls, including many of the great *curacas* of Tahuantinsuyo, were killed "like ants" that evening in the plaza of Cajamarca, while the horses sent flying down the road to Cunú after those who had escaped accounted for an untold number of others. The vast camp at the baths dissolved instantaneously into the night. Rumiñaui, who could have successfully taken the Spaniards in the rear, deserted his charge and with his regiment fled far away into the north. Thus the year 1532, whose predecessor had witnessed the humbling and seizure of one emperor, had completed its own full harvest of deeds with the capture of another.

《 4 》

THE AMAZING FINALITY of the collapse of the imperial structure at the hands of so few has intrigued both chroniclers and historians. Fray Buenaventura de Salinas y Córdoba, an uncritical guide at best, was nevertheless expressing that wonder when he said, "Great were the deeds of Cortez in Mexico and few ever equalled them, but my admiration is most kindled and stirred at the resolution with which Pizarro entered Peru." Few will disagree. But there are other respectable historians who additionally ponder with amazement the utter totality of the subsequent imperial ruin. Rowe has pointed out the continuing character of armed resistance to the Spaniards all through the colonial period, but of all the uprisings only the Rebellion of Manco Inca in 1536 was fully Inca and therefore represented an effort by the empire itself to survive—all the rest were indiscriminately Indian. The suddenness of Tahuantinsuyo's going is a fact, and we believe the reasons are to some extent definable.

The most salient of these causes is the War of the Two Brothers, a major piece of self-surgery on the Inca body social which, however much a degenerate Cuzco may have merited it, radically weakened Inca resolution. That Atahualpa was aware of the need for a hardening of Inca confidence is evident from the sequel to the incident of De Soto's horse. His extirpation of Pachacutean legitimacy, wherein that weakness was enshrined, had previously been designed to achieve such a renovation. But history was more devious than Atahualpa, and his atrocities in Cuzco produced in the end only a capital that prayed for the entry of the Spaniards. The Inca sense of mission had disappeared whether among legitimate rulers or usurpers. But the War of the Two Brothers had done even more: it had burned up amounts of the human resources of the empire which cannot be calculated but which must have been considerable. An equally evident part was played by the plague which had struck the empire perhaps several times in the years since 1514. On a heaven-supported empire the effects of such a visitation can be more appalling than a war. What rendered the epidemic even more lethal to the state was the coupling of its ravages with the rumors of the strange bearded beings who brought it, for these rumors spoke of the return of Viracocha, offering new hope to oppressed groups, provinces, and factions, and terror to those who held power.

These reasons—civil war, plague, and rumor—were contributory and general. What is more specific as an occasion for the swift fall of Tahuantinsuyo is the fact that Pizarro struck at the very moment of a serious hiatus between dispensations. Atahualpa had not even had time to enter Cuzco in triumph, settle his power there in some fashion, rebuild a new aristocracy, and organize a peace. Thus what fell on November 16, 1532, was indeed not Tahuantinsuyo at all but a great Peruvian *sinchi* who was about to reassemble the pieces of an empire he had just spilled to the ground. Cotapampa and the affair at Cajamarca were simply the last two great emergencies which had to be met by him before he could remodel the empire, and only he had the right to say what the model was to look like. With him removed, a long Inca resistance to the Spaniards was unthinkable, for there was neither an old nor a new empire from which to make it possible.

Like a burdensome phoenix Tahuantinsuyo had come to its end, splendid only in the suddenness of its fall, while out of the fires in which it was consumed arose the bedraggled bird of New Castile. On the morrow of November 16, Inti and the gods had been flung out of their house in Cajamarca and the gentle St. Francis installed in their place.

« 5 »

TWO ISSUES IN PARTICULAR were now to swamp the captivity of Atahualpa in a morass of intrigue: one Spanish, namely the ransom issue; the other Inca, the continuing existence of Huascar. All other issues were somehow to be caught up in these.

Pizarro had a legal document drawn up between himself and the captive Atahualpa containing the contractual arrangements for the ransom—its general terms well known to posterity. A room in the palace of Atahualpa's captivity was to be filled up to the sacred line with objects of gold and another room with silver. If this were performed within a certain number of days, Atahualpa was then to be assigned his freedom according to Pizarro's bond as well as the sanctity of Spanish legal procedure. But a new body of Spaniards under Pizarro's partner Almagro had just entered Peru, producing the natural suspicion on their part that as late-comers they might be excluded from their share of the loot. According to Zárate, this might well have aided in bringing about the treacherous execution of Atahualpa, an act designed, by the revival of the appearance of danger, to throw the situation back into one of active looting again.

The other issue concerned the curious and indeed unheard-of anomaly in history of one emperor's being held captive by invaders, representing an overseas emperor, while he was holding a third emperor captive. Three claims of imperial sovereignty could thus be simultaneously advanced: one on the grounds of legitimacy and seniority, the second on the grounds of consanguinity and conquest, and the third on the historic mission of Christianity and the evidence of the Papal bulls of 1494. This extreme situation was to last up to the very end of that fateful year.

From reports previously submitted to him Atahualpa was clearly aware of the overmastering passion of the Spaniards for gold. His calculated offer of the ransom was based on this. His mistake was in assessing the dignity of Pizarro's word as the equal of his own, and he therefore leaned on the ransom as the only means available to him to recover his freedom for he seems not to have dared to order either a rescue by force or the countervailing capture of Pizarro. His orders to the various parts of the empire for the delivery of all stocks of gold and silver objects, even those used in royal and divine services, were implicitly obeyed except in Pachacamac. As long as Atahualpa lived, the ingrained respect of the Peruvian for imperial authority could make itself felt.

One serious defection in his camp had already occurred, auguring the full disintegration soon to come. At the noise of the Spanish artillery, Rumiñaui had fled with his five thousand back to Quito, his native pueblo. Originally the captain of the guard and special confidant of Huayna Capac, he had been continued in this career by Atahualpa. Once back in Quito he usurped the authority, deposing Atahualpa's governor and ruling with a ferocity remarkable even for that day and age. His later career is symptomatic. After Atahualpa's death brought the whole Inca design into ruins, Rumiñaui was to butcher the remnants of the royal house in Quito. Illescas, Atahualpa's brother, was skinned and made into a drum. In consequence of these and similar horrors, the Cañars were to call in the Spaniard Benalcazar, who in hard fighting forced the Inca captain back through Riobamba. Burning and pillaging all the Inca tambos behind him in his slow retreat northward, Rumiñaui finally fell back on Quito. What Benalcazar was to find on entering that city was only what could attract the jackal and the thistle, for that capital had suffered the worst fate of all the cities. The aqueducts of the city were permanently destroyed, the stones of the city toppled, and the whole gutted by fire. The *acllas* and harem women the sadistic Rumiñaui was unable to take with him in his flight were killed and flung into the embers of the burning capital. Nothing, in short, was left to the Spaniards. The last days of this captain are unknown, for he departed into the volcanic east where today a mountain still bears his name. The other two great captains, Challcochima and Quizquiz, made no such attempt to clip off parts of the empire while Atahualpa was alive, no doubt because they were so closely tied to the still unresolved Huascar question. Let loose by the wild flight from the plaza of Cajamarca, the news of their master's capture speedily reached their ears. Until the success of the ransom and Atahualpa's freedom had been achieved their actions perforce had to be indecisive.

The news from Cajamarca, however, had fanned the flames of hope in the breasts of the partisans of Huascar in Cuzco, proving to them that the bearded ones were indeed the angelic Viracochas so long predicted in the old prophecy. It was equally obvious to them that Huascar from his captivity should now make to these Viracochas an offer of gold and silver greater than Atahualpa's promise and thus reverse the present intolerable situation.

Not content with Atahualpa's word that the ransom metal was being collected with all dispatch, Francisco·Pizarro had sent two Spanish inspection parties to the major centers of wealth, Cuzco and Pachacamac. In fast litters two Spaniards, Pedro de Moguer and Martín Bueno, with one Negro were sent over the great road to the capital, their passport being the person of one of Atahualpa's magnates. The Negro was dropped off in Jauja to organize gold collection in that city, which at the time was ecstatically celebrating its release from Inca rule, and thus Moguer and Bueno—otherwise unsung—became the first Europeans ever to enter the holy city of Cuzco. Quizquiz with a large garrison still had the city locked in an iron vise, but he honored Atahualpa's orders to give the Spaniards what facilities they needed, even though he did it with an open air of hostility.

The oppressed population received the two Viracochas who came gliding through their streets one dingy December day with a wild clamor, beseeching them for release from their captivity. Those violent and hostile layers of history out of which the city had originally been built could now be clearly seen. The ancient Alcaviza families which had never forgotten that they had once been the original possessors of Haucaypata broke into unrestrained rejoicing, and on learning that the Viracochas had come to secure gold, they rushed to contribute from their own stocks. The few Cañar and Chachapoya *mitmacs* remaining in the colonies near by—bitter converts at best to the Inca *raj*—showered friendliness upon the Spaniards and looked upon them as harbingers of better treatment. These and other dissident members of the city—some for hatred of Atahualpa, some for hatred of the Inca race in general—blew kisses to the Viracochas, worshipped them, and provided them with *acllas* and serving women.

But this holiday spirit was not to last long, for very soon the city learned of what manner of clay these beings were made. The two Spaniards misused the noblewomen, and when they burst into Coricancha equipped with crowbars to prize off the gold plates lining some of the walls, no Peruvian could be found to help them. Even

Quizquiz had not so deeply insulted their most sacred *huaca*. The two entered all the public buildings, palaces, repositories, and *canchas* of the dead kings, ordering the removal of every piece of gold or silver seen. Final disillusionment fell upon the city when news of the murder of their prince Huascar was received. It was then apparent that the Viracochas had come to loot the empire, not to preserve it for legitimacy. There was even talk of having the Spaniards put to death.

It was in this fashion that Christian Europe flung open the portals of the Andean world. The feeling which possessed James Bryce when he visited Cuzco comes to mind: "A strange and dreamy melancholy, a melancholy all the deeper because there was little in its past that one could wish restored. There were dark sides to the ancient civilization. But was it worth destroying in order to erect on its ruins what the Conquerors brought to Peru?"

The second and well-mounted gold-gathering patrol had gone out to Pachacamac under Hernando Pizarro. While on the site he destroyed the famous idol, which must have been to some degree pleasing to Atahualpa who had himself ardently desired to do the same, believing as he did that the *huaca* had been a tool of the Huascar faction. But the Spaniards were bitterly disappointed in the amount of gold they collected here, for the priesthood had spirited it away on news of their arrival. No doubt those treasures lie today on the far offshore bottom of the Pacific visited only by the fish. In returning via Jauja, Hernando Pizarro found Challcochima there with the last large organized Inca army in the field under his personal command. He had been terrorizing the Huancas and met the Spaniards with heads and hands spitted on his lance-points. Only after extended pressure from Hernando Pizarro, and because he felt unable to deal with the anomaly of the situation, did Challcochima entrust the army to a subordinate and accompany the Spaniards sullenly back to Cajamarca. By separating that army from its head, the Spaniards cut off the last hope of an organized Inca stand. Huascar had already been killed when Chalcochima left Jauja.

The decision previously taken by the Cuzco partisans, that their captured emperor should compete with Atahualpa for the Spaniards' favor, had signed Huascar's death warrant. Atahualpa, on receiving the word, was aware of the deepening gravity of the situation, and he adopted a plan that should be correct whatever attitude the Spaniards might adopt. He therefore one day presented to Pizarro a dejected and frightened air, and on being asked the reason, replied that his captain to the south had killed Huascar out of hand and contrary to orders. Pizarro, considering that after all he still had a worth-while bird in the hand, assured Atahualpa that it would make no difference in the terms of the contract or in their relationship. Thus assured that his own life would not be forfeit for the death of Huascar, Atahualpa dispatched a secret and urgent message to Challcochima to have Huascar destroyed. The year was approaching its end.

This was before Challcochima met Hernando Pizarro in Jauja. He had been moving north with a sizeable force and accompanied by the royal captives, including Huascar, the two queens, and such of the grandees as remained. It had been considered prudent not to have them in Cuzco, where sentiment showed still a propensity to flare up in their favor. Challcochima had planted his camp in Jauja, where he could stand between the Spaniards and his captives, for he had now had them sent off the route to the Inca station of Andamarca. While he waited, he campaigned locally among the Huancas. When Atahualpa's angels of death slipped down from the *puna* about Jauja with the command to do away with the embarrassing captives, Challcochima shot the word back into the hinterland. Here at Andamarca, Huascar, his shoulders threaded for leading, was dragged out and butchered. Here his *coya* Chuqui Huipa and the queen mother Rahua Ocllo similarly met their ends as well as the remaining male members of Huascar's partisans, their dismembered limbs being tumbled into the foaming waters below. The twelfth emperor was dead. The story of Tahuantinsuyo closed on a proscription whose unthinkable secrets only the mighty Amazon would then whisper for a while along her ten thousand banks.

« 6 »

ON THE RETURN OF Challcochima to Cajamarca in the company of Hernando Pizarro, Atahualpa pretended pleasure, but a grim story allows us to realize that this capture of Challcochima—for that is what it was—gave his master only a closer foreboding of his own demise. Dissatisfied with the gold deliveries and fearful of unknown Inca machinations, Francisco Pizarro ordered information to be extracted from Challcochima. Tied to a stake with heaped-up brush around him, he was threatened with burning if he did not divulge the truth. Atahualpa was brought to the scene but glared so menacingly at his great general that that individual requested the Spaniards to remove his royal master from his sight. Thereupon he confessed that Atahualpa had three or four times ordered him to prepare large groups to attack the Christians but each time countermanded the order in fear of his own jeopardy. As for the gold, he stated that Quizquiz still controlled large amounts of it in Cuzco. He was then released but kept under close surveillance. Rapidly Atahualpa's ability to conceive and activate plans was being sheared away.

Further insight into the intrigues swirling under the surface of this famous captivity is gained from the incident of those two half-brothers of Huascar who had escaped the proscriptions and sought refuge with Pizarro. They requested permission from the Spaniards to return to Cuzco. Unable to prevent in Cajamarca what he foresaw as an important linking-up of the chain of his eventual deposition as emperor, Atahualpa had them murdered on the road, even though they carried a Spanish steel sword as a passport of safety.

When the ransom had been all collected the Spaniards divided it up, sending the royal fifth back to Charles V in charge of Hernando Pizarro—a man whom Atahualpa knew to favor reasonable treatment for him as a prisoner. This removed an important check on that cabal which every day, to Atahualpa's certain knowledge, was advocating his death. Rumors of secret Inca armies gathering in hidden rendezvous began to appear with regularity. The Spanish cabal increasingly believed, or professed to believe, these rumors, while among his own magnates Atahualpa's illegitimacy and usurpation—hitherto forbidden subjects—began now to enter ominously into their conversation.

Through his spies Atahualpa could follow this process. He was surely not surprised therefore when, after some ominous activity, his other solitary supporter among the Spaniards, Hernando de Soto, was sent out on a wild-goose chase to reconnoiter the near-by valleys. In the interval of his absence it was finally decided—against some who advocated that Atahualpa be sent back to Charles V in Spain—that Atahualpa be summarily executed. The illegality or the expediency of the decision is not our subject here. Briefly the charges preferred were Atahualpa's treachery in raising armies (for evidence of which the Spaniards were even then fruitlessly scouring the country side) to which was added Huascar's murder and possibly the Inca lord's incestuous marriage to his sister.

When informed of the verdict of the drumhead court, Atahualpa is reported to have replied in the following vein to Pizarro and his captains: "How can you take me for one so depraved of sense as, in my position, to commit treason! The troops you say are gathering outside at my orders could not save me, tied as I am in iron shackles, from your retaliation. If you believe they are gathering without my orders, then you are ill informed as to my supreme power over all beings in this land. If I so desire, no bird flies here and no leaf stirs." In conclusion, he offered immense pledges for the first Spaniard who should be treacherously killed in the land. Over and over he pleaded with them to suspend sentence until the return of De Soto's search party, which would bring in evidence of the falseness of the charges. But this the conquerors had no intention of doing.

The sentence was burning at the stake, an end reserved by the Spaniards for heinous moral crimes, witchcraft, and heresy. Atahualpa and his people were more frightened at this than at the sentence of death itself. That a great lord should be deprived of his mummy after death was an unthinkable abasement and annihilation, and against this he specially pleaded. On condition that he become a Christian, Pizarro agreed that he could be garroted instead. Whereupon Fray Vicente baptized him and named him, after his captor and benefactor, Don Francisco Atahualpa. Atahualpa told his people that he would come to rule over them again for his father Inti would bring life back into his body now that, after death, he would not be dispersed in dust and ashes.

On a Saturday night in the year 1533, the plaza of Cajamarca filled up with Atahualpa's women and courtiers plus a decent party of Spaniards in mourning headed by Francisco Pizarro, white haired, lean, and scarred. At dusk and to the muttered prayers of the Spanish party Atahualpa was escorted into the center of the square and tied to a post. Here he calmly commended his sons to Pizarro, requested that his mummy be taken to Quito, and was strangled by Negroes selected to be his executioners. Hanging on its stake, the body was guarded throughout the night while thousands of Indians groveled round about in the square. Some of his women succeeded in hanging themselves while the two sister-wives performed the ancient funeral rites with drums and wailed appeals to their hero to return from his sleep of death. These ceremonies were brought to a swift end when the Spaniards divided up Atahualpa's women as part of the spoils of the occasion. At dawn the body was cut down and buried with solemn Christian rites in the Spaniards' chapel. Later his body was secretly taken up out of the ground by a party of Indians and borne back into the Ecuadoran hills. No one knows the fate of Atahualpa's remains, for the cortege escorting them was met by Rumiñaui in Liripampa, where all were treacherously slain as they feasted in honor of their dead *sinchi*.

« 7 »

OUR STORY IS DONE. What follows is epilogue. From 1533 to the year 1572 it is a tale which concerns the hopeless quest of the Incas for a proper status within the ambient of Spanish power in New Castile. Atahualpa's son Topa Hualpa (Royal Cock) was created a puppet emperor but was dead in two months, and with this the Atahualpa faction succumbed to the Huascar group which now saw to it that Challcochima, their pitiless destroyer, ended on the Spanish stake. And Quizquiz, joined by Huaypalcon, a brother of Atahualpa, in his dash up to Quito, was slain by that person in a last futile council of war. *Sic semper tyrannis.*

Manco Inca, a half-brother of Huascar who had somehow escaped the proscriptions, was then crowned emperor in October, 1533, but, subjected to the continuous insults of the Spaniards, led a formidable rebellion against the conquistadors in 1536 which proved only that Inca power had been of parochial growth and must wither in a larger world garden. With the collapse of that attempt to drive out the invader, Manco Inca, like the Chancas before him, fled into the montaña, there to rule the province of Vilcabamba as a rump empire. The Vilcabamba state had no polity of its own save mere survival, raiding, and devastation. Assassinated by renegade Spaniards, Manco Inca left three sons, each of whom with varying vicissitudes ruled as relict emperor over the lonesome outpost of Tahuantinsuyo. The last one, Topa Amaru, was finally tracked down in the wilds of the montaña and executed in Cuzco in 1572.

The Spaniards continued to ride like deathly shadows over this land, strong in their quest, voracious in their hungers, unconquerable in their gross visions. From the native race whose well-woven mantle they wrapped so thinly about their shoulders they learned to speak only these words of easy pacification: *Ama mancha ñoca Inca*, "Fear not, I am an Inca."

§   §   §

The *cantut*-flowers, crimsons and yellows, bloomed as ever by the roads leading in and out of the Spanish *cabildo* of Cuzco. Cuzco was a colonial city of violence, strange aberrant murders, masked stabbings of both men and women, a city of floods, hail, lightning, terrible plagues, and even more terrible earthquakes. Periodically it would be seized by sudden and unaccountable panic which would in a matter of moments pour into the central square great crowds of abject and trembling Indians. It was also a city of fantastic wealth, being an entrepôt for the silver of Potosí. Today the walls of Coricancha blandly survey the trucks and foot traffic that squeeze past them along the road leading out to the airport. The wonderful cathedral stands on the site of Viracocha Inca's great establishments, and the curious tourist may even see bits of their ancient masonry still in place. The unheeding who warm themselves on the benches of the Plaza de Armas are inhabiting a bit of this earth's surface both resplendent and tragic with the events of history. Bryce said of it: "The feeling of a vista stretching far back filled with many specters of the past is overpowering."

CHRONOLOGY

The Spanish dates in this table are certain. The Inca dates are purely conjectural and have no foundation in attested fact, being set down purely to display the chronological structure of this history. Dates marked with an asterisk are taken from Cabello Valboa. Spanish events are in italic type.

1250	Incas enter Cuzco
1391	Pachacuti born
1400	Accession of Viracocha Inca
*1438	Chanca war
1440	Antisuyo campaigns; rebuilding of Cuzco begins
1441–44	Vilcas campaign
1448	Topa Inca born
1445–50	Collao campaign
*1463	Topa commands army; coregency
1463–70	Chinchaysuyo campaign
1471–74	Conquest of south coast
1473	Pachacuti dies
1473–75	Madre de Dios campaign
1474–80	Collao rebellion
1480–82	Charcas campaign

1482–85	Chilean campaign
1485–89	Topa's grand tour
1488	Huayna Capac born
1492	*Columbus discovers America*
*1493	Topa Inca dies
1511	Huayna Capac goes north
1513	*Balboa discovers the Pacific*
1522	End of Carangui war; *Andagoya's voyage; Cortez conquers Mexico*
1523	Chiriguana raid.
1524	Huayna Capac in lowlands
1524–25	*Pizarro's first voyage*
1526	Huayna Capac dies; *Pizarro's second voyage begins, January*
1527	*Pizarro on the coast of Peru*
1528	Quilaco embassy
1530	War of the Two Brothers begins
1531	*Pizarro's third voyage begins, January; Pizarro in Coaque, April to September*
1532	Battle of Cotapampa, very early in the year; Atahualpa captured, November 16; *San Miguel founded, September*
1533	Atahualpa executed, late June or July

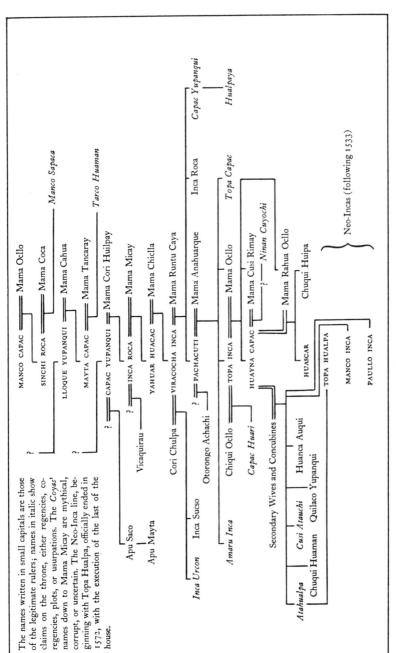

The names written in small capitals are those of the legitimate rulers; names in italic show claims on the throne, either regencies, co-regencies, plots, or usurpations. The *Coyas'* names down to Mama Micay are mythical, corrupt, or uncertain. The Neo-Inca line, beginning with Topa Hualpa, officially ended in 1572, with the execution of the last of the house.

MANCO CAPAC ══ Mama Ocllo

SINCHI ROCA ══ Mama Coca
              ══ *Manco Sapaca*

LLOQUE YUPANQUI ══ Mama Cahua

MAYTA CAPAC ══ Mama Tancaray
            ══ *Tarco Huaman*

? ══ CAPAC YUPANQUI ══ Mama Cori Huilpay
  │── Apu Saco
  │── *Vicaquirau*
  │── Apu Mayta

? ══ INCA ROCA ══ Mama Micay

YAHUAR HUACAC ══ Mama Chicla

VIRACOCHA INCA ══ Mama Runtu Caya
  │── Cori Chulpa
  │── *Otorongo Achachi*
  │── *Inca Urcon*   Inca Sucso

? ══ PACHACUTI ══ Mama Anahuarque   Inca Roca   *Capac Yupanqui*
                                                            │── *Hualpaya*

TOPA INCA ══ Mama Ocllo   *Topa Capac*
  │── *Amaru Inca*
  │── Chiqui Ocllo ══
  │── *Capac Huari*

HUAYNA CAPAC ══ Mama Cusi Rimay
             ══ ?── *Ninan Cuyochi*
             ══ Mama Rahua Ocllo   Chuqui Huipa
             ══ Secondary Wives and Concubines

HUASCAR

Atahualpa   *Cusi Atauchi*   Huanca Auqui
  │── Chuqui Huaman   Quilaco Yupanqui

TOPA HUALPA

MANCO INCA

PAULLO INCA

⎫
⎬ Neo-Incas (following 1533)
⎭

Genealogical Table of the Imperial Inca House

NOTES ON SOURCES

I HAVE ESSAYED no overall bibliographical task of exegesis here, though this would have strengthened the work. The list of abbreviations of sources shows only a part of the published material I have consulted. For more complete information in this regard the reader is encouraged to go to the bibliographies in the works of John Howland Rowe, J. Alden Mason, Louis Baudin, Philip Ainsworth Means, and others.

The indispensible sources are of course Sarmiento and Cabello Valboa, Cieza de León, Betanzos, and Cobo. Others such as Polo, Las Casas, Pachacuti, Cristóbal de Molina, and Fernandez are invaluable, often for specific topics, but in the main the bulk of the works fall into families descended from one or other of the basic sources, some of which have disappeared. Some works such as Montesinos and Velasco are puzzles, though the latter has many nuggets to be mined out if one is perceptive. Garcilaso, the Livy of the group, is novelistic and romantic. In a few spots he is indispensable. Huaman Poma I have cited in two editions, as the facsimile version (GPF) carries the story farther than the printed one (GP).

In citing the works of Santa Cruz Pachacuti, two editions were inadvertently used—the one listed below as published in Madrid,

and another published in Asunción, Paraguay, in 1950. If the page
citations are incorrect for one edition, they will be correct for the
other. This error was discovered too late to regain consistency.

Because I have written this *de novo* out of the primary sources,
reference to secondary works has been generally eschewed. A major
exception has been made in the case of Rowe's studies, all of
which are impressively scholarly. He is cited as RAC for "Absolute
Chronology in the Andean Area," *American Antiquity*, Vol. X
(1944–45), and as RIC for "Inca Culture at the Time of the Spanish
Conquest," *Handbook of the South American Indians*, Vol. II
(1946). Where works by authors other than Rowe from the *Handbook* are cited, the abbreviation is HSAI. Rowe's article on Viracocha,
"The Origins of Creator Worship among the Incas," in *Culture in
History: Essays in Honor of Paul Radin* (1960), appeared after
this work reached its final form. I am pleased that my conclusions
agree with his, except that I have put more stress on the importance
of the reign preceding that of Pachacuti in the growth of that religion.

In the spelling of Quechua words the ideal would have been to
follow the system enunciated first in Rowe and Escobar, *Los sonidos
quechuas de Cuzco y Chanca* (1943). Owing to the conquistadors' in-
competence in transcribing Quechua words into Spanish, plus garbled
texts, this has been impossible. I have therefore adopted no system
at all, which includes of course tolerance of inconsistencies such as
bamba or *pampa*; Topa, Tupa, or Tupac; Andamarca or Antamarca;
etc. I believe no real harm will eventuate from this, and indeed the
general reader may even learn to revel, as I do, in the bizarre charm
of the original Spanish spellings. After all, when behind the single
Spanish spelling *tanta* lurk three differently pronounced Quechua
words, meaning either "bread," "heap," or "ragged," then the trans-
lator's task is formidable indeed. As for the citations in the Notes on
Sources, the reader should not be puzzled; when he has the volume
in hand it will be apparent whether the numerals refer to books,
chapters, or pages. I have used only the dictionaries of Gonzalez
Holguín and Domingo de Santo Tomás for translations of Quechua
words, as these are nearest to the Incaic period.

We might add here that the first two chapters are an exercise in
possibilities. Another historian could arrange the pitiful remnants

of our information in a totally different fashion and with justification. May he be encouraged to do so.

THESE NOTES bear the following code references:

ABC   Alonso Borregán, *Crónica de la conquista del Perú*, Seville, 1948.

AC   Anon., *Anales del Cuzco, 1600 a 1750*, Lima, 1901.

ACCM   Antonio de la Calancha, *Corónica moralizada del órden de San Augustín en el Perú*, Barcelona, 1638.

AEI   Pablo José de Arriaga, *La extirpación de la idolatría en el Perú*, Lima, 1920.

ARGCS   Alonso Ramós Gavilán, *Historia del célebre santuario de Nuestra Señora de Copacabana*, Lima, 1621.

AZH   Agustín de Zárate, *Historia del descubrimiento y conquista de la provincia del Perú*, Madrid, 1853.

BC   Bernabé Cobo, *Historia del nuevo mundo*, Vols. III, IV, Cuzco, 1956.

BLC   Bartolomé de las Casas, *Apologética historia de las Indias*, Madrid, 1909.

BSC   Buenaventura de Salinas y Córdoba, *Memoriál de las historias del nuevo mundo . . . Piru*, Lima, 1957.

BV   Blas Valera, *Relación de las costumbres antiguas de los naturales del Pirú*, in *Tres relaciones de antigüedades peruanas*, Madrid, 1879.

CA   Anon. *La conquista del Perú*, in *Proc. Amer. Acad. Arts and Sciences*, Vol. LXIV, No. 8 (1930).

CCDM   Cristóbal de Castro and Diego de Ortega Morejón, *Relación y declaración del modo que este valle de Chincha y sus comarcanos se governavan antes que oviese Yngas*, in H. Trimborn, *Quellen zur Kulturgeschichte des praekolum—bischen Amerika*, Stuttgart, 1936.

CL   Pedro de Cieza de León, *Segunda parte de la crónica del Perú*, Madrid, 1880.

CLPP   Pedro de Cieza de León, *Primera parte . . .* , many eds.

CLTP   Pedro de Cieza de León: *Tercera parte . . .* , in the *Mercurio Peruana, revista mensual de ciencias sociales y letras*, Lima.

CM   Cristóbal de Molina, *Fabulas y ritos de los Incas*, Lima, 1916.

CV   Miguel Cabello Valboa, *Miscelanea antártica*, Lima, 1951.

DF	Diego Fernandez, *Historia del Perú (Libro tercero de la segunda parte)*, Lima, 1876.
DIIH	Francisco Dávila, *Idolatrías de los Indios de Huarochirí*, Lima, 1918.
FJ	Francisco de Jerez, *Verdadera relación de la conquista del Perú y provincia del Cuzco*, Madrid, 1853.
FS	Fernando de Santillán, *Relación del origen, descendencia, política, y gobierno de los Incas*, in *Tres relaciones de antigüedades peruanas*, Madrid, 1879.
GBH	Girolamo Benzoni, *History of the New World*, London, 1857.
GGO	Gregorio García, *Origen de los Indios del nuevo mundo*, Madrid, 1729.
GHLQ	Diego Gonzalez Holguín, *Vocabulario de la lengua general de todo el Perú llamada lengua Qquichua o del Inca*, Lima, 1952.
GHV	Francisco López de Gómara, *Hispania Victrix (o La Historia general de las Indias)*, *Primera parte*, in *Historiadores primitivos de Indias*, Vol. I, Madrid, 1852.
GP	Huaman Poma de Ayalá, *Primera nueva crónica y buen gobierno*, *Primera parte*, Lima, 1956.
GPF	Huaman Poma de Ayalá, *Nueva crónica y buen gobierno*, Paris, Institut d'Ethnologie, 1936 (facsimile version).
GSC	Gutiérrez de Santa Clara, *Historia de las guerras civiles del Perú*, Madrid, 1905.
GVCR	Garcilaso de la Vega, *Comentarios reales de los Incas*, Buenos Aires.
IH	Roberto Levillier, ed., *Información hecha en el Cuzco por orden del rey y encargo del Virrey Martín Enríquez acerca de las costumbres que tenían los Incas del Perú*, in *Gobernantes del Perú*, Vol. IX, Madrid, 1925.
ISP	Anon., *Informaciones sobre el antiguo Perú*, Lima, 1922.
ISP-HP	*Relación de Hernando Pizarro acerca de la conquista.*
ISP-IH	*Información sobre idolatrías en Huacho.*
ISP-TY	*Relación de señores Indios que sirvieron a Tupac Yupanqui y Huayna Capac.*
ISP-VC	*Declaración de los quipocamayos a Vaca de Castro.*
ISP-VT	*Informaciones al virrey Toledo.*
JA	José de Acosta, *Historia natural y moral de las Indias*, Mexico, 1940.

JB	Juan de Betanzos, *Suma y narración de los Incas*, Madrid, 1880.
LAC	Lope de Atienza: *Compendio historial del estado de los Indios del Perú*, Quito, 1931.
LDB	Reginaldo de Lizárraga, *Descripción breve de toda la tierra del Perú, Tucumán, Río de la Plata, y Chile*, Madrid, 1909.
LTOP	Roberto Levillier, ed., *Don Francisco de Toledo, supremo organizador del Perú*, Vol. II, *Sus informaciones sobre los Incas*, Buenos Aires, 1940.
MGP	Juan Matienzo, *Gobierno del Peru*, 1910.
MHVE	Marie Helmer, *La vie économique au XVIᵉ siècle sur le haut-plateau andin, Chucuito en 1567—d'après un document inédit des archives des Indes*, in *Travaux de l'Institut français d'Études andines*, Lima, 1951.
MM	Martín de Morúa, *Historia del origen y genealogía real de los reyes Incas del Perú*, Lima, 1922–25.
MM-DN	Martín de Morúa: *Declaración del nombre deste reino del Perú con las ciudades que hay en él*.
NC	Anon., *Nouvelles certaines des isles du Perú*, translated by Raul Porras Barrenechea, *Las relaciones primitivas de la conquista del Perú*, in *Cuadernos de historia del Perú*, No. 2, Paris, 1937.
OV	Gonzalo Hernandez de Oviedo y Valdés: *Historia general y natural de las Indias*, Madrid, 1851–55.
PO	Polo de Ondegardo, *Del linage de los Ingas y como conquistaron*, Lima, 1917.
PO:Error.	Polo de Ondegardo, *Los errores y supersticiones de los Indios*, Lima, 1916.
PO:Fund.	Polo de Ondegardo, *Relación de los fundamentos acerca del notable daño que resulta de no guardar a los Indios sus fueros*, Lima, 1916.
PO:Tras.	Polo de Ondegardo, *Traslado de un cartapacio a manera de borrador*, Lima, 1917.
PPR	Pedro Pizarro, *Relación del descubrimiento y conquista de los reinos del Perú*, Madrid, 1844.
PRN	Pedro Ruiz Naharro, *Relación de los hechos de los Españoles en el Perú*, Madrid, 1855.

RGI	*Relación geográficas de Indias, Peru,* 4 vols. Madrid, 1881–97.
RHA	*Relación de la religion y ritos del Perú hecha por los primeros religiosos agustinos,* Lima, 1918.
RZ	Jerónimo Román y Zamora, *Republicas de Indias; idolatrías y gobierno en Mexico y Perú antes de la conquista,* Madrid, 1897.
SG	Pedro Sarmiento de Gamboa, *Segunda parte de la historia general llamada Indica,* in *Abhndl. Konig. Gesell. Wissensch. zu Göttingen,* neue Folg. Band VI aus den Jahren 1902–1906. Berlin.
SPY	Juan de Santa Cruz Pachacuti Yamqui Salcamaygua, *Relación de antigüedades deste reino del Perú,* in *Tres relaciones de antigüedades peruanas,* Madrid, 1897.
TCYI	Diego de Castro Tito Cusi Yupanqui Inca, *Relación de la conquista del Perú y hechos del Inca Manco II,* Lima, 1916.
VRQ	Juan de Velasco, *Historia del reino de Quito,* 3 vols. Quito, 1841–1849.

PREFACE and IN THE BEGINNING . . .

Preliminaries: For "*Ñaupa pacha,*" GSC III, 56; GHLQ 259; GP 204. For fourfold classification of sierra history, GP 35–58. We treat this scheme with a certain credence firstly because there is agreement elsewhere (SG 10, 32; ISP-VT 106) on the heroic caste of the fourth age and on an age of the *purun-pacha* (SPY 235), and secondly because the Rucanas had memories, as well as ruins, of a pre-Inca culture of stone-builders and missionaries among them, whom they called Viracochas just as in Huaman Poma's golden age (RGI I, 210). I have translated *huari* as origin here, rather than the place name, in view of GP 55. Huaman Poma's attempt to disestablish the Incas as the inventors of all the best in sierra life is upheld by considering the noncontiguous civilization of the Chibchas where the following traits, all of which are characteristic of the Incas, are also found: gold-hunger, servile and exaggerated obeisance to the ruler, large armies, child sacrifice, use of ancestral mummies or relics as battle standards, segregation of princes in temples before investment with the royal power, wearing of earplugs, and worship of the sun as an ancestor, OV XXVI, 30f.

CHAPTER I—THE SETTLEMENT OF CUZCO IN LEGEND AND FACT

The Sacred Legend: Sarmiento is fundamental here; his information came out of the various Inca barrios of Cuzco with their local memories of the early situation. He has a full itinerary of the Wandering and much ethnic information. Santa Cruz Pachacuti is as good in detail not found elsewhere; his knowledge covers areas farther to the southeast of Cuzco, as we might expect from his provenience. Cabello Valboa follows Sarmiento closely. Though he rationalizes some of his material and presents the Incas as clever charlatans, he seldom twists the facts; he lacks Sarmiento's fullness of detail on the tribal situation. Cieza has a streamlined, official version of the Wandering but deals only shortly with the Founding. The same is true of Betanzos, though he does include some information from the Alcavizas. Garcilaso knew the story but did not consider it the official version, which was otherwise related to him by his uncle, GVCR I, 15–18. Gavilán gives us a ridiculously rationalized and local piece of nonsense. Morúa has two or three bits which are useful. Almost every chronicler has some reference to the story. When the tale comes from the confines of the empire—Ecuador, for instance—Manco Capac alone of the brothers appears, LAC I. For the three names of Pacaritambo, SG II, 33; SPY 244f. The name Huanacauri is given in GHLQ, 73 (if *huayahuari* is in error for *huanacauri*?) as a word synonomous with "rainbow" (corroborated in SG 12).

The Huallas: The presence of the Hualla cave of origination in the area proves them to have been autochthonous to Cuzco, BC XIII, 14. The Quechua names found among the Huallas in the days of Toledo can be attributed to their years as subjects of the Inca empire. It is an interesting if dangerous speculation to equate them archaeologically with a Chanapata people (see J. H. Rowe, *Introduction to Archaeology of Cuzco*, Peabody Museum Papers [1944]; also Rowe, *Archaeological Exploration of Southern Peru*, in *American Antiquity* [Oct., 1956]) who survived through the Huari-Tiahuanaco occupation.

The Sinchis: For the bringing in of *sinchis* from other groups, SG 8. For the "tyrannies" which, like the Incas, they set up, SG 10. For their titles, GP 45–50, 107. For election to the office and relinquishment of same, ISP-VT 106; SG 8; BLC 250.

The Sauasirays: For origins from the cave of Sutictoco and settlement on the uninhabited site of the later Santo Domingo, ISP-VT 133; SG 13. For the four building enclosures on the early site, SG 13. The first Incas in the valley, before their final push into Cuzco proper, were for a while resident in Cayaocachi, the present parish of Belén, south of the Chunchulmayo, FS 2. According to our reconstruction these first Incas should therefore have been the Sauasirays.

The Antasayas: The Cuzco Indians (also called Antasayas) were certainly among the first to enter the valley. The Antasaya *ayllus* testified that Manco Capac, coming into the Huatanay area, found their ancestors already settled there, ISP-VT 134b. The identification of Ayar Auca as the *genius* of the Antasayas is evident from the fact that when he alighted in his last flight to Cuzco he became a stone *huaca* called Cuzco Huanca (Field-Guardian of the Cuzcos), SG 39. Cuzco Huanca is even specifically classed as one of the four Ayar brothers, MM-DN 2 (this source adds that he was the "first" Inca to conquer the city though he died before becoming king). The flight of Ayar Auca and his translation into a *huaca* is therefore that relic of the Antasaya version of their entry which for later reasons of policy the Tambos welded onto their own. Manco Capac has thus nothing to do with the center of Cuzco—his role in the legend stops when he settles on the fields of Huaynapata.

The Alcavizas: This group had seized the Huatanay ford, perhaps from the Sauasirays, and settled there, ISP-VT 135; JB 3; SG 14. For their later banishment from the triangle by Pachacuti, JB 16. For the identification of Ayar Ucho as the *genius* of the Alcavizas, ISP-VT, 135. An Ayar Ucho *ayllu* existed even in Toledo's day, ISP-VT, 135.

Manco and the Tambo Group: An official hymn to the sun (J. H. Rowe, *Eleven Inca Prayers from the Zithuwa Ritual*, in Kroeber, *Anthropological Society Papers*, Nos. 8 and 9 [1953], Hymn No. 10) makes clear that the nuclear Incas were either "Cuzcos or Tambos." Manco is never said to be a Cuzco Indian; thus he has to be a Tambo for only these two groups were the true and original children of the Sun. For Manco as of Tambo lineage, JA I, 25. His father was Apu Tambo (The Tambo Captain), SPY 240–46. Manco has a servant of his called Tambo Chacay (Tambo Plug) sent back for a special purpose to his cave of origination, the name of which was Tambotoco (Cave of the Tambos), cv III, 9f. For Caxatambo as the real name of Pacaritambo, ISP-TY, 57. For Manco as a war-standard, see the analogy with the Chanca ruler whose mummy led his people into battle, SG 26.

The Attack on the Ridge: For the attack on the Huallas, SG 13; cv III, 10; JB 4. The field of Huaynapata had belonged to the Huallas. For Hualla retirement from the valley, ISP-VT 141f; cv III, 10; JB 4. The attack is allotted in the Sacred Legend however to Manco, who must have launched it against the Antasayas—if he fought here at all. Copali Mayta is said to have led the Sauasirays, SG 40, and again the Huallas, cv III, 10. For Copali Mayta's quotation, cv III, 10. For Manco's division of the conquered lands in the triangle into four parts, ACCM I, 15.

The Itinerary: The best account is SG 12f. For the settlement at Matahua, cv III, 9f. For birthplace of Sinchi Roca, cv III, 9–10. For his marriage, CL 31; cv III, 10; BC XII, 4; SG 15; JB 5. This sañu marriage must have been the first triumph of Inca policy, for there is unusual unanimity among the chroniclers about it. For Huanacauri as the sacred mountain of the Sañus, cv III, 9 (this is no doubt the *huaca* near Sañu referred to in SPY 240–46). For the entry of the Sañu people under their *sinchi* into Cuzco along with the Tambos, CL 32.

Mama Huaco: For her name as Pachamama Achic, SPY 240–46. The equation between Pachamama the Earth Mother and Mama Huaco is strengthened by the remark that Pachamama was worshipped as an open field above Cuzco, BC XIII, 14 (this probably refers to the lands seized from the Huallas and turned over to Mama Huaco, cv III, 10; CM 86). On Mama Huaco, her attributes as witch, oracle, snake-goddess, and giver of fertility, GP 60f., 90f. For Mama Huaco's decimation of Huallas and Sauasirays, ISP-VT 136f. Garcilaso, either from inspired confusion or a true memory, gives her name as

Mama Ocllo Huaco (Holy Mother Wisdom-Tooth). By splitting off the adjective and deifying it, two aspects of one goddess could thus be achieved—a common procedure in cult—which may explain the indecision in our sources as to whether Mama Ocllo or Mama Huaco was Manco's wife.

Primitive Inti Cult: The sacred bird of the Incas was no doubt a hawk or similar bird of prey, GP 61f. It was the Quiquijana (Conquest Sign?).

CHAPTER II—THE FIRST SEVEN RULERS

The Ethnic Situation in the Valley: Eighteen of the thirty-eight pueblos in the valley southeast of Cuzco were Ayamarca, GVCR I, 20. For Huaro, BC XII, 6. On Pikillacta, Rowe, *Archaeological Exploration of Southern Peru, passim*.

The Term Inca: For meaning of word, SG 11; GP 59; ARGCS I, 2; AZH 11; Matienzo, *Gobierno del Peru*, I, 1; DF V; CV XLVII, 9; RGI II, 25; GSC III, 49f. For the Hahua Inca, GP 171. For the two Inca dynasties, GP 59f., 66, 108f. These two dynasties were first the legitimate Intip Churin, Children of the Sun (worshipping the well-known Inca gods), and secondly a usurping group of Amaru (Serpent) people whose totem was the Quiquijana bird and who are the historic Incas as we know them. For their respective blazons, GP 59–62. The last ruler of the first dynasty was Tocay Capac, who fought either Sinchi Roca or Lloque Yupanqui. Huaman Poma's two Inca dynasties are a puzzle—invented perhaps to discredit the historic Incas as usurpers. For the military character of the early constitution, SG 14.

Sinchi Roca and Lloque Yupanqui: For Sinchi Roca at Matahua, CV III, 10f. For his marriage with Mama Coca, SG 15; CV III, 10; JB 5. For Manco Sapaca, SG 13, 16; CV III, 10f. For Lloque Yupanqui as unwarlike, SG 16; CV III, 12; GSC III, 49; GP 72; ACCM I, 15; DF V; ARGCS I, 3. For the connection between Lloque and Huaro, CV III, 12; BC XII, 6. For the *coya's* name, SG 16; CV III, 12; GSC III, 49; BLC 250.

Mayta Capac: For the struggle with the Alcavizas, ISP-VT, 137f. We

attribute the invention or first regular use of *mitmacs* to Mayta Capac
on the basis of ISP-VT 137f., though it was probably Topa Inca who
geared it to empire. For Mayta's attitude toward the cults of the
conquered, CV III, 12; SPY 155. Mayta is once said to have been the
first Inca to rule in Cuzco, DF V.

Capac Yupanqui: BC XII, 8, attributes the division of the emperors
into residents of either Upper or Lower Cuzco to Capac Yupanqui.
SG says that the point of division begins with his son Inca Roca. We
have accepted Cobo as he seems to be corroborated in CL 34, where
we find that Capac Yupanqui was the first to build a palace for himself. SG 19 says that the first palace (which he attributes to Inca Roca)
was in Upper Cuzco.

Inca Roca: Huayllacan was in the Yucay Valley, RZ II, 11; BLC 250.
The name Ayhuairo is found today in the northwestern part of the
Anta Basin, near Maras—could this serve to locate the center of
Tocay's power? For Sumac Inca of Huayllacan (or Patahuayllacan),
SG 19, 23. Luis Pardo, *Ruinas precolombinas de Cuzco* (Cuzco,
1937), gives a story whose setting he says was in Pikillacta in the
days of Huayna Capac and is reminiscent of the story of Mama
Micay and the bringing of water to Cuzco; it concerns the *curaca*'s
daughter Sumac Tica, for whose hand the neighboring suitors performed prodigies of irrigation—Pardo gives no source for this tale.
For the statement that Inca Roca's sons "hastened his death," ACCM
I, 15. Vicaquirau is said to have reduced the twin pueblos of Muhina
and Pinahua, but this occurred after Inca Roca had died, SG 23. For
the presumed physical characteristics of Inca Roca, GP 77.

Yahuar Huacac: For his full name as Titu Cusi Hualpa, SG 20. For
his name alternately as Mayta Yupanqui, ISP-VC 14. Knowledge of
this reign must be had from a painstaking critique of SG 20–23.
Herein is a curious doublet of the Yahuar Huacac abduction story,
where the pueblo of Huayllacan is again involved in a plot over the
Inca succession, but regarding now the heir of Yahuar Huacac, not
of Inca Roca. This plot resulted, however, in the murder of the heir
and second son Pahuac Hualpa Mayta in the town of Paullu to
which he had been treacherously invited. This conspiracy involved

the old Huayllacan *curaca* Sumac Inca, the father of the *coya*. In revenge the Incas almost exterminated the Huayllacans. This story may be the original version—it reads less romantically—and folk-tale ingenuity may have passed it back and imposed it upon the more colorful father, Yahuar Huacac. This would then explain the difficulties of the Inca historians in keeping the twice-abducted young prince alive for so long a period and amid such hostile surroundings. The doublet also, if it is true, would help to explain why the third of the legitimate sons of Yahuar Huacac succeeded to the rule—the second having been assassinated. Compare also the account in DF V, where, though Yahuar Huacac is confused with his father, a simpler version is given—this has the abducted three-year-old prince kept by the *curaca* of Jaquijahuana, finally to be discovered and rescued by his uncle Huaylla Cancaca (Huayllacan Curaca?). For the statement that Yahuar Huacac renounced the throne for the last seven years of his life, VRQ II, 24.

Early Chronology: See Rowe, *Introduction to Archaeology of Cuzco*, 55–59, for a summary of his position with supporting tabulations.

CHAPTER III—BASIC FORMS OF PERUVIAN RELIGION

General Statements: On the deep religiosity of the Indians, LAC 4: "It happens many times, in pointing out the places, whether close by or far, where the sacrificial objects were buried, that the indians so fear their devils that they fall speechless and almost paralyzed. No human power can force them to tell in words where the treasures are and only after a while will they open their eyes and—biting the cloak with which they cover themselves from sheer anxiety—finally designate with their glance the spot where one is to dig. And this being started, if anything is uncovered, nothing in the world will prevail upon them to touch the object brought out."

Pachamama: For the Sun and the Earth as the the two high deities, BC XIII, 23. For Pachamama modeled in clay, GSC III, 56. A possible exception to our theory of the "unofficial" status of Pachamama in Inca cult may appear in the royal prayer where the Earth mother is petitioned to take the Inca ruler, "thy child, in thine arms" and to lead him by the hand, Rowe, *Eleven Inca Prayers*, 93. For the oracular shrine of Pachamama on the Rímac just above Chosica, RGI I, 75, appendix cxx (see also map reproduced on p. 6of.). For the special *huaca* of a confluence of two streams (tinco yaco), GP 216. For cult of Pachamama as belonging intimately to women, AEI II; FS 27. For myth of Pariacaca and Chuqui Suso, DIIH 7. For Pachamama adored as a field above Cuzco, BC XIII, 14. For the Aymoray festival, CM 86; PO:Error. VIII. For the Inca cult of Pachamama which was taken down to Copacabana, ARGCS I, 29. For her connections with the Virgin Mary, ARGCS I, 27.

Mamacocha: For worship of the sea down on the coast, ACCM II, 11. For Lake Titicaca as the mother of the Collas, GVCR II, 19. For springs as Daughters of the Sea, JA V, 18; BC XIII, 22. For the prayer to the spring, BC XIII, 21. For the myth of Coniraya, DIIH 2.

Concept of Huaca: For *huac* and *huaccay*, GHLQ 164, 166f. Note however that Gómara says that the word *huaca* comes from *huay*, an exclamation of lament, a wail, GHV 227, 232 (see also GHLQ 164f.), and he backs up his statement by adverting to the wailing and weeping which was indeed the customary approach to a *huaca*. For a *huaca* in Huamachuco that patronized weaving and dying, RHA 30. For the legend of Mama Coca, LTOP 10; ISP-VT 114.

Andean Sun Cults: The Chibchas worshipped Usa, the Sun, and his wife Chia, the Moon, in temples which were pilgrimage centers and where the sun-god was fed with the blood of children; as a people they considered themselves to be brothers of the Sun, OV XXVI, 3of. For human sacrifice to the Sun in the coastal valleys of Peru, OV XLVI, 17. The Chachapoyas adored the Sun before the coming of the Incas, CLPP 78. The coastal valleys of Végueta and Huacho utilized the Sun in their myths, AEI 7, but Chincha and Icá seem to have had no important sun-worship. Sun and Moon were most highly honored in the Quito area, LAC XLI; RGI III, 167, 172, 193.

Atmospheric Huacas: For the legend of Pariacaca and Huallallo, RGI I, 71f. For the storm as a heavenly slinger, JA V, 4; PO:Error. I. For the storm-god as Santiago, AEI 6; PO, *Instr. contra las cerem. y ritos*, chap. 1. Two items confirm the fact that serpents were sym-

---

bolical of the lightning; modern survivals in Peru and Bolivia where crossed snakes indicate lightning, and an explicit testimony from the colonial period that Chuqui-illa (Illapa as the lightning) once endowed Pachacuti with two-headed snakes as a charm, sg 31. For the contemporary cat-god Ccoa, hsai 463f. For the volcanic Ccoa of northern Ecuador who strangles women today, E. C. Parsons, *Cosmography of the Indians of Imbabura Province Ecuador, Journal of American Folklore*, Vol. LIII (1940).

Stellar Huacas: For the stars as sources of the fertility of all forms of animal life po:Error. L; ja V, 4; bv 139; bc XIII, 6; accm II, 11. The Pleiades were called Chuchococ in Huamachuco and were thought to be close to the creator-god, rha 40. In the coastal valleys they were known as Fur, accm III, 2. For the Oncoy Mita, aei V; rgi I, 205f. For the morning star, bv 138, and for her shrine in Cuzco, gp 187. For the moon as the superior deity on the coast, accm III, 2. For the moon as a woman's deity, bv 138.

Cults of Stone: For the *conopa*, aei 2, 8, 10; accm II, 11. The *conopa* could be dried maize, bony concretions from the viscera of animals, or any other unusual substance, but stone seems to have been the most usual. The small household fetishes of the Chibchas, ov XXVI, 30, may have been similar to the Peruvian *conopas*; they were treated as intercessors between the family or person involved and the supreme sun or moon deity. The "*curaca*-stones" of the northern coastal valleys were both the sons of the Sun and the ancestors of the local folk, accm III, 2; Rowe, *Kingdom of Chimor*, 49–52. For ancestral stone *huacas* in the Huamachuco pueblos, rha 32. For the Manta emerald as a stone *huaca* of great power, gsc III, 56. For families of *huacas*, aei 15. For the *huaca* Hilavi, aei 9. For the *huaca* Tantazoro, rha 32f. For the sons of Catiquilla, rha 24f. For the marriage of the virgin to a tribal *huaca*, aei III. For the marriage of Titicaca to Coati, bc XIII, 18. For the material on Chimborazo, rgi III, 150–52.

Oracles: The oracle of Coropuno in Contisuyo was unique in giving utterances frequently and at off intervals, cl 28. For night worship of oracles, jb V, 12. For the wealth of Pachacamac, ppr 241; ja V.

For the population figures, ov XLVI, 17. For the description of
Pachacamac, ACCM II, 19; BLC 131; CLPP 72; FJ 339; ISP-HP 176f.;
Hernando Pizarro's letter to the Audiencia at Santo Domingo quoted
in ov XLVI, 15. The identification of Urxayhuachac as the form of
Mamacocha worshipped in the Lurín Valley is based on the myth
of Coniraya, DIIH 2. For Catiquilla's cult, RHA 19–21. For his anti-
Inca oracles, AEI II. For Aconcagua, CL 28, 42; CLPP 97. Aconcagua
may also be called Ausangate and Vilcañota from the neighboring
peak and river. For the oracle of Apurimac, PPR 259f.; BC XIII, 20;
CLPP XCI.

Peruvian Priests and Shamans: Cobo is best on this subject, BC XIII,
33–35, but see also CM 20–23; AEI III; RHA 18; PO:Error. 10. Interesting on the hierarchy of native wizards, but to be used with caution,
is BV 164f., 174–78. For three ways of becoming a diviner, AEI III.
For present-day superstitions about people destroyed by lightning
(by the Ccoa), B. Mishkin, *Cosmological Ideas among the Indians
of Southern Peru, Journal of American Folklore*, Vol. LIII (1940).
On the people's dependence on the sorcerors for their contacts with
the *huacas*, FS 31. For the *ichuri*-confessors, BC XIII, 24; PO:Error.
5; JA V, 25; FS 33; BV 165–69. That confession was an Andean and
not just a Bolivian Indian rite is proved by its presence among the
Chibchas, ov XXVI, 30. For the rite with the colored powders and
the confessor's invocation, RGI I, 205 (quoting Avendano, an archepiscopal *visitador* in the year 1617).

CHAPTER IV—PERUVIAN MYTHS OF CREATION

Myth of the Cuyos: Found in CM 13f. The tale was probably widespread for a close variant is found in DIIH 4, where a different sacred
mountain is mentioned; here the llama shepherd is made the ancestor of all men, and the mountain peak is the refuge of birds and
animals as well.

Myth of the Quitos and the Cañars: The Quito myth comes from a
lost source (Fray Marcos Niza), quoted in VRQ I, 142. This tale
should be compared to the flood-serpent story of the modern Jivaros,
Rafael Karsten, *Head Hunters of Western Amazonas* (Helsinzfors,

1935), 532–35. For the Cañar myth, sg 6; cm 12f.; bc XIII, 2. A close variant of the myth belonged to the Mainas Indians of the Marañón montaña, rgi IV, lxxii f.

Myth of Catiquilla and Pariacaca: Found only in rha 13f., 19–21. For the destruction of Catiquilla, aei II; rha 23f.; sg 64. The Spaniards succeeded in destroying this formidable idol, but the fragments, recovered by the Indians, came alive in their hands and announced themselves as various sons of Catiquilla; the Augustinians had finally to sequester some three hundred of these sons, rha 24f., 30. For the myth of Pariacaca, diih 6 (the Huathiacuri doublet is found in chap. 5).

Myth of Coniraya: Taken from diih 2. The Pachacamac section of the tale is undoubtedly an inorganic appendage, possibly reflecting a hostility between the worshippers of Pachacamac and those of Viracocha. If so, then this appendage dates to a period no later than the reign of Topa Inca, who absorbed the region. The version found in gsc III, 56, and ggo V, 8, shows that the Dávila version is incomplete, stopping as it does with the highland creator's return to the sky and failing to add the account of the destruction of the world by the coastal Pachacamac or his subsequent reordering of the same. For Pachacamac's claim to be a creator, bc XIII, 2. Con changed men because of their ingratitude into evil and unlucky animals, after which his more merciful son Pachacamac re-created them, vrq II, 27. A slightly different version exists where Con turns all the lands into desert because of man's wickedness; his brother Pachacamac (also a son of the Sun) changed that generation of men into cats, but then proceeded to re-create them, ghv 233.

Coastal Myths of the Sun as a Creator-God: Important here is accm II, 19. For the sun's appearance in Végueta and leaving two (not three) eggs, the golden egg producing all the magnates while the silver egg produced the rest of mankind, aei 7. On the coast near Végueta it was believed that mankind in his various social and sexual differences came not from eggs but from four stars, accm II, 19; accm III, 2.

Flood Motif: For a generalized flood tale, ghv 233. In this the only unique elements are the dispatch of dogs from the cave to ascertain if the waters have receded, and the creation of great serpents from the slime of the receding waters. The Jivaro flood story (see Karsten) tells that there were once two brothers whose daily food, brought from the hunt, was stolen by the *pangi* or *amaru* (the giant anaconda). They accordingly killed it and one brother ate its flesh. He began to suffer thirst and wallowed in a lake that increased as he expanded in size. Finally he himself became a *pangi* and warned his brother that the uncontrollable lake would drown all men. The brother climbed the highest palm on the highest hill and escaped the flood, but all the people whom he had warned were drowned. For connections of local *huacas* with an antecedent flood, CM 7. For the name *uno pachacuti*, SG 6; GP 37. On the widespread belief in Peru in an original flood, CV III, 6; BC XIII, 2; JA I, 25. For Huanacauri as a flood-mountain, BC XIII, 2, 15. For the *pacarina*, Anello Oliva, *Historia del reino y provincias del Peru* (Lima, 1895), I, 4, 1.

Viracocha Myth in the Sources: The following are basic: BC XIII, 2; JB I; SG 6f; CL 5. For more local versions, SPY 236–40, 262; ACCM II, 10. See also CM 5–11; GGO V, 7.

The Name Viracocha: For his name as Con Ticci Viracocha, GGO V, 8; JB I; BLC 126. He is called Cons in GSC III, 56. Cons may have been the god's real name. For his full name and titles, BV 147. He must be related to the Con in GGO V, 8, though the relationship is not clear.

The Sons of Viracocha: For their appearance as angels or soldiers, BV 140. For their being as pure duplicates of Viracocha, CM 9–12. In JB I they are not two but a multiplicity.

The Evil Son Tahuapaca: The name is variously written: SG 7; BLC 126; CL 5; SPY 236–40; ARGCS I, 7f. The features of this deity are outlined in RZ I, 3, where, however, he is not specifically named. The best sources identify the journey as across Titicaca, not over the sea. A god Tahuapaca was undoubtedly worshipped down near the Desaguadero, a deity whose tales and rites were later transferred to the mythology of the Inca creator. For the rites of setting his victim adrift on the lake and/or impaled on a chonta-palm stake, ARGCS I, 7f., 10. Perhaps the Cross of Carabuco was a transferred relic of his cult, ARGCS I, 10. Tahuapaca has interesting analogies in myth with Ayar Cachi, i.e., leveling mountains, dissolving landscapes, stirring up fear and enmity, and being sent underground finally.

The Two Parts of the Viracocha Myth: The artificial separation is ours. The elements we have extracted to produce the priestly version are stressed in our better sources, but are jumbled with more primitive elements. For tolerably pure forms of the myth, CM 7–9; GSC III, 56. For the specifically Inca addition to the Viracocha myth, BC III, 2f.; ACCM II, 10. Illiterate peasants of Peru today tell garbled versions of the myth, W. S. Stein, *Hualcán, Life in the Highlands of Peru* (Cornell, 1961), 298–302.

The Site of Tiahuanaco: For the theory of a swift imperial impulse out of the highlands and an equally sudden collapse (dated with hesitation 1,000–1,300 A.D.), Wendell C. Bennet, *Ancient Arts of the Andes* (N. Y., 1954), 67, 76f. Huari, the vast ruins near Ayacucho, has a good claim to be the capital site of this pre-Inca empire. For traditions and description of the site, BC III, 19. For connections between the widely separated sites of Huari and Tiahuanuco, CLPP 105, LDB I, 18, 88.

The God of the Tiahuanaco Sun-Gate: He is probably a composite astral and atmospheric deity, for he wields serpents (the lightning) and shows rays issuing from his head. Such a god appears approximately a millenium earlier in the highlands at Chavín de Huantar (the Raimundi stele). For a standing statue at Tiahuanaco wearing a crown and buckled with a sword-belt, LDB I, 18, 88, By way of comparison see the bearded god of the Collas called Tonapa, SPY 236–40, 262. The name Tonapa is said to have meant "great wise man" or "lord," ARGCS I, 7f.

CHAPTER V— VIRACOCHA INCA AND THE CHANCA WAR

His Dates: We follow Rowe in accepting Cabello Valboa's dates as the best available from this reign on. For this ruler's advanced age, CL 43; SG 25. For the tradition that he ruled thirty-six years, VRQ II, 24.

Life and Family: For the fullest pictures of the reign, CL 38–45; SG 23–25 (only the latter gives his pre-throne name). The element *caya* in the *coya*'s name refers to a preparation of *oca*, sliced and dried, GP 50, 135, 251. A suspect list of his brothers is given in DF V. For the tradition that he was wise and amicable, GP 79; ACCM I, 15; JB 5; RZ II, 11; BC XII, 11; BLC 250. As heroically active in warfare, CL 39; ARGCS I, 3; MM I, 10; CV III, 14; ISP-VC 17. For his learning in astrology and ceremonial inventiveness, RGI II, appendix 31.

Assassination of Yahuar Huacac: On the assassination and the consequent tumult, CL 37f; SG 24. The expunging of the story from the official records may come from Pachacuti's desire to preserve a tradition of uninterrupted legitimacy. For hints that the transition between the rule of Viracocha Inca and his father was troubled, see the remark that the older ruler had renounced his crown seven years before he died, VRQ II, 24.

Warfare and Revolt: For the attack on Calca and the treaty terms CL 38; SG 25. For the league of Muhina, BLC 250; RZ II, 11 (Muhina is erroneously given as Mechina in the latter). For the would-be usurper Capac and his revolt, CL 40. Cieza makes some kind of connection between this revolt and the cultic problem, where he shows the initial attack as made on the religious establishment in Coricancha.

Expansion to the Southeast: For the intense struggle with the Cavinas, CLPP 97. For the Inca victory at Compapata and the later surrender of the Canas, CLPP 47; CL 41f. For the reputed entry of Viracocha Inca into the Titicaca area, CL 42f.

Titles: For the title *capac*, JB 6. In Pachacuti's time many chieftains around Cuzco were thus titled, JB 18. The reference to the *curaca* of Huaro who boasted the title of Pachachulla Viracocha in the days of the third Inca ruler is a reference on the contrary to a *huaca*, CV III, 12, 14; BC XII, 6.

The Temple of Viracocha: For description of the idol, CL 5. This idol as described seems to be similar to the monolithic god found by Bennet at Tiahuanaco and now in La Paz. For references to this temple under two different designations (Aconcagua and Vilcañota), CL 42.

The Revelation to Viracocha Inca: For the revelation as being at Urcos, SG 24. For a slim version of the event, JB 5. For the rebuilding of the shrine and the statue of the god, BC XII, 11. A confusion exists in the chronicles between the shrines at Cacha and Urcos; in the latter the god's statue was the Hatun Viracocha (The Great Lord).

Viracocha in Cuzco: For his cult here previous to the reign of Viracocha Inca, BC XII, 12. For a hint of a connection between the establishment of the office of high priest and the introduction of the new cult (where it is stated that the office was the permanent possession of the descendents of Viracocha Inca), CV III, 24. For statement that Inca cults were subject to change to conform to new ideas of empire, BC XIII, 1. For religious unrest in Cuzco in days of Viracocha Inca, BV 172. For Viracocha Inca's desire to destroy the *huacas*, GP 79f. For the breaking of the *huacas* and the voice from heaven, RGI II, appendix 33. For the precedence of the god, BC XII, 11. For Huanca belief in a pre-Inca creator, RGI I, 85. For Rucana testimony regarding a pre-Inca Viracocha people, RGI I, 210.

Viracocha Inca's Sons and the Yucay Valley: For Pachacuti's birthplace in Cusicancha, BC XIII, 13, carelessly displaced to south of the Huatanay, GPF 1051. For the four legitimate princes had by Viracocha Inca from Mama Runtu Caya (Roca Inca, Topa Yupanqui, Inca Yupanqui, Capac Yupanqui) and the two bastards from the concubine Cori Chulpa (Inca Urcon, Inca Socso), SG 24. For the masonry dwellings in the Vilcañota Valley, JB 10. For contradictions regarding the place of Viracocha Inca's retirement before and after the Chanca war (a *pucara* in the Yucay, a place on the west side of the Vilcañota between the confluence of that river with the Huatanay and Quispicancha, a place near Calca, as Caquia Jaquijahuana, and as a place called Pomamarca) PO 49; GVCR V, 20; JB 6; SG 28; CL 44; SPY 269–72. The truth may be that he retired to the Plain of Anta before the Chanca war and to the Yucay after, CL 43f.

Reign of Inca Urcon: For his deposition after only eleven days of rule following the death of his father, VRQ II, 24. We are faced with a difficult conflict of evidence regarding the coregency in our best sources. For a strong statement of the bastardy of Inca Urcon with details of the name and native pueblo of the concubine who was his mother, sg 24f. For his legitimacy, cl 43. For his marriage, cl 44.

Pachacuti's Conspiracy: For Pachacuti's official appointment as Urcon's representative in Cuzco, cl 44. For Pachacuti's early career, sg 25. For Topa Huarochiri, cv III, 14; spy 269–72 (erroneously given in the latter as Topa Huanachire). We assume from the name Viracocha Inca Paucar the filiation of this prince to the old ruler, sg 26. For lists of the conspirators, sg 26; jb 6. For the seduction of the royal women, sg 25. At least one name in the garbled list of Pachacuti's legitimate brothers in df V may be brought into connection with the conspiracy.

The Chancas and Their Advance: On the Chancas, clpp 90; jb 6; gvcr IV, 15; sg 26. For Chanca pressure on Cuzco previous to final attack, cv III, 14. A gauge of the consternation they aroused is to be found in the Inca tag *auca* (tough, warlike) appended to their name, gvcr V, 24. For the two Chanca captains, sg 26; cv III, 14; gvcr IV, 23. For Uscovilca, sg 27; jb 6. More specifically he is called leader of the Chanca tribe of the Hancohuallus gvcr IV, 15, 24; spy 269. For Chanca envelopment tactics, jb 6. For the embassy calling for the Inca surrender, sg 27. Viracocha Inca stayed for a while on his flight at Chita, sg 27.

Pachacuti's Vision: The exiled-prince version is found in bc XII, 10; gvcr 20–23. The scene of the revelation is characteristically said in spy 269–72 to have been at Lucre, just beyond Muhina. For the spring at the site of the revelation (present Tambo Machay?), bc XIII, 14. For attribution of the revelation to Viracocha Inca, jb 8. For the interesting version that Pachacuti's mother dreamed that the reason for the initial successes of the Chancas had been Inca neglect of the cult of Viracocha in favor of that of Inti, po:Fund. 54. For the magic-mirror tale, cm 17, 18; sg 27; bc XII, 12.

The Battle for Cuzco: There is an Ichupampa Hacienda today on the approximate spot where logic would place the Chanca camp in the Anta Basin, some four miles west-southwest of Surite. All details are uncertain—this is like Arthur's victory at Mount Badon. For Pachacuti's request to his father for aid, gvcr IV, 24; jb 7; spy 269–

72. For the hiring of Canas and Canchas, PO:Fund. 54. For the aid from Contisuyo, GVCR V, 17f. For the offer of Incaship in return for aid, CL 45. For the Chanca embassies, JB 7. For the story of the faithful "eight," JB 6–8 (the number being based no doubt on the Sacred Legend; there were the three generals, Inca Roca, Vicaquirau, and Apu Mayta, plus Pachacuti himself, each with a heroic squire). For the location of Quiachilli, which literally means "pus oozings," SPY 269–72; BLC 250f.; CV III, 14. For the Paul Revere and the Molly Pitcher stories, SG 27; SPY 269–72. For the barricades in Cuzco, CL 45. For the *puruaucas*, SPY 269–72. These angelic warriors are mentioned under different names, BV 140. For the augmentation of the Chanca forces at Ichupampa, JB 8. For the Inca attack there, SG 28. For the victory hymn stating that Uscovilca and the Chanca captains were all killed at Ichupampa, JB 13.

Chapter VI—Pachacuti: Father of Victory

Chronology and Pachacuti's Age: Pachacuti was no callow youth at the time. The Collao campaign was to come when Pachacuti was "cargado de dias" (corroborated in PO:Tras. 115), and we know that he died at an advanced age, LTOP 173; GVCR VI, 34; CV III, 18; JA VI, 21; BLC 259. If we arbitrarily set his age at death as eighty years and accept Cabello Valboa's date of this event as 1471, then he will have been born about 1391. Cabello Valboa's date of 1438 as the first year of his rule would then make him a middle-aged man about forty-seven years of age at the time of the Chanca attack. For his conquest of Chucuito, RAC 278. Considerable overlap must be allowed for the campaigns from 1438 to 1445, Pachacuti no doubt organizing one before the others had been completed. For Pachacuti's early turning to the planning and the setting up of administrative procedures, JB 11–13; SG 32. No block of time sufficient for his cultic and theological innovations can be found except the period when he was no longer devoting himself in person to the campaigns, i.e., after his return from Collas—this is confirmed in CV III, 15, where it is attested that Coricancha was reconstructed only at the time of the Collao campaign.

Relations with Calca: For battle trophies, CL 46; CV III, 14; JB 10.

For Urcon's outlawry and death, CL 46; CV III, 14. For the death of Urcon in battle with a local *sinchi* of the Canchas, SPY 269. For a variant account where he is defeated near Ollantaytambo by Inca Roca, Pachacuti's brother, SG 33. For the tale—which we reject—that Viracocha Inca twice refused the spoils offered to him by Pachacuti unless he should deliver them first to Urcon; SG 27f.; JB 9.

Coronation: For full details, JB 17. Who the *coya* was at this ceremony is uncertain. The only named wife of Pachacuti is Mama Anahuarque, of the pueblo of Chuco, BLC 250; RZ II, 11. For the possibility that Pachacuti's *coya* had been Urcon's wife, CL 46. For the statement that Mama Anahuarque was not Pachacuti's sister, ISP-VC 21. For marriage of Pachacuti to Mama Anahuarque *after* his father's death, CV III, 15. Both Pachacuti and Viracocha Inca wore the fringe simultaneously following the Chanca victory, GVCR V, 20. For Viracocha Inca's death and mummy, ACCM I, 15.

Names and Titles: For previous rulers who bore the name of Pachacuti, GP 71. For the possible use of the name in Collasuyo, SPY 269, 273. For the meaning of the name as "Renewer of the Ages," ISP-VC 19; as "Earthquake," GP 71; as "Engulfer," SG 6. It is the equivalent of our Armageddon, GHLQ 270. For his titulary, JB 13f., 17; SG 29; RZ II, 12. The full imperial title was Capac Apu Inca, GP 84.

The Generals: For Inca Roca, SG 35. For a brother noted for his swiftness, Pahuac Mayta Inca, GVCR V, 23.

Pacification of the Area around Cuzco: Most of the campaigns were to the south and east, SG 35; CV III, 14. For the Cuyo conspiracy, SG 34; CV III, 14; SPY 279. Cabello Valboa places these campaigns before the Chanca attack.

The Yucay and Vilcabamba Campaigns: For Spanish remarks on the valley, GVCR V, 27; CLPP 94; RGI II, 182, appendix 10. For the attack on Ollantaytambo, BC XII, 12; SG 35. For the Inca bridge erected at Pachacuti's orders, BC XII, 12. For the Vilcabamba campaign, CV III, 14. On the Amazons, GP 56f., 240. For the wild men born of female monkeys, CLPP 95. For Inca remains at Vitcos and surrounding areas, H. Bingham, *Vitcos, the Last Inca Capital, Pro-*

ceedings of the American Antiquarian Society, Vol. I, No. 5 (1912). For textual record of buildings erected in Vitcos by both Pachacuti and Huayna Capac, TCYI 82.

Vilcas Campaigns: For escape of the Chanca captain Hastu Huaraca, CL 45. But for his death at Ichupampa see SG 28; CV III, 14; JB 8, 10. For Hastu Huaraca's reluctant homage, CL 46. I place this during or after Pachacuti's invasion of Andahuaylas, CV III, 15; CL 47. For differing opinions regarding which brother was left in Cuzco as governor, GVCR V, 24; CL 47. On the campaigns in general, CL 47f.; CLPP 88; CV III, 15; SG 35. On the Apurimac bridge, RGI II, 218; CLPP 91; E. G. Squier, *Peru—Incidents of Travel and Exploration in the Land of the Incas* (New York, 1877), 544–50. The interpretation of the dispatch of Chanca forces into Collao as a policy to weaken them is purely ours, CLPP 89; CL 48. Challcomarca was also called Auquimarca, RGI II, 9. The rock Pillucho was situated in the territory of that group of Soras called the Challcos; it served also as a refuge for the loyalist forces of Ayacucho during Gonzalo Pizarro's rebellion. For the ranking of Vilcas with Cuzco, CLTP (Feb., 1956), 86f. For a description of Vilcas, CLPP 89. For the victory chant, GGO III.

Pachacuti and His Family: For his advanced age on return from Vilcas, PO:Tras. 115. For the physical description of Pachacuti, GP 80–82. Some of the lists of sons are merely corrupt copies of each other, GSC III, 49; DF V. The highest number of legitimate sons reported is six, BLC 259. For Amaru Topa Inca, his selection as heir and subsequent rejection, SPY 281–85, 293; BLC 259. For the seven-year drought, ACCM I, 15.

Collao Campaigns: That the Chancas had previously advanced to Chucuito (CL 48) is somewhat suspect, for Pachacuti, in following with a much larger army, had difficulty getting past Ayavire. For Carabaya as meaning "the Sack," GHLQ 191. For Amaru Inca in command of the initial phases of the campaign, BLC 259. It is difficult to decide whether there were two or three Collao campaigns: there were the Chanca advance, the advance past Ayavire which went into the Carabaya country, and the victory over the coalition at Hatun-

Colla or Chucuito. The second and third may have been the same, but we have assumed differently. For the battle of Ayavire, CLPP 98; CL 52. For the Carabaya expedition, CLPP 102; CL 52; SPY 273. For Carabaya as a gold producer, OV XLVI, 9. For the process of gold-washing under the Incas here, CA 278. For the campaign against Chuchi Capac, SG 37; CV III, 15. Sarmiento claims that the Collas held territory from the montaña to the Atacama, including the province of Arequipa up to some sixty miles from Cuzco.

Deposition of Amaru Inca: Pachacuti tried to train him for leadership for a period of five or six years, i.e., the length of his coregency. For the deposition, BLC 259.

The Inca Army: See mainly BC XIV, 9; BLC 256. For the Chucuito levies of three thousand and six thousand men, MHVE 137. For the dual command reflecting the two Cuzco moieties, CV III, 21. For sacrifices before a campaign, JA V, 18. For a description of the Inca army encamped, OV XLVI, 6. For the age limits of the *auca* classification as twenty-five to fifty, GP 137. It is given as thirty to sixty in MHVE 129.

Terror: For Inca atrocities, BC XII, 35. Examples were the systematic starving of a whole province (here the Lupacas), ARGCS I, 20, and the wiping out of all the *curacas* of Chincha as well as their sons in retribution for the seduction of one of the *acllas*, CCDM 242.

The Mitmacs: For *mitmacs* among the Lupacas, ARGCS I, 29; MHVE 129. For Chachapoyas among the Huancas, LTOP 22, and Acos in Huamanga, SG 74. For general discussions of the system, BC XII, 23; SG 39; CL 22; ARGCS I, 9. For their use as garrison troops, MHVE 130. Cieza discards the theory that Viracocha Inca created the system, CL 22. For the tied-in economy of the Lupaca *mitmacs* and their highland kinsmen, MHVE 131.

Capac Yupanqui and the Chincha Raid: For this, see CLPP 74; CL 59; FS 5. We have placed it after the Rucana surrender inasmuch as these people controlled the passes down into the Chincha and the near-by valleys. Rowe tentatively dates it 1440; see RAC 279. For Capac Yupanqui as a half-brother of Pachacuti, CL 56; SG 24, 38; LTOP 40,

44; GVCR VI, 10, 22f. The theory that he was a son of Pachacuti (PO:Tras. 115; LTOP 19) is surely based on the confusion of his Chinchaysuyo campaign and that of Pachacuti's son Topa Inca.

The Yanamayo River: It may have been one of the swift tributaries of the upper Marañón rising in the Cordillera Blanca (SG 38), though we should note that SG 69 seems to contradict this when he makes the Yanamayo the scene of Huascar's death, which surely did not occur so close to Cajamarca. While no identification brings confidence, I strongly suspect that the Yanamayo was the present Mantaro. The statement that Vilcas was the limit of Capac Yupanqui's tether (LTOP 19, 44; PO:Tras. 115) could be accepted if this territory were not already integrated into Tahuantinsuyo or if more campaigning around Huamanga had to be undertaken. Atahualpa as overlord of Quito had originally claimed the Yanamayo as the frontier between his and Huascar's possessions, SG 69. For the boundary of Capac Yupanqui's authority as near Jauja, CL 49.

Chinchaysuyo Campaign through Parcos: Cieza, with the doubtful support of GVCR VI, 10, 21, curiously diverges from the bulk of the sources, CL 49f., 53, 56. The officers under Capac Yupanqui were Huayna Yupanqui (another of Pachacuti's brothers), a bastard son of the emperor, Apu Auqui (or Yanqui) Yupanqui, and the Chanca leader Ancoayllu, SG 38; CV III, 16. On the Chanca leader's identity, GVCR V, 27; CLPP 78; CL 49. For the Inca humiliation at Parcos, CV III, 16. For Parcos, CLPP 85. For Huanca testimony that Capac Yupanqui was the first Inca to subdue Jauja, RGI I, 80.

Chinchaysuyo Campaign from Parcos to Cajamarca: For the Chanca desertion, SG 38; CV III, 16; CL 49. For the Chanca route into the Huallaga country, GVCR VIII, 1–3. For the four-month campaign against Cajamarca, GVCR VI, 24. For the retention of the house of Cusmanco in power, SG 38. For the execution of the Inca generals at Limatambo, LTOP 40.

CHAPTER VII—PACHACUTI: ORGANIZER OF THE STATE

Office of Sinchi: Our summary is from information in LTOP 4, 18f., 22f., *passim*. The quotation is from LTOP 34f. For a typical trophy

head, CA 250. For the tendency to primogeniture in the office of
sinchi, LTOP 39. The Chibchas also had the custom, as did the Peruvians, of sending their women out to treat for peace, or on other embassies, OV XXVI, 31. For the growth of kingship in the fifteenth
century, Rowe, *Kingdom of Chimor*, 42.

The Succession: For early Inca succession, SG 16. The *ayllus custodias*
acted as sworn thanes of the *sinchi* and his heir, SG 14. For the election
of Manco Inca and later of Amaru Inca, following the death of Sayri
Topa, FS 18. For legitimacy and not seniority as the overriding cri-
terion in the choice of a successor, GP 89.

The Coya *and Incestuous Marriage*: For attribution of incestuous
marriage to Pachacuti, ISP-VC 201. For his marriage to all his sisters,
SG 47. For the statement that Topa's was the first incestuous marriage
in Inca policy, imposed on him by his father, BC XIV, 7. It may be
that Mama Anahuarque was not identical with the full-sister whom
Pachacuti seized from Urcon, ISP-VC 21. For the resemblance between the names of the *coyas* of Pachacuti, Topa Inca, and Huayna
Capac on the one hand and those of the ancestral four sisters on the
other, note that Mama Anahuarque was also called Ipa Huaco, MM
I, 24, that Topa Inca married Mama Ocllo, and that Huayna Capac
produced his legitimate heir on a sister called Rahua Ocllo. For the
adoption by an infertile *coya* of the sons of her husband by other sisters, DF 60; JB 16.

The Royal Wedding: For the title "Daughter of the Sun," JB 16.
For her replacement by next sister in case of sterility, JB 16. For the
marriage rites, JB 17; ISP-VC 24–26; DF 9. For the *cuicuchicoy*,
ARGCS I, 23; SPY 247. For the menstruating girl's new name, CM
87; ISP-VC 26.

The Harem: For the emperor's custom in the harem, PPR 235. For
the eight-day harem shift, BC XII, 36. Numbers in the harem range
from a minimum of two hundred, BC XII, 8, to not less than seven
hundred, CL 10, and up to Huayna Capac's establishment of six
thousand (split between Cuzco and Quito), CL 63. For the custom
that only the heir could marry a sister, DF 9.

The Regalia and Crest: For the *mascapaycha* borne on a staff-head in making an arrest, GP 257, 260. Other items in the regalia included the sandals, the coca-bag, the litter, the stool, the mace, etc. For the items in the royal crest, BC XII, 36; JA V, 4; CL 20; RHA 37f.; RGI II, appendix 32. For a picture of it, GP 59, 62. For Manco Capac's serpent parentage, GP 60f. For serpents depicted on tambo walls, RHA 37f., and on the royal litter, CL 20. For the woolen "serpent" of the Inca clans, BC XIII, 26. For the *achihua* or royal canopy, RGI I, 166f.

The Panaca: Our sources often confuse *ayllu* for *panaca*, the former often standing for the latter. For the Spanish translation as *cofradía*, GSC III, 50. For Manco as the reputed founder of the *panaca* system, SG 14. For Inca Roca as the real founder, JA 6; SG 19. For a bastard daughter of Huayna Capac who belonged to the Vicaquirau *panaca* (of Inca Roca), ISP-VC 45–47. For Pachacuti's reform of the system, SG 19. For statement that the *panaca* did not exist before Pachacuti, ISP-VT 133. All sons except the heir continued in their father's *panaca*, BC XII, 4. For the meaning "descent," SG 14. An interesting example is seen in Pachacuti's appointment of Amaru Inca after his demotion to the leadership of the Capac Ayllu (i.e., Topa Inca's *panaca*), BLC 259. Note than an emperor could appoint a bastard son as head of his *panaca*, in this case concerning Viracocha Inca, SG 24f. For five lists of the *panacas*, GVCR IX, 40; BLC 251; ISP-VC 12; DF 7; D. de Santo Tomás, *Grammatica o arte de la lengua general de los Indios de los reynos del Peru* (Lima, 1951), 128f. (where Santo Tomás however gives only the eight, ninth, and tenth *panacas*). The only confusion in these lists comes with the *panacas* of the third, fourth, and fifth rulers. Sarmiento's list gives not the names of the royal *panacas* reformed by Pachacuti but tribal names from the foundations of Inca history, SG 11. That Upper Cuzco included those *panacas* subsequent to Topa Inca can be deduced from the fact that Huascar's *panaca* claimed inclusion in it, CLTP (May, 1957), 259, 263. The twelve *ayllus* were able to gather 2,200 braves on the death of Pachacuti, SG 48.

Court Protocol: The ruler bathed every other day, GP 249. For court etiquette under Atahualpa, PPR 224–51; JB 8. For the sons of the *curacas* each in their national dress, GHV 232. For the emperor's progress in his litter, CL 20; ISP-HP 171. Atahualpa's bodyguard consisted of four hundred selected men, CV XLVI, 6.

The Incas: For a physical description, GP 225. For the prerogative of private confession, CM 23. For Huanca belief in the Inca ruler's affiliation to the sun and the moon, RGI I, 85.

The Capac Raymi: For a similar rite among the highland Indians of Ecuador, LAC 27. The proper sequence of the ceremonies performed in this month is not always certain; I have made a composite of CM 57f.; BC XIII, 25; JB 14; CL 7; DF 6. The *huarachicoy* was last celebrated on Mount Anahuarque by Manco Inca, but the Spaniards scattered the celebrants before its completion, TCYI 57f. For Huanacauri as the focal *huaca* in the rites, BC XIII, 15. My interpretation of the mountain race as being partially a test of the new sexual powers of the boys is suggested by the allied Quiteño ritual where the youths received the breechcloth *"en conociendo mujer,"* LAC 27. For the white llama, BC XIII, 25. Pachacuti designated Yahuira, a peak sacred to the Maras tribe, as a locus in the knighting ceremonies, CM 72. For the four judges sitting in Haucaypata, GGO IV, 16 (this purification may really belong in the Situa). For the *chocano*, the mock fight in the square, CM 78. The dance belonging to the Incas as a whole was the *huayyaya*, BC XIV, 17 (elsewhere called the *yauayra*, CM 80). It was danced by both sexes, GVCR IX, 1, notwithstanding. The woolen serpent or cable was the *moroy urco* (parti-colored male), CM 80; SG 31. Pachacuti had embellished this cable with gold from the Soras campaign, CL 49. On the fifth of the final eight days the Incas by privilege were admitted, DF 6; BC XIII, 25; JA V, 23. For Pachacuti explaining the symbolism of these rites, JB 14.

The Inca Aristocracy: Greater Cuzco extended from Urcos as far as Huana, five and six leagues away from Cuzco respectively, PO 45. For distinction of Incas living in Cuzco (*"señores"*) and the remaining Incas (*"orejones"*), JB 16. For the same distinction between princes and common Incas, GP 253 (see also GP 63, 171, 227, 260). *"Caballeros exentos"* as a term descriptive of the aristocracy occurs in the letter written by Manco Inca to Almagro, OV XLVII, 8, 13. For Incas by adoption and exemptions given to them for their military service, cv III, 16. Incas by adoption were the "Hahua Incas," Outer Incas, GP 171. For Inca women given to distant *curacas*, RGI II, 60. For sons of royal concubines being denied high provincial offices, CL 10; JB 16. For three levels of dignity, litter-borne, hammock-borne, and those who walked, GHV 232. For the ruler's prerogative of granting earplugs, RZ III, 13. For the expansion of the Inca class during the Chanca crisis, CL 45, and for granting of Incahood to the Cotapampas and the Cotaneras specifically, GVCR V, 23.

Pachacuti's Organization of the Core-State: The best source is JB 11–13, 16. For evidence that forced and controlled marriages had replaced the imperial population by the reign of Topa Inca, RGI 170, 200. For losses among Soras, Rucanas, and Huancas thereafter, RGI I, 82, 181. For types of dwellings on a nobleman's country estate, GP 254. For the uprooting of the surrounding pueblos and the reassignment of their lands, SG 32. For agricultural terraces built by Pachacuti near Cuzco, SG 30.

CHAPTER VIII—CUZCO: THE LION IN THE MOUNTAIN

Haucaypata and Cusipata: For the spring near the Huatanay crossing wherein they bathed the *huaca* Illapa—no doubt as rain-magic—BC XII, 13. It can probably be identified as the one called Teccecocha just under Collcampata, running down the street which today bears its name. For the early filling of the swamp, CLPP 92; RGI II, 180. For the name Haucaypata, GVCR VII, 10. Cusipata was the site of a market, MM-DN 2; GVCR VII, 11. For Haucaypata as reserved for Incas of the blood and Cusipata for Incas by privilege, GVCR VI, 21. (This plainly appears in the drawing in GPF 1051 from the colonial period.) For Cusipata as the scene of military reviews, GHLQ 155. For the covering of the Huatanay as a drain, GVCR VII, 10. The Monroy Panorama which hangs in the church of the Triunfo shows the two squares as they appeared in the seventeenth century, and here they are separated by a line of *portales* over the course of the buried Huatanay— it is probable that they were duplicating in Spanish terms some earlier Inca structures, possibly *galpones*. For a description of the two squares tallying with this, see the Anonymous, *Descripción del Virreinato del Perú* (Rosario, Argentina, 1958), 94.

For reproductions of the Monroy Panorama, H. E. Wethey, *Colonial Architecture and Sculpture in Peru*, (1949), Fig. 21, and also the UNESCO report on Cuzco (Paris, 1952). For the sacredness of Haucaypata's soil, PO:Fund. 109, 111. For the *usno*, SPY 199; GP 186. For the stone which received the god's *chica*, JB 11; PPR 264f.; CM 37, 44.

Traffic and Foreigners in Cuzco: Quotation on the view of Cuzco, CL 13. For the *huaca* where the first glimpse of Cuzco was secured, BC XIII, 14. For the labor *corvée* working in Cuzco, CLPP 93. For fish brought in two days from Titicaca to Cuzco, MHVE 138. For the Lupaca *quinoa* offerings, MHVE 138. For check-points and searches outside of Cuzco, CL 55; CLPP 97; RZ II, 14. For restrictive law on Collas coming into Cuzco, CL 55. For the barrio of Chimor craftsmen in Cuzco, CL 58. For the barrio of buffoons, GP 253. For Cañars and other groups in Cuzco, CL 56; CLPP 92f. For the dole in Cuzco, JB 13. The population estimate in CM 141 adds that there were two hundred thousand Indians within a radius of thirty to thirty-five miles of Cuzco. For comparison we might note that in 1950, Cuzco had a total population (not just *vecinos*) of eighty thousand persons. We have accepted a six-mile radius out from Haucaypata as defining the area of Cuzco's diffused sanctity, and therefore the greater metropolitan area; this is based on CM 35.

Cuzco as a Sacred Lion: For Cuzco as created by the word of the sun-god, BC XIII, 23. For Pachacuti's definition of Cuzco as a lion-body, JB 17; SG 53. Besides the example of this in the name Pumapchupan (Lion's Tail), the street that forms the backbone and shoulders of the lion is called today Pumacurco (Lion Beam, Lion Ridgepole), with amazing anatomical exactness if the allusion is to the spine.

Cuzco Rebuilt: For the rebuilding of Cuzco, JB 11–13, 16; SG 30. For the date 1440 A.D., see RIC 225. The unbonded Inca masonry was called *choco pirca*, GHLQ 116.

General Appearance: For the first Spanish report on the city, CV XLVI, 13. For contrasting opinions of the early Spanish Cuzco, LDB I, 80; Anon., *Descripción del Peru*, 94. For Garcilaso's plan of the city, GVCR VII, 8–10. For the division of the city into ten *ayllus*, five to each moiety, RZ II, 12; BC XII, 8; BLC 25. For the contrasting division of the city into four parts (to contain *mitmacs* and foreign artisans), AZH I, 9. For a description of a Cuzco *cancha*, PPR 264. For the rooms, apartments, and outhouses of a greater royal *cancha*, GP 245. For Collcampata, GVCR V, 2.

Palace Area: Casana is erroneously assigned to Huayna Capac in PPR 319; BC XIII, 13. It was a section of Cuzco, SG 58. Pachacuti resided in Condorcancha during his lifetime, BC XIII, 14. Pachacuti's establishment contained at least the area today between Plateros and Suecia, and probably also the block between Suecia and Ataud. For the site of Viracocha Inca's palace, AC 123. For Polo's uncertainty in regard to Viracocha's shrine, PO:Fund. 92. For the Triunfo as the true site of this shrine, BV 148 (corroborated by BC XIII, 13, where it is placed in Pucamarca, which directly adjoins Hatuncancha on the southeast). For attribution of the shrine to Pachacuti, BC XIII, 4; MM IV, 44. For the image of Viracocha in the shrine, BC XII, 12; BC XIII, 4; BV 148; MM IV, 44; CM 16f. Our sources confuse this image with that of Inti in Coricancha; one of these was recovered in 1572. We assume that Hatuncancha included both the living quarters of Viracocha Inca and the shrine to Viracocha, GVCR VII, 9; PPR 264. Topa Inca's palace probably extended from the Triunfo to the Callejón Romero; its back wall ran along San Augustín, and its façade may have been either Arequipa or Loreto, probably the former. Huayna Capac probably reclaimed and built up the riverbank on which to terrace his palace.

Acllahuasi: For Santa Catalina as the traditional site, AC 8. The nuns of Santa Catalina did not acquire the site until 1605. For the best picture of the *acllahuasi* and its inmates, BC XIII, 34, 37. Blas Valera throws a rosy Christian interpretation over the institution, BV 179–85. For attribution of the system to Pachacuti, MM-DN 60; ARGCS I, 19. For Topa Inca as its originator, SG 52. For the triennial collection of girls, BLC 140; MM-DN 60. For the three provinces most heavily taxed, BV 180. For the number of three thousand *acllas* in Cuzco, BV 182. Provincial establishments numbered up to two hundred girls, DF XI. Velasco calls the establishments *panahuasis* (a *panan* being a girl from seven to twelve years of age) and gives a maximum figure of six hundred, vrq II, 56. For the teaching of weaving to four-year-old girls there, GP 218. For training in singing, GP 218. For the possibility that the establishments, at least on the coast, may have been houses of courtesans, ov XLVI, 15; CLTP (April, 1951), 158; CL 61. These may have been the "common" girls, *pampa aclla*, of GP 218. Could the "orgy house" recorded of the Ecuadoran tribes have lent something to the concept of the *acllahuasi* of the Incas (RGI III, 153)? For classes of *acllas*, GP 75, 136, 176, 206, 216–19.

Prisons: For Pumapchupan as a favored location, JB 16. For the park there, BC XII, 8. For the shrine of Mama Quilla in Pumap-chupan, GP 187 (there is a strong possibility that this shrine was really the one which in Coricancha was dedicated to the moon). For aviaries and gardens, GP 249. For the spellings of the name *sankahuaci* (Sam-kihuaci in GHLQ 323), SG 76; SPY 267, 309; CV III, 20; ISP-VT 137; GP 221. For its location as inside the city (probably greater Cuzco), BC XII, 26. GPF 1051 puts the Sankayhuaci on the south bank of the Huatanay below Cusipata. For Bimbilla as a prison for magicians only, CV III, 20. For a contrasting view of it as a place of permanent detention for Incas quilty of great crimes, RZ II, 14. Bimbilla is more correctly spelled as Vinpilla in GHLQ 353 and is defined as the place where the rope-treatment was meted out to malefactors. The name of the place of execution is borne today by the hill Arahuaycata (or Arahay) just south of the city. It was just outside the city by a river, CL 26; BC XII, 26. More specifically it was in Tancar "opposite Cayaocachi," which would place it close to the Chunchulmayo, CV III, 20.

Environs: In Garcilaso's day Cayaocachi had shrunk to three hundred householders and was separated by a thousand paces of open ground from the city, GVCR VII, 8. For the terraces of Cuzco, SG 30; PPR 297.

Sacsahuaman: For early Inca artifacts here, RIC 199. For the spring in the area, CM 76. Oviedo says the Inca name of Sacsahuaman was Calispo, ov XLVI, 17, which looks like a Spanish error for the name of the spring Calispuquio, see also GP 253. For the Cañar and Cha-chapoya guards, RGI II, appendix p. 10. For the numbers of workers on the project, CL 50; BC XIV, 12. For the architects, GVCR VII, 29. For Sacsahuaman as a dwelling for ten thousand and as an arsenal, PPR 275f. As a house of the Sun, CL 51; MM 163. For the wall names, CL 50.

Sacredness of Cuzco: For Cuzco as the *"casa y morada de dioses,"* PO:Fund. 54f. For the *pururauca* niches, BC XIII, 15f. The serpent shrine, supposedly in Amarucancha (BV 149), is curiously called *chacara* in BC XIII, 6. For its oracles, ACCM II, 11. For an analogous House of the Serpent in Cajamarca, OV XLVI, 7. For the house of heads, SG 37. For the shrine of Pirhua, BV 149, and for the deity himself, BV 138. For mention of a shrine to the Lightning in Pucamarca, CM 36. For the temple of the star Venus, Chasca Cuillor Chuquilla, GP 187. For the *ceque*-system, BC XIII, 13, 16.

Coricancha: For the relative poverty of the site before Pachacuti, CM 16f. For Inticancha as the home of the four sister-wives of Manco Capac, BC XIII, 16. For its name as Chumbicancha, LTOP 185; ISP-VT 133; BLC 126, though in garbled fashion. Intihuasi alternates as a name of Inticancha, CL 27. For the name Coricancha as given by Pachacuti, LTOP 185; BLC 126. For the beginning of the rebuilding with spoils of the Chanca war, CL 27. For its completion after the Collao campaign, SG 31, 37; CV III, 15. For the installation ceremonies, JB 11. For the sun-idol with ashes and gold dust contained in it, BC XIII, 5. The painted bar still to be seen around the interior of the Sala Capitular in the monastery may be a statement in permanent paint of the blood-line blessing the walls (for a photograph, see Rowe, *Introduction to Archaeology of Cuzco*, Plate IV, No. 2). The lands and flocks given to Coricancha were from Sora, Chanca, and Colla loot, CV III, 15. For the holy fire, *nina villca*, BV 182.

Layout of Coricancha: For the present remains, Rowe, *Introduction to Archaeology of Cuzco*, 26–41, 62f. For a description of the suntemple in Cajamarca, OV XLVI, 6; FJ 330—this temple was girdled by a great adobe temenos and contained an artificial grove inside, the *mamaconas* being housed apparently just outside the enclosure. For a sun-temple plated inside and out with gold, north of Cajamarca, OV XLVI, 19. For a sun-temple unlike Coricancha, BLC 131.

The temple in vrq II, 37f., recalls Coricancha, consisting as it did of a large enclosure with seven intercommunicating parts; the rainbow Cuychic was housed in one. For the pound for children and llamas awaiting sacrifice, cl 27. The number of inmates as four thousand is much too high; see Cristóbal de Molina de Santiago, *Relación de muchas cosas acaecidas en el Peru* (Lima 1916), 146. For the number of sun-women as something over two hundred, ppr 266f., and as five hundred, jb 11. On analogy of the Titicaca cult we believe the high priestess in Coricancha was a proxy for Mama Quilla, argcs I, 28. The fountain was called Pilcopuquio, bc XIII, 16. For the emperor in the gardening ritual, blc 126. For the golden garden, ppr 266; gsc III, 50; cl 27. The gold lid of the god's *chicha*-basin became famous in the tale of the conquistador Mansio Serra, to whose share it fell, losing it in a night of gambling, ldb I, 80.

Coricancha as a Pantheon: For Coricancha as a pantheon, argcs I, 26; ggo IV, 5; po:Error. 15; gsc III, 63. Some provincial *huacas* were stationed on the highways leading out from the city to their particular province, po:Error. 15. For Coricancha as a pilgrim center, bc XIII, 12. For the three great gods in Coricancha, sg 31; argcs I, 26. For the moon in Coricancha, bv 178. For the image of Punchao, argcs I, 26; gsc III, 50; blc 131; bc XIII, 5. For Mama Ocllo in Coricancha, cv III, 18. For the daily service in Coricancha, bc XIII, 21, 37.

CHAPTER IX—PACHACUTI: CREATOR OF THE IMPERIAL MYSTIQUE

Inti: For the Inti-bird, sg 12, 17. For the Punchao disc as a giver of oracles, bc XII, 243f. For the Inti trinity, ja V, 28; argcs I, 24; bc XIII, 5. "Inti the son" was also called Huayna Punchao, cm 77. For the god's weapons, ppr 265. For Inti as leader of the army, bc XIII, 21; XIV, 9.

Illapa: For the overall picture, bc XIII, 7. Illapa is also given the name Libiac, aei II: accm II, 11 (see Llipiyak, ghlq 214). On Illapa's three names, bc XIII, 7; ja V, 4; accm II, 11; po:Error. 1. For Illapa's shrine in Tococachi, bc XIII, 7, 13. It appears as Illapa Cancha in gpf 1051. For Illapa as Pachacuti's *huaoqui*, bc XIII, 7; sg 69.

Mama Quilla and the Stars: For the moon cult as reserved for women, BC XIII, 6, 37; GP 187. For mummies of the *coyas* in the shrine of the moon, VRQ II, 38. For a separated shrine of the moon at Vilcas, RGI I, 166. For the hierarchy of stars, CV III, 15. Urcochillay is also identified as the Southern Cross, BC XIII, 6. For the stars as daughters of Inti, BC XIII, 5. For the Rucanas' testimony on the order of precedence among the stars (they called Venus, Auquilla, and the Pleiades, Larilla), RGI I, 205.

Council of Coricancha and Inca Pantheon: The most detailed account is in CV III, 15. Cabello Valboa says Pachamama—not Mama Quilla —follows Illapa in the order of precedence. For the council as a part of the dedication ceremonies of the building, BLC 126. On the great importance of the stars in Inca cult, see the famous diagram in SPY, accessible in a reproduction in Means, *Ancient Civilizations of the Andes* (N. Y., 1931), Fig. 168. For a shrine of Chasca Cuillor in Cuzco, GP 187. For her position next to Inti, see SPY diagram. The Hyades are said to be one of the three great stellar *huacas*, VRQ II, 38, where they are called the Tapir's Jawbone, Ahuara Caqui.

Council of Coricancha and Viracocha: For Pachacuti's mocking of all *huacas* as lesser, RZ I, 3; CV III, 15; BLC 126. For the "three sentences," ACCM II, 10 (only the third is mentioned in CM 16f., and only the second in CV III, 15, and BSC Disc. I, 1). For Inti and the *huacas* as intercessors and kinsmen of the Creator, LTOP 129. For the malleability of the Incas' religious ideas, BC XIII, 1. Quishuarcancha, built by Pachacuti, was distinct from Viracocha's shrine in Coricancha, CM 16f. We assume that this was a rebuilding and not a new erection.

Council of Coricancha and the Provincial Problem: For the squalor of the local shrines and the commanding position of Inti's temples, BLC 131; RZ I, 3. For a *curaca* demoted for personally invading the cult of Inti, LTOP 108f. For the hundred sun temples, JA VI. "Lo principál con que tienen (los Incas) toda la gente sujeta, era con este color de la observancia de este religión y adoración," FS 33; see also GSC III, 49. For the proscription of certain *haucas*, BSC Disc. I, 1; CV III, 15. The sons sent as *visitadores* were Amaru Topa Inca and a certain Huayna Yanqui Yupanqui, sg 37 (the latter also called Huayna Auqui Yupanqui, cv III, 15).

Viracocha's Attributes: For early Inca worship of Viracocha, cm 16. For pan-Peruvian tradition of the Creator as supreme and the Sun as subordinate, gsc III, 56. For Viracocha as judge and principal of life, bc XIII, 23. As an absolver of the Incas, bc XIII, 24. For confusion between Viracocha and Inti as state gods, bc XIII, 23, 32; jb 11; cv III, 9. For the emperor as the son of Viracocha, Rowe, *Eleven Inca Prayers*, No. 8. For the tone of Viracocha prayers, bc XIII, 23.

The Viracocha Prayers: The only authoritative translation of the prayers in Cristóbal de Molina is Rowe, *Eleven Inca Prayers*. The hymns quoted here are Numbers 1 and 4. For a longer version of first prayer, mm I, 7. For the query form of Viracocha prayers as possibly pre-Inca, gp 37, 58 (where it is attributed to the fourth age of man). For other prayers, gp 35, 39, 135, 172, 179, 206. For important details on prayers, bc XIII, 23.

Cult of Viracocha: For an Inca ceremony in Urcos, abc 80f. For the rebuilding of Viracocha's temple at Cacha, gvcr V, 22; this temple is in Racchi in the district of San Pedro, province of Canchis. For the cult of Viracocha among early Incas in Cuzco, bc XII, 12; XIII, 13–16. For woolen statue of Viracocha in Coricancha, bc XIII, 5. For sacrifice to him first in coronation ceremonies, bc XIII, 32. For nonassignment of women to his cult, cm 43. For belief that offerings and prayer made to a *huaca* were in turn offered by them to Viracocha, bc XIII, 4. 7; po:Error. 1; bv 154. Viracocha had no special endowments or herds, bc XIII, 4, 21 (Polo's denial of this, po 85, is probably based on his knowledge that Viracocha did in fact receive sacrifices, though apparently from the general religious fund).

The Trinity: Viracocha, Inti, and Illapa all had trinitarian aspects, bc XIII, 5, 7; sg 31; po:Error. 8. The concept of an all-male trinity is put as far back as the second age of man in gp 40.

Priesthood: For Pachacuti as the one who rearranged or set up the expanded priesthood, bsc Disc. I, 1; bv 172f. The reason for our ignorance on the subject is found in BLC 140. For historical background of Inca priesthood, BV 157–63, 172f. The high priest is once referred to as Intip apu, SG 29. For the high priest as also the chief priest of Inti, Cristóbal de Molina de Santiago 146f. He was always one of the Tarpuntay family or college, BC XIII, 33; CM 34. For his residence inside Coricancha, CL 27. Under Huascar the high priest belonged to the *ayllu* of Viracocha Inca (if different from the Tarpuntay college?), CV III, 24. For the high priestess of Punchao, the *"coya pacasa,"* CM 43. For the sun-women, BC XIII, 12. For the appointive powers of the villacumu, ARGCS I, 12. For nomination and appointment by state of certain of the local holy men, BC XIII, 34. For Pachacuti's demotion of the local cults, BLC 131.

Fear of Local Huacas: Quotation from BC XII, 22. For Pachacuti's campaigns seen in the light of attacks against demons, SPY 273–76. Huacas brought to Cuzco for the annual Situa were returned afterward if in good standing, CM 56. For profanation of *huacas* by Inca armies, BC XIII, 1; ARGCS I, 27. For control of *huacas*, CM 95. For Inca espionage against *huacas*, BV 160. For *huacas* grouped about the mummy of that ruler in Coricancha who had conquered them, PO: Fund. 96f. For local *huacas* as intercessors before Inti, RGI I, 85. For Capac Yupanqui's victory over a local *huaca*, SPY 259–61. For the part played by dissident priestly elements in Inca history, CV III, 12. For Topa Inca's hostility, RGI I, 169. For Manco Inca's hostility, TCYI 86f.

Supay: For the devil worshipped throughout Peru, BC XIII, 36; CLPP 62. We note him in Jauja in colonial times, Anon., *Descripción del Peru*, 82; in Huamachuco, RHA 43; in the Quito area, RGI III, 93; while the modern Titicaca Indians know him as the evil hail, Bandelier, *Titicaca and Coati*, 50, 93. The Supay of the modern Ecuadoran montaña is often a sorcerer's soul resident in a jaguar or anaconda. Huascar referred to the *huacas* supporting Atahualpa as "supayllulla," lying devils, SPY 316. For designation of ordinary oracular *huacas* as Supay, GP 186. For devils in the underworld, CM 79; GP 51. For shamans serving Supay, RHA 15–17. For Manco Inca's remarks on Supay, TCYI 31.

The Calendar: For Pachacuti as the author of Inca ceremonialism,

CM 82; BC XIII, 23. As the creator of the complete calendar, CM 15f.; PO:Error. 7. Beginning in December/January, the Inca calendar differed from the other common Peruvian one based on the Pleiades, which began in March, VRQ II, 39. For Pachacuti's reorientation of the fiestas, JB 14f.

Capacocha *and* Itu: For Pachacuti as inventor of the *capacocha*, CM 88–91; BC XIII, 21. For child-sacrifice, ARGCS I, 5. For the *itu*, BC XIII, 31. For transferal of dances to the Corpus Christi, JA V, 28; PO:Error. 9.

Mayocati: This festival is sometimes classed with the closing rites of the Camay, both being in January. For the Camay, GP 165–67, 206. For a clear distinction, DF X. For the Mayocati, CM 83f.; BC XIII, 26. It was attributed to Pachacuti, JB 18. For its other name, JB 15.

Inti Raymi: On this festival, RZ I, 21; BV 186–89. As an anniversary of the Chanca defeat, JB 14. The adoration of the sun is variously put in Coricancha, on Mount Manturcalla, in Haucaypata, and in a meadow east of Cuzco, CM 24–32; BC XIII, 28; GVCR VI, 20f.; Cristóbal de Molina de Santiago 160f.—all could be in part correct as the feast lasted at least eight or nine days (CL 30 says fifteen to twenty days). It may have been from the solstitial fires here that Coricancha received its new fire for the year, GVCR VI, 22.

Situa: The festival of the early sowing was the *Yapaquis*, CM 33–37; BC XIII, 29; CV III, 19; ARGCS I, 24; GVCR VII, 6. Pachacuti is said to have invented the imperial communion meal as an act of fealty, JB V, 23.

Inca Historiography: Quotation on Pachacuti, SG 30. For Inca heroic lays, FS I; CL 11f. For the dirges ordered by Huayna Capac, CLPP 53. For folkloristic remnants of biographies of the *coyas*, GP 91–100. Huaman Poma was certainly acquainted with pictured representations of the rulers, GP 76. For wooden tablets bearing these pictures, CM 4. For messages passed among Incas by pictures, ISP-VC 45. For the tablets stored on Puquín, CM 4, 77. For Inca Roca as the founder of the Yachahuasi, GVCR VII, 10. Quotation on Inca respect for tradition, BC XIII, 1. For appointment of the *amautas*, BV 161. There were one thousand *amautas* in Cuzco, BC XIII, 1. For the four-year curriculum, MM III, 4. Two good descriptions of the *quipu* are BC XII, 37; ACCM I, 14. For state support of *amautas*, ISP-VC 4f. For the *amauta* versus the bard, GVCR VI, 9. For "*amauta*" as a general term covering all sciences, GP 53. For the lays of each ruler, CL 11f. For popular, nonofficial interpretations of Inca history, ISP-VC 7–12.

Historical Drama: For the ancestral dance-drama, GHLQ 297; BC XIV, 12; SG 31. On the ancestral mummies, JB 17; BV XIV, 12; MM III, 6.

Royal Mummies: For the cult, BC XIII, 10; PPR 238f., 268; PO:Fund. 123f. For Huayna Capac's establishment, GA 256ff. A ruler's gold was noninheritable, CA 266. For Toledo's burning of the mummies in public, ARGCS I, 22.

Burial: For Peruvian burial customs and the chullpa-type tomb, BLC 249. For *illapa* as against *aya*, GP 208; GPF 377f. For the ability of the *illapa* to desert the mummy, BLC 259. For "*malquis*," the common term for ancestral mummy, AEI II. For worship accorded these mummies and their *huaoquis*, PO:Error. 3. For the fertilizing power of mummies, BC III, 10. For the mourning festival, GP 208; RZ III, 9. The suttee is attested for all of Peru, PPR 251; BV 150–53; RZ III, 9; BC XIV, 19; JA V, 7. For imperial mourning, CL 60.

The Huaoqui: For Pachacuti's *huaoqui*, BC XIII, 7; SG 31, 47. For the *huaoqui* in general, BC XIII, 9. For the *huaoquis* of Manco Capac and Sinchi Roca, SG 14; BC XIII, 5.

The Afterlife: For the name Upamarca, AEI 7. For the names of heaven and hell, GVCR II, 7; GP 51. For remarks on the subject, BC XIII, 3; CM 79; PO:*Instruc. contra Cerem. y ritos*, 3; ACCM II, 12. But see the curious inversion in FS 32, where to the underworld are assigned the good and to the heavens, which are fiery, are sent the evil. For the four parts of heaven, CL 26.

Armegeddon and Resurrection: For the classic statement, GHV 233. There are strong hints of ideas here similar to the Mexican and Mayan beliefs; this allows us to accept the Inca picture as essentially uncontaminated by Christian ideas. For Peruvian belief in revival, *porque había de venir un Viracocha que revolviese la tierra,* LTOP 7. See also LTOP 135; GSC III, 56. For the belief that the soul will revive in the body, BV 153; OV XLVI, 17; LTOP 127. For the return of Atahualpa's soul to his mummy, PPR 251. For the necessity of the mummy to a resurrection, GHV 234.

Incas as an Elect Group: For obeisance to a ruler, BC XIII, 23. For prohibition against divinization of rulers, BV 155. For confession of sin by ruler, PO:Error. 5; BV 169f.; BC XIII, 24. For the *pururaucas* as visible only to Pachacuti, BC XIII, 8. For the Incas as ecclesiastical geniuses, BC XII, 35. For a Tupí-speaking people today showing interesting ideological affinities with the Incas (but unconnected, of course), C. Wagley, "World View of the Tapirapé Indians," *Journal of American Folklore,* Vol. LIII (1940).

CHAPTER X—TOPA INCA: CHIMOR AND THE NORTH

Age and Youth: Confusion is introduced by the fact of the coregency which allowed sources to attribute undertakings both to Pachacuti and to his son. For the prince's name and mother's identity, GSC III, 49; DF V; GP 100; ISP-VC 20; BLC 259. For Topa's birth late in his father's life, SG 40. Topa will have become a co-emperor about 1448 (at age of fifteen or sixteen during a combined *huarachicoy* and coronation) as Pachacuti was finishing the Collao campaign—this checks well with the date 1445 for that campaign in RAC 278. For Pachacuti's part in the events of co-optation and coronation, SG 42f.

Trouble under the Coregency: For the seven-year drought which filled most of the coregency, SPY 282; ACCM I, 15—for the drought as seven or ten years, GP 82. For earthquakes and eruption of Misti, MM-DN 11. The ructions in Cuzco at this time may be connected with the appearance there of fifteen thousand Cañar *mitmacs* in the area, CL 56, who had been introduced by Topa, ISP-VT 123. For the name Pachacuti as meaning a public calamity, GHLQ 16.

The Army: For Topa's army at Jauja as numbering ten thousand, LTOP 19. The estimate of two hundred thousand is exaggerated, CL 56. The three generals are named in CV III, 16, 18.

Cuzco to Cajamarca: For Topa's building at Vilcas, RGI I, 166–68.

For the reduction of three Quechua hill forts, cv III, 16. For the submission of Jauja, LTOP 19f.; ISP-VT 119. The Spaniards estimated that the Vilcas plaza held one hundred thousand people, BLC 57. For Huánuco, GP 55. Huánuco lay under the peak of Yaropaja, almost as famous a *huaca* as Pariacaca (with which it is sometimes confused), RGI I, 71 f. For severe fighting in the area between Jauja and Cajamarca, CL 56. For Topa's palaces at Huánuco, CL 56. For an easy victory over the Huacrachucos farther down the Marañón, GVCR VIII, 1 f. For a description of Cajamarca, OV XLVI, 6.

The Chachapoyas: For the unusual beauty of the women, PPR 255; CLPP 78. For the capture of a *pucara* here and a *sinchi* named Chuqui Sota, SG 44. Details on this campaign must be treated cautiously in GVCR VIII, 1–3.

Chimor: J. H. Rowe, "Kingdom of Chimor," *Acta Americana*, Vol. VI (1948), is indispensible here particularly as he gives the only accessible text of the *Anonymous History of Trujillo* (1604 A.D.). For hints of an elaborate court etiquette, cv III, 17. Eunuchism is mentioned for the harem guard in GHV 233, 237. For facial mutilation, see examples in Mochica ceramics. For religion in the coastal area of Chimor, ACCM III, 2. My remarks on the king's relationship with the goddess are based on the Lambayeque legend of the evil king Fempallec, cv III, 17. For cultic homogeneity on the coast, CLPP 61. For the reputation of Chimor on the coast, cv III, 16. For sodomy and the invading giants, CLPP 52, 64; GSC III, 66; JA I, 19; ACCM III, 2. The legend of the giants' landing in northern Peru or Ecuador may well refer to the landing of the Marquesans on *Te Fiti* or the "Land of Ridges" of the people of Rarotonga, R. C. Suggs, *Island Civilizations of Polynesia* (N. Y., 1960), XV. For mutual feelings of sierra and coastal peoples, BLC 257. Rowe gives the third ruler as roughly 1370, with Minchançaman as *c.*1461 (we have changed this to 1460). For Canda as the name of Chimor, OV XLVI, 17. Minchançaman is said to have imposed his language Quingnam in the wake of his armies quite like the Inca custom, ACCM III, 2. When Capac Yupanqui got to Cajamarca, Chimor extended south only to Huarmey, cv III, 16. Its final extension south was at or near Paramunca, ACCM III, 2.

Source Criticism for Inca Attack on Chimor: Topa's first raid via Huamachuco, cv III, 16, was probably a different and later attack from that in GVCR VI, 32; ACCM III, 2. Cieza reverses Garcilaso's northward push up the coast, CL 58, beginning the Inca conquest at Tumbez and ending at Paramunca, no doubt in conformity with the direction of his own travels.

Cuismancu: For this area at the time of the founding of Lima in 1534, see ACCM II, 19. For the heavy theocratic bias on the coast, CLPP 72. In the days of Huascar, Pachacamac had a *curaca* named Taurichumbi as well as a high priest, FJ 339. For confusion between Rímac and Pachacamac, GVCR VI, 30; SPY 302, 304. For oblique mention of an unsuccessful push against the Yauyos by the pre-Inca people of the Rímac Valley, RGI I, 71f. For the site of San Pedro de Mama, RGI I, 15, appendix cxx (and see map on p. 60). For political and linguistic diversity in Cuismancu, RGI I, appendix xxviii f.

Thrusts out of Cajamarca: For thrusts against Chimor via Huamachuco and against Palta and Cañar groups, cv III, 16; sg 44. For the five-month campaign against the Paltas, Huancabambas, etc., CL 56. For the submission without a fight of Huancabamba, Cajas, and some coastal groups, VRQ II, 10. For Topa's army of forty thousand attacking Huancabamba, GVCR VIII, 3. Cusibamba is today Loja, LDB I, 72. For the martial reputation of the Cañars, LDB I, 71. For the Cañar *mitmacs*, LTOP 22; LDB I, 71; ISP-VT 123; CL 56.

Topa's First Chinchaysuyo Triumph: If we accept that the second half of the campaign lasted six years, then the initial part of the campaign up to the seizure of Tumibamba lasted only two years. We can thus tentatively set the date of Topa's first triumph back in Cuzco as 1465 or 1466. This break in the campaign is undoubtedly that two-year period of building in and around Tumibamba before the push against the Puruháes, VRQ II, 11.

From Tumibamba to Quito: For the four-year limit on the second part of the campaign, sg 46. On the battle of Latacunga, CL 56. For the capture of the Quito *sinchi*, cv III, 17. This battle is probably that one referred to as being close to St. Andrés Xunxi, RGI III, 150–52. For Topa's daily round of activities in Quito, CL 57. For the quotation attributed to Topa, CL 56. For the appointment of Challco Mayta as viceroy in Quito, CL 57.

The Kingdom of Quito: The traditions on the Caras are from Velasco, about whose credibility there is much question, HSAI 48, 792f. Velasco's source from the regime of Benalcazar has disappeared, VRQ II, 4–22, 33, 46, 142, 156f., 207f. Inasmuch as Quito lay exactly on the common border of the Caras and the Panzaleos, it is permissible to infer that the two people joined to found the city.

From Quito to Tumbez: For the slaughter of envoys sent to Puerto Viejo (Guayaquil), CL 57. Topa probably approximated the present Calpi-Babahoyo route. He embarked twenty thousand men on balsa rafts, SG 46. For a picture of such raft transportation on this river route, RGI I, 13. Following his pet Galapagos theory, Sarmiento erroneously states that they had *already* arrived on the coast and that the embarkation was therefore on the high seas; the reference however is obviously to river transportation. For the two mysterious islands reputedly discovered by Topa in the ocean, Aguachumbi and Ninachumbi, SG 46; CV III, 17. These names may stand for Ninachhumpi (Deep Maroon) and Ahuachhumpi (Twin Maroon), GHLQ 17, 121, 260. The merchant princes assigned to these islands practically identify them with the middleman island of Puná. For the two thousand inhabitants of pre-Hispanic Manta, GBH 241. For the slaughter of garrisons in the estuary area, CLPP 47. For the *capullana*, LDB I, 8; ISP-VC 15f.; BSC Disc. I, 5. The unplaced tale of Topa's *coya* and the *capullana*, BC XII, 15, probably refers in a popular way to the stratagem used by the Incas in capturing Tumbez: the luring away of their fleet to allow an attack on the city. For the demolition of the thousand-year-old fortress of Tumbez and the erection on the site of an Inca fort, palace, and *acllahuasi* about the year 1475 by an Inca emperor (erroneously identified as Huayna Capac), VRQ II, 13.

End of Chimor Campaign: Topa turned off from his main army at Pachecos to come out on the sierra road at Huancabamba, CV III, 17f. A return to Tumibamba is undoubtedly in error, SG 46. For the resistance of Chimor in Santa Valley, GVCR VI, 32. The Inca army did not have to fight until it came to Jayanca, cv III, 17. The unsupported assumption that the wall of Santa is of Chimor date is mine. For the Chimor governor of Lambayeque named Llempisan, RAC 280—Rowe places this event about 1470 A.D. The Incas nearly lost the final battle in Moche, CL 58. *The Anonymous History of Trujillo* has the conquered ruler of Chimor replaced by his son (contradicted by ACCM III, 2, where it is said that Minchançaman was not carried off to Cuzco but was reconfirmed in his office).

Inca Coastal Policy: For comparative clemency shown by Topa to Chimor, CL 58. For similar clemency to the coastal *curacas*, CLPP 70. For the replacement of the captured Jayanca *curaca* by his son and the carrying off of the father to Cuzco, cv III, 17.

Return to Cuzco: The army from the coast joined Topa at Cajamarca, cv III, 17. Three possible reasons for the execution of Tillca Yupanqui are: first, if Tillca Yupanqui is Apu Yupanqui, SG 46, then he was executed for ordering fiestas of rejoicing at the news that Topa and his army had disappeared in the Pacific Ocean; second, he disobeyed Pachacuti's four-year limit on the campaign by extending it to six, SG 46; and third, he had been commanded not to go beyond a certain point, cv III, 18. The first is not only uncertain but incredible. The second would imply that he was in complete command of the forces, which he was not. The last is simply a duplication of the Capac Yupanqui story. For the Cuzco triumph, SPY 284. For the loot offered in Coricancha, cv III, 18; CL 54. For Topa's remarriage at this time, cv III, 18.

The South Coast: For interesting information on the populations of these valleys, ov XLVI, 17. Sources for this campaign are cv III, 18; CL 59; CLPP 73; GVCR VI, 17, 29 (Garcilaso confuses this with Capac Yupanqui's earlier campaign). Cieza says that Chincha surrendered without a fight (the other two imply a bitter struggle) while Nazca offered resistance (whereas Cabello Valboa classifies Nazca as friendly). For the population of Chincha, LDB I, 59. Atahualpa credited Chincha with being the greatest power on the coast, PPR 365f., as well as being a center for treasure in silver, CA 250.

Topa at Pachacamac: For Inca fear of Pachacamac, BC XIII, 17. The idol supported Huascar against Atahualpa, PPR 242 (this is both denied and asserted in OV XLVI, 9f.). The Interlocking and early Lima ceramics of this area of the coast have decided connections with styles in Pucara and Tiahuanaco roughly dated to 450 B.C.–200 A.D. For exemptions granted by the Council of Coricancha, CV III, 18. The first Spaniards reported that the coast paid tribute to Pacha-camac and not to Cuzco, ISP-HP 176; OV XLVI, 15. For Inca buildings there, BC XIII, 17; CV III, 18; CL 58. For two of the local folk tales relating to Topa Inca and the idol, FS 28; CCDM 246.

Campaign on the South Coast: The figure of thirty thousand warriors available to Chincha implies that it controlled outside areas. For the situation encountered at Cañete Canyon, CL 59; CLPP 73; GVCR VI, 29. Runahuana is up in the Cañete Canyon and was called New Cuzco by the Incas. For Topa's presence among the Chachapoyas after the fall of Huarco, CV III, 18. The *pucara* of Huarco was used as a Spanish prison by the Marquis de Cañete, RGI I, 40.

Death of Pachacuti: Using Cabello Valboa, Pachacuti's rule ran from 1438 to 1471, a thirty-three-year span, but CV III, 18, also says that he died as an old man after a rule of thirty-six years. We may thus assume that he lived only a while after resigning, and died about 1472 A.D. For his age as over seventy or eighty, JA VI, 21. For the prophecy of the end of empire, BLC 259. For dragons and comets, SPY 276. For the palaces of Pachacuti in the Yucay Valley and at Patallacta, SG 41, 47; BC XIII, 13. For the death scene, SG 47; SPY 286. The poem exists only in its Spanish translation: "Nací como lirio en el jardín, y ansí fuí criado, y como vino mi edad, envejecí, y como había de morir, así me sequé y morí." For Topa's taking power, SG 48. For Pachacuti's mummy, JA VI, 21.

CHAPTER XI—TOPA INCA: REBELLION AND THE SOUTH

The Eastern Forests: For old tales of the Amazons, GP 57, 240. For the realm of the Amazonian queen Conori, OV XLIX, 4. For the Amazons as the *huarmi aucas* and for the cannibalistic "Double-Faces," the *Iscayoyas*, SPY 289–91. For Inca rumors of a populous kingdom in the jungle, CL 53. For enchanted anacondas, CLPP 95.

For modern tales of the two-faced creatures, I. Goldman, "Cosmological Beliefs of the Cubeo Indians," *Journal of American Folklore*, Vol. LIII (1941).

Advance into the Montaña: On the levy of the new army, CL 60; SG 49. For the assignment of commands to Otorongo Achachi and Challco Yupanqui, SG 49; CV III, 18. For the officers under Otorongo, SPY 289–91. For Otorongo himself, GP 112. For the name Achachi as meaning "old" or "grandfather," GP 192. For Amaru Inca as governor of Cuzco, CV III, 18. For the three passes, Agua Tona, Amaru, and Pilcopata, SG 49 (they are no doubt the present routes leading down into the Tono, the Cosnipata, and the Pilcopata, three adjacent feeder streams of the Madre de Dios). Sarmiento's Opatari may be the modern frontier post of Alicta. For the Amarumayo, GVCR VII, 13f. For the penetration of Opatarisuyos, Manusuyos, Mañaries, Chunchos, and Chipomaguas, CV III, 18; SG 49; SPY 289. If the Paititi River is the present Tambopata, then the Incas may have reached the site of Puerto Maldonado. On Incas and Mojos, BC XII, 4; GVCR VII, 13f. On a populated but unnamed land to the east, CL 53.

Topa's Recall: For the Colla contingent with Topa and the mutinous attitude of the army, CV III, 18. The Colla *sinchi* who took Pachacuti's name was Chucachucay Coaquiri, CV III, 18; SG 50 (he was a son of Chuchi Capac, SG 40). For Topa's return, BC II, 14. For Topa's instructions to Otorongo, BC II, 14; CV III, 18; SG 49. For Incas left in the montaña, SPY 289–91.

Collao Campaign: The best account is in CL 53–55. For Colla slavery in the Yucay Valley, SG 40. For the Colla uprising at time of Pachacuti's death, SPY. For the extension of the revolt of Collao north to the Vilcañota watershed, CL 53. For Topa's new levies, CV III, 18; SG 40. For the enemy confederation, CL 53. For the four enemy *pucaras*, CV III, 18. For massacre of Incas in Collao, CL 53. For the loyalty of Canas and Canchis, CL 54. For the siege of Pucara, CLPP 102. For fate of the Colla *curacas*, BC XII, 14. For Mama Ocllo's fiestas, CL 55.

Reorganization of the Titicaca Basin: For an example of this among the Pacasas, RGI II, 58–60. For a general account of the procedure, BC XII, 24. For the meeting at Chucuito, CL 54. For special treatment of the Urus, RGI II, 53, 55, 57; MHVE 129, 131. I take the round number of five thousand Urus from MHVE 129, reading it back from the last days of the empire. Figures from the last census are also from MHVE 129.

Topa's Provincial Government: For an example of Inca colonial administration in Ecuador, RGI III, 172. For the tendency for *sinchis* in empire to make their power hereditary, SG 52. For *visitadores* sent into eastern and western quarters, CL 55. For the office of *tocricoc*, BC XII, 25; FS 10; RGI I, 99; 188f.; IH 272, 277. For the moieties, BC XII, 24. For governors who were sons or kinsmen of the Incas or of an allied caste, RGI III, 179. For *orejones* as governors, CL 20. For the governor's remuneration, BC XII, 27. For succession preferred for *curaca* class, RGI II, 45, 240; FS 20; RGI I, 189; LTOP 5f., 21; BC XII, 25. For the residence of sons in Cuzco, LTOP 132, 140; FS 37; OV XLVI, 17; CL 14; BLC 255; RGI I, 101. For the *micho*, SG 50; CV III, 18; GP 260; ISP-TY 72; RGI I, 100. For liquidation of the old title of *sinchi*, SG 8. It was probably Topa who instituted the decimal system, LTOP 51. For the Inca *visitadores* at both regular and irregular intervals, GP 82–84; SG 51f.; GP 135f., 151; RGI I, 100; ISP-TY 68f.; FS 15. For the mass marriage, RGI I, 100. For classification of special officials, ISP-TY 68f.; GP 271–73. For the *tocoyricoc*, SG 52; IH 277f., 287. For the spy called *quillescachi equeco*, GP 271–73; SG 27. For the system of awards, ISP-TY 83–85.

Organs of the Central Government: For the imperial council, BC XII, 25; BV 181; FS 9; MM III, 6; ISP-TY 60; IH 278. For the interesting coincidence of the names of the four *apuconas* who served under Huayna Capac with those of Topa's Collao generals, CV III, 18; FS 9. For the seven or eight coregents set up by Huayna Capac's will, CV III, 24. For the ruler's ratification of the council's decisions, ISP-TY 60. For the ruler's secretary, deputy, and treasurer, GP 82, 130f., 269. The *Incap ranti* was invested with his office on the day of the emperor's coronation by the priests of the Sun, IH 280.

Topa Capac's Conspiracy: For Topa Capac's relationship to the emperor, cv III, 16. For the conspiracy, sg 51, 98f.; cv III, 19. Garbled memories of this plot probably explain the stories of treason in cl 56 and po:Tras. 115. The Apu Achachi in sg 52 may be either the famous Otorongo Achachi or perhaps the Achachi (if this is not Otorongo himself) who was one of Topa's four generals in Collao and was a brother of his, cv III, 18.

Sources for Study of Inca Law: For detail on Inca laws, S. F. Moore, *Power and Property in Inca Peru* (1958), chaps. 3–5 and Appendix. My own analysis has been made independently of this work. Three lists of Inca laws are bv 199–205; gp 129–37; bc XII, 26. For Topa's reputation as a lawgiver, cv III, 20; gvcr VI, 34.

Inca Law: For the trial circle, rgi I, 101f. For the Cuzco court of twelve, ggo IV, 16; ih 284f. For oaths to the Sun and Earth as well as for the generally personal nature of Inca justice, ih 272, 276, 282. For the resentments of local peoples, here the Huamangas, rgi I, 149. For Jesuitical interpretations of the *amautas*, bv 201. For the regulation of conservation practices and the protection of llamas, cl 16. For Inca coca-terracing in the montaña, Isaiah Bowman, *Andes of Southern Peru* (N. Y., 1916), 77. Bowman picked up traditions of a paved road into this area but saw no remains. For coca-chewing as reserved to the upper classes, ppr 270; ja IV, 22. For Topa as the ruler introducing it, blc 261. For its use later, ltop 131, 139. For the Cuzco monopoly on metals, cl 14; clpp 97; ppr 277; cv III, 19; abc 81 f. For laws prohibiting divine honors to private persons, bv 155 (undoubtedly one of Topa's regulations). For Topa's anti-*huaca* reputation, spy 283f.

Pre-Inca Titicaca: For the pre-Inca cult here, bc XIII, 18. For historical ignorance of the Pacasas, bc XII, 14. For archaeological proof that the island was a pre-Inca cult site, Bandelier, *Titicaca and Coati*, 236; argcs I, 4. On a meaning (dubious) of the word "titi," argcs I, 13. For the serpent coiled about the island, argcs I, 5. This serpent, the *yaurinka* of the present inhabitants, is said to have appeared on the shore during this century, Bandelier, *Titicaca and Coati*, 48. For adornment of the rock, argcs I, 24. For the shining cat on the rock, ARGCS I, 13. For the pre-Inca Colla priests and priestesses, ARGCS I, 4.

Population at Copacabana: For the expulsion of the Yunguyos and the retention of some priests, BC XIII, 18; ARGCS I, 4, 28. For the forty-two groups among the *mitmacs*, ARGCS I, 12. For the division between them, ARGCS I, 9, 12. For Apu Inca Sucso, ARGCS I, 12. For the pre-Inca blue stone idol at Copacabana, ARGCS I, 32. The two hills by Copacabana were Copacati and Copacabana itself, the former connected with rain, ARGCS I, 32. The Incas seem to have renamed these hills Quisani (or Sirocani where rebels were executed) and Llallagua (or Yaca Llallagua), ARGCS I, 1.

Topa's Reorientation of Titicaca Religion: For the story of Topa and the Colla priest, ARGCS I, 4. For Topa's son at Pacaritambo, CV III, 19 (this may be the Manco Capac Inca of GP 114, who was one of Topa's captains in Chile). For Inti at Copacabana as both trinity and a golden statue, ARGCS I, 24, 29. For Viracocha's worship there, BLC 182; ACCM II, 10. For the temple in Copacabana, BC XIII, 18. For confusion between the goddesses Titicaca and Mama Quilla, BC XIII, 18. For the modern tradition that the mother rock was Mama Ocllo, Bandelier, *Titicaca and Coati*, Pt. V and p. 275 particularly (this is in line with the tendency for folk memory in the southern Andes today to preserve Inti Huayna Capac and Manco Capac as alternate names for the sun); B. Mishkin: "Cosmological Ideas among the Indians of the Southern Andes," *Journal of American Folklore*, Vol. LIII (1940). For the temple on Coati, Squier, *Peru*, 360–65. For the status of Mama Quilla, BC XIII, 18. For priestly visitations to the holy islands, BC XIII, 18; ARGCS I, 28. For the displaying of the high priestess, BC XIII, 18.

The Area as a Pilgrimage Site: The two all-important sources here are BC XIII, 18; ARGCS I, 1, 5, 12ff., 20, 24, 28f. For the architectural feature of five doors in a temple, Squier, *Peru*, 368f. For the *pillco*-bird, CM 42. Child sacrifice on Titicaca is also mentioned in BLC 182. Modern natives tell of mothers anciently on the island secluding their illegitimate children (whose fathers had been white

Viracochas on the island) in caves where dripping water kept them alive; thus nourished by the rock, the children emerged to become the Incas who thereupon drove out the white Viracochas, Bandelier, *Titicaca and Coati*, 294f. Here are undoubted memories of child sacrifice mingled with the tale of the Incas' origin.

Three-pronged Offensive South of the Lake: For the army of twenty thousand in Bolivia, SPY 292. For the five thousand who went into the montaña and never returned, SG 41. For the ingenious capture of the *pucara* of the Charcas, BC XII, 14. For the Tucumán incident, BC XII, 14. For the Porco mines, CV III, 18. For the Lupacas as miners there, MHVE 137f. For the failure of the montaña venture, GVCR VII, 17, 18. For the Chiriguanas, LDB I, 99. The Chiriguanas may have given rise to tales of the Amazons, SPY 292. The women of related groups (i.e., the Tupinambas) did sometimes accompany their men to the attack and help to eat captured males (whom sometimes they married first), Steward and Faron, *Native Peoples of South America* (1959), 326f., 334. The Paititi referred to in RGI IV, cxcviii ff., was undoubtedly a foreign name for the Bolivian highland, as it is described as raising maize and llamas, having many mines, and possessing a famous house of the Sun in a large lake; beyond it lay Paneca, the land of the Amazons. For the Chilean campaign, CL 60; GVCR VII, 18. For the garrison in Coquimbo, CV III, 18. For fighting there, SPY 292. This campaign became a sensational popular tale, GP 114; BC XII, 14. The southernmost Chilean river reached is said additionally to be the Arauco, RGI II, 8, and the Chachapoal, FS 6.

Topa's Last Years: For the four-year progress through the realm, BC XII, 15. For Inca troops in Chachapoyas after the Chilean campaign, SG 50. For Huayna Capac's birth in Tumibamba, SG 46; CL 56. For his birth in Quito, LTOP 152. For Topa as the one who carried Sacsahuaman almost to completion, BC XII, 15; MM I, 12; CV III, 18; DF 5. For Chinchero as built by Topa and as the place of his decease, SG 54; LTOP 148. Cobo says that he died in Cuzco; if by this he means the province of Cuzco, he is of course correct, BC XII, 15. For the burning of Topa's mummy by Atahualpa, BC XII, 14; SG 54.

CHAPTER XII—HUAYNA CAPAC: ABSENTEE EMPEROR

Background on Huayna Capac: For the court tale about Topa, BC XII, 15. For Huayna Capac's name, SG 54. It is confused in ISP-VC 21. The other legitimate prince, Auqui Topa Inca, is wrongly broken into misnamed doublets, BLC 261; DF 5, and into a worse triplet, GSC III, 50. For Huayna Capac as the youngest, GP 85f. There were only two legitimate princes, SG 102. For his accession as a small boy, SG 57.

Conspiracy of Chiqui Ocllo: For the plot, SG 55; CV III, 20. Huayna Capac's first official act was the execution of his brothers, GP 84f.; this is probably an oblique reference to this conspiracy.

Mama Ocllo: For her intervention, CV III, 20. For her villa on Picchu, BC XIII, 13. For a description of her, GP 101f. The *coya* in the tale of the Cacica on the coast is unnamed but must be Mama Ocllo, witness the correct detail of the Inca general who was a brother of Topa, BC XII, 15.

The Hualpaya Plot: For the sources, CV III, 20; SG 57; BC XII, 16; SPY 293–96. A person called Gualepaya occurs in ISP-TY 60 as one of the four prefects under Huayna Capac. The list is Auqui Topa Inca as secretary of the Council, Capac Ancha, Chularico, Coyoche, and Gualepaya.

Huayna Capac's Accession: For Auqui as the emperor's councilor, CV III, 20; SG 57. For the nuptials, SPY 297–99. For Cusi Rimay as a legitimate sister, BC XII, 14; SG 60. Cieza has the emperor marry a sister Chimpu Ocllo instead of Cusi Rimay, CL 62.

The Emperor and His Court: For Huayna Capac as the most splendid of the emperors, CL 61; PPR 236. For the unique adoration of him as a living god, JA 6; BC XII, 17. For his title Shepherd of the Sun, SG 57. For his purge of the *huacas*, GP 84, 186.

The Mourning Pilgrimage: For the suttee and events in connection with the mourning, CL 60; CV III, 20f.; BC XII, 16. For the progress, CL 62. For Quito as the ultimate stop, BC XII, 16. The Chachapoyas were certainly intimidated at this time, SG 58; BC XII, 16.

Early Building: Huayna Capac's temporary residence was called Uchullo, cv III, 21. Sinchi Roca undertook the channeling of the Vilcañota while he was governor of Cuzco under Huayna Capac, cv III, 21; LTOP 130.

Adolescence: For his lengthy residence in the new Cuzco palace and then in his Yucay dwellings previous to the Collao campaign, sg 59; BC XII, 16.

Problem of the Legitimate Heir: The exceptionally confused problem revolves around Ninan Cuyochi, about whom the following facts are pertinent: his mother was Caya Cuzco, GP 84–86; his mother was Huayna Capac's sister and a concubine, and he was older than Huascar, ISP-VC 26; he was a bastard and taken when full-grown north to Ecuador, sg 60; he was the only son of that one of the emperor's wives who predeceased her husband, BC XII, 16; Cusi Rimay was childless, sg 60; his mother Cusi Rimay died soon after (his birth?), SPY 299f.; he fought the Pastos, sg 60; Huayna Capac left him the kingdom, inasmuch as Huascar's mother was not the *coya* at the time she bore Huascar, cv III, 31; he is mentioned with Atahualpa in a list of sons, DF 5; his selection as Huayna Capac's successor—against Huascar's claims—was left to an omen, but *orejones* in Quito wanted him as ruler, sg 62; his selection by Huayna Capac as heir surprised the *orejones*, who had assumed Huascar's title to be incontestable, cv III, 24. There was thus obviously a weakness in the prince's claims. Could it be that Cusi Rimay was barren and adopted Nina Cuyochi as her son at a time when Mama Rahua (the legitimate sister who was to succeed her as *coya*) had already borne Huascar? In such a hypothetical case Huascar will have been a bastard at birth, and only the later marriage of his father to his mother will have raised him to the legitimacy. The statements about Huascar are as follows: Huascar was the oldest son, PRN 239; he was beloved as the natural heir in Cuzco, CL 69; he was a bastard until he forced his mother to marry his father's mummy, SPY 308; he began to rule at twenty-five, more or less, CL 71 (using Cabello Valboa's dates, this would put his birth about 1500, at the beginning of his father's adolescence, which would be consonant with Cobo's statement that he was the oldest bastard prince).

Atahualpa: At his death Atahualpa was just noticeably over thirty years of age (thirty, says FJ 336; more than thirty, says CL 69; thirty or thirty-two, says OV XLVI, 9). He is said to have been four or five years older than Huascar, CL 62, 69, which is not probable. He is called the "second son," BC XII, 18. We have arbitrarily settled on his birth as in the same year as Huascar's, 1500 A.D. That he was a bastard and born in Cuzco is certain, CL 62, 69; CLPP 37. For Tocto Coca, SG 63 (a fuller version of her name at Tocto Ocllo Coca occurs in SPY 299f.; it is garbled in the Tutu Palla of CL 62 and the Tupac Palla of CL 69). For her death by the time of the move into Ecuador, CV III, 21. For the favors lavished on Atahualpa by his father, CL 62, 68f. For his move north along with Ninan Cuyochi while Huascar, Manco Inca, and Paullo remained in Cuzco, SG 60.

Huascar: For Huascar's birthplace as the Muhina area, CV III, 24. For Kenko and its traditions, RGI II, appendix 10. Huascar's given name is curiously said to have been Atoco ("a species of bird"), VRQ II, 19, 62. The word is not given in our dictionaries.

Other Sons: For the birth of Manco Inca in Tiahuanaco, CLPP 105; BC XIII, 19. For his mother as a woman from Anta named Chuquillanto, MM II, 13. She is also called Mama Runto, DF 5, and is said to have been Huayna Capac's third wife, VRQ II, 62f. For his full name as Paullo Topa Inca, ARGCS I, 31. He was to be baptized a Christian in 1543 and to die probably in 1549. Two other names prominent in later warfare appear as sons of Huayna Capac: Huari Tito, MM IV, 16 (son of Anahuarque in GP 84–86), and Quiso Yupanqui, son of a Huánuco princess, who led the attack on Lima during the siege of Cuzco, GP 84ff.

Collao Campaign: For this, see SG 59; CV III, 21. Sarmiento takes Huayna Capac as far south as Coquimbo (he was a year in Chile, says CL 62), but Cabello Valboa, supported by BC XII, 16, omits the Chilean march. Cieza has probably confused this campaign with that of Topa Inca previously.

Huayna Capac at Titicaca: For the appointment of a princess as chief vestal, ARGCS I, 31. Don Cristóbal Paullo Inca was later to marry this half-sister; she was Doña Catalina Toctoc Oxica, a member of the

Vicaquirau *panaca*, ISP-VC 45ff. As Azca or Ozeca she is erroneously called his mother, GP 86, 127. For the building on Coati, ARGCS I, 18. For the unsuccessful attempt of Huayna Capac to spread the Titicaca cult to other islands, ARGCS I, 30 (see on this J. H. Rowe, "The Origins of Creator Worship among the Incas," in *Culture in History* [1960]).

Announcement of Revolt in the North: Specifically the Pastos, Quitos, Cayambis, Caranguis, and Huancavelicas had revolted, SG 60. For Chucuito as the scene of the parley, BC XII, 16 (otherwise Tiahuanaco in CV III, 21, and Titicaca in SG 59). For Auqui Topa Inca as the generalissimo and Michi as the co-ordinate, SG 60; CV III, 21 (the latter is named as Mihicnaca Mayta in SPY 301). Ilaquita or Larquita is elsewhere substituted for Michi, SG 60.

Appointment of Huascar as Heir: For a categorical statement to this effect, FS 18. For Huaman Achachi as governor of Cuzco, SG 60. The four members of the Council are in ISP-TY 60, undoubtedly garbled.

Progress Northward: For this advance, CL 63; ABC 82. The emperor sent back for Huanacauri while at Vilcas, SPY 301. For the idol later in Quito, BC XIII, 15. For the defeat of the Chachapoyas, CL 63. For the Bracamoros, CL 64. For the military effort in Tumbez and on the coast, ABC 82; SG 60; CL 64.

The Carangui War: The entire war consumed ten years, BC XII, 17, and we have assumed it as 1511–22. This is perhaps the ten-year period of residence in Tumibamba recorded in RGI III, 158. The events of the war are recorded in SG 60; CV III, 21–23; BC XII, 16f.; CL 66f. The name of the Carangui leader is given as Pinto (Wild Cane) in GP 84, 247, and it is hinted that his son carried on the struggle.

Geography of the Campaigns: Confusion between the sieges of Cochisque (near Cayambe) and Carangui create difficulties here. Sarmiento implies that Yahuarcocha was next to Cayambe (confirmed in RGI III, 113). Cieza places it between Carangui—three miles from Spanish Ibarra—and the Mira River, CLPP 37 (the great *pucara* overlooked the Mira River, VRQ II, 43). Yahuarcocha is said to be a mile from Ibarra, vrq II, 44, and to be on the edge of the province of Mira, abc 82. Cabello Valboa similarly agrees with Cieza by placing the *pucara* last attacked north of Otavalo. Rumichaca was between Tulcan and Ipiala. The probe northward got to within a day's journey of Pasto, rgi III, 178 (the point is identified as the valley of Atres, cv III, 23).

Revolt of the Orejones: Cabello Valboa is our source here, though his literary trimmings must be suspect. For the claim that the *orejones* deserted Huayna Capac out of annoyance and that they seized not Huanacauri but Inti, spy 305. The rebellion in Cuzco in abc 83 is probably a memory of this time.

Chiriguana Incursion: On the dating and details of the Portuguese side of this adventure, C. E. Nowell, "Aleixo García and the White King," *Hispanic-American Historical Review* (Nov., 1946). As García was killed in the latter part of 1525 near Asunción on his return, this would date the raid on Chuquisaca to 1523 or thereabouts. For this invasion, sg 61; cv III, 23. The Chiriguana advance was halted just to the east of Sucre at Tarabuco and Presto.

Inca Cities in Ecuador: For Huayna Capac's pleasure lake in Quito, rgi III, 55. Tumibamba was designed to be another Cuzco, abc 84. For a description of Tumibamba, clpp 44. For the warm springs there, rgi III, 159. The *usno* in the plaza was called Huacha Opari Pampa, cv III, 21f. For the gold statues in Mollecancha, blc 56. For the cult of Mama Ocllo, cv III, 21. For the emperor's placenta, sg 60; cv III, 21.

Ecuador in the Empire: For Ecuador as a semi-independent appanage, cv III, 21. For the three hundred provinces in the empire, ov XLVI, 9. For the death of Cusi Rimay and the emperor's marriage to Rahua Ocllo, cv III, 21.

Preliminary Tumbez Expedition: For the expedition's dropping off at Cajas, abc 82. For the decimation of twenty communities near Piura, ov XLVI, 3. For the Inca buildings in Tumbez as well as the disaster of the rafts, clpp 53.

Coastal Campaign: The accepted interpretation has been that Huayna Capac turned down the Ancasmayo River to the coast, SG 62; CV III, 23. This is contradicted in CV III, 24, where the route given is the same as Topa Inca's (which was neither the Tumaco nor the Esmeraldas route). This common-sense view is corroborated in BC XII, 17, where Puná is the objective. For the hostilities necessary to gain the island, OV XLVI, 2. For the Inca garrison on Puná (probably of this period), OV XLVI, 17.

First Knowledge of Spaniards: The Incas heard of the Spaniards eight years before Pizarro entered Cajamarca, CV III, 32—this would place it in 1524, the year of Pizarro's first expedition, when he reached four degrees north. The gift of gold sent by Huayna Capac to Pizarro (fruitlessly, as he had already turned back) undoubtedly is to be placed here, BLC 261. Considering the mercantile interests of Tumbez and Puná in the north, rumors of the Spaniards must have been heard as early as 1513, the year of Balboa's appearance on the Pacific.

The Epidemic and Return: Huayna Capac first learned of the epidemic either at Puná, CV III, 24, or while returning from coast, SG 62. More improbably the coming of the first news is placed after Yahuarcocha and before the advance to the Ancasmayo, SPY 306. Nothing is known of the manner in which the epidemic spread—the interpretation is solely ours. For the *modorra* epidemic of 1514 in Darien, K. Romoli, *Balboa of Darien* (1953), 224. For the return route and the decimation in Cuzco, CV III, 24. Two governors of Cuzco died, Auqui Topa and the emperor's uncle Apu Illaquita, CV III, 21, 24; SG 62. Elsewhere it is said that Auqui Topa lived long enough to counter Ninan Cuyochi's attempts on the crown, ISP-VC 26. For Mama Coca as the abbess of the Cuzco *acllahuasi*, SPY 300. For the silence of most of the *huacas*, GP 186. For the emperor's intention to leave for Cuzco, SG 62. For two hundred thousand dead in Ecuador, CL 68.

The First Spaniards in Peru: Huayna Capac had died the year Pizarro first made landfall at Tumbez, CLTP (April, 1951), 159. Yet the news of the landfall was apparently received by the emperor, BC XII, 17; BSC Disc. I, 6. For seizure of the two Indians at the Chira

River, GHV 225. For the probably erroneous story that Molina and Hernandez, the two Spaniards left in Tumbez, were sent to the emperor in Quito, where they were sacrificed and eaten, BSC Disc. I, 6 (a doublet of this story calls them Sanchez and Martín and has them sacrificed by Atahualpa near Quito, CV III, 27). For the contrary statement that the people of Tumbez killed them, CL 68.

The Portents: For the portents announcing the Spaniards, ACCM I, 17f. For the oracle ending the Inca line at the twelfth ruler, ACCM I, 16; GPF 378. For the oracle of the Apurimac *huaca*, PPR 380. For the execution and proscription of *huacas*, GP 186.

Huayna Capac's Last Days: The house where Huayna Capac retired to escape the plague, SPY 307, was probably rather where he underwent his penitential fast. For the dream of the three dwarfs, BC XII, 17; PPR 235f. The tale of the Pandora's box, SPY 307, is indigenous to Peru as witness the Ecuadoran belief that if the box containing the ashes of the double-faced *chipicha*-demon is opened, the evils which fly out will become fierce insect pests and briars. For the early death of Michi, SPY 307. For the emperor's death in the sunlight, PPR 236, which is probably a rationalization of BC XII, 17, where it is the *huaca* of Inti and not the actual sun which is in question. The year of his death is given as 1524 in SG 62; this would put it during Pizarro's first voyage.

The Testament: Royal commissions painted on batons are also known from Topa Inca's reign, SPY 291. For the prophecy that the Viracochas would return, CL 68; ACCM I, 16; ISP-VC 22. The limits of the province of Ecuador are given as from Quito north to Popayan, CL 68; as everything north of Mocha (which was sixty miles south of Quito), RGI III, 158; as from Tiqui Cangui north to Pasto, ABC 84. In any case the Cañars are never included. It was commonly believed to be a division of the empire between two sons, ISP-VC 22. For the third item of the will, SG 62; CV III, 24; CL 68. For a definite statement that the kingdom was left to Ninan Cuyochi, CV III, 31.

CHAPTER XIII—HUASCAR: TWELFTH EMPEROR

Chronology of Reign: The battle of Cotapampa preceded Atahualpa's capture by about six months, ov XLVI, 5, 9. Pizarro captured Atahualpa on November 16, 1532. *Ergo* Cotapampa was fought about April, 1532. Atahualpa said that his father died eight years before, or 1524 (this is supported in cv III, 32; FJ 334; GSC III, 51). Others say that the lapse of time was eight to ten, ten, and five years respectively, ISP-VT 108; PPR 236; GVCR IX, 32. Our date for Huayna Capac's death is confirmed in VRQ II, 24f., where it is said that Atahualpa reigned in Quito six years and four months. VRQ II, 66, gives December, 1525, as the date of Huayna Capac's death, which is close to our conjecture of 1526. Both GSC III, 51, and ov XLVI, 9, say that seven years of peace between Atahualpa and Huascar was ended by the War of the Two Brothers, this making that conflict about one year in duration. The Quilaco embassy is roughly dated in cv III, 30, where we have a four-year interval between Quilaco's introduction to Golden Star and his reappearance to her at Yanamarca. Inasmuch as Yanamarca must have been fought very soon before Cotapampa, this puts the Quilaco embassy in 1528. The battle of Cusipampa was fought while Pizarro was still in Puná, CLTP (Feb., 1956), 89, and thus occurred in 1531 (indirectly confirmed in FJ 328f., where it is shown that the Spaniards heard of that portion of the brothers' war relating to Ecuador while they were in Puná). Inasmuch as Atahualpa received news of Cotapampa a few days before he heard of Pizarro's landing at Tumbez, cv III, 32, and JA VI, 22, which happened early in 1532, this confirms the synchronization of the two events.

The Imperial Council: There were seven or eight members, probably divided between Cuzco and Ecuador; among them were Colla Topa, Catumgui, Tauri Machi, and Auqui Topa Yupanqui, cv III, 24 (the latter is undoubtedly Auqui Topa Inca, ISP-VC 26). Colla Topa was a brother of Huayna Capac and led the funeral cortege back to Cuzco, CL 68, 70; cv III, 25 (it is doubtful if he is the Colla Topa in MM IV, 16—but see CL 70).

Ninan Cuyochi: His attempt on the succession is once called a conspiracy, ISP-VC 26, for which his partisans were punished. For the embassy to him in Tumibamba, SG 62.

Huayna Capac's Funeral: For the burial of his entrails near Quito,

LAC I; JA VI; BC XII, 17; VRQ II, 65. For a picture of the funeral cortege, GPF 377. For the mourning, CL 68. For his gold *huaoqui* called Huaraqui Inca, SG 62. For the *coya*'s return ahead of the mummy, CV III, 24; SG 62. While the funeral party was in Tumibamba the executors appointed Inguil Topa, one of Huayna Capac's sons, as governor there, with part of the army for his use, CV III, 24; DF 5; GP 84–86; GSC III, 50.

Huascar Seizes Power: For the appointment of Tito Atauchi and Topa Aatach (Atauchi?), two of Huascar's uncles, as counselors, CV III, 24. The former either went to Cuzco immediately or was there already at the time of appointment, CV III, 25. For Huascar's prompt seizure of power, CV III, 24; CL 70. For the priests who crowned him, CV III, 31 (they belonged to the *panaca* of Viracocha Inca, inasmuch as we are informed that this family held the office of high priest under Huascar, CV III, 24). For Atahualpa's retention of some of his father's women, CL 70. For the three councilors appointed by Huascar, CV III, 24.

Conspiracy of Cusi Atauchi: For the forty sons of Huayna Capac, CL 70. The story is given only in CV III, 25.

Slaughter of the Executors: For the funeral party near the Apurimac, SG 63; CV III, 25. For the official line, GVCR LX, 33. For the questioning of the victims, SPY 309.

Coronation and Wedding: The sister Chincha Ocllo had earlier been designated by Huayna Capac as Huascar's bride, CL 68. This *coya*'s name was Chuqui Huipa, ISP-VC 23, 47f. (Chuqui Uzpai in CV III, 25, and Chuquillanto in GP 86ff., 104). Huascar is called Topa Cusi Hualpa Huascar Auqui in RGI III, 178; (Inca substitutes for Auqui, GPF 376). Huascar's birthsite was called Huascar Quiguar, SG 63. For his building and residence at Collcampata and Amarucancha, SG 63; CV III, 24; GVCR VII, 8. For the Chachapoya campaign, CV III, 25.

Events Preceding the Quilaco Embassy: For Atahualpa's title of *Incap ranti*, SPY 310. For Atahualpa's request for reconfirmation of his post, ISP-VC 26ff. For Atahualpa's gifts to the queens and for

Huascar's accusations, cv III, 26. For the *coya*'s unhappiness and indulgence in coca, GP 104.

The Quilaco Embassy: Sources are cv III, 26f.; LTOP 21; SPY 310; FJ 328f. For inclusion of a half-brother on embassy, ov XLVI, 5. For the fictitious parentage of Atahualpa, GHV 230, 232; GSC III, 50; ABC 83; LAC I; VRQ II, 62f., 67. For Quilaco forced by Huascar to wear women's clothes, GP 86ff.

The Quilaco Love Story: Found only in cv III, 26–33. The activities of the aunt, Caua Ticlla (Skein of Two Colors), seem those of the abbess of an *acllahuasi*.

Description of Huascar: For a description, GP 86ff. For hatred of him, BC XII, 18. For his arrogance, GPF 386. For slanderous tales about him, SPY 308f. For a view of him as childish, ISP-VC 27. For massacres near Cuzco, MGP I. For a moderate account, CL 69. For the Inca procession of the year 1610 A.D., BC XII, 2. For the poisoning of harem girl, cv III, 26. For Huascar's hatred of ancestral cults, PPR 240; BC XII, 18. For cause of war as Huascar's fear of Atahualpa, LAC I.

Atahualpa's Capture and Escape: For events before the capture, VRQ II, 67–70. For agents of both parties among the Cañars, CL 71. For the delivery from prison, CL 71; AZH I, 12; cv III, 28; ZR III, 15; BSC Disc. I, 6; GSC III, 51; ov XLVI, 17. For the military review in Quito, cv III, 27. For Huascar's power among the Cañars, SPY 310; CL 70.

Atahualpa's Generals: For suppression of the Huancavelica revolt, SG 63. For cabals among generals, CL 70. For a list of anti-Huascar generals surrounding Atahualpa, VRQ II, 71. Atahualpa's later statement that his council dragged him into anti-Spanish hostilities does not prove him a weak ruler, but simply one trying to placate his captors, FJ 333.

Remarks on the War: Cabello Valboa has been our indispensible source here. The estimate of one hundred thousand casualties in CLPP 77 may be close to the truth. For three thousand deaths among the Lupaca contingents, MHVE 129.

Situation on North Coast: For Tumbez split into a Cuzco and a Quito faction, ACCM I, 17f. For the repulse at Puná, AZH I, 12; VRQ II, 72; GHV 230. I am assuming that Huascar's governor on Puná was the Atauchi (spelled Atoche) mentioned in Maggs Brothers (comp.), *From Panama to Peru* (London, 1925) 149. The facts exactly fit the overall picture. For the loyalty of the north coast to Huascar, OV XLVI, 3. For the complicated situation between Puná and Tumbez as well as Atahualpa's failure there, GHV 227. For the loyalty of Lambayeque to Huascar, CV III, 27. For war between Jayanca and Tucumes, CV III, 32. For Atahualpa's fifty thousand troops (exaggerated) on the coast, OV XLVI, 4.

Cañar Phase of the War: For Atoc in Tumibamba, GHV 230. For first battle at Ambato, CL 72 (not Riobamba, SG 63). For the blinding of Atoc, SPY 311f.; CL 72. For the bones on the field of Ambato, SG 63. For the effect of the news, CL 73. For the estimates of Huanca Auqui, SG 63; CV III, 28; CL 73; SPY 312f. For refutation of the treason charge, CV III, 28. For the numbers of Cañars destroyed, ABC 84f.; AZH I, 12, 60; GHV 230; OV XLVI, 17; RGI III, 159. For the effects of the news of massacre, FJ 329; OV XLVI, 5. For the *itu* in Cuzco, CV III, 29.

Recruitment of Armies: Atahualpa recruited among the Quixos in the montaña, CV III, 29. For the veteran army in Quito, OV XLVI, 8. This army numbered forty thousand, BLC 261; FJ 335. What part of this the thirty thousand with Atahualpa in Cajamarca made up is unclear, FJ 331. For exaggerated figure of one hundred thousand, see RGI III, 178. For the officers and contingents, BSC Disc. I, 7; GP 9f., 117ff.; SPY 308.

Campaigns in Center: For the Pacamoros campaign, SG 63. For Atahualpa's accusations against Pachacamac, PPR 242; OV XLVI, 10. The episode of Catiquilla is tied up surely with the massacre of the Huamachucos, CA 250. For the destruction of this oracle, SG 64; RHA 23f.

Campaigns in the Jauja Area: For orders to Huanca Auqui to stand firm at Jauja and for his reinforcement, CLTP (Feb., 1956), 89. For casualties of ten thousand on each side at the Pumpu crossing of the

Mantaro, SPY 321ff. Yanamarca must have been fought between Jauja and Tingo Paccha. Huascar's general Avante (no doubt garbled from Ahuapanti) fled with Huanca Auqui (Quancanque), CLTP (Feb., 1956), 91ff. After Yanamarca, Mayta (Mayca?) Yupanqui took over from Huanca Auqui, SG 63. Huascar's forces reformed at Paucaray or Huarachaca, SG 63; CLTP (Feb., 1956), 91ff. The battle of Ancoyaco is probably referred to in FJ 324; OV XLVI, 12.

Huascar's Last Measures: For his suicidal intentions and advice of the council, CLTP (Feb., 1956), 89. For his embassy to Pizarro, PRN 237; GHV 227; GPF 375f. For his consultation of *huacas*, SPY 312–24. For the oracular responses to Huascar, CV III, 30f.

Battle of Cotapampa: For the date of battle as at the beginning of April, 1532, see VRQ II, 76f. For Huanca Auqui's defeat at Pincos and between Abancay and Andahuaylas, BC XII, 18. A stand was made at the Cochacajas crossing of the Pachachaca River. SG, CV, and SPY have the most detail on the main battle, while BC concentrates on the push at Corahuasi. The site of Huascar's capture is variously called Mount Chontacaxas, Huazavara, Huanacopampa, or the Pass of Cotapampa. For the eight hundred men with Huascar when he was captured, GHV 230. The battle at Limatambo can only be clarified by assuming that Huanca Auqui withdrew from the Apurimac at Huascar's news too slowly and was taken in the rear, BC XII, 18. Quihuipay is called a battle, ACCM I, 17f., and DF 5, but it was more correctly the scene of the surrender of Cuzco. For Huascar's personal orders to his army to surrender, GHV 230; VRQ II, 76f.

Massacres at Quihuipay and Cuzco: The main sources are CV III, 31; SG 65–67; SPY 312–24; GVCR IX, 37. Minor sources, such as GPF 389, mention the disembowelment of Huascar's pregnant women. Three of Huascar's women who escaped were Huarcay, Quispicusi, and Usica, DF 5; GVCR LX, 37; GSC III, 51; ACCM I, 17f.; CV III, 31. For four women escaping and several men of Huascar's line, BC XII, 230. They took refuge in the montaña or Collao, ISP-VC 26ff. For the thirty or forty-three brothers, CL 5; CLTP (May, 1957), 263; ACCM I, 17f.

Tyranny of Quizquiz: Huayna Capac's establishment was not invaded or looted by Quizquiz as the Spaniards found it intact, CA 258. For the decimation of near-by pueblos, GVCR IX, 39. For the tyranny of Quizquiz, PPR 243. His underling in this terror was Yucra Hualpa, ISP-VC 26ff. For the occupation troops as ten thousand, FJ 335; as fifteen to twenty thousand, CM, 155; as thirty thousand, OV XLVI, 13. For the burning of records and the quipucamayocs, ISP-VC, 3–5. For the sacrifice to Viracocha, BC XII, 226. For the move against Collao, VRQ II, 88. For the revolt of the Yunguyos, ARGCS I, 28.

CHAPTER XIV—THE ADVENT OF THE BEARDED MEN

Atahualpa in Huamachuco: For his victory celebration and the reception of news of Pizarro's Tumbez landing while still in Huamachuco, SG 68; OV XLVI, 4.

Atahualpa's Character: For his reputation with the army, BC XII. For his *huaoqui* called Ticci Capac, SG 65. For the concept of Atahualpa as beginning a new era, ISP-VC 4. For a personal description, FJ 336; OV XLVI, 9; PPR 247f.; GHV 231. Pizarro apparently ordered a soldier named Mora to make a portrait of Atahualpa, from which later copies were made. It hung in Cajamarca, VRQ II, 74f.

Spaniards on the Coast: For the six months' stay at Coaque, NC 69f. For events from Esmeraldas to San Miguel, PRN 237–40. For hostilities between Puná and Tumbez, CLTP (Jan., 1956), 77–84. For the prisoners on Puná and Pizarro's release of them, CV III, 32. For Spanish attacks on Puná and Tumbez, NC 70f. For Atahualpa's first embassy, OV XLVI, 15. For the belittling reports sent to Atahualpa of the Spaniards, GBH 177; VRQ II, 88f. For the council of war, OV XLVI, 7—supported by SG 68. For the general's boast, CLTP (Feb., 1956), 95; GHV 227. For Pachacamac's favorable oracle, OV XLVI, 10. For Rumiñaui's embassy, GPF 380. For levies from the coast, OV XLVI, 4. For pro-Huascar sentiment on the coast, OV XLVI, 3; GBH 176; NC 71f. For full warehouses along the Spaniards' route, CLTP (Feb., 1956), 94. For Pizarro's flirtation with the Huascar party, PPR 223; PRN 241; CLTP (Feb., 1956), 90. For Pizarro's reasons for leaving Tumbez, OV XLVI, 2. Huaman Mallqui (the father of Huaman Poma) at Tumbez was undoubtedly Huascar's ambassador to Pizarro, GP 11, 14; VRQ II, 86f.; PRN 241.

Cajamarca: For best contemporary description, FJ 330, 334. For the near-by royal baths, ov XLVI, 8; PPR 224f.

Atahualpa Awaits Pizarro: For the embassies to Pizarro, CA 230. For withdrawal of troops from the passes, CA 224, 228. The area around Cajas was unfriendly to Atahualpa because of war exactions, CA 224, 226; VRQ II, 72; PRN 241. For the alliance between Pizarro and Chimor, PRN 240. For the embassy informing Pizarro that Huascar was a captive, ov XLVI, 15. For the embassy to Pizarro in Cajas which brought him *"patos dessollados"* and *"fortalezas"* in clay, CA 226; FJ 326 (for a different view of what these objects were, GHV 227). The skinned ducks and toy fortresses were threats or insults, CLTP (May, 1957), 247f., or perhaps a warning to approach no further, CV III, 32. For the report to Atahualpa of the similarity among the Spaniards, GPF 381. For plans to cut off the Spaniards, CLTP (May, 1957), 247f. The Inca army at Cunú was estimated at thirty thousand, FJ 331; ov XLVI, 6, or at forty thousand, CA 238; PPR 224f.; NC 72. These guesses were based not on men seen but on tents, an easily camouflaged number. For the Hernando Pizarro–De Soto embassy, AZH II, 4; CA 236f.; PPR 224f.; PRN 242; CLTP (May, 1957), 249f.

Events of November 16, 1532: The sources are too well known to be here cited. For Atahualpa's remarks in the square, PRN 243; GHV 228f. Most of the great *curacas* of the empire were involved in this disaster, RGI I, 198; ov XLVI, 7; FJ 332f. For the quotation comparing Cortez and Pizarro, BSC Disc. I, 7.

The Ransom Agreement: The terms are variously reported, inasmuch as the document quickly disappeared, PPR 230f.; ov XLVI, 15.

Intrigues: For injection of the Almagrists into the situation, AZH II, 7. For the rumor that Pizarro all along intended to kill his prisoner, GBH 182. Huascar was killed probably in late December, 1532, according to VRQ II, 24. For the Rumiñaui case, VRQ I, 9; VRQ II, 111f.; AZH II, 5, 8f.; ov XLVI, 17, 19; BSC Disc. I, 6; MM II, 14. For the indecision of Quizquiz and Challcochima regarding Huascar, PPR 230ff. For the Cuzqueño view of the Spaniards as Viracochas, CL 5; BC XII, 227; CLTP (May, 1957), 259. The rumor that Huascar conversed with some Spaniards on his freedom is obviously false, ABC 86; AZH II, 6; ISP-VC 28–31; CV III, 32.

Spanish Patrols out of Cajamarca: Our sources have often confused three patrols, i.e., to Cuzco, to Pachacamac, and the third to investigate rumors of Inca armies. Pedro de Moguer and Martín Bueno were probably the first Spaniards to see Cuzco, RGI I, 80, after dropping a Negro off at Jauja. For the Alcaviza reaction, ISP-VT 138. For the enthusiasm with which cities like Jauja and Chincha at first received the Spaniards, NC 75. Chachapoyas and Cañars in Cuzco threw in their lot with the Spaniards, RGI II, appendix 10f. The quotation is from James Bryce, *South America* (N. Y., 1912), 117. The second and third patrols are hopelessly confused in CV III, 32.

Death of Huascar: Any of three places, each called Andamarca, could be the scene of Huascar's death. There was an Andamarca on the upper San Fernando River emptying into the Mantaro, one in the upper basin of the Pampamarca River, and one on the Royal Road at its junction with the Pariacaca road down to the coast (i.e., on the Mantaro River just west of Jauja). The following texts are important in attempting to identify the site: SG 69; CV III, 32; BC XII, 18; VRQ II, 89; CLTP (May, 1957), 265; ISP-VC 31; PPR 232. We must remember that at the time of Huascar's death, Challcochima was at Jauja with a large army, FJ 338; OV XLVI, 15. Logic would choose therefore the Andamarca on the Mantaro River as the one intended.

Disintegration of Atahualpa's Position: For Atahualpa's lament in Quechua on the rape of his *coya*, GPF 388. For Challcochima's treason, CA 264ff. For the reputedly nefarious part played by Felipillo the interpreter, AZH II, 7; GBH 182. For the murder of Huascar's two brothers, Mayta Yupanqui and Huaman Tito, PPR 233. For the comet portending Atahualpa's death, OV XLVI, 14; FJ 345. For Atahualpa's defense, AZ II, 7. There is confusion about Atahualpa's Christian name, whether Carlos or Francisco, GSC III, 55. The common sources are used for the execution, with snippets from GBH 183; GHV 231. The date of execution is given as August 29, 1533, in VRQ II, 106. For a report that the body was burned after garroting, NC 75. For the massacre of the funeral party carrying the corpse back to Quito, GHV 234. For the death of Quizquiz, GHV 236. Quiso Yupanqui had also fled from the Spaniards, GPF 391. For Spanish use of "*Ama mancha ñoca Inca*," GPF 395.

INDEX

SOME FEW GENERAL TOPICS are listed in this index, but rulers such as Pachacuti, Huayna Capac, and Atahualpa are noted only when mention of them appears outside the chapters specifically devoted to them.

Chaquillchaca: 151
Charca Indians: 234, 236, 246, 258
Chasca Cuillor: 50, 162
Chasqui: 141, 262
Chavín de Huantar: 49, 337
Chibcha Indians: 325, 332–35, 346
Chicha Indians: 235
Chilca: 204
Chile: 235f., 247
Chillo River: 257
Chimborazo: 52, 196, 199
Chimor: 116f., 121, 142, 188, 190–95, 200f., 207, 214, 281, 299
Chimor Capac: 192
Chimpu Cisa: 294
Chimpu Ocllo: 372
Chincha Indians: 112f., 121, 203, 301, 345
Chincha Ocllo: 379
Chinchaysuyo: 14, 113, 117, 188, 196
Chinchaysuyo road: 35, 103, 113, 141, 275, 288, 292
Chincheros: 237f., 240
Chingana: 233
Chiqui Ocllo: 240
Chira: 299, 376
Chiriguana Indians: 235, 247, 258f., 298
Chita: 86f.
Choclococha: 84
Chontacaxas: 290
Chosica: 193
Chronology: 41, 72
Chuchi Capac: 107, 212, 214
Chucuito: 76, 108, 111, 121, 216, 280
Chullpa: 360
Chuncho Indians: 110, 367
Chunchul River: 29
Chuño: 109, 111
Chuqui Huaman: 270, 273
Chuqui Huipa: 272, 294, 311
Chuqui Illa: 158, 161, 334
Chuquimancu: 204
Chuquipampa: 153, 155
Chuqui Sota: 361
Chuqui Suso: 44
Churi Inti: 160

Desaguadero River: 68, 216
De Soto, Hernando: 287, 302, 304, 313
Diaguita Indians: 236
Drama: 178
Duchicela: 198

Esmeraldas River: 197
Espionage: 112, 217, 219f., 272, 275f.

Festivals: 168, 171
Flood, the: 60, 62, 66–69, 71
Flood Serpent: 59f., 334
Funerals: 180f., 244f., 265, 267f., 270, 314

Galapagos Islands: 364
García, Aleixo: 258f.
Giants: 70, 361
Gold: 100, 102, 106, 224f., 247, 309, 312
Guaraní: 235
Guayas River: 199, 262

Hahua Inca: 26, 36, 40, 349
Hanan Cuzco: 33, 145, 222, 272
Hanan Pacha: 182
Harem: 124
Hastu Huaraca: 85, 91, 101f.
Hatuncancha: 148, 315
Hatun Colla: 76, 107
Hatun Topa Inca (same as Viracocha Inca): 40
Hatun villac: 169
Haucaypata: 14, 18, 131, 139f., 145, 147f., 155, 160, 172, 174, 208, 223, 231, 277, 294, 309, 315
Heaven: 182
Hilavi: 52
Huaca: 11, 20, 22, 32, 44, 46–52, 56, 64, 66, 68, 70f., 80, 109, 125, 141, 153ff., 158, 163, 165, 169–72, 175f., 209, 226, 258, 263, 268, 288, 303, 331f.
Huachala: 250
Huacho: 60
Hualcopo: 198
Hualla Indians: 11–14, 22, 155

Empire of the Inca has been set in Caslon, an English type design of the eighteenth century which was transplanted to the American colonies. Because of its easy legibility, it soon gained wide acceptance among typesetters of all the English-speaking world, and has continued to be one of the most popular book faces in use today.

UNIVERSITY OF OKLAHOMA PRESS

Norman